AMERICA IN CRISIS

AMERICA

IN CRISIS

Contemporary Political Dilemmas

Edited by
Raymond L. Lee
and
Dorothy A. Palmer

Winthrop Publishers, Inc.

Cambridge, Massachusetts

Cover design and cartoons by Dave "Omar" White.

Copyright © *1972 by Winthrop Publishers, Inc.*
17 Dunster Street, Cambridge, Massachusetts 02138

Library of Congress Catalog Card Number: 70–181337.

CONTENTS

PREFACE

This book is important. It is important because the authors represented here are among the most perceptive observers of the contemporary American scene, and because the issues they discuss concern the critical dilemmas of our time. Our role as editors is a minor one— that of collecting and organizing these diverse materials into a coherent pattern.

We share the concern of most of our countrymen, who believe that America is faced today with crises that challenge her basic beliefs, her institutions, her domestic tranquillity, and her survival as a free nation. We reject the long-time, comfortable American assumption that we have a special arrangement with the Deity that exempts us from the historical forces that have toppled other great nations. Instead, we share the views of U.S. Senate majority leader, Mike Mansfield:

We can't give up!
This country is too young to die.
We'll have to work our way through our problems and find a greater maturity. We've been lucky for too many decades. Now our luck is running out and we have do some thinking.

In spite of the foregoing, we are cautious optimists. We believe that Americans, if alerted, will make the hard choices that will give the United States "a new birth of freedom, and that government of the people, by the people, and for the people shall not perish from the earth."

A casual glance at the Table of Contents may suggest that we have ignored major crises. At no point, for instance, have we separately identified the racial tensions that seem to be tearing America asunder; the youthful rebellion against the existing Establishment; the drug abuse that is destroying millions of individual lives. But this organizational approach is a deliberate decision. We do not believe, for instance, that "racial crisis" as an abstract term exists in isolation. Nor can this crisis be dealt with politically except in its component parts. In other words, we have examined this issue in each chapter, insisting that every aspect of "America In Crisis" has racial implications. As for the alleviation of this overriding crisis, political realism dictates that the issue will be resolved, if at all, in an uneven pattern involving a multitude of programs. To a lesser degree, this approach covers such issues as the "youth crisis" and the "drug crisis." None of the foregoing should be misread as a claim that we have within the covers of a 480 page book examined all issues or even all aspects of any specific issue. We privately mourn for the many authors and articles lost on the cutting room floor.

Finally, we owe a note of appreciation to those publishers and authors whose permission to reprint has made these ideas accessible to a new audience. And we would be remiss, indeed, if we did not cite our indebtedness to James J. Murray, III, President of Winthrop Publishers, Inc., with whom we have worked in one capacity or another over the past fifteen years. His low-key questions have at many points forced us to revise our original concepts and the final manuscript is a far better product because of his patience and encouragement.

Raymond L. Lee
Dorothy A. Palmer

PART ONE

Crises of the System: People, Ideas, and Institutions

America faces multiple crises in her political life. As used here, the word "crisis" does not merely imply an inconvenience or a mild disruption of the status quo; rather, it refers to political life or death. America's failure to cope successfully with current political and social challenges may assign our present system to history's scrap heap.

The first "crisis" of the system involves the people themselves. Our original democratic framework was designed for a small rural nation. That structure now shows signs of strain and fatigue as our population passes the 200,000,000 milestone with little evidence of approaching stability. Urbanization of our population is a further strain on the system, creating super-cities that seem to be ungovernable.

To a large extent, these cities are filled with uprooted black and white migrants who appear to have lost a basic component of the old system— a sense of community—somewhere along the way.

This mass society that we have created does not fit neatly into our political heritage. Citizens in traditional democratic theory were deeply involved in making the system work. In theory, at least, they were concerned with public affairs and felt a responsibility for the general welfare. Government was a highly personalized affair, with a great many face-to-face relationships. Today, many Americans find government to be a vast, anonymous, bureaucratized organization that responds only in terms of computers and form letters. This alienation from the world of politics leads to a "we" vs. "they" attitude and a widespread cynicism about the democratic system and its leadership. In a word, millions of Americans no longer believe that we have government by the people.

Although American democracy as a system of government is still widely accepted as an ideal, both the informal and formal institutions

1

of government show signs of age and obsolescence. Our interest groups often seem to pervert the public interest. The political parties are charged with thwarting the popular will. Our election system, say the critics, is manipulated by public relations techniques and money. The Congress, entangled in its own procedures, has become an institution for the prevention of legislation. The Supreme Court has been tarnished by recent resignations, nominations and deaths. Our expectations for the Presidency far outrun the ability of any one man. Behind him lies the self-perpetuating bureaucracy, bumbling and poorly-organized.

Even the original concept of a federal system does not escape the critics. Although the division of power between state and nation may have matched political reality in 1787, it does not square with political reality in the 1970's. Authority, money, and problems are gravely mismatched today. As an example, we have no political or tax unit that matches the geographic reality of the megalopolis (super-city).

Summary

The case put forth here can be challenged at every point. In its totality, however, it is a serious charge that must be examined. The best refutation, of course, would be reform of the system in all of its parts. For American democracy, in the words of Abraham Lincoln, is "the last best hope on Earth."

1. The People Problem: A Population Bomb and Migration In Black and White

We begin with the American people, for it was for them that the American government was created. When our Declaration of Independence was written, nearly two centuries ago, Americans numbered fewer than 4 million. Today there are 200 million more. Tomorrow (1980) there will be over 230 million; by the time that you are middle-aged the total may run over 300 million—half again as many people as there are today. In fact, half the people that have ever lived in the United States are alive today.

Population Growth and Government Problems

What do all of these dry statistics have to do with government? Plenty! Many parts of our governmental system were planned to handle the problems of a small, rural nation. This system today shows signs of being overloaded— like the electrical wiring of a house built long ago. More people require more and different government. They need and expect more and better education, housing, recreation, highways, and pollution control—the list is very long.

Furthermore, this population growth has been unevenly distributed. In fact, as you will learn in this chapter, several states actually lost population between 1960 and 1970. Impossible as this may seem, more than half the nation's counties lost population in the 1960's. Contrast this, however, with the fact that one out of every eight Americans now lives in either California or Florida. The multiplying problems of their political leaders are obvious. The mayors of New York, Chicago and Los Angeles are responsible for more people than most governors. A half-dozen megalopolises are emerging that spill over state lines without any government to match. The largest of these (nicknamed Bo-Wash) runs 450 miles from Boston to Washington and is the home of one out of every six Americans.

Americans On The Move

The 1970 Census pictures a nation troubled by central city decay and suburban sprawl. In the past ten years millions of white Americans have fled to the suburbs, so that today for the first time, more Americans live in the suburbs than in the core cities themselves. Most suburbs suffer from helter-skelter planning and a lack of government services. But the people keep coming!

These more affluent white migrants are being replaced in the core city by refugees from rural America; southern blacks, Chicanos, Indians, Puerto Ricans, and Appalachian whites. These migrants inherit an abandoned central city with a sagging tax base and rising social troubles.

Such migration patterns, that resemble the old game of musical chairs, result in big problems for representative government. If we are to have a government of "one man, one vote," every population shift is also a shift of political power. The 1970 Census shows that some regions will lose power: others will gain. And, in our great metropolitan regions, we have the makings of a suburban white noose tightening around the black central city. These wealthy white suburbs appear to be divorcing themselves from the myriad problems of the inner city.

This emerging political split poses a basic question: does our traditional division of government into national, state and local levels fit an urbanized society? We seem to have created a dilemma where authority, problems, and tax funds are badly mismatched.

Coping With the Population Explosion

Finally, we must take another look at future population growth. Americans have usually linked together growth and progress. Every Chamber of Commerce cheers if the census shows more people: they demand a recount if population declines. How realistic is this? Does bigger mean better? More pessimistically, can democracy survive in a human anthill, where people are massed together and where the demand for regimentation mounts?

Up to this point all decisions on population have been individual choices. Should government idly stand by and watch its problems being compounded by soaring birth rates? Or should it actively intervene to discourage births? Should it distribute contraceptive information? Should it repeal all laws on abortion?

What about population mobility? Is the decision as to where one will live an American birthright? Or, if we agree that large metropolitan areas are headed toward a disaster point at which they "will be socially intolerable, politically unmanageable, and economically inefficient," should government attempt to direct the pattern of national population distribution? These and other dilemmas will be examined in more detail in the readings that follow.

THE RISE OF SUBURBAN POWER *

CHRISTIAN CENTURY

In terms of population growth, the future clearly belongs to the suburbs. What does such an evolution mean in political-economic-sociological terms? What effect does this population growth have on integration? On job opportunities? On urban legislation?

William Cowper's classical observation that "God made the country, and man made the town" is no longer pertinent in the United States. Towns are rapidly disappearing, obliterated by super highways or swallowed up by encroaching cities. Indeed, most cities can no longer be adequately described in municipal or political terms that draw sharp boundaries. Most cities today are vast, fluid complexes of interdependent urban and suburban areas. Moreover, just as towns disappeared into expanding cities, so cities today spread and overlap to form megacities. Last summer we drove from Boston to Washington, D.C., by way of New York City, Phila-

delphia, Baltimore and numerous smaller cities that are being sucked into the orbits of the larger ones. Although the connecting parkways were sometimes reminiscent of the countryside, we were never actually outside the huge urban complex as we drove for 400 miles through traffic that threatened to gel at any moment into immobility and beneath a smog that covered all the east coast under one blanket. So we must update Cowper's aphorism and now say that God made the country, and man made the megacity. There is too much good in the megacity to credit it to the devil and too much evil to blame it on God. It is man's—his glory and his shame, his possibility and his peril. What happens in the cities and in the metropolitan clusters in the next decade will in large measure determine the shape and fate of human life in the United States for the next century. Here if anywhere we have the indices to man's future; for man, however else he may be defined, will be misdefined if he is interpreted apart from his habitat, apart from what he does to the city and what the city does to him.

I

What is happening in and to the cities? What are the deep, slowly flowing currents and the rapid, superficial changes? What are these urban movements doing to us? We shall never have final answers to these questions, but for a starter we suggest some hard facts and some suppositions that appeared in the opening article of the July issue of *City,* a magazine dedicated to illuminating the city's problems and hopes and improving its quality of life. . . . The points made in this article are simple, but they are basic to our understanding of current trends in the nation's metropolitan areas. First, during the present decade the suburbs assumed for the first time a clear population majority over central cities. In 1966, according to the annual April estimates of the Census Bureau, the population of the major central cities of the United States was 59,418,000 and the population of their suburbs was 65,815,000. This shift of the population from urban to suburban locations has racial as well as numerical significance. During the past six years the white population of the suburbs increased 21.3 percent, the nonwhite population of the central cities 23.9 percent. During the same period the nonwhite population of the suburbs increased only 10.1 percent. Since the suburbs began the decade with a very small nonwhite population, this 10.1 percent increase was actually insignificant. So the shrinking urban areas become more and more nonwhite, the growing suburban areas more and more white.

Chicago—the city in which our staff sees and feels this development most sharply—is an apt illustration of this nationwide trend. In 1960 Chicago proper, occupying only 5.5 percent of its metropolitan area, had 57.1 percent of that area's population. During the 1960's

the population of the Chicago suburbs has increased rapidly and has done so along the racial lines noted by *City.* The nonwhite population of Chicago has increased, as has the white population of the Chicago suburbs; but there has been no significant increase in the suburbs' nonwhite population. On September 23, 1967, the *Chicago Daily News* carried a partial report on the racial situation in the Chicago suburbs. The area surveyed included 770,000 people in 26 suburbs. Only 17,000 of these people—roughly 2 percent—are Negroes; of these, nearly 10,000 live in Evanston and 1,600 live in La Grange. In suburb after suburb the reports read: no Negroes, two Negroes, five nonwhites, 41 Chinese and Japanese, etc. The crescent surrounding Chicago proper grows bigger and whiter. And if the Black Power idea becomes widely popular among Negroes—if resegregation becomes a symbol of racial pride and loyalty—the reports of desegregation may be more depressing in the future than they are now. The growing suburbs remain a white preserve, and the central cities increasingly become Negro ghettos.

Second, the U.S. labor department has concluded on the basis of the valuation of nonresidential building permits issued from 1954 to 1965 that job opportunities are following the people to the suburbs. *City* states that the labor department "found 49 percent [of nonresidential building permits] accounted for in the suburbs, including 63 percent of the valuation of new industrial buildings and 53 percent of the new stores." The effect of this development on Negroes and poor whites can easily be imagined. Economist Dorothy K. Newman says that the new jobs are precisely those "for which the unemployed and underemployed in cities could be hired directly, or trained by employers or the government with little effort or expense. But these jobs are not accessible or always open to unemployed or underemployed city dwellers." Slowly but certainly, then, the jobs are moving away from the people who need them most and who are prohibited by their race and by other less indelible circumstances from pursuing them.

The third trend in the metropolitan clusters is a logical and practical consequence of the first two: the shift of political power from the central cities to their suburbs. The 90th Congress, says *City,* "includes 20 freshman representatives of districts that became suburban, or more suburban, as a result of reapportionment since the previous election. . . . The House vote on an amendment to trim model cities appropriations to the bone of planning funds provided a test of how these spokesmen for suburban growth would treat urban legislation. Of the 20, only five voted against the drastic cutback, 15 for it (and thus against model cities)." This may be too small a sampling to test which way the political wind will blow as political power moves to the suburbs, but the logical supposition to be drawn from this sampling is that suburban political power will be more concerned about and partial to the suburbs than to the central cities.

II

These three trends—continuing racial segregation in the suburbs, the flow of job opportunities to the suburbs and the transfer of political power from the central cities to the suburbs—create in combination an extremely dangerous situation for the nonwhites and the poor whites in the inner city and compound and prolong the nation's racial problem.

If we think that the present rebellious mood in the central cities endangers the whole public, these three trends portend racial crises and rebellions that will make the present revolts in the ghettos seem preliminary skirmishes. It is possible that the parochial attitude of suburban politics will change for the better as the suburbs, invaded by "creeping urbanization," more and more share the problems of the central city. But whether that awakening will come soon enough remains to be seen.

THE 1970 CENSUS:
MORE AND MORE A
NATION OF SUBURBANITES *
U. S. NEWS & WORLD REPORT

*Growth patterns highlighted by the
1970 Census are continuing. What
is happening to the birth rate?
What regions have had the greatest
growth? How has farm population
changed? How have city growth
rates altered? Why was suburban
growth a surprise to statisticians?
What is the largest state? The
largest city? What state had the
highest growth rate? Which had
the largest decline? How does your
own state's growth compare with
national averages? Which states
have lost political power? Which
have gained? At whose expense has
suburbia gained its political power
within the states?*

A new picture of America is emerging from the figures of the 1970
Census.

The picture is still incomplete.
But, as illustrated on these pages,
the broad sweep of population

* "The 1970 Census: How Many Americans and Where They Are," U. S. News
& World Report, September 14, 1970,
pp. 22–25. Copyright 1970 U. S. News
& World Report, Inc.

growths and shifts is already in
sharp outline—

• The total number of Americans, when the full count is in, is
expected to be between 204 and
205 million. That will signal a
growth in the decade of the '60's of
about 24.5 million—a steep drop
from the 28.3 million increase in
population during the '50's.

• People are continuing to "go
west." Among regions, the Pacific
States showed the biggest gain by
far—more than 23 percent over
the 1960 census. Following were
the Mountain States and the South
—with the East, the Midwest and
the Border States trailing behind.
In the table you get the picture of
which States are growing faster
than the national average, which
have a slower growth, which have
lost population.

• Figures also illustrate a shift
in the preferences of a large number of people for the type of surrounding in which they wish to
live. In 1960, more people preferred
city life to suburban life. But in
1970 there were 12 million more
persons in suburbia than there were
in central cities.

• People continued to leave the
farm or, if they stayed on the land,
sought jobs in industries that are
increasingly moving to the countryside.

The farm population dropped
from 15 million in 1960 to 10 million
in 1970. In 1960, farmers and their
families comprised about 8 percent
of the U.S. population. In 1970, the
ratio had fallen to about 5 percent.

Count in Progress

The preliminary field count for persons with fixed residences in the U.S. was announced on September 1 by Secretary of Commerce Maurice Stans. The figure: 200.3 million persons.

But Mr. Stans estimated that about 4 million more will be added before the census is complete and official. They will include the more than 1 million members of the armed forces now overseas, the crews of naval and merchant vessels, transients who were counted away from home but not yet allocated to their residences, and persons discovered by postal checks and those living in housing units classified as vacant.

Thus, if the final count is around 204.5 million, the growth during the '60's was about 13.6 percent, the slowest rate for any decade since the depression years of the '30's. It is in marked contrast to the 18.6 percent rise during the post World War II years of the '50's when the population grew faster than during any decade since the period of 1900–10.

Few Surprises, But—

The headcount results, so far, include few surprises, although the magnitude of the shifts was greater than anticipated by the Census Bureau.

Many large cities lost population faster than expected, and the suburbs around those cities grew more rapidly than foreseen.

A tabulation by the Economic Unit of "U. S. News & World Report" of the 230 officially designated "standard metropolitan statistical areas"—based on census data—showed that the population of those areas amounted to 136.4 million in 1970, against 118.4 million in 1960, a rise of about 15 percent.

However, 84 percent of the growth in those areas occurred in the suburban rings surrounding the central cities. The suburban population—at 74.2 million—rose 15.2 million, or 26 percent.

There were also shifts in ranking among the 25 largest areas. The Washington area, including suburbs of Virginia and Maryland, moved from tenth to seventh in the nation, with an increase of 38.4 percent. That gain was exceeded only by the Anaheim, Calif., area, which jumped 100 percent.

The declining fortunes of the large cities can be seen by examining the changes in population from 1950 to 1960 and from 1960 to 1970 for the 50 largest cities in the U.S.

During the '60's of those 50 cities, 23 lost population and 27 showed some increases. During the '50's 20 lost population and 30 gained.

Moreover, as a general rule the cities which showed gains during the '60's posted smaller increases than they had recorded the previous decade. Those which showed losses generally lost even more than they had during the '50's.

Biggest City, Biggest State

New York City continues as the nation's largest, with a preliminary count of 7,771,730. That is a small decline of 10,254 from the 1960 census—although the figure could turn into a gain when the count is complete.

Houston, with a gain of 29.3 percent, moved up in rank from seventh place to sixth, displacing Baltimore. Dallas, rising 23 percent, jumped from fourteenth to eighth.

The real gainers—largely because they took over surrounding suburbs—were Indianapolis and Jacksonville. Indianapolis went from 26th place to 10th, Jacksonville from 61st to 23rd.

The most populous State now is California, which exceeded New York State's population by 1.7 million.

Nevada was the fastest-growing State with a rise of 68.9 percent, followed by Florida and Arizona, with increases of almost 35 percent.

Move by Regions

Another way the U.S. population has shifted is shown by these figures:

In 1950, the States of the Southern, Mountain and Pacific regions contained only 37.5 percent of the nation's people. Now they have 41.6 percent.

In 1950, the States of the Eastern, Midwest and Border regions accounted for 62.5 percent of the population. Now they have only 58.4 percent.

The movement of the population during the '60's followed the same pattern as during the '50's—south and west, with particular emphasis on coastal areas.

The center of population, which in 1960 was 6.5 miles northwest of Centralia, Ill., will move farther west and south.

A Political Shift

The population changes will mean, too, a reallocation of political power, which could come about in these ways:

• Within States, suburbia in general will gain State and national representation, largely at the expense of the big cities.

• Among States, those which showed the biggest increases will pick up additional seats in Congress, effective with the 1972 election. The expected gainers: California, 5 seats; Florida, 3; Arizona, Colorado, Connecticut and Texas, 1 each. Those which are likely to lose seats: New York and Pennsylvania, 2 each; Alabama, Iowa, North Dakota, Ohio, Oklahoma, Tennessee, West Virginia and Wisconsin, 1 each. These shifts are based on preliminary figures and could be different when the final census tally is finished. . . .

HOW THE STATES HAVE CHANGED
IN THE PAST DECADE

National average growth since 1960: 13.6%

GROWING FASTER THAN NATIONAL AVERAGE

	1970 Population	Change Since 1960
Nevada	481,893	Up 68.9%
Florida	6,671,162	Up 34.7%
Arizona	1,752,122	Up 34.6%
Alaska	294,607	Up 30.3%
California	19,696,840	Up 25.3%
Colorado	2,195,887	Up 25.2%
Maryland	3,874,642	Up 25.0%
Delaware	542,979	Up 21.7%
New Hampshire	722,753	Up 19.1%
Utah	1,060,631	Up 19.1%
Hawaii	748,575	Up 18.3%
Connecticut	2,987,950	Up 17.9%
Washington	3,352,892	Up 17.5%
New Jersey	7,091,995	Up 16.9%
Oregon	2,056,171	Up 16.3%
Texas	10,989,123	Up 14.7%
Virginia	4,543,249	Up 14.5%
Georgia	4,492,038	Up 13.9%

GROWING MORE SLOWLY THAN NATIONAL AVERAGE

Vermont	437,744	Up 12.3%
Michigan	8,776,873	Up 12.2%
Wisconsin	4,366,766	Up 10.5%
Minnesota	3,767,975	Up 10.4%
Indiana	5,143,422	Up 10.3%
Louisiana	3,564,310	Up 9.4%
Massachusetts	5,630,224	Up 9.4%
Illinois	10,973,986	Up 8.9%
North Carolina	4,961,832	Up 8.9%
Ohio	10,542,030	Up 8.6%
Tennessee	3,838,777	Up 7.6%
Missouri	4,636,247	Up 7.3%
Oklahoma	2,498,378	Up 7.3%
Rhode Island	922,461	Up 7.3%
New York	17,979,712	Up 7.1%
South Carolina	2,522,881	Up 5.9%
Arkansas	1,886,210	Up 5.6%
New Mexico	998,257	Up 5.0%
Idaho	698,275	Up 4.6%
Kentucky	3,160,555	Up 4.0%
Nebraska	1,468,101	Up 4.0%
Alabama	3,373,006	Up 3.3%
Pennsylvania	11,663,301	Up 3.0%
Kansas	2,222,173	Up 2.0%
Iowa	2,789,893	Up 1.2%
Montana	682,133	Up 1.1%

| Maine | 977,260 | Up 0.8% |
| Dist. of Columbia (est.) | 764,000 | No change |

LOSING POPULATION

West Virginia	1,701,913	Down 8.5%
North Dakota	610,648	Down 3.4%
South Dakota	661,406	Down 2.8%
Mississippi	2,158,872	Down 0.9%
Wyoming	328,591	Down 0.4%

NOTE: Preliminary State-by-State figures do not add up to the estimated total U.S. population of 204.5 million because they do not include about 4 million Americans—servicemen abroad and people who were counted while away from home. Final population figures will place these people in their various States, raising each State total a little.

WHAT'S HAPPENED TO THE 50 BIGGEST CITIES

From preliminary census reports, subject to later revision—

1970 Rank	1970 Population	Change Since 1960	1960 Rank
1. New York	7,771,730	Down 0.1%	1
2. Chicago	3,325,263	Down 6.3%	2
3. Los Angeles	2,782,400	Up 12.2%	3
4. Philadelphia	1,926,529	Down 3.8%	4
5. Detroit	1,492,914	Down 10.6%	5
6. Houston	1,213,064	Up 29.3%	7
7. Baltimore	895,222	Down 4.7%	6
8. Dallas	836,121	Up 23.0%	14
9. Washington (est.)	764,000	no change	9
10. Indianapolis	742,613	Up 55.9%	26
11. Cleveland	738,956	Down 15.6%	8
12. Milwaukee	709,537	Down 4.3%	11
13. San Francisco	704,209	Down 4.9%	12
14. San Diego	675,788	Up 17.9%	18
15. San Antonio	650,188	Up 10.6%	17
16. Boston	628,215	Down 9.9%	13
17. Memphis	620,873	Up 24.8%	22
18. St. Louis	607,718	Down 19.0%	10
19. New Orleans	585,787	Down 6.7%	15
20. Phoenix	580,275	Up 32.1%	29
21. Columbus, Ohio	533,418	Up 13.2%	28
22. Seattle	524,263	Down 5.9%	19
23. Jacksonville	513,439	Up 155.4%	61
24. Denver	512,691	Up 3.8%	23
25. Pittsburgh	512,676	Down 15.2%	16
26. Kansas City, Mo.	495,405	Up 4.2%	27
27. Atlanta	487,553	no change	24
28. Buffalo	457,814	Down 14.1%	20
29. Cincinnati	448,444	Down 10.8%	21
30. Nashville	444,489	Up 160.1%	73

31. San Jose	436,757	Up 113.9%	57
32. Minneapolis	431,977	Down 10.5%	25
33. Fort Worth	388,225	Up 9.0%	34
34. Toledo	379,104	Up 19.2%	39
35. Newark	378,222	Down 6.7%	30
36. Portland, Oreg.	375,161	Up 0.7%	32
37. Oklahoma City	363,225	Up 12.0%	37
38. Oakland	358,198	Down 2.5%	33
39. Louisville	356,982	Down 8.6%	31
40. Long Beach	347,072	Up 0.8%	35
41. Miami	331,554	Up 13.7%	44
42. Tulsa	328,219	Up 25.4%	50
43. Omaha	327,789	Up 8.7%	42
44. Honolulu	319,784	Up 8.7%	43
45. El Paso	317,462	Up 14.7%	46
46. St. Paul	308,686	Down 1.5%	40
47. Birmingham	297,364	Down 12.8%	36
48. Rochester, N.Y.	293,695	Down 7.8%	38
49. Wichita	274,448	Up 7.8%	51
50. Tampa	274,359	Down 0.2%	48

NOTE: In some cases, Jacksonville, Nashville and Indianapolis, for example, increase in population since 1960 is due at least in part to annexation of suburban areas.

BLACK MIGRATION: THE SEARCH FOR THE PROMISED LAND *

JOSEPH BOSKIN

For most black migrants the northern industrial cities, when viewed from afar, were a Promised Land. The reality has been a slum ghetto from which few escape. According to Joseph Boskin this

* *Reprinted from Joseph Boskin, "The Revolt of the Urban Ghettos," The Annals of the American Academy of Political and Social Science, (March, 1969), pp. 4–7. Reprinted with permission of the author.*

feeling of entrapment is a basic cause of urban riots.

What image of the city has been portrayed by TV, literature and the movies? Where was the white man's "Promised Land"? How did blacks originally view the city? Why did they change their minds? In what ways did the big city slum create black solidarity?

. . . Throughout the 1950's and 1960's, television portrayed the city as a violent, unhealthy, dirty, corrupt, lonely, unseemly place for people to live, develop, and grow. Survival appeared to be the main component dramatized in series after series. With the exceptions of such productions as were borrowed from earlier successful radio shows, the bulk of television performances were antiurban in substance. In such medical series as "Ben Casey," "The Young Interns," and "The Nurses," psychological maladies or life and death were constant themes. The decade of the 1920's, depicted in such series as "The Roaring Twenties" and "The Untouchables," consistently associated the city with gang violence. In such outstanding series as "Naked City," which dealt with some realistic problems of life in New York, and "East Side, West Side," a series based on the experiences of a social worker, the promise and potential of the city were lacking. Television largely reinforced the image of the city earlier perpetuated by literature and the movies. As Herbert Kosower has correctly noted: "Almost all of Hollywood's films deal with contemporary urban life on a superficial fantasy plane." Even *Street Scene, On the Waterfront, The Naked City, The Pawnbroker,* and *A Thousand Clowns* tended to reflect the harsh aspects of urban life.

Resistance to city living grew from several sources. The organization of the city was felt to be antagonistic to basic American values. It bred impersonality, detachment, and unhealthy conditions. Criticism stemmed from the conception of the city as being anti-individualistic. Groups of people were herded together in living and working conditions which placed a premium on co-operative

and collectivistic solutions to social problems.

The city was further indicted for altering the landscape of America, for denying its past and playing havoc with its future. As Anselm Strauss has accurately written, the United States managed to develop an industrial economy without developing a thoroughly urbanized citizenry. Americans, he noted, entered upon the great urbanization of the nineteenth century "protestingly, metaphorically walking backward."

The image of the city was capped in the catch phrase originally ascribed to New York City: "It's a nice place to visit but I wouldn't want to live there." Living was to be done in the suburbs, away from the source of corruptions. The "Promised Land," then, was to be sought outside the city.

Aided by affluence, millions fled from the city into the landscaped suburbs—leaving the core cities to the newer migrant and immigrant groups. Negro-, Puerto Rican-, Mexican-, and Japanese-Americans, and other smaller American minority groups with dark or nonwhite skins, filled the central cities. By the 1960's, all major and most smaller cities had sizeable numbers of various ethnic groups in the downtown areas, living in slum ghettos, breathing the increasingly foul urban air, and becoming increasingly alienated. They gradually developed an urban consciousness—a consciousness of the entrapped underclass.

The sense of entrapment stemmed

from the inability of the ethnic groups to break out of the urban ghetto and become part of the burgeoning middle classes. Alienation grew out of the anger of betrayal, a betrayal that began when the inner-city dwellers were made the inheritors of decaying cities. That they were being deserted, that the promised land in the North and West was drying up, as Langston Hughes caustically expressed it, "like a raisin in the sun," became increasingly clear in the decades of the 1950's and 1960's. Claude Brown, in his *Manchild in the Promised Land,* an affectionate portrayal of Harlem, began his sketch with this denial of the promise:

I want to talk about the first Northern urban generation of Negroes. I want to talk about the experiences of a misplaced generation, of a misplaced people in an extremely complex, confused society. This is a story of their searching, their dreams, their sorrows, their small and futile rebellions, and their endless battle to establish their own place in America's greatest metropolis— and in America itself.

The characters are sons and daughters of former Southern sharecroppers. These were the poorest people of the South, who poured into New York City during the decade following the Great Depression. These migrants were told that unlimited opportunities for prosperity existed in New York and that there was no "color problem" there. They were told that Negroes lived in houses with bathrooms,

electricity, running water, and indoor toilets. To them, this was the "promised land" that Mammy had been singing about in the cotton fields for many years. . . . It seems that Cousin Willie, in his lying haste, had neglected to tell the folks down home about one of the most important aspects of the promised land: it was a slum ghetto. There was a tremendous difference in the way life was lived up North. There were too many people full of hate and bitterness crowded into a dirty, stinky, uncared-for closet-sized section of a great city.

Before the soreness of the cotton fields had left Mama's back, her knees were getting sore from scrubbing "Goldberg's" floor. Nevertheless, she was better off; she had gone from the fire into the frying pan.

The children of these disillusioned colored pioneers inherited the total lot of their parents—the disappointments, the anger. To add to their misery, they had little hope of deliverance. For where does one run to when he's already in the promised land? [1]

One runs to one's soul brother.

The significant consequences of the great migration along the hallelujah trail was the development of an urban consciousness in the ghettos of the industrial cities. Alain Locke, in his important book in the 1920's, *The New Negro,* took cognizance of the ecological forces at work in Harlem. Proscription

[1] Claude Brown, *Manchild in the Promised Land* (New York: New American Library, 1965), pp. vii–viii.

and prejudice, he noted, had thrown dissimilar black elements into a common area of contact and interaction. Prior to the movement into Harlem, the Negro was "a race more in name than in fact, or to be exact, more in sentiment than in experience." The central experience between these groups, he continued, was that of "a common condition rather than a life in common. In Harlem, Negro life is seizing upon its first chances for group expression and self-determination." [2] The fusing of sentiment and experience in Harlem was repeated over and again in ghettos across the country. Indeed, ghetto experience became a common denominator, its lifestyle and language and conditions a similarity of experiences.

Had the ghetto become a viable environment within a dynamic city existence, the level of grievance-consciousness shared by Negroes would have been muted. But the opposite occurred. Instead, the ghetto became a dead-end to those who lived in it. It became an object of loathing, a mirror of a squalid existence. Feelings of hopelessness and isolation were recurrent themes in the testimony of the slum residents, wrote the United States Commission on Civil Rights in 1967. When asked what she would do if she had sufficient income, one resident declared, "The first thing I would do myself is move out of the neighborhood. I

[2] Alain Locke, *The New Negro* (New York: Albert and Charles Boni, 1925), pp. 6–7.

feel the entire neighborhood is more or less a trap."

Compounding these antagonisms were, of course, the intensifying antiurban attitudes of whites. "The people in Harlem," wrote James Baldwin in *Nobody Knows My Name*, two years before the first protest riot, "know they are living there because white people do not think they are good enough to live elsewhere. No amount of 'improvement' can sweeten this fact. . . . A ghetto can be improved in one way only: out of existence." These resentments were further exacerbated by the obvious disparity between the Caucasian and black neighborhoods. Said a young man to Budd Schulberg in the Watts Happening Coffee House immediately after the riots:

The contrast: the spectacular growth of central and west L.A. vs. the stagnation of Watts. . . . You've conquered it, baby. You've got it made. Some nights on the roof of our rotten falling down buildings we can actually see your lights shining in the distance. So near and yet so far. We want to reach out and grab it and punch it on the nose.

The mythical urban melting pot began to simmer and finally boiled over.

The protest riots which occurred in massive profusion were thus the consequence of a myriad of historical and ecological factors which fused in the 1960's. Their outstanding feature was a collective mode of attitude, behavior, and sense of power. . . .

OUR NATION IS MOVING
TOWARD TWO SOCIETIES *
NATIONAL ADVISORY
COMMISSION ON CIVIL
DISORDERS

---

*When riots and violence boiled up
out of the ghettos in the summer
of 1967, President Johnson appointed an investigating committee,
headed by Governor Otto Kerner
(the Kerner Commission). At the
outset of their report this Commission offered their conclusions
in a two-page summary that follows.
From the vantage point of the
1970's we can now measure the
Report's analysis and predictions.
Why did the Commission conclude that we were moving toward
two societies? Is there any evidence
that this trend has been halted?
Have we applied massive national
resources to this issue? Has the
nation displayed the new attitudes
called for by the Commission?
Can blacks gain their objectives
by a resort to violence? Why is
white society responsible for ghetto
problems? Can our nation exist if
it is organized into two societies,
"separate and unequal"?*

* Reprinted from Report, National Advisory Commission on Civil Disorders
(U.S. Government Printing Office, 1968)
pp. 1–2.

The summer of 1967 again brought
racial disorders to American cities,
and with them shock, fear and be-
wilderment to the nation.

The worst came during a two-
week period in July, first in Newark
and then in Detroit. Each set off a
chain reaction in neighboring communities.

On July 28, 1967, the President
of the United States established
this Commission and directed us to
answer three basic questions:

What happened?

Why did it happen?

What can be done to prevent it
from happening again?

To respond to these questions, we
have undertaken a broad range of
studies and investigations. We have
visited the riot cities; we have heard
many witnesses; we have sought the
counsel of experts across the country.

This is our basic conclusion: Our
nation is moving toward two societies, one black, one white—
separate and unequal.

Reaction to last summer's disorders has quickened the movement and deepened the division.
Discrimination and segregation
have long permeated much of
American life; they now threaten
the future of every American.

This deepening racial division is
not inevitable. The movement apart
can be reversed. Choice is still possible. Our principal task is to define
that choice and to press for a national resolution.

To pursue our present course

will involve the continuing polarization of the American community and, ultimately, the destruction of basic democratic values.

The alternative is not blind repression or capitulation to lawlessness. It is the realization of common opportunities for all within a single society.

This alternative will require a commitment to national action—compassionate, massive and sustained, backed by the resources of the most powerful and the richest nation on this earth. From every American it will require new attitudes, new understanding, and, above all, new will.

The vital needs of the nation must be met; hard choices must be made, and, if necessary, new taxes enacted.

Violence cannot build a better society. Disruption and disorder nourish repression, not justice. They strike at the freedom of every citizen. The community cannot—it will not—tolerate coercion and mob rule.

Violence and destruction must be ended—in the streets of the ghetto and in the lives of people.

Segregation and poverty have created in the racial ghetto a destructive environment totally unknown to most white Americans.

What white Americans have never fully understood—but what the Negro can never forget—is that white society is deeply implicated in the ghetto. White institutions created it, white institutions main-

tain it, and white society condones it.

It is time now to turn with all the purpose at our command to the major unfinished business of this nation. It is time to adopt strategies for action that will produce quick and visible progress. It is time to make good the promises of American democracy to all citizens—urban and rural, white and black, Spanish-surname, American Indian, and every minority group.

Our recommendations embrace three basic principles:

- To mount programs on a scale equal to the dimension of the problems;
- To aim these programs for high impact in the immediate future in order to close the gap between promise and performance;
- To undertake new initiative and experiments that can change the system of failure and frustration that now dominates the ghetto and weakens our society.

These programs will require unprecedented levels of funding and performance, but they neither probe deeper nor demand more than the problems which called them forth. There can be no higher priority for national action and no higher claim on the nation's conscience. . . .

POPULATION BOMB, U.S.A. *

PAUL R. EHRLICH

---

*Americans are increasingly aware
that our major social, economic
and political problems are a by-
product of our rising population.
This concern is dramatized by such
terms as "population explosion"
and "population bomb." Both at
home and abroad our hopes for
the good life may be drowned in a
sea of human fertility.*

*What are the projections for
population growth in the developed
countries? The underdeveloped
countries? Why can't the developed
nations escape the food crisis?
What current U.S. problems does
Ehrlich link to our soaring population? Could the United States avoid
the worldwide population crisis
by becoming totally self-sufficient?
Why does Ehrlich discount optimistic reports of declining birth
rates? Does he offer any solutions?*

. . . I have understood the population explosion intellectually for a
long time. I came to understand
it emotionally one stinking hot night
in Delhi a couple of years ago. My
wife and daughter and I were re-

° *From* The Population Bomb *by Dr.
Paul R. Ehrlich. Copyright © 1968 by
Paul R. Ehrlich. Reprinted by permission
of Ballantine Books, Inc.*

turning to our hotel in an ancient
taxi. The seats were hopping with
fleas. The only functional gear was
third. As we crawled through the
city, we entered a crowded slum
area. The temperature was well
over 100, and the air was a haze of
dust and smoke. The streets seemed
alive with people. People eating,
people washing, people sleeping.
People visiting, arguing, and
screaming. People thrusting their
hands through the taxi window,
begging. People defecating and
urinating. People clinging to buses.
People herding animals. People,
people, people, people. As we
moved slowly through the mob,
hand horn squawking, the dust,
noise, heat, and cooking fires gave
the scene a hellish aspect. Would
we ever get to our hotel? All three
of us were, frankly, frightened. It
seemed that anything could happen—but, of course, nothing did.
Old India hands will laugh at our
reaction. We were just some over-
privileged tourists, unaccustomed
to the sights and sounds of India.
Perhaps, but since that night I've
known the *feel* of overpopulation. . . .

. . .

Too Many People

Americans are beginning to realize
that the undeveloped countries of
the world face an inevitable population-food crisis. Each year food
production in undeveloped countries falls a bit further behind
burgeoning population growth, and

people go to bed a little bit hungrier. While there are temporary or local reversals of this trend, it now seems inevitable that it will continue to its logical conclusion: mass starvation. The rich are going to get richer, but the more numerous poor are going to get poorer. Of these poor, a minimum of three and one-half million will starve to death this year, mostly children. But this is a mere handful compared to the numbers that will be starving in a decade or so. And it is now too late to take action to save many of those people.

In a book about population there is a temptation to stun the reader with an avalanche of statistics. I'll spare you most, but not all, of that. After all, no matter how you slice it, population is a numbers game. Perhaps the best way to impress you with numbers is to tell you about the "doubling time"—the time necessary for the population to double in size.

It has been estimated that the human population of 6000 B.C. was about five million people, taking perhaps one million years to get there from two and a half million. The population did not reach 500 million until almost 8,000 years later—about 1650 A.D. This means it doubled roughly once every thousand years or so. It reached a billion people around 1850, doubling in some 200 years. It took only 80 years or so for the next doubling, as the population reached two billion around 1930. We have not completed the next doubling to four billion yet, but we now have well over three billion people. The doubling time at present seems to be about 37 years. Quite a reduction in doubling times: 1,000,000 years, 1,000 years, 200 years, 80 years, 37 years. Perhaps the meaning of a doubling time of around 37 years is best brought home by a theoretical exercise. Let's examine what might happen on the absurd assumption that the population continued to double every 37 years into the indefinite future.

If growth continued at that rate for about 900 years, there would be some 60,000,000,000,000,000 people on the face of the earth. Sixty million billion people. This is about 100 persons for each square yard of the Earth's surface, land and sea. . . .

. . .

Doubling times for the populations of the DCs [Developed Countries] tend to be in the 50-to-200-year range. Examples of 1968 doubling times are the United States, 63 years; Austria, 175; Denmark, 88; Norway, 88; United Kingdom, 140; Poland, 88; Russia, 63; Italy, 117; Spain, 88; and Japan, 63. These are industrialized countries that have undergone the so-called demographic transition—a transition from high to low growth rate. As industrialization progressed, children became less important to parents as extra hands to work on the farm and as support in old age. At the same time they became a financial drag—expensive to raise and educate. Presumably these are the reasons for a slowing of population growth after industrialization. They boil down to a simple fact—people just want to have fewer children.

This is not to say, however, that population is not a problem for the DCs. First of all, most of them are overpopulated. They are overpopulated by the simple criterion that they are not able to produce enough food to feed their populations. It is true that they have the money to buy food, but when food is no longer available for sale they will find the money rather indigestible. Then, too, they share with the UDCs [Under-developed Countries] a serious problem of population distribution. Their urban centers are getting more and more crowded relative to the countryside. This problem is not as severe as it is in the UDCs (if current trends should continue, which they cannot, Calcutta could have 66 million inhabitants in the year 2000). As you are well aware, however, urban concentrations are creating serious problems even in America. In the United States, one of the more rapidly growing DCs, we hear constantly of the headaches caused by growing population: not just garbage in our environment, but overcrowded highways, burgeoning slums, deteriorating school systems, rising crime rates, riots, and other related problems.

From the point of view of a demographer, the whole problem is quite simple. A population will continue to grow as long as the birth rate exceeds the death rate—if immigration and emigration are not occurring.

· · ·

There are some professional optimists around who like to greet every sign of dropping birth rates with wild pronouncements about the end of the population explosion. They are a little like a person who, after a low temperature of five below zero on December 21, interprets a low of only three below zero on December 22 as a cheery sign of approaching spring. . . .

· · ·

The battle to feed all of humanity is over. In the 1970's the world will undergo famines—hundreds of millions of people are going to starve to death in spite of any crash programs embarked upon now. At this late date nothing can prevent a substantial increase in the world death rate, although many lives could be saved through dramatic programs to "stretch" the carrying capacity of the earth by increasing food production. But these programs will only provide a stay of execution unless they are accompanied by determined and successful efforts at population control. Population control is the conscious regulation of the numbers of human beings to meet the needs, not just of individual families, but of society as a whole.

Nothing could be more misleading to our children than our present affluent society. They will inherit a totally different world, a world in which the standards, politics, and economics of the 1960's are dead. As the most powerful nation in the world today, *and its largest consumer,* the United States cannot stand isolated. We are today involved in the events leading to famine; tomorrow we may be destroyed by its consequences.

Our position requires that we take immediate action at home and promote effective action worldwide. We must have population control at home, hopefully through a system of incentives and penalties, but by compulsion if voluntary methods fail. We must use our political power to push other countries into programs which combine agricultural development and population control. And while this is being done we must take action to reverse the deterioration of our environment before population pressure permanently ruins our planet. The birth rate must be brought into balance with the death rate or mankind will breed itself into oblivion. We can no longer afford merely to treat the symptoms of the cancer of population growth; the cancer itself must be cut out. Population control is the only answer.

IN SEARCH OF A POPULATION POLICY *
POPULATION REFERENCE BUREAU

The idea of a national population policy is completely foreign to our tradition. Americans have always lived where they pleased: likewise, procreation has always been a private affair. The march of events now challenges these assumptions. As more and more people crowd into a few megalopolises—as the relationship between difficult political problems and population growth becomes clear—the line between government policy and private decisions becomes blurred.

What kind of national growth policy has President Nixon proposed? Why is population distribution a critical problem? Why is a U.S. growth rate of one per cent a cause for concern? What has been done by government to encourage family planning? What changes in abortion policy have occurred? In the ongoing debate over population policy what position has been taken by the American Medical Association? The

* Extracted from "Population Developments in 1970," Population Bulletin, December, 1970, pp. 8–10. Copyright © 1971 by Population Reference Bureau, Inc., 1755 Massachusetts Avenue, N.W., Washington, D.C. 20036.

Catholic Physicians Guild? The
Presbyterian Church? What is the
general public attitude as reflected
in the Harris Poll?

. . .

President Nixon set the tone for the discussion of population distribution policy in his January 22 State of the Union Address. "For the past 30 years," he told Congress, "our population has . . . been growing and shifting. The result is exemplified in the vast areas of rural America emptying out of people and of promise—a third of our counties lost population in the '60's. The violent and decayed central cities of our great metropolitan complexes are the most conspicuous area of failure in American life today.

"I propose that before these problems become insoluble, the nation develop a national growth policy. . . . In particular, the federal government must be in a position to assist in the building of new cities and the rebuilding of old ones. . . . We must create a new rural environment which will not only stem the migration to urban centers but reverse it."

This was the opening shot in a barrage of resolutions during 1970 to develop a national growth policy to influence the future location of the next 50 million Americans. The assumption of a population imbalance went unchallenged. With rare unanimity, planners and politicians agreed that the growth of BosWash, ChiPitts, SanSan and other mega-

lopolises was a bad thing and that the development of smaller communities nearer the countryside would be a good thing.

Almost all the participants in this non-debate treated migration as a cause rather than a symptom of social and economic problems. The underlying causes of migration from rural areas to central cities and from decaying central cities to suburbs tended to be glossed over or ignored.

Typical of this rhetorical habit, which has not led to a single promising solution or even a demonstration project in the field of "balanced" growth, was a speech given at American University on February 24 by Secretary of Commerce Maurice H. Stans. Reiterating President Nixon's call for a national growth policy, he flatly predicted that by the year 2000 "85 percent of our population of 300 million will be urban" and concluded that "it is not very pleasant to contemplate what such an anthill society would mean to this nation."

. . .

But by far the most comprehensive government statement on population distribution policy was issued by the National Goals Research Staff, set up by President Nixon in 1969. Its report, *Toward Balanced Growth,* attempted the difficult feat of clarifying a gamut of public policy options. On the subject of population, Leonard Garment's team, which produced the report, dismissed overall growth as a non-problem. On matters of distribution, however, the report found a very real and important challenge.

"Plainly the country faces a problem in the distribution of its population regardless of policies to control its overall size," it said. "Assuming that the trends continue unabated, most of the U.S. population growth over the next few decades will be concentrated in the 12 largest regions. . . . These trends have led to a prevalent sense of gloom for the future of both urban and rural America. . . . Hence, the choice of no change in public policy would run the high risk of bringing about the kind of future in which the communities of both urban and rural America would further deteriorate. It means that hundreds of American towns will continue to lose young people and economic opportunity and that the large metropolitan areas, already burdened with social and fiscal problems and characterized by fragmentation of governmental responsibility, may reach a size at which they will be socially intolerable, politically unmanageable and economically inefficient."

The Goals report, noting that the federal government can "provide leadership" for a national strategy of balanced population growth, defined what it construed to be the current debate over tactics. It identified three choices: (1) generating growth in underpopulated rural areas; (2) generating growth in existing small towns and cities in nonmetropolitan areas; and (3)

creating new cities outside the big metropolitan regions. . . .

. . .

The Growth Debate

In its concluding passages on population, the Goals report struck a note which recurred through much popular and learned commentary in the past year. "One problem which appears not to be urgent," it said, "is that of overall size of the population. . . . The issue of population distribution is a different matter, and one to be taken seriously."

The implication that a U.S. growth rate of 1 per cent per year and an annual increase of more than 2 million are not *serious* matters may seem unwarranted to those who view them in terms of resource consumption, the loss of open space, pollution and the stubborn persistence of social problems whose resolution is made more difficult by growth. . . .

. . .

The wave of optimism was countered from expected sources. Writing in the November 4 *New York Times*, Stanford University biologist Paul R. Ehrlich asked: "Assume for a moment that . . . in the year 2000 the population of the United States is 'only' some 280 million people. What might that mean to us and to the world?

"Each American has roughly 50 times the negative impact on the earth's life-support systems as the average citizen of India. Therefore, in terms of ecosystem destruction, adding 75 million more Americans will be the equivalent of adding 3.7 billion Indians to the world population. . . . Clearly population growth among Americans is much more serious than population growth in underdeveloped countries."

Ehrlich did not disclose the data which led to his 50:1 ratio of environmental damage as between the average North American and the average Indian. About the message of the projections themselves, however, the author of *The Population Bomb* was more precise. Referring to the new low projection based on replacement-level fertility, he observed: "Even with luck we are doomed to continued population growth until at least 2045, and the projected population size then will be over 300 million. Hardly a pleasant prospect for a nation now failing to provide properly for 205 million people."

In May, the Population Reference Bureau pointed out that a wave of U.S. women had begun to flood the prime reproductive ages of 20–29, and that this trend might offset the drop in age-specific fertility (the number of children per 1,000 women in each age cohort). "In 1960," it said, "there were only 11 million women aged 20–29; by 1980 there will be nearly twice as many [about 20 million]." This population bulge is made up of the children of the post-World War II "baby boom."

. . .

Family Planning's Greatest Year

The single most definitive achievement of the population community in 1970 was the passage, in both the Senate and House, of companion bills to make family planning services and information available to every woman in the United States who presently cannot afford them. The services would include birth control pills and other means of contraception along with consultations, examinations, instruction and referral to other medical programs where necessary.

Both bills would significantly expand the government grants for family planning services, training and research, but construction of population research centers did not survive opposition by the Nixon administration, which generally favored the two bills. To coordinate these grants and to serve as a clearing house for population and family planning information, the legislation creates a national center for population and family planning in HEW.

. . . Dr. [Charles F.] Westoff [Princeton University demographer who now heads the staff of the Commission on Population Growth and the American Future] reports: "For the nine years from 1960 through 1968, we estimate that between 35 and 45 per cent of the natural increase that occurred in the United States could be attributed to unwanted fertility."

"In other words, a national family planning program with the capacity to prevent all unwanted births would have gone far to substantially slow our population growth and reduce the financial burdens on communities forced to provide for increased services such as highways, school construction and welfare."

. . .

Abortion

There is an analogy between family planning programs and abortion reform or repeal: Both are advocated principally as humane welfare and health measures, and both may lead to a lower birth rate. The past year was a breakthrough year for those groups which have been fighting the restrictions on abortion that have been in effect for decades (though at one time in the United States abortion was available to most women who could afford it). In all, 12 states have reformed their abortion laws since 1967, some in small ways, some drastically. Three states repealed their restrictive abortion laws in 1970. To date eight states have had their abortion laws declared unconstitutional by the courts and four more have cases pending.

The closest step toward outright repeal of all restrictions on abortion was taken by New York which wiped a 140-year-old law off the books. The old law had permitted abortions only to save the pregnant woman's life; the new law leaves the decision to have an abortion entirely up to the woman and her doctor. Requiring no in-state residency, the law sanctions virtually all abortions within the first 24 weeks of pregnancy—before the fetus becomes viable.

In all the states where abortion laws were reformed, the Women's Liberation movement played a significant role. It is also a leading force in the drive to secure a uniform national sanction for abortions on demand. A bill to accomplish just that was introduced by Senator Packwood in April. Its operative clause states: "Any physician is authorized to perform, in any state, by such means as he deems appropriate, an abortion on any female person who requests that action."

. . .

Complementing the legislative advances in abortion reform (a major setback occurred in Maryland, whose governor vetoed the reform bill), the House of Delegates of the American Medical Association voted twice, in June and November, to allow doctors to perform abortions for social and economic reasons as well as for medical ones. The Association stipulated that the operations be performed by properly licensed doctors in accredited hospitals, and that two other doctors be called on for consultation with the operating doctor in each case. Voting in favor of the new policy after a long, bitter debate, the Association reversed its former 123-year-old position by a 103 to 73 margin.

The new resolution was angrily opposed by the 6,000-member National Association of Catholic Physician's Guilds. Its president, Dr.

Gino Papola, asserted: "The AMA has made it ethical for doctors to become formal executioners." In a related move, the General Assembly of the Presbyterian Church, meeting in Memphis on June 18, declared that economic straits were a valid justification for abortion. And four days later the Harris Poll reported that the U.S. public was 50-40 percent opposed to passage of state laws "permitting abortion for almost any reason," but that when the question was put, "until good, safe birth control methods can be found, abortions should be legalized," the public agreed by 49–39 percent. Support for reform of abortion laws was strongest in the East and far West, and among the college educated and the young. . . .

2. Basic Beliefs In Question: The Who, What, Why of American Democracy

Contemporary American society, with 200-plus million people concentrated in six super-cities, does not easily fit the assumptions of time-honored democratic theory. Until some acceptable compromise is reached to bridge the present gap between theory and reality the nation will be ill-at-ease, since all legitimate governments are based on ideas that have widespread acceptance.

America As A Mass Society

Ours is a totally different nation than the nation for which the Constitution of 1787 was drafted. Ours is a mass society, where people are identified by Social Security numbers. In housing "developments," variants of little boxes in assorted colors stretch from horizon to horizon. Automobiles six abreast jam the freeways in an unending stream. The Holiday Inn in Wichita Falls, Kansas resembles in every way the Holiday Inn in Sharon, Pennsylvania. College students are packed into lecture halls, graded by IBM computers, and have their degrees conferred in mass exercises. Sports and amusements are mechanized and commercialized: everyone is a spectator. Most human contacts are casual: we have many acquaintances; few true friends. The great moments of human experience—birth, marriage, retirement, death—are celebrated by a trinket bought out of the office "welfare kitty."

Ours is a society of planned obsolesence. It is a consumer-oriented culture where nothing is permanent. Everything's plastic! Aluminum-foil pie pans, last-year's wife, and the old moral values are equally expendable in the giant contemporary American Disposall.

Values of A Mass Society

In a society where everything has become relative—where values are unranked—tradition and the ideas of the Founding Fathers carry little weight. History and experience are easily discounted in favor of glittering new ideas. Careful, rational thought is rejected for government by bumper stickers. "America: Love It or Leave It" allows no reasoned discussion.

Extreme individualism seems to be the order of the day. Everyone does his own thing, unchallenged by his peers. The welfare of the group, the state, the nation is nobody's business. These tendencies are encouraged by an urbanization that has shattered old groupings—family, church, community—and raised doubts about basic democratic beliefs.

Traditional Democratic Beliefs

Americans did not invent democracy, but they have certainly played a major role in making it a practical theory. The hard-headed men who drafted our Constitution did not believe that men were angels, nor that they would ever become angels. They also discarded the opposing theory that men were basically evil. They believed that the average citizen would be involved in public affairs and have a concern for the public interest. He need not necessarily participate in every decision, but he would be involved in determining major public policy. The Founding Fathers greatly feared the potential tyranny of government. The Constitution created a federal system that delegated certain powers to the national government, while it reserved other powers to the states. National power was balanced between the executive, legislative and judicial branches, with each having a check on the others. Very quickly a Bill of Rights was added that protected citizens from arbitrary governmental action. Many of these restrictions were extended to the states by the Fourteenth Amendment.

A gross oversimplification would say that the authors of the Constitution feared simple majority rule. They devised a system under which each branch of government was selected through a different procedure by a different constituency. Each held office for a different term. The minority gained protection from the Bill of Rights. They could also block amendments to the Constitution by mustering slightly more than one-third of either House of Congress or one-fourth of the state legislatures. Before bills could become law they normally had to clear several hurdles, including approval by each House of Congress and the President.

These examples are only illustrations of the intricate devices created to thwart simple majorities.

The Founding Fathers had great misgivings about the ability of ordinary people to function as voting citizens. Excluded completely from the process were women, non-propertied citizens and blacks. Bit by bit these exclusions have been erased, but authority in the 1970's still is concentrated in the hands of white, upper-class males.

Questioning Basic Beliefs

This concentration of authority is perhaps the major cause of widespread alienation from the present political system. Quite simply, millions of Americans believe that our present government is run by "them" rather than by "us." They believe that they are manipulated by an "Establishment" for its own ends. Some of the most vocal protest has come from young people on college campuses, who are distressed by the emerging mass society, and deeply concerned with evidence of injustices at home and abroad. They have heretofore been excluded completely from the decision-making process. In reaction some have staged protests to reform the political system. Some have forsworn politics in favor of a life style that concentrates on personal fulfillment. Others find the existing system to be beyond reform and are committed to its destruction.

But this political disenchantment reaches far beyond the college campus. Millions of middle-class white Americans believe that they have lost control of a system that was once theirs. They deem themselves an outwitted majority whose government responds only to "kooky kids," "pointy-headed" professors, "pinkos," lazy welfare mothers, and "uppity" blacks. Archie Bunker of TV's "All In The Family" vividly portrays the frustrations of these "forgotten Americans."

In essence, the cement that formally held Americans together appears to be crumbling before the stresses of a mass society. To further complicate this widespread political sickness, we are living in a period of high-speed change in every department of human existence. One middle-aged economist is quoted as saying, "I was born in the middle of human history . . . Almost as much has happened since I was born as happened before." In summary, basic democratic beliefs are being questioned today as never before.

Does Democracy Have A Future?

What political beliefs square with the realities of an urbanized America? What parts of traditional theory remain valid? Can we in pragmatic fashion pick and choose from our heritage those concepts that will give us a revitalized democratic framework? Can we broaden the base of participation to reestablish legitimate governmental authority? As it stands today that legitimacy is being steadily eroded.

History suggests that men do not long endure disorder in society. If the legitimacy of American democracy is not restored, some type of authoritarian rule could very well fill the vacuum. A century ago, caught up in the civil strife of his day, Abraham Lincoln at Gettysburg raised the question of "whether this nation or any other nation so conceived and so dedicated can long endure?" Recent hand-to-hand conflict between "hard hats" and peace marchers is a sample of present tensions.

Most of the pages of history are given over to tyranny of one sort or another (ancient Assyria, Babylon, Egypt, Sparta, Rome, the Aztec and Inca kingdoms; modern states such as Hitler's Germany, Mussolini's Italy, Stalin's Russia, Napoleon's France, Mao's China). Far fewer pages are required to record the story of such democratic states as Athens, the Roman Republic, the Italian city-states, the French, Dutch and Scandinavian democracies and the long-enduring British experiment. Supporters of the New Left who hope to create an unstructured communal society can cite from the historical record mostly short-lived attempts such as New Economy, The Oneida Community, Ephrata, and New Harmony.

Summary

If we agree that more people should be involved in the decision-making process, what are they to decide? Can we realistically expect to create a town meeting of over 200 million people, with everyone linked to a central computer? Or should we restrict citizens to broad policy decisions? These are indeed hard questions. But if we avoid hard answers our survival as a democratic nation is in jeopardy.

FUTURE SHOCK *

ALVIN TOFFLER

Jet travelers several years ago invented the phrase "culture shock" to describe the reaction of some tourists who were set down without preparation in a totally new culture. Unable to cope with the different environment, these people withdrew and became erratic in their behavior. According to the author of Future Shock *this phenomenon now occurs within American culture. The speed of change is so rapid that middle-aged people are left behind by the mad rush of the cultural mainstream.*

Of the 800 lifetimes the author cites in his book, man spent the first 650 in caves. We have had precise measurement of time for only four lifetimes. Toffler believes that in a single century we have moved through the industrial period, with its emphasis on the production of goods, to a post-industrial society, dedicated to services.

What symptoms of severe social dislocation are apparent in modern society? How does Toffler's forecast differ from Huxley's, Brave New World? *From Orwell's* 1984? *Can*

. . .

We are creating a new society. Not a changed society. Not an extended, larger-than-life version of our present society. But a new society.

This simple premise has not yet begun to tincture our consciousness. Yet unless we understand this, we shall destroy ourselves in trying to cope with tomorrow.

A revolution shatters institutions and power relationships. This is precisely what is happening today in all the high-technology nations. Students in Berlin and New York, in Turin and Tokyo, capture their deans and chancellors, bring great clanking educational factories to a grinding halt, and even threaten to topple governments. Police stand aside in the ghettos of New York, Washington and Chicago as ancient property laws are openly violated. Sexual standards are overthrown. Great cities are paralyzed by strikes, power failures, riots. International power alliances are shaken. Financial and political leaders secretly tremble—not out of fear that communist (or capitalist) revolutionaries will oust them, but that the entire system is somehow flying out of control. . . .

In the 1920's and 1930's, communists used to speak of the "general crisis of capitalism." It is now clear that they were thinking small. What is occurring now is not a crisis of capitalism, but of industrial society itself, regardless of its political form.

Reaching deep into our personal lives, the enormous changes ahead will transform traditional family structures and sexual attitudes, they will smash conventional relationships between old and young. They will overthrow our values with respect to money and success. They will alter work, play and education beyond recognition. And they will do all this in a context of spectacular, elegant, yet frightening scientific advance. . . .

THE CULTURE OF
MASS SOCIETY *

MAX LERNER

The environmental and cultural background of Americans has changed radically during the past two generations. In 1900 most of them lived on farms or in small towns; now the vast majority live in metropolitan areas (cities and their suburbs). In 1900 most Americans depended on horse-

* From Max Lerner, America As A Civilization, Vol. I, pp. 167–168; 260–261. Copyright © 1957 by Max Lerner. Reprinted by permission of Simon and Schuster, Inc.

and-buggy transportation and high speed communication was epitomized by the telegraph. Today's world is characterized by its airplanes, TV and computers. Above all else the machine dominates modern life in the United States. What impact have such changes made on the American personality? How has the governmental process been affected? Is classical democratic theory valid in this "brave new world"?

The new urban personality which is emerging in America is the product of the machine—but also of a good deal more. The machine aspects of city living are obvious enough. Who can forget the swift tunneling of the machine-as-subway in the earth, the scurrying of the machine-as-automobile over its surface, the exacting regularity of the machine-as-traffic-light, the droning of the machine-as-television, the stream of print emerging from the machine-as-press, the silent power and precision of the machine-as-dynamo? Who can escape the tempo of the mass city—hurrying to work, to appointments, to crises, to pleasure, to tragedy?

Yet what gives the city its character as living is not the tempo or discipline of the machine but the effort to reach for values beyond it. The youngster becomes a member of the city gang, partly at least because the gang gives him a chance for a sense of belonging and feudal allegiance. Similarly with mechanized sports and amusements in the big city. Prize fighters pummel each other like gladiators before thousands; baseball contests are commercial events staged on schedule, with team standings calculated down to the fourth decimal point; movies and TV project the same image on thousands of screens to the accompaniment of millions of fluttering pulses; choruses of dancing girls tap out their rhythms in night clubs with machinelike precision. Yet the big fact about all of them is not that they are mechanical, which is true enough, but that they furnish channels for mass emotion which relieve the tension of machine living.

Within this frame the city has developed a type of American character different from the type that de Crevecoeur, de Tocqueville, or even Bryce depicted. It is less conditioned to the soil and the seasons, less religious, more skeptical about motives and chary of being "played for a sucker," less illusioned in the sense in which illusions—about friendship, work, sex, love, and God—provide an internal sustaining force for the personality. It has been psychologically hardened by innumerable brief encounters—in public schools, on subways and busses, in restaurants, in the course of shopping—which would become intolerable if one did not sheathe oneself against them with a constricted response. It is precocious about money matters and sex, since so many city people grow up in crowded quarters where few things are concealed from them. It is stoical in the face of hardship and the man-made catastrophes of economic life. It is not "urbane" except in the small groups in which one can afford to be generous, but it is much more likely to strip the jungle life of the city down to the nakedness of the human animal. It economizes time with an almost manic earnestness during the hours of pleasure and recreation. It lays stress (within limits) on individual traits of personality, on uniqueness in dress and sophistication in taste, on awareness, on the dramatic impact that the individual makes in his brief meetings with others. It has replaced fear by anxiety, and the concern about danger from elemental forces with a vague concern about security, safety, and the opinions of others.

What this means is that city living has carried men and women ever further away from their instinctual endowment. The city is not the root of the planlessness, the tensions, and the conformism of American life, but it is the envelope that encloses them. Or, to change the figure, the city is the battleground of the values of the culture.

It is here, moving from machine living to cultural standardization, that the picture becomes bleaker. Henry Miller's phrase for its American form is "the air-conditioned nightmare." Someone with a satiric intent could do a withering take-off on the rituals of American standardization.

Most American babies (he might say) are born in standardized hospitals, with a standardized tag put around them to keep them from getting confused with other standardized products of the hospital.

Many of them grow up either in uniform rows of tenements or of small-town or suburban houses. They are wheeled about in standard perambulators, shiny or shabby as may be, fed from standardized bottles with standardized nipples according to standardized formulas, and tied up with standardized diapers. In childhood they are fed standardized breakfast foods out of standardized boxes with pictures of standardized heroes on them. They are sent to monotonously similar schoolhouses, where almost uniformly standardized teachers ladle out to them standardized information out of standardized textbooks. They pick up the routine wisdom of the streets in standard slang and learn the routine terms which constrict the range of their language within dishearteningly narrow limits. They wear out standardized shoes playing standardized games, or as passive observers they follow through standardized newspaper accounts or standardized radio and TV programs the highly ritualized antics of grownup professionals playing the same games. They devour in millions of uniform pulp comic books the prowess of standardized supermen.

As they grow older they dance to canned music from canned juke boxes, millions of them putting standard coins into standard slots to get standardized tunes sung by voices with standardized inflections of emotion. They date with standardized girls in standardized cars. They see automatons thrown on millions of the same movie and TV screens, watching stereotyped love scenes adapted from made-to-order stories in standardized magazines.

They spend the days of their years with monotonous regularity in factory, office, and shop, performing routinized operations at regular intervals. They take time out for standardized "coffee breaks" and later a quick standardized lunch, come home at night to eat processed or canned food, and read syndicated columns and comic strips. Dressed in standardized clothes they attend standardized club meetings, church services, and socials. They have standardized fun at standardized big-city conventions. They are drafted into standardized armies, and if they escape the death of mechanized warfare they die of highly uniform diseases, and to the accompaniment of routine platitudes they are buried in standardized graves and celebrated by standardized obituary notices.

Caricature? Yes, perhaps a crude one, but with a core of frightening validity in it. Every society has its routines and rituals, the primitive groups being sometimes more tyrannously restricted by convention than the industrial societies. The difference is that where the primitive is bound by the rituals of tradition and group life, the American is bound by the rituals of the machine, its products, and their distribution and consumption.

The role of the machine in this standardized living must be made clear. The machine mechanizes life, and since mass production is part of Big Technology, the machine also makes uniformity of life possible. But it does not compel such uniformity. The American who shaves with an electric razor and his wife who buys a standardized "home permanent" for her hair do not thereby have to wear a uniformly vacuous expression through the day. A newspaper that uses the press association wire stories and prints from a highly mechanized set of presses does not thereby have to take the same view of the world that every other paper takes. A novelist who uses a typewriter instead of a quill pen does not have to turn out machine-made historical romances.

The answer is that some do and some don't. What the machine and the mass-produced commodities have done has been to make conformism easier. To buy and use what everyone else does, and live and think as everyone else does, becomes a short cut involving no need for one's own thinking. Those Americans have been captured by conformist living who have been capturable by it.

Cultural stereotypes are an inherent part of all group living, and they become sharper with mass living. There have always been unthinking people leading formless, atomized lives. What has happened in America is that the economics of mass production has put a premium on uniformity, so that America produces more units of more commodities (although sometimes of fewer models) than other cul-

tures. American salesmanship has sought out every potential buyer of a product, so that standardization makes its way by the force of the distributive mechanism into every life. Yet for the person who has a personality pattern and style of his own, standardization need not mean anything more than a set of conveniences which leave a larger margin of leisure and greater scope for creative living. "That we may be enamored by the negation brought by the machine," as Frank Lloyd Wright has put it, "may be inevitable for a time. But I like to imagine this novel negation to be only a platform underfoot to enable a greater splendor of life to be ours than any known to Greek or Roman, Goth or Moor. We should know a life beside which the life they knew would seem not only limited in scale and narrow in range but pale in richness of the color of imagination and integrity of spirit."

Which is to say that technology is the shell of American life, but a shell that need not hamper or stultify the modes of living and thinking. The real dangers of the American mode of life are not in the machine or even in standardization as much as they are in conformism. The dangers do not flow from the contrivances that men have fashioned to lighten their burdens, or from the material abundance which, if anything, should make a richer cultural life possible. They flow rather from the mimesis of the dominant and successful by the weak and mediocre, from the intolerance of diversity, and from the fear of being thought different from one's fellows. This is the essence of conformism.

THE NEW YOUTH CULTURE *
PRESIDENT'S COMMISSION ON CAMPUS UNREST

"Apathy" was the most frequently used word to describe college students in the 1950's. By 1965 college campuses were seething with unrest and revolt against "The Establishment." Society's most favored young people in economic and social terms were in rebellion against that society.

What were they in revolt against? What fraction of the college generation was involved? Was it a unified movement? Was the revolt a college phenomenon, or did all young people share it? What is meant by the term "counter culture"? Why do these critics concentrate on American shortcomings? Do they have an alternate program? Is the entire youth movement part of a maturation process, or is a new culture being born?

In early western societies, the young were traditionally submissive to adults. Largely because adults retained great authority, the only way for the young to achieve wealth, power and prestige was through a cooperative apprenticeship of some sort to the adult world. Thus, the young learned the traditional adult ways of living, and in time, they grew up to become adults of the same sort as their parents, living in the same sort of world.

Advancing industrialism decisively changed this cooperative relationship between the generations. It produced new forms and new sources of wealth, power and prestige, and these weakened traditional adult controls over the young. It removed production from the home, and made it increasingly specialized; as a result, the young were increasingly removed from adult work places and could not directly observe or participate in adult work. Moreover, industrialism hastened the separation of education from the home, and the young were increasingly concentrated together in places of formal education that were isolated from most adults. Thus, the young spent an increasing amount of time together, apart from their parents' home and work, in activities that were different from those of adults.

This shared and distinct experience among the young led to shared

* *Report of President's Commission On Campus Unrest (Government Printing Office, 1970), pp. 61–69.*

interests and problems, which led, in turn, to the development of distinct subcultures. As those subcultures developed, they provided support for any youth movement distinct from—or even directed against—the adult world.

A distinguishing characteristic of young people is their penchant for pure idealism. Society teaches youth to adhere to the basic values of the adult social system—equality, honesty, democracy, or whatever—in absolute terms. Throughout most of American history, the idealism of youth has been formed—and constrained—by the institutions of adult society. But during the 1960's, in response to an accumulation of social changes, the traditional American youth culture developed rapidly in the direction of an oppositional stance toward the institutions and ways of the adult world.

This subculture took its bearings from the notion of the autonomous, self-determining individual whose goal was to live with "authenticity," or in harmony with his inner penchants and instincts. It also found its identity in a rejection of the work ethic, materialism, and conventional social norms and pieties. Indeed, it rejected all institutional disciplines externally imposed upon the individual, and this set it at odds with much in American society.

Its aim was to liberate human consciousness and to enhance the quality of experience; it sought to replace the materialism, the self-denial, and the striving for achievement that characterized the existing society with a new emphasis on the expressive, the creative, the imaginative. The tools of the workaday institutional world—hierarchy, discipline, rules, self-interest, self-defense, power—it considered mad and tyrannical. It proclaimed instead the liberation of the individual to feel, to experience, to express whatever his unique humanity prompted. And its perceptions of the world grew ever more distant from the perceptions of the existing culture: what most called "justice" or "peace" or "accomplishment" the new culture envisioned as "enslavement" or "hysteria" or "meaninglessness." As this divergence of values and of vision proceeded, the new youth culture became increasingly oppositional.

And yet in its commitment to liberty and equality, it was very much in the mainstream of American tradition; what it doubted was that America had managed to live up to its national ideals. Over time, these doubts grew, and youth culture became increasingly imbued with a sense of alienation and of opposition to the larger society.

No one who lives in contemporary America can be unaware of the surface manifestations of this new youth culture. Dress is highly distinctive; emphasis is placed on heightened color and sound; the enjoyment of flowers and nature is given a high priority. The fullest ranges of sense and sensation are to be enjoyed each day through the cultivation of new experiences, through spiritualism, and through drugs. Life is sought to be made as simple, primitive, and "natural" as possible, as ritualized, for example, by nude bathing.

Social historians can find parallels to this culture in the past. One is reminded of Bacchic cults in ancient Greece, or of the wandering bands of German students in the early 19th century, the Wandervoegelen, or of primitive Christianity. Confidence is placed in revelation rather than cognition, in sensation rather than analysis, in the personal rather than the institutional. Emphasis is placed on living to the fullest extent, on the sacredness of life itself, and on the common mystery of all living things. The ancient vision of natural man, untrammeled and unscarred by the fetters of institutions, is seen again. It is not necessary to describe such movements as "religious", but it is useful to recognize that they have elements in common with the waves of religious fervor that periodically have captivated the minds of men.

It is not difficult to compose a picture of contemporary America as it looks through the eyes of one whose premises are essentially those just described. Human life is all; but women and children are being killed in Vietnam by American forces. All living things are sacred; but American industry and technology are polluting the air and the streams, and killing the birds and the fish. The individual should stand as an individual; but American society is organized into vast structures of unions, corporations, multiversities, and government bureaucracies. Personal regard for

each human being and for the absolute equality of every human soul is a categorical imperative; but American society continues to be characterized by racial injustice and discrimination. The senses and the instincts are to be trusted first; but American technology, and its consequences, are a monument to rationalism. Life should be lived in communion with others, and each day's sunrise and sunset enjoyed to the fullest; American society extols competition, the accumulation of goods, and the work ethic. Each man should be free to lead his own life in his own way; American organizations and statute books are filled with regulations governing dress, sex, consumption, and the accreditation of study and of work, and many of these are enforced by armed police.

No coherent political decalogue has yet emerged. Yet in this new youth culture's political discussion there are echoes of Marxism, of peasant communalism, of Thoreau, of Rousseau, of the evangelical fervor of the abolitionists, of Gandhi, and of native American populism.

The new culture adherent believes he sees an America that has failed to achieve its social targets; that no longer cares about achieving them; that is thoroughly hypocritical in pretending to have achieved them and in pretending to care; and that is exporting death and oppression abroad through its military and corporate operations. He wishes desperately to recall America to its great traditional goals of true freedom and justice for every man. As he sees it, he wants to remake America in its own image.

What of the shortcomings of other societies, especially the Soviet Union? Why does the new culture denounce only the United States? On this question, Drs. Heard and Cheek said in a memorandum to the President:

The apparent insensitivity of students to Soviet actions and to evils in the Soviet system is at least partly explainable by considerations like these: *First,* they feel that by the wrongness of our own policies, such as the war in Vietnam, we have lost our moral standing to condemn other countries. *Second,* there is an obsession with our own problems, a feeling that our own crises should occupy all our attention. *Third,* the fear of Communism is less than existed a decade ago.

Students perceive the Czech invasion as one more evil action by a powerful imperialist government, but they don't perceive it as a threat to the United States. Since the Sino-Soviet split, they see Communism as consisting of different and often competing national governments and styles. The Russians appear to repress their satellite countries, but students see that fact as parallel to American domination in *its* sphere of influence (the Dominican Republic, Guatemala, economic exploitation, etc.). They see the Russians as no better than we, maybe not as good, but feel more responsibility for our actions than for those of foreign powers.

The dedicated practitioners of this emerging culture typically have little regard for the past experience of others. Indeed, they often exhibit a positive antagonism to the study of history. Believing that there is today, and will be tomorrow, a wholly new world, they see no special relevance in the past. Distrusting older generations, they distrust the motives of their historically based advice no less than they distrust the history written by older generations. The anti-rationalist thread in the new culture resists the careful empirical approach of history and denounces it as fraudulent. Indeed, this anti-rationalism, and the urge for blunt directness often leads those of the new culture to view complexity as a disguise, to be impatient with learning the facts, and to demand simplistic solutions in one sentence.

Understandably, the new culture enthusiast has, at best, a luke-warm interest in free speech, majority opinion, and the rest of the tenets of liberal democracy as they are institutionalized today. He cannot have much regard for these things if he believes that American liberal democracy, with the consent and approval of the vast majority of its citizens, is pursuing values and policies that he sees as fundamentally immoral and apocalyptically destructive. Again, in parallel with historical religious movements, the new culture advocate tends to be self-righteous, sanctimonious, contemptuous of those who have not yet shared the vision, and intolerant of their ideals.

Profoundly opposed to any kind of authority structure from within or without the movement and urgently pressing for direct personal participation by each individual, members of this new youth culture have a difficult time making collective decisions. They reveal a distinct intolerance in their refusal to listen to those outside the new culture and in their willingness to force others to their own views. They even show an elitist streak in their premise that the rest of the society must be brought to the policy positions which they believe are right.

At the same time, they try very hard, and with extraordinary patience, to give each of their fellows an opportunity to be heard and to participate directly in decision-making. The new culture decisional style is founded on the endless mass meeting at which there is no chairman and no agenda, and from which the crowd or parts of the crowd melt away or move off into actions. Such crowds are, of course, subject to easy manipulation by skillful agitators and sometimes become mobs. But it must also be recognized that large, loose, floating crowds represent for participants in the new youth culture the normal, friendly, natural way for human beings to come together equally, to communicate, and to decide what to do. Seen from this perspective, the reader may well imagine the general student response at Kent State, to the Governor's order that the National Guard disperse all assemblies, peaceful or otherwise.

Practitioners of the new youth culture do not announce their program because the movement is not primarily concerned with programs; it is concerned with how one ought to live and what he ought to consider important in his daily life. The new culture is still in the process of forming its values, programs and life style; at this point, therefore, it is primarily a *stance*.

A parallel to religious history is again instructive. For many (not all) student activists and protestors, it is not really very important whether the protest tactics employed will actually contribute to the political end allegedly sought. What is important is that a protest be made—that the individual protestor, for his own internal salvation, stand up, declare the purity of his own heart, and take his stand. No student protestor throwing a rock through a laboratory window believes that it will stop the Indochina war, weapons research, or the advance of the feared technology—but he throws it in a mood of defiant exultation—almost exaltation. He has taken his moral stance.

An important theme of this new culture is its oppositional relationship to the larger society, as is suggested by the fact that one of its leading theorists has called it a "counter culture." If the rest of society wears short hair, the member of this youth culture wears his hair long. If others are clean, he is dirty. If others drink alcohol and illegalize marijuana, he denounces alcohol and smokes pot. If others work in large organizations with massively complex technology, he works alone and makes sandals by hand. If others live separated, he lives in a commune. If others are for the police and the judges, he is for the accused and the prisoner. By these means, he declares himself an alien in a large society with which he fundamentally is at odds.

He will also resist when the forces of the outside society seek to impose its tenets upon him. He is likely to see police as the repressive minions of the outside culture imposing its law on him and on other students by force or death, if necessary. He will likely try to urge others to join him in changing the society about him, in the conviction that he is seeking to save that society from bringing about its own destruction. He is likely to have apocalyptic visions of impending doom of the whole social structure and the world. He is likely to have lost hope that society can be brought to change through its own procedures. And if his psychological make-up is of a particular kind, he may conclude that the only outlet for his feelings is violence and terrorism.

In recent years, some substantial number of students, in the United States and abroad, have come to hold views along these lines. It is also true that a very large fraction of American college students, probably a majority, could not be said to be participants in any significant aspect of this cultural posture, except for its music. As for the rest of the students, they are distributed over the entire spectrum that ranges from no participation to full participation. A student may feel strongly about any one or more aspects of these views, and wholly reject all the others. He may also subscribe wholeheartedly to many of the philosophic assertions implied while occupying any of hundreds of different possible positions on the questions of which tactics, procedures, and actions he considers to be morally justifiable. Generalizations here are more than usually false.

One student may adopt the outward appearance of the new culture and nothing else. Another may be a total devotee, except that he is a serious history scholar. Another student may agree completely on all the issues of war, race, pollution, and the like, and participate in protests over those matters, while disagreeing with all aspects of the youth culture life style. A student may agree with the entire life style, but be wholly uninterested in politics. Another new culture student who takes very seriously the compassion and life aspects may prove to be the best bulwark against resorts to violence. A student who rejects the new youth culture altogether may, nevertheless, be in the vanguard of those who seek to protect that culture against the outside world. And so forth.

As is observed elsewhere in this report, to conclude that a student who has a beard is a student who would burn a building, or even sit-in in a building is wholly unwarranted.

But almost no college student today is unaffected by the new youth culture in some way. If he is not included, his roommate or sister or girlfriend is. If protest breaks out on his campus, he is confronted with a personal decision about his role in it. In the poetry, music, movies, and plays that students see, the themes of the new culture are recurrent. Even the student who finds older values more comfortable for himself will, nevertheless, protect and support vigorously the privilege of other students who prefer the new youth culture.

A vast majority of students are not adherents. But *no* significant group of students would join older generations in condemning those who are. And almost *all* students will condemn repressive efforts by the larger community to restrict or limit the life style, the art forms, and the non-violent political manifestations of the new youth culture.

To most Americans, the development of the new youth culture is an unpleasant and often frightening phenomenon. And there is no doubt that the emergence of this student perspective has led to confrontations, injuries, and death. It is undeniable, too, that a tiny extreme fringe of fanatical devotees of the new culture have crossed the line over into outlawry and terrorism. There is a fearful and terrible irony here as, in the name of the law, police and National Guards have killed students, and some students under the new culture's banner of love and compassion have turned to burning and bombing.

But the new youth culture itself is not a "problem" to which there is a "solution;" it is a mass social condition, a shift in basic cultural viewpoint. How long this emerging youth culture will last, and what course its future development will take, are open questions. But it does exist today, and it is the deeper cause of the emergence of the issues of race and war as objects of intense concern on the American campus. . . .

THE FORGOTTEN AMERICAN *

PETER SCHRAG

Frustration is not a monopoly of any single American minority today. While the peculiar problems of the Negro have attracted special attention in recent years, children and grandchildren of the "new immigration" (1890–1920) have their own frustrations and value conflicts. In many ways these

* Copyright © 1969 by Peter Schrag. Reprinted from Out of Place in America by Peter Schrag, by permission of Random House, Inc.

people (who represent a great voting bloc) represent an older America that praised thrift, hard work, law and order. On American TV this "forgotten American" is brought to life in the person of Archie Bunker of "All In The Family."

Why is the "forgotten American" frustrated? Does the American lower middle class represent a voting majority? What statistics describe this group's education, income, housing, transportation? How do they react to the welfare poor? The Negro protest? The student revolt? Do they accept the goals of the intellectual elite?

There is hardly a language to describe him, or even a set of social statistics. Just names: racist-bigot-redneck-ethnic-Irish-Italian-Pole-Hunkie-Yahoo. The lower middle class. A blank. The man under whose hat lies the great American desert. Who watches the tube, plays the horses, and keeps the niggers out of his union and his neighborhood. Who might vote for Wallace (but didn't). Who cheers when the cops beat up on demonstrators. Who is free, white, and twenty-one, has a job, a home, a family, and is up to his eyeballs in credit. In the guise of the working class—or the American yeoman or John Smith—he was once the hero of the civics book, the man that Andrew Jackson called "the bone and sinew of the country." Now he is "the forgotten man," perhaps the most alienated person in America.

Nothing quite fits, except perhaps omission and semi-invisibility. America is supposed to be divided between affluence and poverty, between slums and suburbs. John Kenneth Galbraith begins the foreword to *The Affluent Society* with the phrase, "Since I sailed for Switzerland in the early summer of 1955 to begin work on this book . . ." But *between* slums and suburbs, between Scarsdale and Harlem, between Wellesley and Roxbury, between Shaker Heights and Hough, there are some eighty million people (depending on how you count them) who didn't sail for Switzerland in the summer of 1955, or at any other time, and who never expect to. Between slums and suburbs: South Boston and South San Francisco, Bell and Parma, Astoria and Bay Ridge, Newark, Cicero, Downey, Daly City, Charlestown, Flatbush. Union halls, American Legion posts, neighborhood bars and bowling leagues, the Ukrainian Club and the Holy Name. Main Street. To try to describe all this is like trying to describe America itself. If you look for it, you find it everywhere: the rows of frame houses overlooking the belching steel mills in Bethlehem, Pennsylvania, two-family brick houses in Canarsie (where the most common slogan, even in the middle of a political campaign, is "curb your dog"); the Fords and Chevies with a decal American flag on the rear window (usually a cut-out from the *Reader's Digest*, and displayed in counter-protest against peaceniks and "those bastards who carry Vietcong flags in demonstrations"); the bunting on the porch rail with the inscription, "Welcome Home, Pete." The gold star in the window.

When he was Under Secretary of Housing and Urban Development, Robert C. Wood tried a definition. It is not good, but it's the best we have:

He is a white employed male . . . earning between $5,000 and $10,000. He works regularly, steadily, dependably, wearing a blue collar or white collar. Yet the frontiers of his career expectations have been fixed since he reached the age of thirty-five, when he found that he had too many obligations, too much family, and too few skills to match opportunities with aspirations.

This definition of the "working American" involves almost 23-million American families.

The working American lives in the gray area fringes of a central city or in a close-in or very far-out cheaper suburban subdivision of a large metropolitan area. He is likely to own a home and a car, especially as his income begins to rise. Of those earning between $6,000 and $7,500, 70 percent own their own homes and 94 percent drive their own cars.

94 percent have no education beyond high school and 43 percent have only completed the eighth grade.

He does all the right things, obeys the law, goes to church and insists—usually—that his kids get a better education than he had. But the right things don't seem to be paying off. While he is making more than he ever made—perhaps more than he'd ever dreamed— he's still struggling while a lot of others—"them" (on welfare, in demonstrations, in the ghettos) are getting most of the attention. "I'm working my ass off," a guy tells you on a stoop in South Boston. "My kids don't have a place to swim, my parks are full of glass, and I'm supposed to bleed for a bunch of people on relief." In New York a man who drives a Post Office trailer truck at night (4:00 P.M. to midnight) and a cab during the day (7:00 A.M. to 2:00 P.M.), and who hustles radios for his Post Office buddies on the side, is ready, as he says, to "knock somebody's ass." "The colored guys work when they feel like it. Sometimes they show up and sometimes they don't. One guy tore up all the time cards. I'd like to see a white guy do that and get away with it."

What Counts

Nobody knows how many people in America moonlight (half of the eighteen million families in the $5,000 to $10,000 bracket have two or more wage earners) or how many have to hustle on the side. "I don't think anybody has a single job anymore," said Nicholas Kisburg, the research director for a Teamsters Union Council in New York. "All the cops are moonlighting, and the teachers; and there's a million guys who are hustling, guys with phony social-security numbers who are hiding part of what they make so they don't get kicked out of a housing project, or guys who work as guards at sports events and get free meals that they don't want to pay taxes on. Every one of them is cheating. They are underground people— *Untermenschen.* . . . We really have no systematic data on any of this. We have no ideas of the attitudes of the white worker. (We've been too busy studying the black worker.) And yet he's the source of most of the reaction in this country."

The reaction is directed at almost every visible target: at integration and welfare, taxes and sex education, at the rich and the poor, the foundations and students, at the "smart people in the suburbs." In New York State the legislature cuts the welfare budget; in Los Angeles, the voters reelect Yorty after a whispered racial campaign against the Negro favorite. In Minneapolis a police detective named Charles Stenvig, promising "to take the handcuffs off the police," wins by a margin stunning even to his supporters: in Massachusetts the voters mail tea bags to their representatives in protest against new taxes, and in state after state legislatures are passing bills to punish student demonstrators. ("We keep talking about permissiveness in training kids," said a Los Angeles labor official, "but we forget that these are our kids.")

· · ·

Stability is what counts, stability in job and home and neighbor-hood, stability in the church and in friends. At night you watch television and sometimes on a weekend you go to a nice place—maybe a downtown hotel—for dinner with another couple. (Or maybe your sister, or maybe bowling, or maybe, if you're defeated, a night at the track.) The wife has the necessary appliances, often still being paid off, and the money you save goes for your daughter's orthodontist, and later for her wedding. The smoked Irishmen—the colored (no one says black; few even say Negro) —represent change and instability, kids who cause trouble in school, who get treatment that your kids never got, that you never got. . . . The black kids mean a change in the rules, a double standard in grades and discipline, and —vaguely—a challenge to all you believed right. Law and order is the stability and predictability of established ways. Law and order is equal treatment—in school, in jobs, in the courts—even if you're cheating a little yourself. The Forgotten Man is Jackson's man. He is the vestigial American democrat of 1840: "They all know that their success depends upon their own industry and economy and that they must not expect to become suddenly rich by the fruits of their toil." He is also Franklin Roosevelt's man—the man whose vote (or whose father's vote) sustained the New Deal.

At the Bottom of the Well

American culture? Wealth is visible, and so, now, is poverty. Both have become intimidating clichés. But the rest? A vast, complex, and disregarded world that was once—in belief, and in fact—the American middle: Greyhound and Trailways bus terminals in little cities at midnight, each of them with its neon lights and its cardboard hamburgers; acres of tar-paper beach bungalows in places like Revere and Rockaway; the hair curlers in the supermarket on Saturday, and the little girls in the communion dresses the next morning; pinball machines and the *Daily News*, the *Reader's Digest* and Ed Sullivan; houses with tiny front lawns (or even large ones) adorned with statues of the Virgin or of Sambo welcomin' de folks home; Clint Eastwood or Julie Andrews at the Palace; the trotting tracks and the dog tracks —Aurora Downs, Connaught Park, Roosevelt, Yonkers, Rockingham, and forty others—where gray men come not for sport and beauty, but to read numbers, to study and dope. (If you win you have figured something, have in a small way controlled your world, have surmounted your impotence. If you lose, bad luck, shit. "I'll break his goddamned head.") Baseball is not the national pastime; racing is. For every man who goes to a major-league baseball game there are four who go to the track and probably four more who go to the candy store or the barbershop to make their bets. (Total track attendance in 1965: 62 million plus another 10 million who went to the dogs.)

There are places, and styles, and attitudes. If there are neighborhoods of aspiration, suburban enclaves for the mobile young executive and the aspiring worker, there are also places of limited expectation and dead-end districts where mobility is finished. But even there you can often find, however vestigial, a sense of place, the roots of old ethnic loyalties, and a passionate, if often futile, battle against intrusion and change. "Everybody around here," you are told, "pays his own way." In this world the problems are not the ABM or air pollution (have they heard of Biafra?) or the international population crisis; the problem is to get your street cleaned, your garbage collected, to get your husband home from Vietnam alive; to negotiate installment payments and to keep the schools orderly. Ask anyone in Scarsdale or Winnetka about the schools and they'll tell you about new programs, or about how many are getting into Harvard, or about the teachers; ask in Oakland or the North Side of Chicago, and they'll tell you that they have (or haven't) had trouble. Somewhere in his gut the man in those communities knows that mobility and choice in this society are limited. He cannot imagine any major change for the better; but he can imagine change for the worse. And yet for a decade he is the one who has been asked to carry the burden of social reform, to integrate his schools and his neighborhood, has been asked by comfortable people to pay the social debts due to the poor and the black. In Boston, in San Francisco, in Chicago (not to mention Newark or Oakland) he has been telling the reformers to go to hell. The Jewish schoolteachers of New York and the Irish parents of Dorchester have asked the same question: "What the hell did Lindsay (or the Beacon Hill Establishment) ever do for us?"

The ambiguities and changes in American life that occupy discussions in university seminars and policy debates in Washington, and that form the backbone of contemporary popular sociology, become increasingly the conditions of trauma and frustration in the middle. Although the New Frontier and Great Society contained some programs for those not already on the rolls of social pathology—federal aid for higher education, for example—the public priorities and the rhetoric contained little. The emphasis, properly, was on the poor, on the inner cities (e.g., Negroes) and the unemployed. But in Chicago a widow with three children who earns $7,000 a year can't get them college loans because she makes too much; the money is reserved for people on relief. New schools are built in the ghetto but not in the white working-class neighborhoods where they are just as dilapidated. In Newark the head of a white vigilante group (now a city councilman) runs, among other things, on a platform opposing pro-Negro discrimination. "When pools are being built in the Central Ward—don't they think white kids have got frustration? The white can't get a job; we have to hire Negroes first." The middle class, said Congressman Roman Pucinski of Illinois, who represents a lot of it, "is in revolt. Everyone has been generous in supporting anti-poverty. Now the middle-class American is disqualified from most of the programs."

"Somebody Has to Say No . . ."

The frustrated middle. The liberal wisdom about welfare, ghettos, student revolt, and Vietnam has only a marginal place, if any, for the values and life of the working man. It flies in the face of most of what he was taught to cherish and respect: hard work, order, authority, self-reliance. He fought, either alone or through labor organizations, to establish the precincts he now considers his own. Union seniority, the civil-service bureaucracy, and the petty professionalism established by the merit system in the public schools become sinecures of particular ethnic groups or of those who have learned to negotiate and master the system. A man who worked all his life to accumulate the points and grades and paraphernalia to become an assistant school principal (no matter how silly the requirements) is not likely to relinquish his position with equanimity. Nor is a dock worker whose only estate is his longshoreman's card. . . .

THE DEMOCRATIC CREED *

JAMES BRYCE

Lord James Bryce was a perceptive, sympathetic English observer of the worldwide thrust toward democracy in the early twentieth century. In the passage that follows he attempted to capture the essential democratic philosophy of the American and French revolutionary periods. What was the source of their axioms about the end and purpose of government? How did they cope with the problem of human selfishness? What were the two main ends of government? How would the model citizen conduct himself? Why was violence unnecessary? How was democracy to be regenerated?

"We hold these truths to be self-evident, that all men are created equal, that they are endowed by their Creator with certain inalienable Rights, that among these are Life, Liberty, and the pursuit of Happiness, that to secure these rights, Governments are instituted, deriving their just powers from the

* Reprinted with permission of The Macmillan Company from Modern Democracies by James Bryce. Copyright 1921 by The Macmillan Company, renewed 1949 by Margaret Vincentia Bryce, Roland L'Estrange Bryce and Rosalind L'Estrange Tudor Craig.

consent of the governed." (American Declaration of Independence, 1776).

"Men are born and continue equal in respect of their rights.

"The end of political society is the preservation of the natural and imprescriptible rights of men. These Rights are liberty, property, security, and resistance to oppression.

"The principle of all Sovereignty resides essentially in the nation. No body, no individual, can exert any authority which is not expressly derived from it.

"All citizens have a right to concur personally, or through their representatives in making the law. Being equal in its eyes, then, they are all equally admissible to all dignities, posts, and public employments.

"No one ought to be molested on account of his opinions, even his religious opinions." (Declaration of the Rights of Man made by the National Assembly of France, August 1791.)

These two declarations, delivered authoritatively by two bodies of men at two moments of far-reaching historical importance, contain the fundamental dogmas, a sort of Apostles' Creed, of democracy. They are the truths on which it claims to rest, they embody the appeal it makes to human reason. Slightly varied in expression, their substance may be stated as follows.

Each man who comes into the world comes into it Free, with a mind to think for himself, a will to act for himself. The subjection of one man to another except by his own free will is against Nature. All men are born Equal, with an equal right to the pursuit of happiness. That each man may secure this right and preserve his liberty as a member of a community, he must have an equal share in its government, that government being created and maintained by the consent of the community. Equality is the guarantee of independence.

These axioms, being delivered as self-evident truths, antecedent to and independent of experience, require no proof. They are propounded as parts of the universal Law of Nature, written on men's hearts, and therefore true always and everywhere.

While the Declarations of the Natural Rights of Man made at Philadelphia and at Paris were resounding through the world there were other thinkers who, like some Greek philosophers more than two thousand years before, were drawing from the actual experience of mankind arguments which furnished another set of foundations on which democracy might rest. Testing the value of a principle by its practical results, they propounded a number of propositions, some of which may be given as familiar examples.

Liberty is a good thing, because it develops the character of the individual, and conduces to the welfare of the community. When one man, or a few men, rule over others, some of the subjects are sure to resent control and rebel against it, troubling the general peace. No one is good enough to be trusted with unlimited power. Unless he be a saint—perhaps even if he be a saint—he is sure to abuse it.

Every man is the best judge of his own interest, and therefore best knows what sort of government and what laws will promote that interest. Hence those laws and that government will presumably be the best for a community as a whole which are desired by the largest number of its members.

Two men are presumably better able than one to judge what is for the common good. Three men are wiser still, and so on. Hence the larger the number of members of the community who have a right to give their opinion, the more likely to be correct (other things being equal) is the decision reached by the community.

Individual men may have selfish aims, possibly injurious to the community, but these will be restrained by the other members of the community whose personal aims will be different. Thus the self-regarding purposes of individuals will be eliminated, and the common aims which the bulk of the community desires to pursue will prevail.

As every man has some interest in the well-being of the community, a part at least of his own personal interest being bound up with it, every man will have a motive for bearing his share in its government and he will seek to bear it, so far as his personal motives do not collide therewith.

Inequality, by arousing jealousy

and envy, provokes discontent. Discontent disturbs the harmony of a community and induces strife. Hence equality in political rights, while it benefits the community by opening to talent the opportunity of rendering good service, tends also to peace and good order.

To sum up, government by the whole people best secures the two main objects of all Governments—Justice and Happiness. Justice, because no man or class or group will be strong to wrong others; Happiness because each man judging best what is for his own good, will have every chance of pursuing it. The principles of liberty and equality are justified by the results they yield.

From these propositions it follows that the admission on equal terms of the largest possible number of members of a community to share in its government on equal terms best promotes the satisfaction of all the members as individuals, and also the welfare of the community as a whole; and these being the chief ends for which government exists, a government of the people by themselves is commended by the experience of mankind.

An Ideal Democracy—the expression comes from Plato's remark that a pattern of the perfect State is perhaps stored up somewhere in heaven—may be taken to mean a community in which the sense of public duty and an altruistic spirit fill the minds and direct the wills of the large majority of the citizens, so that the Average Citizen stands on the level of him whom we sometimes meet and describe as the Model Citizen. What then, expressed in the terms of our own day, would such a community be?

In it the average citizen will give close and constant attention to public affairs, recognizing that this is his interest as well as his duty. He will try to comprehend the main issues of policy, bringing to them an independent and impartial mind, which thinks first not of his own but of the general interest. If, owing to inevitable differences of opinion as to what are the measures needed for the general welfare, parties become inevitable, he will join one, and attend its meetings, but will repress the impulses of party spirit. Never failing to come to the polls, he will vote for his party candidate only if satisfied by his capacity and honesty. He will be ready to serve on a local Board or Council, and to be put forward as a candidate for the legislature (if satisfied of his own competence), because public service is recognized as a duty. With such citizens as electors, the legislature will be composed of upright and capable men, single-minded in their wish to serve the nation. Bribery in constituencies, corruption among public servants, will have disappeared. Leaders may not be always single-minded, nor assemblies always wise, nor administrators efficient, but all will be at any rate honest and zealous, so that an atmosphere of confidence and good-will will prevail. Most of the causes that make for strife will be absent, for there will be no privileges, no advantages to excite jealousy. Office will be sought only because it gives opportunities for useful service. Power will be shared by all, and a career open to all alike. Even if the law does not—perhaps it cannot—prevent the accumulation of fortunes, these will be few and not inordinate, for public vigilance will close the illegitimate paths to wealth. All but the most depraved persons will obey and support the law, feeling it to be their own. There will be no excuse for violence, because the constitution will provide a remedy for every grievance. Equality will produce a sense of human solidarity, will refine manners, and increase brotherly kindness.

The abstract doctrines of the Revolutionary epoch and the visions of a better world that irradiated those doctrines, blurred as they have been in the lapse of years, have never ceased to recommend popular government to men of sanguine temper. But the Vision, the picture of an Ideal Democracy, a government upright and wise, beneficent and stable, as no government save that of the people for the people can be, has had greater power than the abstract doctrines, mighty as was their explosive force when they were first proclaimed. It is the conception of a happier life for all, coupled with a mystic faith in the People, that great multitude through whom speaks the Voice of the Almighty Power that makes for righteousness —it is this that constitutes the vital impulse of democracy. The country where the ideal democracy exists has not yet been discovered, but the faith in its existence has survived many disappointments, many disillusionments. Many more will follow, but in them also the faith will survive. From time to time hope is revived by the appearance of a group of disinterested reformers, whose zeal rouses a nation to sweep away abuses and leaves things better than it found them. It is only sloth and torpor and the acquiescence in things known to be evil that are deadly. So we may hope that the Ideal will never cease to exert its power, but continue to stand as a beacon tower to one generation after another.

THE SEMI-SOVEREIGN PEOPLE *

E. E. SCHATTSCHNEIDER

Classical definitions of democracy emphasize government by the people rather than by a single

* Reprinted from E. E. Schattschneider, The Semi-Sovereign People (Holt, Rinehart, Winston, 1960) by permission of the author. Copyright © 1960 by E. E. Schattschneider.

ruler. As an extension of that theory there is a common belief that the extent of democracy can be measured by the number of decisions made by the people. Professor Schattschneider challenges these assumptions. What role does he assign to political parties and leaders? Why do we need conflict and competition? How does he respond to critics who cite public opinion polls to prove that the people are ill-informed? How have American intellectuals failed democracy? What is the central problem in organizing a democratic political system? What is the unforgivable sin of democratic politics?

The classical definition of democracy as government by the people is predemocratic in its origins, based on notions about democracy developed by philosophers who never had an opportunity to see an operating democratic system. Predemocratic theorists assumed that the people would take over the conduct of public affairs in a democracy and administer the government to their own advantage as simply as landowners administer their property for their own profit. Under this historical circumstance this over-simplification is easy to understand. There is less excuse for the failure of modern scholars to re-examine the traditional definition critically in the light of modern experience.

Perhaps as good a point as any at which to test our ideas about democracy is in the general area of public opinion research. This research is based on the assumption that public opinion plays a great role in a democracy. Lurking in the background is the notion that the people actually do govern.

One implication of public opinion studies ought to be resisted by all friends of freedom and democracy; the implication that democracy is a failure because the people are too ignorant to answer intelligently all the questions asked by the pollsters. This is a professorial invention for imposing professorial standards on the political system and deserves to be treated with extreme suspicion. Only a pedagogue would suppose that the people must pass some kind of examination to qualify for participation in a democracy. Who, after all, are these self-appointed censors who assume that they are in a position to flunk the whole human race? Their attitude would be less presumptuous if they could come up with a list of things that people must know. Who can say what the man on the street must know about public affairs? The whole theory of knowledge underlying these assumptions is pedantic. Democracy was made for the people, not the people for democracy. Democracy is something for ordinary people, a political system designed to be sensitive to the needs of ordinary people regardless of whether or not the pedants approve of them.

It is an outrage to attribute the failures of American democracy to the ignorance and stupidity of the masses. The most disastrous short-comings of the system have been those of the intellectuals whose concepts of democracy have been amazingly rigid and uninventive. The failure of the intellectuals is dangerous because it creates confusion in high places. Unless the intellectuals can produce a better theory of politics than they have, it is possible that we shall abolish democracy before we have found out what it is!

The beginning of wisdom in democratic theory is to distinguish between the things the people can do and the things the people cannot do. The worst possible disservice that can be done to the democratic cause is to attribute to the people a mystical, magical omnipotence which takes no cognizance of what very large numbers of people cannot do by the sheer weight of numbers. At this point the common definition of democracy has invited us to make fools of ourselves.

What 180 million people can do spontaneously, on their own initiative, is not much more than a locomotive can do without rails. The public is like a very rich man who is unable to supervise closely all of his enterprise. His problem is to learn how to compel his agents to define his options.

What we are saying is that conflict, competition, leadership, and organizations are the essence of democratic politics. Inherent in the operations of a democracy are special conditions which permit large numbers of people to function.

The problem is how to organize the political system so as to make the best possible use of the power of the public in view of its limitations. A popular decision bringing into focus the force of public support requires a tremendous effort to define the alternatives, to organize the discussion and mobilize opinion. The government and the political organizations are in the business of manufacturing this kind of alternative.

What has been said here has not been said to belittle the power of the people but to shed some light on what it is. The power of the people is not made less by the fact that it cannot be used for trivial matters. The whole world can be run on the basis of a remarkably small number of decisions. The power of the people in a democracy depends on the importance of the decisions made by the electorate, not on the number of decisions they make. Since the adoption of the Constitution the party in power has been turned out by the opposition party fourteen times, and in about six of these instances the consequences have been so great that we could not understand American history without taking account of them.

The most important thing about any democratic regime is the way in which it uses and exploits popular sovereignty, what questions it refers to the public for decision or guidance, how it refers them to the public, how the alternatives are defined and how it respects the limitations of the public. A good democratic system protects the public against the demand that it do impossible things. The unforgivable sin of democratic politics is to dissipate the power of the public by putting it to trivial uses. What we need is a movement for the conservation of the political resources of the American people.

Above everything, the people are powerless if the political enterprise is not competitive. It is the competition of political organizations that provides the people with the opportunity to make a choice. Without this opportunity popular sovereignty amounts to nothing.

The common definition of democracy may be harmless if it is properly understood, but the fact is that it is very commonly misunderstood. It would be more imaginative to say that some things we now are actually doing are democratic even though they do not fit the traditional definition. Definitions of democracy since the time of Aristotle have been made on the assumption that the "many" in a democracy do the same things that the "one" does in a monarchy and the "few" do in an aristocracy. But obviously the shift from the "one" to the "many" is more than a change in the number of people participating in power but a change in the way the power is exercised. The 180 million cannot do what a single ruler can do. This is not because the 180 million are stupid or ignorant but because it is physically impossible for 180 million to act the way one acts. In the interests of clarity and the survival of the political system we need a definition of democracy that recognizes the limitations that nature imposes on large numbers.

A working definition must capitalize on the limitations of the people as well as their powers. We do this when we say that liberty and leadership are the greatest of democratic concepts. Democracy is a competitive political system in which competing leaders and organizations define the alternatives of public policy in such a way that the public can participate in the decision-making process. The initiative in this political system is to be found largely in the government or in the opposition. The people profit by this system, but they cannot by themselves, do the work of the system. We have already had a great deal of experience with this kind of system. Is it not about time that we began to recognize its democratic implications?

Conflict, competition, organization, leadership and responsibility are the ingredients of a working definition of democracy. Democracy is a political system in which the people have a choice among the alternatives created by competing political organizations and leaders. The advantage of this definition over the traditional definition is that it is operational, it describes something that actually happens. It describes something feasible. It does not make impossible demands on the public. Moreover, it describes a going democratic concern whose achievements are tremendous.

The involvement of the public in politics is a natural outgrowth of the kind of conflict that almost inevitably arises in a free society. The exploitation of this situation by responsible political leaders and organizations is the essence of democracy; the socialization of conflict is the essential democratic process.

PARTICIPATORY DEMOCRACY FOR EVERYONE *

HERBERT J. GANS

Many sizable groups are excluded from social and political decision-making under existing American democratic procedures. Among these are college and high school students, blue-collar and lower middle-class workers, blacks in the ghetto, wives and children within the family. Nearly all existing institutional authority patterns are being called into question. At

* From Herbert J. Gans, "The Equality Revolution," New York Times Magazine, November 3, 1968. Copyright © 1968 by The New York Times Company. Reprinted by permission.

the root of this argument is the demand for liberty on the part of the "haves" and for equality on the part of the "have nots." How can the "have nots" achieve greater equality? How rapidly will it occur? How is it geared to prosperity? What groups will play a key role in determining the limits of the equality revolution?

. . . "In a large and complex society, inequality and the lack of control over one's life are pervasive and are often thought to be inevitable by-products of modernity and affluence. We are learning, however, that they are not inevitable—that there can be more equality, democracy and autonomy if enough people want them.

"In the past, when most people earned just enough to 'get by,' they were interested mainly in higher incomes and did not concern themselves with equality or autonomy in their everyday lives. For example, the poor took—and still take—any jobs they could get because they needed the money to pay for the week's food and the month's rent. Working-class and lower-middle-class people were, and are, only slightly more able to choose; they take whatever job will provide the most comfortable lives for themselves and their families. But in the upper-middle class, the job is expected to offer personal satisfactions, and upper-middle-class people gravitate to the jobs and careers that provide more equality and autonomy. The huge increase in graduate-school enrollments suggests that many college students want the personal freedom available in an academic career; their decreasing interest in business careers indicates that they may be rejecting the autocracy and lack of autonomy found in many large corporations.

"Today, as more people approach the kind of economic security already found in the affluent upper-middle-class, they are beginning to think about the noneconomic satisfactions of the job and of the rest of life; as a result, aspirations for more equality, democracy and autonomy are rising all over America.

"Some manifestations of 'the equality revolution' are making headlines today, particularly among students and blacks. Whatever the proximate causes of college protests and uprisings, the students who participate in them agree on two demands: the right to be treated as adults—and therefore as equals— and the right to participate in the governing of their schools. Though the mass media have paid most attention to the more radical advocates of these demands, equality and democracy are sought not just by the Students for a Democratic Society but by an ever-increasing number of liberal and even conservative students as well.

"Similar demands for equality and democracy are being voiced by the young people of the ghetto. Only a few years ago, they seemed to want integration, the right to become part of the white community.

Today, recognizing that white America offered integration to only a token few and required with it assimilation into the white majority, the young blacks are asking for equality instead. When they say that black is beautiful, they are really saying that black is equal to white; when the ghetto demands control of its institutions, it asks for the right to have the same control that many white neighborhoods have long had.

"And although the call for 'participatory democracy' is voiced mainly by young people of affluent origins in the New Left, a parallel demand is manifesting itself among the young blue-collar supporters of Governor Wallace. What they are saying, in effect, is that they are tired of being represented by middle-class politicians; they want a President who will allow the working class to participate in the running of the Federal Government and will get rid of the upper-middle-class professionals who have long dominated the formulation of public policies, the people whom the Governor calls 'pseudo-intellectuals.'

"Many other instances of the equality revolution are less visible, and some have not made the headlines. For example, in the last two generations, wives have achieved near equality in the family, at least in the middle class; they now divide the housework with their husbands and share the decision-making about family expenditures and other activities. Today, this revolution is being extended to the sexual relationship. Gone is the day when women were passive vessels for men's sexual demands; they are achieving the right to enjoy sexual intercourse.

"Children have also obtained greater equality and democracy. In many American families, adolescents are now free from adult interference in their leisure-time activities and their sexual explorations, and even preteens are asking to be allowed their own 'youth culture.'

"Man's relationship to God and the church is moving toward greater equality, too. The minister is no longer a theological father; in many synagogues and Protestant churches, he has become the servant of his congregation, and the unwillingness of many Catholics to abide by the Pope's dictates on birth control hides other, less publicized, instances of the rejection of dogma that is handed down from on high. The real meaning of the 'God is Dead' movement, I believe, is that the old conception of God as the infallible autocrat has been rejected.

"In the years to come, the demand for more equality, democracy and autonomy is likely to spread to many other aspects of life. Already, some high-school students are beginning to demand the same rights for which college students are organizing, and recipients of public welfare are joining together to put an end to the autocratic fashion in which their payments are given to them. Public employees are striking for better working conditions as well as for higher wages; teachers are demanding more freedom in the classroom and—in New York—the right to teach where they choose; social workers want more autonomy in aiding their clients, and policemen seek the right to do their jobs as they see fit, immune from what they call 'political interference.' The right of the individual to determine his job is the hallmark of the professional, and eventually many workers will seek the privileges of professionalism whether or not they are professional in terms of skills.

"Eventually, the equality revolution may also come to the large corporations and government agencies in which more and more people are working. One can foresee the day when blue-collar and white-collar workers demand a share of the profits and some voice in the running of the corporations.

"Similar changes can be expected in the local community. Although the exodus to suburbia took place primarily because people sought better homes and neighborhoods, they also wanted the ability to obtain greater control over governmental institutions. In the last 20 years, the new suburbanites have overthrown many of the rural political machines that used to run the suburbs, establishing governments that were responsive to their demands for low taxes and the exclusion of poorer newcomers. In the future, this transformation may spread to the cities as well, with decentralized political institutions that respond to the wants of the neighborhood replacing the highly centralized urban machines. . . .

"Consumer behavior will also undergo change. The ever-increasing diversity of consumer goods represents a demand for more cultural democracy on the part of purchasers, and the day may come when some people will establish consumer unions and cooperatives to provide themselves with goods and services not offered by large manufacturers. Television viewers may unite to demand different and perhaps even better TV programs and to support the creation of UHF channels that produce the types of quality and minority programming the big networks cannot offer.

"It is even possible that a form of 'hippie' culture will become more popular in the future. Although the Haight-Ashbury and East Village hippies have degenerated into an often-suicidal drug culture, there are positive themes in hippiedom that may become more acceptable if the work-week shrinks and affluence becomes more universal; for example: the rejection of the rat race, the belief in self-expression as the main purpose of life, the desire for a more communal form of living and even the idea of drug use as a way to self-understanding. . . .

"These observations suggest that the future will bring many kinds of change to America, producing new ideas that question beliefs and values thought to be sacrosanct. Who, for example, imagined a few years ago that the ghetto would reject the traditional goal of integration or that college students would rise up against their faculties and administrations to demand equal rights? Thus, nobody should be surprised if in the next few years adolescents organize for more freedom in their high schools or journalists decide that their editors have too much power over their work.

Liberty Versus Equality

"These demands for change will, of course, be fought bitterly; protests will be met by backlash and new ideas will be resisted by old ideologies.

"Today many argue that college students are still children and should not be given a voice in college administration, just as many say that women do not really need orgasms or that men who help their wives at home are becoming effeminate. Undoubtedly, the defenders of outmoded traditions will argue sincerely and with some facts and logic on their side, but processes of social change have little to do with sincerity, facts or logic. When people become dissatisfied with what they have and demand something better they cannot be deterred by facts or logic, and the repression of new ideas and new modes of behavior is effective only in the very short run.

"But perhaps the most intense struggle between new ideas and old ideologies will take place over America's political philosophy, for a fundamental change is taking place in the values which guide us as a nation. In a little-noticed portion of the 'Moynihan Report,'

Daniel P. Moynihan pointed out that the civil rights struggle, which had previously emphasized the achievement of liberty, particularly political liberty from Jim Crow laws, would soon shift to the attainment of equality, which would allow the 'distribution of achievements among Negroes roughly comparable to that of whites.'

"Moynihan's prediction was uncannily accurate with respect to the civil rights struggle, and I would argue, as he does, that it will soon extend to many other struggles as well and that the traditional belief in liberty will be complemented and challenged by a newly widespread belief in the desirability of equality.

"Since America became a nation, the country has been run on the assumption that the greatest value of all is liberty, which gives people the freedom to 'do their own thing,' particularly to make money, regardless of how much this freedom deprives others of the same liberty or of a decent standard of living. Whether liberty meant freedom to squander the country's natural resources or just to go into business for oneself without doing harm to anyone else, it was [our] guiding value.

"Today, however, the demand for liberty is often, but not always, the battle cry of the 'haves,' justifying their right to keep their wealth or position and to get more. Whether liberty is demanded by a Southern advocate of states' rights to keep Negroes in their place or by a property owner who wants to sell his house to any white willing to buy it, liberty has become the ideology of the more fortunate. In the years to come, the 'have-nots,' whether they lack money or freedom, will demand increasingly the reduction of this form of liberty. Those who ask for more equality are not opposed to liberty *per se*, of course; what they want is sufficient equality so that they, too, can enjoy the liberty now virtually monopolized by the 'haves.'

"The debate over liberty vs. equality is in full swing, and one illuminating example is the current argument about the negative income tax and other forms of guaranteed annual incomes for the underpaid and the poor. The advocates of guaranteed annual incomes want greater equality of income in American society; the opponents fear that the liberty to earn as much as possible will be abrogated. However, neither side frames its case in terms of equality or liberty. The advocates of a guaranteed annual income rely on moral argument, appealing to their fellow Americans to do away with the immorality of poverty. The opponents charge that a guaranteed annual income will sap the incentive to work, although all the evidence now available suggests that professors and other professionals who have long had virtually guaranteed annual incomes have not lost their incentive to work, that what saps incentive is not income but the lack of it.

"Being poor makes people apathetic and depressed; a guaranteed income would provide some emotional as well as economic security, raise hopes, increase self-respect and reduce feelings of being left out, thus encouraging poor people to look for decent jobs, improve family living conditions and urge their children to work harder in school. A guaranteed annual income may reduce the incentive to take a dirty and underpaid job, however, and at the bottom of the debate is the fear of those who now have the liberty to avoid taking such jobs that less fortunate Americans may be given the same liberty.

"In the years to come, many other arguments against equality will develop. We have long heard that those who want more equality are radicals or outside agitators, seeking to stir up people thought to be happy with the way things are. This is clearly nonsensical, for even if radicals sometimes lead the drive for more equality, they can succeed only because those who follow them are dissastified with the status quo.

"Another argument is that the demand for more equality will turn America into a society like Sweden, which is thought to be conformist, boring and suicidal, or even into a gray and regimented society like Russia. But these arguments are nonsensical, too, for there is no evidence that Swedes suffer more from ennui than anyone else, and the suicide rate—high in all Scandinavian countries save Norway—was lower in Sweden at last counting than in traditionalist Austria or Communist Hungary and only slightly higher than the rate in *laissez-faire* West Germany or pastoral Switzerland. And current events in the Communist countries provide considerable evidence that the greater economic equality they have achieved does not eliminate the popular desire for freedom and democracy.

"But perhaps the most frequently heard argument is that the unequal must do something to earn greater equality. This line of reasoning is taken by those who have had the liberty to achieve their demands and assumes that the same liberty is available to everyone else. This assumption does not hold up, however, for the major problem of the unequal is precisely that they are not allowed to earn equality—that the barriers of racial discrimination, the inability to obtain a good education, the unavailability of good jobs or the power of college presidents and faculties make it impossible for them to be equal. Those who argue for earning equality are really saying that they want to award it to the deserving, like charity. But recent events in the ghettos and on the campuses have shown convincingly that no one awards equality voluntarily; it has to be wrested from the 'more equal' by political pressure and even by force.

The Timing of Revolution

"Many of the changes that make up the equality revolution will not take place for a generation or more, and how many of them ever take place depends on at least three factors: the extent to which the American economy is affluent enough to permit more equality; the extent to which America's political institutions are able to respond to the demands of the unequal, and—perhaps most important—the extent to which working-class and lower-middle-class Americans want more equality, democracy and autonomy in the future.

"If the economy is healthy in the years to come, it will be able to 'afford' more economic equality while absorbing the costs of such changes as the democratization of the workplace, increased professionalism and more worker autonomy. If automation and the currently rising centralization of American industry result in the disappearance of jobs, however, greater equality will become impossible and people will fight each other for the remaining jobs. This could result in a bitter conflict between the 'haves' and the 'have-nots' that might even lead to a revolution, bringing about formal equality by governmental edict in a way not altogether different from the Socialist and Communist revolutions of the 20th century. But that conflict between the 'haves' and the 'have-nots' could also lead to a right-wing revolution in which the 'haves,' supported by conservatives among the 'have-nots,' would establish a quasi-totalitarian government that would use force to maintain the existing inequalities.

"Although the likelihood of either a left-wing or a right-wing revolution is probably small, even a gradual transformation toward greater equality is not likely to be tranquil. More equality for some means a reduction in privileges for others, and more democracy and autonomy for some means a loss of power for others. Those who have the privilege and the power will not give them up without a struggle and will fight the demand for more equality with all the economic and political resources they can muster. Even today, such demands by only a small part of the black and young population have resulted in a massive backlash appeal for law and order by a large part of the white and older population.

"Moreover, whenever important national decisions must be made, American politics has generally been guided by majority rule or majority public opinion, and this has often meant the tyranny of the majority over the minority. As long as the unequal are a minority, the structure of American politics can easily be used to frustrate their demands for change. The inability of the Federal government to satisfy the demands of the Negro population for greater equality is perhaps the best example. In the future, the political structure must be altered to allow the government to become more responsive to minority demands, particularly as the pressure for equality grows.

"Whether or not such governmental responsiveness will be politically feasible depends in large part on how working-class and lower-middle-class Americans feel about the equality revolution. They are the ruling majority in America, and if they want more equality, democracy and autonomy, these will be achieved—and through peaceful political methods. If the two classes remain primarily interested in obtaining more affluence, however, they will be able to suppress demands for equality by minorities, especially those demands which reduce their own powers and privileges. No one can tell now how these two classes will feel in the future, but there is no doubt that their preferences will determine the outcome of the equality revolution.

"Still, whatever happens in the years and decades to come, the equality revolution is under way, and however slowly it proceeds and however bitter the struggle between its supporters and opponents, it will continue. It may succeed, but it could also fail, leaving in its wake a level of social and political conflict unlike any America has ever known.

"What I have written so far I have written as a sociologist, trying to predict what will occur in coming generations. But as a citizen, I believe that what will happen ought to happen, that the emerging demand for more equality, democracy and autonomy is desirable. Too many Americans, even among the nonpoor, still lead lives of quiet desperation, and the good life today is the monopoly of only a happy few. I think that the time has come when unbridled liberty as we have defined it traditionally can no

longer be America's guiding value, especially if the right to liberty deprives others of a similar liberty. But I believe also that there is no inherent conflict between liberty and equality; that the society we must create should provide enough equality to permit everyone the liberty to control his own life without creating inequality for others, and that this, when it comes, will be the Great Society."

IN PRAISE OF MILITANT DEMONSTRATIONS
W. E. B. DUBOIS CLUBS

The right of the people peaceably to assemble is guaranteed by the Bill of Rights. But the widespread resort to mass marches and demonstrations during the past few years has raised several troublesome questions. Defenders of the demonstrations picture the existing government as an Establishment, organized to maintain the status quo and block the rights of the "real" people. They cite the historical record to prove that oppressed American minorities have always resorted to militant demonstrations. They see the present demonstrations as a successful weapon in squeezing concessions from the Establishment and anticipate the emergence of a new political majority, welded together from the presently oppressed groups.

The militancy of the demonstrators has provoked a series of questions from their critics. Do 500,000 people have the right to march down Pennsylvania Avenue to protest the Vietnam war? What if 1,000,000 people show up? 10,000,000? What if a counter-march is scheduled the same day? If some fringe groups in a protest march engage in violence, should police break up the entire demonstration? How thin is the line between militant demonstrations and violence? Is there a danger that militancy will provoke oppression rather than change? Will counting demonstrators rather than ballots provide a truer gauge of the popular will?

DISRUPTERS!

Why do we demonstrate? Because we live in a corrupt society, one which seems to have grown insensitive to human suffering—whether in Southeast Asia or Southeast U.S.A.—and we can't sit back and allow things to continue that way. It's about as simple as that. We aim to change the world for the better, and demonstrations are one way of attempting to do just that.

In a TV documentary on American youth produced last year by a major network, the narrator commented: "Most of today's youngsters feel a sense of powerlessness to change society." In contrast, a *Holiday* magazine study recently characterized today's young Americans as "more thoughtful, more aggressive, more willing to take chances and learn from occasional mistakes, and more interested in ultimately improving the world about them than earlier generations have been."

There is truth in both of these remarks. Feelings of hopelessness and alienation are prevalent among young people today . . . but they have not infected all of us. Millions of words are being written about our generation's "desperate search for values." It is ironic, then, that when some of us are moved to act according to our society's most cherished values, the mass media and the Establishment gang up to put us down.

A generation intent upon "improving the world" sees the necessity for action; for deliberate steps taken with some assurance that the action will indeed contribute to the changes demanded. Thousands upon thousands have acted, and the ranks of activists grow each day in number and determination. With this growth has come the avalanche of condemnation, the accusation of "beatniks" and "militant hotheads," the Freudian interpretations about "generational conflict," and the unending sermons about "law and order."

Why? Because the principal weapon seized upon by those who

are seeking changes has been the public demonstration. Peace marches, sit-ins, picket lines—these are the order of the day. And somebody up there doesn't like it. Boiled down, about all we can say is: TOUGH! Down here in the streets, we see the necessity for our actions.

But why demonstrations? Aren't demonstrations the wrong way to go about it? Doesn't direct action disrupt society and violate the tradition of orderly democratic progress? Why don't we use the established institutions of government to secure redress of grievances?

Because all too often "order" and democratic institutions are expressions and devices of the *status quo*. We are all for order—for elections, courts, laws and police, when and if they are by, for and of the people. Our whole dream is to create a truly democratic society. But it is wrong to speak of this country as a truly democratic one. For us, democracy must be more than a promise; it must function. That means real people, equipped with knowledge, making the real decisions that affect their lives.

Look at the South. When the whole structure of government and the force of economic power is bent on denying people (white and black) their rights, how can anyone insist that the drive for redress of grievances be contained within the framework of law and order and established political institutions? The law is built to defend the white power structure. "Order"

means keeping people "in their place." The government, courts, and police are manipulated by white-owned big business and the nation's most backward, ignorant politicians.

We have seen time and again in the "liberal" North how well the courts, the police, the legislatures serve the interests of the *status quo*. We have learned how little can be accomplished by polite argument and rational discussion, and we have learned the true meaning of "deliberate speed."

There is great power in the Establishment, and we have no choice but to meet that power with power of our own if we wish to have our voices heard and our demands met. Our most elementary power lies in our bodies and our numbers and our knowledge of what bodies and numbers can do together.

We wonder whether those "liberals" who are so quick to condemn militant demonstrations and yet so pleased with last year's civil rights act really think that act blossomed out of Congressional good will. Do they really believe the President gave his "We Shall Overcome" speech and rushed through his voting rights bill because he suddenly decided it would be a nice thing to do? Even Johnson himself credited the demonstrations with provoking his action. That speech and that legislation (which really does little more than reaffirm the long-standing power of the Federal Government to ensure the rights of citizens) are the direct result of tremendous pressure by a Movement grown strong enough to move Washington.

In the election of 1964, the overwhelming majority of Americans took a stand against the blindly aggressive policies of the extreme right, only to see those policies adopted by the elected government. Can we stand silently by and watch this happen?

No, we must publicly demonstrate our will, and attempt by force of numbers to make our voices heard, to wrest concessions from a power structure whose interests appear to be opposed to our own.

That's the way it has always been. In reality, we see no tradition of "orderly" progress in America. Instead, we see a history of militant struggle. This nation was founded on the rebellious uprising of colonial people, beginning with that grandaddy of all our native civil disobedience, the Boston Tea Party. The Abolitionist movement before the Civil War was a nationwide conspiracy to break the hallowed laws of private property and destroy the established institution of chattel slavery.

Those American workingmen and women who today enjoy a pleasant standard of living owe their comfort to a century of bitter and militant direct action. The strike—called "disruptive" by its enemies—is the worker's right and his power. Without that weapon he would be at the mercy of his employer. And the history of labor organizing testifies that the lawlessness and violence came not from the side of those seeking redress, but from those who would deny it—the owners, their militia, their courts and vigilantes. So it is in the South today: violence injected by segregationists into a nonviolent movement of masses seeking their civil rights.

Would the timid friends of social justice have us hold our peace and stop, just because someone else is going to start trouble? Where is all the dignity, power and grandeur of our democratic institutions when people get shot in Mississippi? Oh, they are being embarrassed into action—slowly; they are being prodded by thousands in the streets with picket signs. But our government has yet to ensure the safety of those who go about doing the work of gaining full citizenship for all Americans—a job the government should have done long ago. It is our right to demonstrate; it is the duty of a democratic government to help us exercise that right.

We are quite aware, as are many others, that the current attacks on young activists are not motivated primarily out of concern over street demonstrations in Mississippi or Alabama cities. They are rather motivated by the knowledge that this current challenge to Southern power will also change the balance on Capitol Hill; that real democracy for people in the Deep South will have far reaching effects across the nation—effects that in time will extend to Vietnam, the Congo and other far-off lands. Indeed, for some sections of the power structure, the threat of that happening makes mere demonstrations preferable.

This is not to say that we consider demonstrations the only or even activity. Until now, the focus for the most viable form of political activists was the sporadic picket, sit-in, strike, march—The Movement growing from action to action, slumping, then gaining larger life in some new and unexpected spot. But behind these outbursts of ever-growing action, something new is coming. The time is ripe for political organization, incorporating all the experiences of recent years, but building on far stronger foundations; uniting activists, racial minorities and great numbers of working people—and those who can't find work—into a permanent political force.

We are not dreaming, or giving advice. We are describing what we see. We see the organization of the forgotten in the United States—the Negro people, Puerto Ricans, Mexican-Americans, the ex-miners of Appalachia. In nearly every community in the land the work is going on: block committees, unionization, tenants' councils, unemployed councils. The most impressive aspect of this emergent political organization is the drive to bring the political process to the grass roots, with such developments as the Mississippi Freedom Democratic Party which has begun to operate on a ward level across the state. Such work will spread, and with it the possibility for the People to assume the power and transform America into a real democracy—a socialist democracy. . . .

PARTICIPATORY DEMOCRACY: COMPUTER STYLE *

HAZEL HENDERSON

If the essence of democracy is government by the people, then the ideal is achieved to the extent that the people are involved in all decisions. Representative government was invented in part because direct participation by all citizens was technically impossible. With the use of computers and television it is now possible to have all voters participate in major decisions.

How would the system work? Would the average citizen do his homework? Would the problems of college students receive greater or less consideration? Do we need to keep representative government to filter out the emotions of the voters? Do you favor letting everyone have a direct voice in public policy?

It is an early February evening in the year 2023, and John and Jane Doe are relaxing before the TV wall in their home communications center. The newly-elected President of the United States is having his first

* Reprinted from Hazel Henderson, "Computers: Hardware of Democracy," Forum, February, 1970, by permission of the author.

"fireside chat" with his fellow-citizens. He maps out the main issues the voters have presented to his administration, together with the widest range of options suggested by citizens from all walks of life. These options have been winnowed and tabulated by computers as to priorities. Priority number six has been flagged for resolution now to meet long-range planning goals. Priorities one through five, while of global importance, need further information input and analysis. "Priority number six," the President continues, "concerns future development plans for U.S. Region Three, which was formerly known as Appalachia; and five major options have been developed from both random voter feedback and scientific and specialist feedback. The options will now be summarized and simulated on your home screen."

The first option is displayed in a series of colorful simulated maps and diagrams. It would designate the whole region as a national park, and the chief recreational playground for the two great adjacent megalopolitan regions: to the east, BOSWASH (formerly known as the northeastern seaboard from Boston to Washington), and to the west, CHIPITTS (formerly the great industrial region of the Ohio river between Chicago and Pittsburgh). The plan entails six new cities of 250,000 people each, to serve as spas and cultural meccas. Their chief industries would be leisure and tourism, health and beauty maintenance, and the performing arts. Now charts appear showing that the economy of the region would grow at 10 percent per year for the first five years, and would require capital expenditures of half of one per cent of current gross national product. Then, expected influxes of construction engineering and planning personnel are shown for the first five years of building; and, thereafter, the needs for increasing numbers of recreational managers and workers, doctors, beauticians, physical education personnel, and, of course, performing artists of all kinds.

"And now to Option Two," the President says. The second option would designate the area primarily as a natural resource bank, with a secondary use as wilderness recreation. The plan calls for filling the old mines with plastics, iron, copper, rubber and other materials salvaged from the nation's waste disposal plants; these items would be stored until needed for recycling into production. A network of small towns would be necessary; their economies would be based largely on caretaker and inventory-control functions, while also providing for campers and hikers using wilderness areas. As each of the additional combinations of alternatives was presented, a new computer simulation would appear on the Does' screen. The President reappears and makes his formal declaration that the referendum on these development plans for U.S. Region Three would be made at 7 PM, one week hence. He adds, "Each voter can, of course, receive his own detailed printout of the plans from the U.S. Government Printout Office by dialing 235-4707 on his computer phone terminal."

At 7 PM, one week later, John and Jane Doe—having discussed the plans with neighbors, and at their community town-hall meeting—have made up their minds. The telecast begins and the President says, "Good evening, my fellow citizens. I hope you have all done your homework, and that those of you who are registered voters will now give America the benefit of your informed, collective wisdom in tonight's very important national referendum on the long-range development of U.S. Region Three. To refresh your memories, we will again simulate on your home screens the five alternate plans prepared with guidelines from your previous feedback. Please have your voting cards ready for the optical scanner to verify. At the end of the review of the five plans, please place your voting cards in the scanner and then punch in your choice of options, one through five, on your computer phone digit buttons."

After the voting John and Jane relax while the returns are being tabulated. It has been a gruelling week of study for both of them, even though the standard work week has been reduced to two days —a result of machines and other capital instruments largely taking over production of wealth. Apart from the U.S. Region Three plan,

they have had to study an important local education proposition involving three options on the "mix" of educational services their growing town will need in the next decade; they also have had to fulfill their voluntary community commitments. The red indicator lights; and the Does return to their home communications center. They learn that Option One for U.S. Region Three has passed.

Next month, their tasks will include determining a 10-year transportation-design mix for their own U.S. Region One, monitoring a new study course given by the University of the Air, and beginning work to establish priorities on national resource allocation for the second phase of the 25-year plan—for the years 2025 through 2050.

Is this the way democracy might be headed? As automation produces more leisure and shorter workweeks, will citizenship itself take up the slack and become more demanding, so that for many it will be a full-time job? Will we use our technology to create a truly participatory democracy? Or will that ideal be prevented by various factors? For instance, will current decision makers be afraid that if citizens have too much undistorted information, and the means of channeling too many informed decisions into the political process, there would be a change in too many power relationships and a reallocation of too many resources, which would, in turn, result in too many new people having access to power? Consider, too, the legitimate fear, shared by our founding fathers, that a truly direct democracy could not sufficiently filter the emotions of the voters, and might lead to a tyranny of the majority. In computer terms, would too much participation make the social system too sensitive to feedback and produce rapid over-corrections, which could lead to destructive oscillation and loss of equilibrium? In short, is man too irrational to build a rational society?

Democracy certainly is a dangerous experiment, and yet our history has demonstrated a continuous movement toward more direct participation. The point is: technology is available, and like all technology will tend to be used, either willy-nilly by private groups as it is now, or systematically to restore power to the voter and to coordinate the interests of all more fairly. The choice is ours.

3. The Institutional Crisis: Progressive Decay or Rehabilitation?

Our growing population and shifting political values have placed a great strain on American governmental institutions. Their laggard response to these challenges is at the root of the institutional crisis. The hopes and expectations of Americans-at-large have been dampened by the failure of government to perform. Our creaking institutional machinery has become in many instances an end in itself rather than an innovative tool for social change.

The Nature of American Institutions

At the outset we need to identify the basic American institutions. Some fall beyond a narrow definition of government—the family, the church, the university. Others are outside the formal governmental structure—interest groups, political parties. Still others are formal in nature—Courts, Congress, President, Federal Communications Commission. These institutions or similar ones are found in all civilizations. They make it possible for men to live together peaceably because they provide established patterns for doing things. In a stable society they intermesh and form a seamless web of social, economic and political relationships. Their authority is so generally accepted there is little need for a resort to force.

The American Institutional Crisis

With this background it is easier to understand the crisis in American

institutions. On every hand, institutional authority is being questioned. University leaders make policy and are immediately confronted by student leaders. City police who attempt to enforce laws may find that they have provoked a ghetto riot. Trial judges who demand orderly courtroom conduct sometimes must physically muzzle defendants. In the midst of battle army lieutenants encounter privates who refuse orders. Roman Catholic church leaders find their stands on birth control and priestly celibacy called into question. Thus far in the United States these challenges to authority are scattered cases that stand as warnings of what may lie ahead. To examine an advanced case of institutional collapse we need only look at Northern Ireland, where outside British soldiers provide the last stand against total chaos.

Some observers believe that we are entering a new age, where individual freedom is breaking the fetters of institutional regimentation. Others believe that if democratic institutions are strangled, raw force will replace this receding social authority. Although it is not a happy thought, the Ohio National Guard did have the greater firepower at Kent State (with middle-America's approval); regular Army detachments did bring Detroit rioters to bay.

Institutional Renewal

What has caused this institutional authority crisis? Opinions vary. One theory suggests that the old institutions are overworked and over-loaded. Another popular analysis talks of the senility of our institutions; their failure to adapt to the realities of the 1970's. Still another theory stresses the inability of large organizations to function efficiently (a kind of institutional giantism).

The most serious charge against our institutions is that government (the total collection of institutions) has been oversold as a device for problem-solving. One article in this chapter by Professor Banfield is dedicated to the proposition that "government can't solve the urban problem." Another author suggests that we must reexamine what government can and cannot do. His specific recommendation is that it restrict itself to making policy decisions.

These opinions suggest something of the scope of the current disillusionment with government and its institutions. In which direction should we move? Should we more narrowly define the role of government? Or should we turn our attention to institutional reform? If reform is attempted, on what defects should we concentrate? The crisis is real. The future of democratic government may hang in the balance.

We have neglected our political governmental institutions. It is ironic that a people who would fight and die for the principle of self-government, neglect the instruments of self-government. As a result, self-government is in a mess. . . . The American people . . . must apply the same philosophy of repair and redesign to their political institutions that they apply to every other part of life. Nothing stands still. You can't neglect anything and expect that it will remain alive and functioning. This society is facing profound changes. Our political institutions must be equal to that challenge. That requires a vital, alive, concerned attention to those institutions.[1]

---

[1] John W. Gardner, *Questions and Answers About Common Cause*, pp. 1, 10.

A NATION IN DEEP TROUBLE *

JOHN W. GARDNER

Our present tensions, according to Mr. Gardner, stem from the fact that our aspirations as a people have outrun our resources and existing institutions. This dilemma has bred widespread public cynicism toward all government.

Who should allocate our resources in the public sector? How can we avoid excessive centralization? Why do all institutions change at a glacial pace? What responsibility do taxpayers and political leaders have for meeting the new challenges? What does the author mean when he says that: "The anarchist plays into the hands of the authoritarian"? What stabilizing elements does he see as necessary counterparts to dissent?

We have seen in the years since 1961 a growth of domestic social programs unrivaled in our history, except during the Depression. These include activities in and out of government in every corner of the land. Americans have experi-

* John W. Gardner, "A Nation In Deep Trouble." Reprinted with permission from The New Leader, February 12, 1968. Copyright © American Labor Conference on International Affairs, Inc.

enced an extraordinary outburst of social conscience, marked first and foremost by a heightened awareness of social problems.

There is no precedent for the scope of goals envisioned by the individuals, public and private, concerned with these matters today. We have declared war on ignorance, disease, poverty, discrimination, mental or physical incapacity—in fact, on every condition that stunts human growth or diminishes human dignity. Though we may be heartened by the progress we have made, it is a struggle all the way and serious difficulties lie ahead.

Consider the coming crunch between expectations and resources. The expectations of the American people for social benefits are virtually limitless. In the past six years we have opened up innumerable areas of constructive governmental activity: in early childhood education; work with handicapped youngsters; special education for the disadvantaged; health research; work on artificial organs; programs for the aged; rural development efforts; conservation and beautification activities; manpower training, and so on. Most of these programs have begun on a modest scale, and the proponents of every social institution or group aided by them believe passionately that support to *their* field must be vastly enlarged in the near future.

The colleges and universities also have ideas for future Federal support that would amount to billions per year, and they ask little compared to the advocates of aid to elementary and secondary education. The annual cost of a guaranteed income would run to scores of billions. Estimates of the cost of adequate air and water pollution control and solid waste disposal run even higher, while estimates for renovating our cities come to hundreds of billions.

Today we attribute budget constraints to the Vietnam war. But if the war ended tomorrow, in 12 months we would be bumping against the ceiling of resource constraints. How then, do we make rational choices between goals when our resources are limited— and will always be limited relative to expectations? How can we gather the data, evaluate it, and accomplish the planning necessary for making rational choices?

We can have our cake and eat at least some of it if we secure a higher yield from the dollars, talent and institutional strength available to us. But this approach raises questions of good management and unit cost that are painful to most people active in the social fields. Once, in talking with a physician who treated poor people, I asked about unit costs of his government supported clinic. He replied, "I'm not an efficiency expert. I just want to heal sick people." What this doctor was refusing to face is that somewhere up the line hard decisions will necessarily be made, and a limit placed on resources available for health care. So if he is in fact functioning with high unit costs, the number of sick people he can treat will be correspondingly few. Without knowing it, he has made a decision on resource allocation.

A forced choice is not the only consequence of limited resources. Any effort to plan and rationalize the allocation of resources tends to reduce pluralism, and to introduce new kinds of institutional controls. If, for instance, we have less than enough to spend in constructing hospitals, then we must be sure that those we do build are properly located and designed to accomplish the greatest good. In doing so, we move toward a measure of social control.

The Federal government has avoided infringement of local autonomy by asking the states to perform the necessary planning functions. But whether the controls are at the Federal, regional or state level, the rational use of resources encourages the creation of large-scale, interconnected systems, and the comprehensive planning of those systems. Traditionally, Americans have no appetite for this kind of systematic planning, and our non-governmental institutions—be they universities or hospitals or scientific laboratories—are not accustomed to thinking of themselves as parts of an immense whole.

It is possible, I believe, to accomplish a substantial measure of rational social planning and still retain the most important features of local and institutional autonomy. It will require a conscious effort, though, and a knowing grasp of what is involved. President Johnson has proposed that the Federal government operate more and more through mutually respecting partnerships with state and local governments, with the universities and corporations, and with the other great estates of the private sector. Rightly designed, these partnerships could maintain the dispersion of power and initiative that we cherish. But it will take a lot of skill and ingenuity to design the partnerships wisely and well.

Meanwhile, our pattern of stumbling into the future is expensive. In our efforts to husband our resources and allocate them intelligently we must be able to predict future needs and expenditures. Proper use of limited resources involves the orderly formulation of goals, the evaluation of means to achieve those goals, and the development of strategies and cost-estimates for getting from where we are to where we want to be.

Yet we must not approach social goals, plans and priorities as though the only significant considerations were rational and technical. In the development of public policy, that can never be. So let us turn to people.

People used to be fatalistic about their problems because they attributed them to the will of God, or the forces of Nature, or simply to the unchanging order of things. For the past three centuries, however, man has gained increasing confidence, justified or not, that he can take a hand in determining his own fate and can rid himself of at least a few of the ancient afflictions. Whatever

else the consequences, that shift places a very heavy burden on man and his institutions. The individual who used to curse his fate now curses himself or his employer or the party in power.

The pressure and strains on institutions are particularly severe when people who have suffered oppression, as have some of our minority groups, begin to envision a better life. Once the grip of tradition or apathy or oppression has been broken and people can hope for more, their aspirations rise very steeply. Unfortunately, the institutions that must satisfy those aspirations change at the same old glacial pace.

As things stand now, modern man believes—if only with half his mind—that his institutions can accomplish just about anything. The fact that they fall very far short of the goal is due, he feels, to the prevalence of people who love power or money more than they love mankind. I find an appealing (or appalling) innocence in this view. I have had ample opportunity over the years to observe the diverse institutions of this society —the colleges and universities, the military services, business corporations, foundations, professions, government agencies, and so on. And I must report that even excellent institutions run by excellent human beings are inherently sluggish, *not* hungry for innovation, *not* quick to respond to human need, *not* eager to reshape themselves to meet the challenge of the times.

I am not suggesting a polarity

between men and their institutions —men eager for change, institutions blocking it. Institutions, after all, are run by men, and often those who appear most eager for change oppose it most stubbornly when their own institutions are involved. I give you the university professor, a great friend of the reformer, provided the patterns of academic life are not affected. His motto is "Innovate away from home." We are going to have to do a far more imaginative and aggressive job of renewing, redesigning, revitalizing our institutions if we are to meet today's challenges.

It should also be stressed that the overall limit on resources available to our government programs is determined not just by the economy and not just by the rational and technical processes of budgeting. It is equally dependent upon the perception of Congress and the public as to what needs doing and how badly it needs doing; upon the willingness of the public to be taxed for relevant purposes; upon the courage of the Administration in calling for taxes and of the Congress in enacting them.

We are now at the point where the gravest consequences for this nation will ensue if we fail to act decisively on the problems of the cities, poverty and discrimination. Human misery in the ghettos is not a figment of the imagination. It can be read in the statistics on infant mortality, in the crime rate, in the unemployment figures, in the data on educational retardation. We must deal responsively and not

punitively with human need. But it does not seem to me that either the Congress or the public is fully aware of the alarming character of our domestic crisis.

We are in deep trouble as a people. And history is not going to deal kindly with a rich nation that will not tax itself to cure its miseries.

The modern belief that man's institutions can accomplish just about anything he wants, when he wants, has led to certain characteristic contemporary phenomena. One is the bitterness and anger that occurs when high hopes turn sour. No observer of the current scene has failed to note the cynicism prevalent today toward all leaders, all officials, all social institutions. That cynicism is continually fed by the rage of people who expected too much in the first place and got too little in the end.

While aspirations are healthy in themselves, soaring hope followed by rude disappointment is a formula for trouble. It breeds leaders whose whole stock in trade is to exploit first the aspirations and then the disappointment. These men profit on both the ups and the downs of the market.

The roller coaster of aspiration and disillusionment is amusing to the extreme conservative, who thought the high hopes silly in the first place. It gives satisfaction to the Left-wing nihilist who thinks the whole system should be brought down anyway. It is a gold mine for mountebanks willing to promise anything and exploit every emotion. And it is a devastating whip-saw for serious and responsible leaders.

This leaves us with crucial and puzzling questions of public policy. How can we make sluggish institutions more responsive to human need and to the requirements of change? How can we mobilize our resources to meet the crises ahead?

How can we preserve our aspirations (the essence of social betterment) and at the same time develop the toughness of mind and spirit to face the fact that there are no easy victories? How can we make people understand that if they expect all good things instantly they will destroy everything? How do we tell them that they must maintain unrelenting pressure on their social institutions to accomplish beneficial change but must not, in a fit of rage, destroy those institutions? How can we caution them against exploitative leaders, leaders lustful for power or for the spotlight, leaders caught in their own vanity or emotional instability, leaders selling extremist ideologies? How can we diminish the resort to violence?

Violence cannot build a better society. No society can live in constant and destructive tumult. We will have either a civil order in which discipline is internalized in the breast of each free and responsible citizen, or sooner or later we will have repressive measures designed to re-establish order. The anarchist plays into the hands of the authoritarian. Those of us who find authoritarianism repugnant have a duty to speak out against all who destroy civil order. The time has come when the full weight of community opinion should be brought to bear on those who break the peace or seek to force decisions through mob action, or those who by-pass established democratic procedures in favor of coercive demonstrations.

Dissent is an element of dynamism in our system. It is good that men expect much of their institutions, and good that their aspirations for improvement are ardent. But the elements of dynamism must have stabilizing counterparts. One is a tough-minded recognition that the fight for a better world is a long one, a recognition that retains high hopes while it immunizes against childish collapse or destructive rage in the face of disappointment. The other is an unswerving commitment to keep the public peace.

We also need something else. An increasing number of very bright and able people must become involved in the development of public policy. Ours is a difficult and exhilarating form of government, not for the faint of heart, not for the tidy-minded, and in these days of complexity, not for the stupid. America needs men and women who can bring to government the highest order of intellect, social motivations sturdy enough to withstand setbacks, and a resilience of spirit equal to the frustrations of public life and the grave difficulties of the days ahead.

THE TWILIGHT OF AUTHORITY *

ROBERT A. NISBET

Some commentators see in the crumbling of existing institutions a new freedom for man. Others predict social anarchy and moral chaos. Mr. Nisbet takes a third position, arguing that as traditional authority recedes it will be replaced by raw power. Why does he believe that total moral permissiveness would not long survive? Unlike power, upon what sanctions does authority rest? What relationship does the author see between boredom and violence? Why are young people bored? Why do they find the New Left attractive? Why does he believe that middle-class America hails the use of police power? What alternative policy does he propose?

The most striking fact in the present period of revolutionary change is the quickened erosion of the traditional institutional authorities that for nearly a millennium have been Western man's principal sources of order and liberty. I am

* *Reprinted from Robert A. Nisbet, "The Twilight of Authority," Public Interest (Spring, 1969), pp. 3–9. Copyright © 1969 by National Affairs, Inc. Reprinted with permission of the author.*

referring to the manifest decline of influence of the legal system, the church, family, local community, and, most recently and perhaps most ominously, of school and the university.

There are some who see in the accelerating erosion of these authorities the beginning of a new and higher freedom of the individual. The fetters of constraint, it is said, are being struck off, leaving creative imagination free, as it has never been free before, to build a truly legitimate society. Far greater, however, is the number of those persons who see in this erosion, not the new shape of freedom, but the specters of social anarchy and moral chaos.

I would be happy if I could join either of these groups in their perceptions. But I cannot. Nothing in history suggests to me the likelihood of either creative liberty or destructive license for very long in a population witnessing the dissolution of the social and moral authorities it has been accustomed to. I should say, rather, that what is inevitable in such circumstances is the rise of *power:* power that invades the vacuum left by receding social authority; power that tends to usurp even those areas of traditional authority that have been left inviolate; power that becomes indistinguishable in a short time from organized and violent forces, whether of the police, the military, or the para-military.

The human mind cannot support moral chaos for very long. As more and more of the traditional authorities seem to come crashing down, or to be sapped and subverted, it begins to seek the security of organized power. The ordinary dependence on order becomes transformed into a relentless demand for order. And it is power, however ugly its occasional manifestations, that then takes over, that comes to seem to more and more persons the only refuge from anxiety and apprehension and perpetual disorder.

So was it in ancient Athens when, after the brilliant fifth century had ended in the disastrous Peloponnesian Wars, when intimations of dissolution were rife, the Athenians turned to despots, generals, and tyrants who could, it was thought, restore the fabric of authority. So was it in Rome after the deadly civil conflicts of the first century. So was it in Western Europe after the French Revolution had mobilized itself into the Terror—the better, it was thought by Jacobins and others, to destroy the final remnants of corrupt, traditional authority, thus freeing forever the natural virtue in man. What France got, as we know, was neither freedom nor virtue, but the police state of Napoleon; and what Western Europe got was an age of political reaction in which governments took on powers over human life never dreamed of by absolute monarchs of earlier centuries. And so was it in the Germany of a generation ago when, after a decade of spiritual, cultural, and material debauchery, of more and more aggressive assaults on the civil order by the political left, Germany got Nazism and Hitler; got these to the open satisfaction at the time of a large part of the German people, the secret satisfaction of many others, and, in due course, very close to the total satisfaction of all.

Authority vs. Power

To see the eruption of organized power and violence as the consequence of a diminishing desire for liberty is easy. What requires more intelligence or knowledge or wisdom is to see such power as the consequence of loss of *authority* in a social order. Authority and power: are these not the same, or but variations of the same thing?

They are not, and no greater mistake could be made than to suppose they are. Throughout human history, when the traditional authorities have been in dissolution, or have seemed to be, it is power—in the sense of naked coercion—that has sprung up. What Aristotle called *stasis*, perpetual civil strife, is at bottom no more than the fragmentation of authority in society. It is *stasis*, warned Aristotle, that democratic societies have to fear above all else. It is the fateful prelude to despotism.

Authority, unlike power, is not rooted in force alone, whether latent or actual. It is built into the very fabric of human association. Civil society is a tissue of authorities. Authority has no reality save in the memberships and allegiances of the members of an organization, be this the family, a political association, the church, or the university. Authority, function, membership: these form a seamless web in traditional society. The authority of the family follows from its indispensable function. So does that of the church, the guild, the local community, and the school. When the function has become displaced or weakened, when allegiances have been transferred to other entities, there can be no other consequence but a decline of authority.

The Importance of Being Bored

Boredom is one of the most dangerous accompaniments of the loss of authority in a social order. Between boredom and brute violence there is as close an affinity historically as there is between boredom and inanity, boredom and cruelty, boredom and nihilism. Yet boredom is one of the least understood, least appreciated forces in human history. A few years ago, the scientist Harlow Shapley listed boredom as third among the five principal possibilities of world destruction. Today it might seriously be considered first.

Nothing so engenders boredom in the human species as the sense of material fulfillment, of goals accomplished, of affluence possessed. It is such a boredom, born of what Eric Hoffer has called the effluvia of affluence, that goes furthest, I think, to explain the peculiar character of the contemporary New Left. I do not deny that youth brings idealism in some degree to this movement, that disenchant-

ment with the more corrupt manifestations of middle-class society plays its part. Youth is beyond question idealistic. But in our present society, youth is also bored. And it is from boredom, more than from idealism, that so much of the intellectual character of radical political action today is derived. I should more accurately say, *non*-intellectual character, for it is the consecration of the *act,* the cold contempt for philosophy and program, and the increasingly ruthless behavior toward even the most intellectual parts of traditional culture that give to the New Left its most distinctive character at the present time.

It is not idealism but *boredom* —boredom born of natural authority dissolved, of too long exposure to the void; boredom inherited from parents uneasy in their middle-class affluence and who mistake failure of parental nerve for liberality of rearing; boredom acquired from university teachers grown intellectually impotent and contemptuous of calling—that explains the mindless, purposeless depredations today by the young on that most precious and distinctive of Western institutions: the university. . . .

The university is the institution that is, by its delicate balance of function, authority, and liberty, and its normal absence of power, the least able of all institutions to withstand the fury of revolutionary force and violence. Through some kind of perverted historical wisdom the nihilism of the New Left has correctly understood the strategic position of the university in modern culture and also its constitutional fragility. Normally there are no walls, no locked gates and doors, no guards to repulse attacks on classroom, office, and academic study. Who, before the present age, would have thought it necessary to protect precious manuscripts from the hands of revolutionary marauders? Above the din of the New Left's incessant and juvenile cry for immediate amnesty can be heard Voltaire's *Ecrasez l'infâme,* directed, however, not at a corrupt feudalism, but at the freest, most liberal, and humane of all Western institutions.

Il dit tout ce qu'il veut—so runs the harsh indictment in the last century of a French critic—*mais malheureusement il n'a rien à dire.* Neither does the New Left, and this is perhaps its most vivid mark of distinction from all previous lefts in Western society. It is free to say all that it wishes, but it has nothing to say. Its program is the act of destruction, its philosophy is the obscene word or gesture, its objective the academic rubble. One need but read the recently published book by Daniel Cohn-Bendit, present philosopher-hero of the New Left, to see the truth of this. Nowhere in its two hundred and fifty pages is there to be found so much as a paragraph that a Robespierre, a Marx, a Proudhon, even—save the mark—an American Communist would not have thrown in the wastebasket as juvenile and inane.

It does not matter. A philosophy and program are not needed. . . . Boredom suffices to win the New Left its constant flow of recruits. *Credo quia absurdum* could be their motto. "Alienation" is the popular and prestigious word to explain the behavior of the New Left. But the word is as ill-fitting as would be a surplice or academic hood on the shoulders of a clown. Alienation is a noble state of the human spirit, one compounded of idealism and suffering and rejection. Alienation compares with boredom as tragedy does with farce. There is no real alienation in the New Left, only the boredom that is itself the result of erosion of cultural authority, of failure of nerve in middle-class society, and of adult fear of youth.

Toward A New Social Contract

It would all be a transitory charade, a tale told by an idiot, were it not for one thing: the fears aroused in this same middle-class society that has lost its anchoring in natural authority. Fear of the void is for human beings a terrible fear, one that will not long be contained. That state of nature that Thomas Hobbes described as one of "continual fear, and danger of violent death," with "the life of man solitary, poor, nasty, brutish, and short" seems always to the anxious and apprehensive to be about to break through the social order, even as it seemed to Hobbes. And in this state of mind, it is only *power* that can seem redemptive, however stained with blood and violence it may be.

The modern media, and especially television, have the capacity for widening and deepening apprehensions beyond anything known before. We are told that a majority of the French people did not know about the storming of the Bastille for months. The entire country watched last summer's confrontation between New Left and police in Chicago. It was violent, ugly, and could only have aroused the chill of fear in those who had chanced to see the rise of Nazism in Germany, the burning of the Reichstag, and the beginnings of a police system that was in time to enclothe German society like a straitjacket. But I know of no national poll or study that has shown other than approval of police actions by a large majority. The size of this majority will grow. People, we say, should know better, should not let civilized restraint be undermined by demons of fear. But, as the great Bishop Butler wrote, "Things and actions are what they are, and the consequences of them will be what they will be; why, then, should we desire to be deceived?"

Human beings, I repeat, will tolerate almost anything but the threatened loss of authority in the social order: the authority of law, of custom, of convention. The void does not have to be great, or seem great, for the fears it arouses to become sweeping, for sanity in politics to disintegrate. We are told by the polls that a large number of people watching their television screens that night in Chicago found even the berserk actions of police and pseudo-police gratifying, reassuring, healing to the sense of security. Let us not forget too that there is a strong upswell of boredom in affluent middle-class society too. And power, as history tells us, is as often the antidote to boredom in society as to anxiety.

We need, as Max Lerner recently wrote in a thoughtful and moving column, a new social contract in our society, one that will do for our violence-torn social order what the doctrine of the social contract in the seventeenth century sought to do in that age, fresh as it was from the horrors of the religious wars. But the task will be far more difficult. The institutions of Western society are less solid and encompassing than they were then. Two centuries of convulsive social change and of remorseless increase in centralized political and economic power have seen to that. We are plagued even by our achievements, for material progress has inevitably taken toll of traditional culture.

There are, as the recent flight of Apollo 8 made clear, great events taking place in our society. But they are events of the technological, not the social, order. If the life of society is to be saved from boredom relieved only by great technological events—if it is to be saved from armed power, from depredations on traditional culture, from mass movements in which exhilaration produced by power is man's substitute for accustomed liberties—ways must be found, and found shortly, of restoring the sense of initiative in the social as well as the technological order. Above all, at this moment, we need a liberalism that is able to distinguish between legitimate authority—the authority resident in university, church, local community, family, and in language and culture—and mere power. Failure to make this distinction between authority and power can only result in the ever-wider replacement of the former by the latter. If our liberalism can see no profound difference between the authority of an academic dean, however fallible this may sometimes be, and the power of the police riot squad, we shall find ourselves getting ever greater dosages of the latter. History, surely, is unmistakable in its testimony on this point.

At the present time, the nearest to a philosophy and program that exists in the political Left is its incantatory phrases about the Establishment, bureaucracy, and technology. But with every fresh assault on the traditional authorities of the social order, the day of what Burckhardt called the "terrible simplifiers," the new men of power drawn precisely from technology in the service of armed force, comes nearer. The impulse to liberty can survive everything but the destruction of its contexts; and these are contexts of authority—a legitimate authority that is inseparable from institutions. . . .

THE SICKNESS OF GOVERNMENT *
PETER DRUCKER

The case against all modern governments has never been made more vigorously than in the indictment offered below. Perhaps the heart of Mr. Drucker's argument is his contention that contemporary governments have been effective in doing only two things: (1) waging warfare; (2) inflating the economy. His list of particulars is long and disturbing. The best we can expect from the welfare state is "competent mediocrity." Modern government has become ungovernable. Government can never innovate. It manages poorly.

What does Drucker believe the purpose of government to be? What new relationship does he propose between governmental and non-governmental institutions? What distinction does he make between "administering" and "governing"? Do these ideas conflict with the concept of participatory democracy?

* Abridgement of "The Sickness of Government" from THE AGE OF DISCONTINUITY by Peter F. Drucker. Copyright © 1968, 1969 by Peter F. Drucker. Reprinted by permission of Harper & Row, Publishers, Inc.

Government surely has never been more prominent than today. The most despotic government of 1900 would not have dared probe into the private affairs of its citizens as income tax collectors now do routinely in the freest society. Even the tsar's secret police did not go in for the security investigations we now take for granted. Nor could any bureaucrat of 1900 have imagined the questionnaires that governments now expect businesses, universities, or citizens to fill out in ever-mounting number and ever-increasing detail. At the same time, government has everywhere become the largest employer in the society.

Government is certainly all-pervasive. But is it truly strong? Or is it only big?

There is mounting evidence that government is big rather than strong; that it is fat and flabby rather than powerful; that it costs a great deal but does not achieve much. There is mounting evidence also that the citizen less and less believes in government and is increasingly disenchanted with it. Indeed, government is sick—and just at the time when we need a strong, healthy, and vigorous government.

There is obviously little respect for government among the young —but the adults, the taxpayers, are also increasingly disenchanted.

· · ·

A Case of Nonperformance

The greatest factor in the disenchantment with government is that government has not performed. The record over these last thirty or forty years has been dismal. Government has proven itself capable of doing only two things with great effectiveness. It can wage war. And it can inflate the currency. Other things it can promise, but only rarely accomplish. Its record as an industrial manager, in the satellite countries of Eastern Europe as well as in the nationalized industries of Great Britain, has been unimpressive. Whether private enterprise would have done worse is not even relevant. For we expected near-perfection from government as industrial manager. Instead we only rarely obtained even below-average mediocrity.

Government as a planner has hardly done much better (whether in Communist Czechoslovakia or in de Gaulle's capitalist France). But the greatest disappointment, the great letdown, is the fiasco of the welfare state. Not many people would want to do without the social services and welfare benefits of an affluent, modern, industrial society. But the welfare state promised to do far more than to provide social services. It promised to create a new and happy society. It promised to release creative energies. It promised to do away with ugliness and envy and strife. No matter how well it is doing its jobs—and in some areas, in some countries, some jobs are being done very well—the welfare state turns out at best to be just another big insurance company, as exciting, as creative, and as inspiring as insurance companies tend to be. This explains why President Johnson's spectacular performance in enacting the unfinished welfare tasks of the New Deal failed to make him a hero with the public.

The best we get from government in the welfare state is competent mediocrity. More often we do not even get that; we get incompetence such as we would not tolerate in an insurance company. In every country, there are big areas of government administration where there is no performance whatever—only costs. This is true not only of the mess of the big cities, which no government—United States, British, Japanese, or Russian—has been able to handle. It is true in education. It is true in transportation. And the more we expand the welfare state, the less capable even of routine mediocrity does it seem to become.

I do not know whether Americans are particularly inept at public administration—though they are hardly particularly gifted for it. Perhaps, we are only more sensitive than other people to incompetence and arrogance of bureaucracy because we have had, until recently, comparatively so much less of it than other people. In any case, we are now appalled to realize that, during the past three decades, federal payments to the big cities have increased almost a hundred-fold for all kinds of programs, whereas results from this incredible dollar-flood are singularly unimpressive. What *is* impressive is the administrative incompetence. We now have

ten times as many government agencies concerned with city problems as we had in 1939. We have increased by a factor of thousand or so the number of reports and papers that have to be filled out before anything can be done in the city. Social workers in New York City spend some 70 or 80 percent of their time filling out papers for Washington, for the state government in Albany, and for New York City. No more than 20 or 30 percent of their time, that is, almost an hour and a half a day, is available for their clients, the poor. As James Reston reported in *The New York Times* (November 23, 1966), there were then 170 different federal aid programs on the books, financed by over 400 separate appropriations and administered by 21 federal departments and agencies aided by 150 Washington bureaus and over 400 regional offices. One Congressional session alone passed 20 health programs, 17 new educational programs, 15 new economic development programs, 12 new programs for the cities, 17 new resources development programs, and 4 new manpower training programs, each with its own administrative machinery.

This is not perhaps a fair example —even of American administrative incompetence. That we speak of "urban crisis," when we face a problem of race, explains a lot of our troubles. But in other areas, the welfare state has not performed much better. Nor is the administrative mess a peculiarly American phenomenon. The daily press in

Great Britain, in Germany, in Japan, in France, in Scandinavia— and increasingly in the Communist countries as well—reports the same confusion, the same lack of performance, the same proliferation of agencies, of programs, of forms— and the same triumph of accounting rules over results. Everywhere, rivalry between various agencies is replacing concern with results and with responsibility.

Power Without Policy

Modern government has become ungovernable. There is no government today that can still claim control of its bureaucracy and of its various agencies. Government agencies are all becoming autonomous, ends in themselves, and directed by their own desire for power, their own narrow vision rather than by national policy.

This is a threat to the basic capacity of government to give direction and leadership. Increasingly, policy is fragmented, and execution is governed by the inertia of the large bureaucratic empires, rather than by policy. Bureaucrats keep on doing what their procedures describe. Their tendency, as is only human, is to identify what is in the best interest of the agency with what is right, and what fits administrative convenience with effectiveness. As a result the Welfare State cannot set priorities. It cannot concentrate its tremendous resources—and therefore does not get anything done.

The President of the United States may still be the most powerful ruler—more powerful than either the prime ministers of parliamentary regimes dependent upon a majority in parliament, or the dictators who can be overthrown by conspiracies against them among the powerful factions within their totalitarian apparatus. And yet even the President of the United States cannot direct national policy any more. The various bureaucracies do much what they want to do. The Anti-Trust Division of the Department of Justice, for instance, has been making its own policies and pursuing its own course these last twenty years, with little concern for what the incumbent President believes or orders. The Soil Conservation Service and the Bureau of Reclamation, the Forestry Service and the Weather Bureau, the Federal Trade Commission and the Army Engineers have similarly become "independent" rather than "autonomous."

Not so long ago, policy control by the political organs of government could be taken for granted. Of course there were "strong" and "weak" presidents as there were "strong" and "weak" prime ministers. A Franklin Roosevelt or a Winston Churchill could get things done that weaker men could not have accomplished. But this was, people generally believed, because they had the courage of strong convictions, the willingness to lay down bold and effective policies, the ability to mobilize public vision. Today, a "strong" president or a "strong" prime minister is not a man of strong policies; he is the man who knows how to make the lions of the bureaucracy do his bidding. John Kennedy had all the strength of conviction and all the boldness of a "strong" president; this is why he captured the imagination, especially of the young. He had, however, no impact whatever on the bureaucracy. He was a "strong" president in the traditional sense. But he was a singularly ineffectual one. His contemporary, Mr. Khrushchev in Russia, similarly failed to be effective despite his apparent boldness and his popular appeal. By contrast, bureaucratic men who had no policies and no leadership qualities emerge as effective—they somehow know how to make red tape do their bidding. But then, of course, they use it for the one thing red tape is good for, i.e., bundling up yesterday in neat packages.

This growing disparity between apparent power and actual lack of control is perhaps the greatest crisis of government. We are very good at creating administrative agencies. But no sooner are they called into being than they become ends in themselves, acquire their own constituency as well as a "vested right" to grants from the treasury, continuing support by the taxpayer, and immunity to political direction. No sooner, in other words, are they born than they defy public will and public policy.

.   .   .

Certain things are inherently difficult for government. Being by design a protective institution, it is not good at innovation. It cannot really abandon anything. The moment government undertakes anything, it becomes entrenched and permanent. Better administration will not alter this. Its inability to innovate is grounded in government's legitimate and necessary function as society's protective and conserving organ.

A government activity, a government installation, and government employment become immediately built into the political process itself. This holds true whether we talk of a declining industry—such as the nationalized British coal mines or the government-owned railroads of Europe and Japan. It holds equally true in Communist countries. No matter how bankrupt, for instance, the Stalinist economic policies have become in Czechoslovakia, Hungary, or Poland, any attempt to change them immediately runs into concern for the least productive industries, which, of course, always have the most, the lowest-paid and the least-skilled—and, therefore, the most "deserving"—workers.

The inability of government to abandon anything is not limited to the economic sphere. We have known for well over a decade, for instance, that the military draft that served the United States well in a total war is immoral and demoralizing in a "cold war" or "limited war" period. No one defends our present system—yet we extend it year after year on a "temporary" basis. The same inability to abandon applies to research projects supported by government. It holds true as soon as government supports the arts. Every beneficiary of a government program immediately becomes a "constituent." He immediately organizes himself for effective political action and for pressure on the decision-maker.

All institutions, of course, find it hard to abandon yesterday's tasks and to stop doing the unproductive. All of man's institutions—and for that matter, all men—are committed to what they are used to and reluctant to accept that it no longer needs doing or that it does not produce results. But government is under far greater pressure to cling to yesterday than any other institution. Indeed the typical response of government to the failure of an activity is to double its budget and staff.

. . .

Government and Mismanagement

Government is a poor manager. It is, of necessity, concerned with procedure, just as it is also, of necessity, large and cumbersome. Government is properly conscious that it administers public funds and must account for every penny. It has no choice but to be "bureaucratic"—in the common usage of the term. Every government is, by definition, a "government of paper forms." This means inevitably high cost. For "control" of the last 10 per cent of any phenomenon always costs more than control of the first 90 percent. If control tries to account for everything, it becomes prohibitively expensive. Yet this is what government is always expected to do. And the reason is not just "bureaucracy" and red tape; it is a much sounder one. A "little dishonesty" in government is a corrosive disease. It rapidly spreads to infect the whole body politic. Yet the temptation to dishonesty is always great. People of modest means and dependent on a salary handle very large public sums. People of modest position dispose of power and award contracts and privileges of tremendous importance to other people—construction jobs, radio channels, air routes, zoning laws, building codes, and so on. To fear corruption in government is not irrational. This means, however, that government "bureaucracy"— and its consequent high costs—cannot be eliminated. Any government that is not a "government of paper forms" degenerates rapidly into a mutual looting society.

The generation that was in love with the state, thirty and forty years ago, believed fondly that government would be economical. Eliminating the "profit motive" was thought to reduce costs. This was poor economics, to begin with. It is worse public administration. The politician's attention does not go to the 90 percent of money and effort that is devoted to existing programs and activities. They are left to their own devices and to the tender mercies of mediocrity. Politics—rightly —is primarily concerned with "new programs." It is focused on crisis and problems and issues. It is not focused on doing a job. Politics, whatever the form of government, is not congenial to managerial organization and makes government defective in managerial performance.

. . .

We can—and must—greatly improve the efficiency of government. There is little reason these days to insist on "100 percent audit," for instance. Modern sampling methods based on probability mathematics actually give us better control by inspecting a small percentage of the events. But we need something much more urgently: the clear definition of the results a policy is expected to produce, and the ruthless examination of results against these expectations. This, in turn, demands that we spell out in considerable detail what results are expected rather than content ourselves with promises and manifestos. In the last century, the Auditor General became a central organ of every government. We learned that we needed an independent agency to control the daily process of government and to make sure that money appropriated was spent for what it was intended for, and spent honestly. Now we may have to develop an independent government agency that compares the results of policies against expectations and that, independent of pressures from the executive as well as from the legislature, reports to the public any program that does not deliver.

We may even go further—though only a gross optimist would expect this today. We may build into government an automatic abandon-ment process. Instead of starting with the assumption that any program, any agency, and any activity is likely to be eternal, we might start out with the opposite assumption: that each is shortlived and temporary. We might, from the beginning, assume that it will come to an end within five or ten years unless specifically renewed. And we may discipline ourselves not to renew any program unless it has the results that it promised when first started. We may, let us hope, eventually build into government the capacity to appraise results and systematically to abandon yesterday's tasks.

Yet such measures will still not convert government into a "doer." They will not alter the main lesson of the last fifty years: *government is not a "doer."*

What Government Can Be

The purpose of government is to make fundamental decisions, and to make them effectively. The purpose of government is to focus the political energies of society. It is to dramatize issues. It is to present fundamental choices. The purpose of government, in other words, is to govern. This, as we have learned in other institutions, is incompatible with "doing." Any attempt to combine government with "doing" on a large scale paralyzes the decision-making capacity.

There is reason today why soldiers, civil servants, and hospital administrators look to business management for concepts, principles, and practices. For business, during the last thirty years, has had to face, on a much smaller scale, the problem that government now faces: the incompatibility between "governing" and "doing." Business management learned that the two have to be separated, and that the top organ, the decision-maker, has to be detached from "doing." Otherwise he does not make decisions, and the "doing" does not get done either.

In business this goes by the name of "decentralization." The term is misleading. It implies a weakening of the central organ, the top management of a business. The true purpose of decentralization, however, is to make the center, the top management of business, strong and capable of performing the central, the top-management task. The purpose is to make it possible for top management to concentrate on decision-making and direction, to slough off the "doing" to operating managements, each with its own mission and goals, and with its own sphere of action and autonomy.

If this lesson were applied to government, the other institutions of society would then rightly become the "doers." "Decentralization" applied to government would not be just another form of "federalism" in which local rather than central government discharges the "doing" tasks. It would rather be a systematic policy of using the other, *the nongovernmental* institutions of the society—the hospital as well as the university, business as well as labor unions—for the actual "do-

ing," i.e., for performance, operations, execution.

. . .

Toward A New Politics

We do not face a "withering away of the state." On the contrary, we need a vigorous, a strong, and a very active government. But we do face a choice between big but impotent government and a government that is strong because it confines itself to decision and direction and leaves the "doing" to others. We do not face a "return of laissez-faire" in which the economy is left alone. The economic sphere cannot and will not be considered to lie outside the public domain. But the choices of economy—as well as for all other sectors—are no longer *either* complete governmental indifference or complete governmental control. In all major areas, we have a new choice: an organic diversity in which institutions are used to do what they are best equipped to do. In this society all sectors are "affected with the public interest," whereas in each sector a specific institution, under its own management and dedicated to its own job, emerges as the organ of action and performance.

This is a difficult and complex structure. Such symbiosis between institutions can work only if each disciplines itself to strict concentration on its own sphere and to strict respect for the integrity of the other institutions. Each, to use again the analogy of the orchestra, must be content to play its own part. This will come hardest to government, especially after the last fifty years in which it had been encouraged in the belief of the eighteenth-century organ virtuosos that it could—and should—play all parts simultaneously. But every institution will have to learn the same lesson.

Reprivatization will not weaken government. Indeed, its main purpose is to restore strength to sick government. We cannot go much further along the road on which government has been traveling these last fifty years. All we can get this way is more bureaucracy but not more performance. We can impose higher taxes, but we cannot get dedication, support, and faith on the part of the public. Government can gain greater girth and more weight, but it cannot gain strength or intelligence. All that can happen, if we keep on going the way we have been going, is a worsening sickness of government and growing disenchantment with it. And this is the prescription for tyranny, that is, for a government organized against its own society.

This can happen. It has happened often enough in history. But in a society of pluralist institutions it is not likely to be effective too long. The Communists tried it, and after fifty years have shown—though they have not yet fully learned—that the structure of modern society and its tasks are incompatible with monolithic government. Monolithic government requires absolute dictatorship, which no one has ever been able to prolong much beyond the lifetime of any one dictator.

Ultimately we will need new political theory and probably very new constitutional law. We will need new concepts and new social theory. Whether we will get these and what they will look like, we cannot know today. But we can know that we are disenchanted with government—primarily because it does not perform. We can say that we need, in a pluralist society, a government that can and does govern. This is not a government that "does"; it is not a government that "administers"; it is a government that governs.

WHY THE GOVERNMENT CANNOT SOLVE THE URBAN PROBLEM *

EDWARD C. BANFIELD

The American tradition has it that no problem is insoluble—that "The impossible takes only a little

* Reprinted from Edward C. Banfield, "Why Government Cannot Solve the Urban Problem," Daedalus (Fall, 1968) by permission of the publisher.

longer." Therefore it is a bit start-
ling to discover one urban expert
who denies that government can
solve the "urban problem." Why
does Professor Banfield believe
that we cannot change the pattern
of metropolitan growth, eliminate
slums, educate slum children, train
unskilled workers, end chronic
poverty, stop crime and delin-
quency or prevent riots? If govern-
ment cannot achieve these goals,
can it make the lot of the patient
more comfortable?

The city as it exists is very largely
the product of tendencies of which we
have as yet little knowledge and
less control.
                    —Robert E. Park, 1928

I shall argue, first, that all of the
serious problems of the cities are
largely insoluble now and will be
for the foreseeable future and, second, that insofar as it is open to
government (federal, state, and
local) to affect the situation, it tends
to behave perversely—that is, not
to do the things that would make
it better, but instead to do those
that will make it worse. These two
arguments prepare the way for the
question with which I shall be
mainly concerned: What is there
about our politics that accounts for
this perversity?

I

By the serious problems of the cities
I mean those that affect, or may affect, the essential welfare (as opposed to the comfort, convenience,
and business advantage) of large
numbers of people or the ability of
the society to maintain itself as a
"going concern," to be in some
sense free and democratic, and to
produce desirable human types. As
examples of serious problems I will
cite chronic unemployment, poverty, ignorance, crime, racial and
other injustice, and civil disorder.
To my mind, these problems are of
a different order of importance
than, say, the journey to work, urban sprawl, or the decline of
department store sales.

What I am calling serious problems exist mainly in the inner parts
of the central cities and of the older
larger suburbs. The large majority
of city dwellers do not live in these
places and have little or no first-
hand knowledge of these problems;
most city dwellers have housing,
schools, transportation, and community facilities that are excellent
and getting better all the time. If
there is an urban crisis, it is in the
inner city. The lowest-skilled, lowest-paid, and lowest-status members of the urban work force have
always lived in the highest-density
districts of the inner city, that being where most of the jobs for the
low-skilled have always been. Improvements in transportation have
in the last thirty years or so hastened a process of outward growth
that has always been going on.
Most of those who could afford to
do so have moved from the central
city to the suburbs and from inly-
ing suburbs to outlying ones. Much
manufacturing and commerce has

done the same thing. The inner city still employs most of the unskilled, but the number (and proportion) that it employs is declining, and considerable numbers of the unskilled are in a sense stranded in the inner city. The presence there of large concentrations of people who have relatively little education and income accounts for—perhaps I should say constitutes—the so-called urban crisis. Most of these people are black. From an objective standpoint, this is of less importance than most people suppose: If all Negroes turned white overnight, the serious problems of the city would still exist and in about the same form and degree; it is the presence of a large lower class, not of Negroes as such, that is the real source of the trouble.

Government can change the situation that I have just described only marginally; it cannot change it fundamentally. No matter what we do, we are bound to have large concentrations of the unskilled, of the poor, and—what is by no means the same thing—of the lower class in the inner parts of the central cities and the larger older suburbs for at least another twenty years. Rich as we are, we cannot afford to throw the existing cities away and build new ones from scratch. The decentralization of industry and commerce and of residential land use is bound to continue, leaving ever larger semi-abandoned and blighted areas behind.

If government cannot change fundamentally the pattern of metropolitan growth, neither can it solve any of the serious problems associated with it. To be specific, it cannot eliminate slums, educate the slum child, train the unskilled worker, end chronic poverty, stop crime and delinquency, or prevent riots. Of course, I do not mean that it cannot eliminate a single slum, educate a single slum child, or prevent a single riot. What I mean is that it cannot put a sizable dent in the problem as a whole. These problems may all become much less serious, but if they do, it will not be because of the direct efforts of government to bring about reforms.

We cannot solve these problems or even make much headway against them by means of government action not because, as many seem to suppose, we are selfish, callous, or stupid, but rather because they are in the main not susceptible to solution. For one reason or another, solving them is beyond the bounds of possibility. In the largest class of cases, solution depends upon knowledge that we do not and perhaps cannot possess. Consider, for example, the problem of educating the lower-class child. In recent years, there has been a vast outpouring of effort on this, and a great many well-thought-out and plausible ideas have been tried, some of them, like Operation Head Start, on a very large scale. So far none of these efforts can be said to have succeeded, and most of them have clearly failed. After surveying the various efforts at compensatory education, the U.S. Commission on Civil Rights said in

Racial Isolation in the Public Schools that "none of the programs appear to have raised significantly the achievement of participating pupils, as a group, within the period evaluated by the Commission." It is probably safe to say that if the leading educators of this country were given first call on all of the nation's resources and told that they could do whatever they liked, they would not succeed in giving what any of us would consider an adequate education to a substantial number of slum children.

The nature of some problems is such that even if we knew how to solve them, we probably could not make use of the knowledge because the cure would be worse than the disease. However attractive they may otherwise be, all "solutions" that are incompatible with the basic principles of our political system must be considered unavailable— that is, beyond the bounds of possibility. If, for example, it were found to be possible to educate the lower-class child by taking him from his family shortly after birth and in no other way, we should have to give up the idea of educating those lower-class children whose parents refused to give them up; a free society cannot even consider taking children from their parents on the mere presumption—indeed not even on the certainty—that otherwise they will grow up ignorant, dependent, lower class.

Incompatibility with the basic principles of the political system is by no means the only ground on which a "solution" may be judged worse than the disease. Consider, for example, the police "crackdown" as a method of reducing crime on the streets. I do not know how well this method really works, but suppose for the sake of argument that it works very well. Even so, it is not a solution because, rightly or wrongly, a "crackdown" would be regarded by Negroes as an affront to the race. What is accomplished if crime is reduced slightly at the cost of deepening the cleavage between the Negro and the rest of society?

It is only because we seldom pay any attention to the indirect, unintended, and unwanted consequences of government actions that we fail to see that they are often worse than the diseases that the actions are supposed to cure. The usual assumption seems to be that a desirable consequence in hand offsets two undesirable ones in the bush. This may be reasonable. But what if the bush is full of extremely undesirable consequences?

II

Although government cannot cure the serious ills of the city, it might make the patient more comfortable and enable it to lead a somewhat more useful life despite its ills. I will list what I think are the more important things that it might do to improve the situation. In general, these are not the things that one would most like to have done (those being in most cases beyond the bounds of possibility for the reasons indicated), but they are all ones that it is possible in principle for government to do and that would make a more than trivial contribution to the improvement of the situation. Some of the items on the list may strike the reader as highly implausible, but this is not the place to try to justify them.

The list is as follows:

1. Use fiscal policy to keep unemployment below 3 percent even though this would entail undesirable inflation. (The possibility of this for more than a few years was denied by Milton Friedman in his Presidential Address to the American Economics Association in 1967. Other leading economists assert it, however, and the question must be considered unsettled.)

2. Eliminate impediments to the free working of the labor market, particularly that for low-skilled labor. This implies removing legal and other barriers to the employment of the young, the unschooled, women, and Negroes. It implies repeal of minimum wage laws and of laws that enable unions to exercise monopolistic powers. It also implies improving the information available to workers about job opportunities in other places.

3. If the second recommendation is not carried into effect, suspend immigration of the unskilled. Also, by bringing about expansion of the rural southern and Puerto Rican economies and by setting welfare allowances so as to favor rural and small-town residence, discourage migration of unskilled Americans to the large cities.

4. Pay the poor to send infants and small children to nursery and pre-schools. Create a competitive school system by giving vouchers for use in any private (including parochial) school to parents of children who do not go to public school. Lower the compulsory attendance age to twelve and the normal school-leaving age to fourteen (grade twelve). Give boys and girls who leave school the choice between taking a job and going into a youth corps. Make it possible for all who qualify to get higher education subject to later repayment.

5. Define poverty in terms of "hardship" (as opposed to "inconvenience" or "relative deprivation") and bring all incomes up to this nearly fixed level. With respect to those competent to manage their own affairs (that is, all but the insane, the severely retarded, the senile, and unprotected children), make the income transfer by means of a negative income tax, leaving the recipients free to spend their money as they please. Public housing, public hospital care, "rehabilitation," and other welfare services in kind rather than in cash should go only to those requiring institutional or semi-institutional care.

6. Allow police officers wider latitude to deal out "curbstone justice"

to petty offenders, especially juveniles. Repeal laws against gambling and usury. Change insurance and police practices (for example, free recovery of stolen cars) so that potential victims of crime will not be deprived of incentive to take precautions to prevent loss.

7. Eliminate impediments to the free working of the housing market. Establish building codes, uniform for the whole of a metropolitan area, that will permit the widest latitude for innovation and economizing consistent with safety. Assure that some part of every suburb is zoned in a manner that does not prevent low-income occupancy.

8. Prohibit "live" television coverage of riots.

9. Avoid rhetoric tending to create demands and expectations that cannot possibly be fulfilled or to excite alarm about nonexistent crises. Above all, stop attributing more importance to racial factors, including discrimination, than the facts warrant. Explain nothing on racial grounds that can be explained as well or better on income or class grounds.

I trust I do not need to say again that this is not a list of "consummations devoutly to be wished." Rather it is one of things that government could do and the doing of which would contribute more than trivially to the amelioration of the serious problems of the city. But even if all of these things were done, the situation would not be fundamentally changed; the improvements would be ones of degree rather than of kind.

III

Although the measures listed are possible, they are not politically feasible. It is safe to say that none of them will be tried in the near future. A politician with a heterogeneous constituency probably could not support any of them vigorously. Indeed, with respect to most of the items on the list, the politically feasible thing is the exact opposite of what has been recommended: for example, to raise the minimum wage, to raise the normal school-leaving age, to encourage immigration of the unskilled, to define poverty as relative deprivation rather than as hardship, to emphasize racial factors while denying the existence of class ones, and so on.

Why this perversity in the choice of policies? Before offering an answer to this question, I should acknowledge that its premises are questionable. Perhaps the recommendations made above are unsound; perhaps, too, the things that I said were beyond the bounds of possibility are not beyond them. Even if the recommendations are sound, the system may not be perverse in rejecting them for their opposites. It may be that "problems" arise only in those instances —which may be a very small proportion of the whole—where the system fails to select a right policy and by so doing fails to prevent a problem from arising. To explain an occasional visible failure on the grounds that the system is perverse is like explaining the presence of a few men in death row on grounds that the threat of capital punishment is not a deterrent. For all we know tens of thousands of men may *not* be in death row precisely because they *were* deterred. Space does not permit me to deal with these objections. All I can do is say that I am aware of them.

Perhaps the most palpable reason for the political infeasibility of most of the items on the list is that they would be instantly squashed by some interest group (or groups) if they were ever put forward. The founding fathers went to great pains to distribute power so widely that "factions" would check one another and prevent the growth of tyranny. This arrangement has the defects of its virtues, of course; one of the defects is that a very small group can often veto a measure that would be of great benefit to a large public. It is laughable, for example, to talk about eliminating impediments to the free working of the labor market so long as labor unions are politically powerful. New York City cannot employ unskilled laborers to repair the slum housing that they live in because to do so it would first have to get them into the building trades unions and then pay them union wages.

There are well-armed and strategically placed "veto groups" (as David Riesman calls them in *The Lonely Crowd*) for almost every item on the list. The organized teachers would veto a proposal to lower the school-leaving age. The organized social workers would veto the substitution of a negative income tax for the traditional arrangements. Civil rights organizations would veto giving policemen more latitude to deal out "curbstone justice." The television industry would veto the prohibition of "live" TV coverage of riots. And so on.

Although interest groups most often exercise their power by vetoing measures that might be injurious to them, they sometimes initiate ones that they think will benefit them. Why, it may be asked, do not the putative beneficiaries of the measures on the list above organize and apply pressure counter to that of the veto groups? The answer (as Mancur Olson has explained in *The Logic of Collective Action*) is that in most instances the benefits are in the nature of what economists call "public goods"—that is, they are such that if anyone benefits, all must benefit. This being the case, no individual has any incentive to support an organization to bring them into existence. TV stations find it to their advantage to maintain an organization that can influence the F.C.C. not to prohibit "live" coverage of riots, but the ordinary citizen, even if he were very much in favor of prohibiting it, would not pay much of anything to have his view urged upon the F.C.C. because he would be sure that his small contribution would not affect the outcome. In a certain sense, therefore, it would be irrational for him to contribute, since he would have the same chance of getting the benefit (prohibition of "live" coverage) if he kept his money in his pocket. For most of the items on the list, the logic of collective action is of this sort.

In the last analysis, however, what makes the items on the list politically infeasible is that promising them would not help anyone to get elected. To some extent this is because public opinion does not favor them. (It is not for this reason entirely, however. As Anthony Downs has explained, candidates and parties offer combinations of measures—"budgets"—that confer on voters large benefits in terms of their primary interests and, at worst, small costs in terms of their secondary and tertiary interests. Thus, in principle, a winning coalition may be built around a "budget" no single item of which is favored by more than a few voters.)

It is pertinent to inquire, therefore, why *public opinion* is perverse. An answer sometimes given is that in matters such as these it is generally dominated by the opinion of the well educated and well off. These people (so the argument runs) are indifferent or downright hostile to the interest of the less well off and the poor. In short, the "masses" are against the recommended measures because they have been misled by an elite that is looking after its own interests.

This explanation does not fit the facts. The perversity of policy does not benefit the well off; on the contrary, it injures them. The well off are not benefited by the minimum wage or by other laws and practices that price low-value labor out of the market and onto the welfare rolls. They are not benefited by laws that keep hundreds of thousands of children who cannot or will not learn anything in schools that they (the well off) must support. They are not benefited by an official rhetoric tending to persuade everyone that the society is fundamentally unjust.

I want to argue that public opinion (which I agree is decisively influenced in many matters by the opinion of the relatively well off) tends to be altruistic and that it is precisely because of its altruism that it opposes the recommendations on the list and favors instead ones that are the reverse of those recommended as well as ones that are beyond the bounds of possibility.

The American cultural ideal, which is most fully exemplified in the upper-middle and upper classes (and within those classes in people of dissenting—Protestant and Jewish—traditions), is oriented toward the future and toward progress. It sees the individual as perfectible by his own effort and society as perfectible by collective effort. Accordingly, it feels a strong obligation to engage in efforts at improvement of self and community. Americans tend to believe that all problems can be solved if only one tries hard enough, and they acknowledge a responsibility to improve not only themselves, but everything else—community, society, the whole world. Ever since the days of Cotton Mather, whose *Bonifacius* was a "how to do it" book on the doing of good, service has been our motto. I do not mean to say that our practice has corresponded to our principles. The principles, however, have always been influential and often decisive. For present purposes they can be summarized in two very simple rules: first, DON'T JUST SIT THERE. DO SOMETHING; and, second, DO GOOD.

It is the application of these two rules that produces most of the perversity that I claim characterizes our choice of policies. Believing that any problem can be solved if only we try hard enough, we do not hesitate to attempt what we do not have the least idea how to do and what may even be impossible in principle. Not recognizing any bounds to what is possible, we are not reconciled to, indeed we do not even perceive, the necessity for choosing among courses of action all of which are unsatisfactory, but some of which are less unsatisfactory than others. That some children simply cannot or will not learn anything in school and that we do not know how to change this are facts that the American mind will not entertain. Our cultural ideal demands that we give everyone a good education whether or not he wants it and whether or not he is capable of receiving it. This ideal also tells us that if at first we don't succeed,

we must try, try again. To suggest lowering the normal school-leaving age is, in terms of this secular religion, out-and-out heresy.

The recommendations listed above are unacceptable—indeed, downright repellent—to public opinion because what they call for does not appear to be morally improving either to the doer or to the object of his doing. It does not appear to be improving to the child to send him to work rather than to school, especially as that is what it is to one's interest as a taxpayer to do. It does not appear to be improving to the delinquent to let the policeman "slap him around a little," especially as that accords with one's feelings of hostility toward the juvenile. It does not appear to be improving to the slum dweller to tell him that if his income is adequate and if he prefers to spend it for other things than housing, that is his affair, especially as that is in one's "selfish" interest. From the standpoint of the cultural ideal, the doing of good is not so much for the sake of those to whom the good is done as it is for that of the doers, whose moral faculties are activated and invigorated by the doing of it, and also for that of the community, the shared values of which are ritually asserted and vindicated by the doing of it. For this reason good done otherwise than by intention, especially good done in the pursuance of motives that are selfish or even "non-altruistic," is not really "good" at all. For this reason, too, actions taken from good motives count as good even when, in fact, they do harm. By far the most effective way of helping the poor is to maintain high levels of employment. This, however, is not a method that affords upper-middle and upper-class people the chance to flex their moral muscles or the community the chance to dramatize its commitment to the values that hold it together. The way to do these things is by a War on Poverty. Even if the War should turn out to have precious little effect on the incomes of the poor— indeed, even if it should *lower* their incomes—the undertaking would be justified as a sort of secular religious revival that affords the altruistic classes opportunities to bear witness to the cultural ideal and, by so doing, to strengthen society's adherence to it. One recalls the wisecrack about the attitude of the English Puritans toward bear-baiting: that they opposed the sport not for the suffering it caused the bear, but for the pleasure that it gave the spectators. Perhaps it is not farfetched to say that the present-day outlook is similar: The reformer wants to reform the city not so much to make the poor better off materially as to make himself and the society as a whole better off morally.

There is something to be said for this attitude. The old Puritans were certainly right in thinking it worse that people should enjoy the sufferings of animals than that animals should suffer. And the reformers are certainly right in thinking it more important that society display a concern for what is right and just than that the material level of living of the poor (which is already well above the level of physical hardship) be raised somewhat higher. There are problems here however. One is to keep the impulse for doing good from gushing incontinently into mass extravaganzas (Domestic Marshall Plans, for example) in which billions are pledged for no one knows what or how; surely if it is to be morally significant, good must be done from motives that are not contrived for the individual by people with big organizations to maintain and foisted upon him by the mass media. Another is to find ways of doing good that are relatively harmless—that do not unduly injure those to whom the good is done (as, for example, children who cannot or will not learn are injured by long confinement in a school), that are not unfair to third parties (taxpayers), and that do not tend to destroy the consensual basis of the society (as headline-catching official declarations about "white racism" may).

Looking toward the future, it is impossible not to be apprehensive. The frightening fact is that vast numbers of people are being rapidly assimilated to the ethos of the altruistic classes and are coming to have incomes—time as well as money—that permit them to indulge their taste for "serving" and "doing good." Television, even more than the newspapers, tends to turn the discussion of public policy questions into a branch of the mass en-

tertainment industry. "Doing good"
is becoming—has already become
—a growth industry, like other
forms of mass entertainment. This
is the way it is in the affluent society. How will it be in the super-
affluent one? How preoccupied can
a society be with reform without
thereby loosening the bonds that
hold it together? If there is an urban crisis, perhaps this is its real
basis.

4. Informal Political Institutions (Interest Groups, Political Parties, Elections): Limited Machinery For Problems Unlimited

Informal political institutions are those organizations that serve as "transmission lines" between the popular will and official governmental machinery. In this chapter we focus our attention on three of these informal organizations: (1) interest groups; (2) political parties; (3) election machinery. Each of these shows signs of institutional fatigue and a crisis syndrome. If these transmission lines are jammed, the formal institutions are cut off from their source of power.

Self Interest and Public Interest

Interest groups arose spontaneously in the United States, completely outside any formal structure. The desire for favorable government action brought together men faced with common problems. Truck owners banned together in the American Truckers Association; teachers joined the National Education Association; policemen became dues-paying members of the Fraternal Order of Police; businessmen organized the U.S. Chamber of Commerce. The effectiveness of this tactic on elected officials is everywhere evident. A single individual's chances of influencing government policy are nearly zero. As part of a group (with expert direction) his political clout may be increased a thousand-fold.

Interest groups are a fundamental part of American political reality. Many citizens have been well served by this arrangement. But it obviously works best for these individuals as private citizens. What of the public interest? Under this system who speaks out when streams are polluted? When the consumer is exploited? Do we not end up by repeating some variety of the slogan: "What's good for me is good for the country"?

And who speaks for unorganized, lower-income Americans? Who champions the migrant grape pickers? The welfare mothers? The physically and mentally handicapped? In a recent year the national government paid out a larger amount to 10,000 farmers for *not growing crops* than it spent on all public housing. Did this action represent the true public interest or did it merely stand as testimony to the effectiveness of the farmer's lobby?

Two proposals for giving priority to the public interest have been suggested. One would curb private groups by publicizing the amount and sources of their income and expenditures. A newer suggestion is the creation of interest groups dedicated to the public interest. The largest of these new groups is Common Cause.

Our Ailing Political Parties

American political parties have long served as rallying points, bringing together most groups under one of two banners. They offer national unity in a diverse society. As a forum they provide a bargaining table where the wishes of conflicting interest groups are compromised.

Recently this search for agreement has been cited as a failure to give American voters a clear-cut choice. Perhaps this charge is only a reflection of changes in American culture. Compromise has become a "cop-out" phrase: in many quarters violence has replaced debate. Economic prosperity seems to have increased rather than reduced tensions: unresolved crises quickly escalate beyond the point where they can be compromised. These tendencies are intensified by the six o'clock TV news, that creates an immediate national awareness of the day's problems. In the face of this awareness, party compromises seem remote, inadequate, glacier-like. Those who engage in militant demonstrations and violence have another explanation of party lethargy. Viewed from the black ghetto, political parties are a tool of "whitey's" establishment, designed to preserve the status quo. The militants feel that effective change can be brought about only by pressure from outside "The System."

Are the old parties finished? Millions of Americans now pride themselves on their lack of party affiliation. Political Johnny-come-latelys leap-frog over the heads of party leaders to gain public endorsement through TV. Under these circumstances can parties as we have known them survive? If parties are weakened—if men are nominated for public office on the basis of personality alone—are we not deserting democratic principles for demagoguery?

Both Democrats and Republicans are actively exploring ways to make their parties more responsive to the public will. Can they recapture the allegiance of voters in a mass society? What is the alternative to a two-party system? Would a dozen parties, with clear-cut policy positions really serve American voters better? How would the majority will then be determined? What if there is no majority? Will citizens recognize that to achieve majority rule they must forego a part of their individual preferences?

The Election Process: Money and Media

In a mass society candidates for public office are heavily dependent on money and a favorable TV image. As we have already noted, the traditional political party machinery can now be bypassed. A contemporary citizen of Pittsburgh may well question whether Pennsylvania's party leaders and machinery have any clear future role. Mayor Peter Flaherty won his office over the solid opposition of his party's leadership; Governor Milton Shapp was nominated despite the united opposition of the 67 county chairmen of his party. In New York, Mayor John Lindsay was defeated in the Republican primary, but bounced back to win the election under the Independent and Liberal party banners. In 1971, with his eyes fixed on the Presidency, he transferred his well-established charisma and TV personality to the Democratic Party.

Richard Ottinger with a $1.3 million TV budget emerged from political obscurity to capture the New York Democratic primary for the U.S. Senate; Millionaire Howard Metzenbaum duplicated this 1970 feat in Ohio.

The new political "medicine men" are the mass media experts who sell the candidates over TV. To the average voter such men as Charles Guggenheim (who managed the Edward Kennedy campaign), David Garth (John Lindsay), Robert Goodman (Spiro Agnew), and Robert Squier (Edmund Muskie) mean nothing, but to candidates eager for victory these men loom large.

Some candidates deliberately avoid party labels. The Senate minority leader, Hugh Scott, won handily in 1970 with state-wide billboards and TV spots that majestically announced "Scott of Pennsylvania," while the rest of the Republican ticket was soundly defeated. For political candidates the greatest recommendation of this new politics can be summed up: "It seems to work."

American elections have become incredibly expensive. For instance, candidates without access to several million dollars should not consider running for the U.S. Senate in New York, Pennsylvania, or California. The candidate with money has always held a great advantage in running for public office. But today that advantage has become a requirement.

Where does this money come from? A private fortune is one handy answer. For the non-millionaire the only answer is "fat cats"—wealthy sponsors who will cover campaign costs. As parties decline, more and more of this money is fed directly to individual candidates. What does this do to the democratic process? A cynical answer would be that "He who pays the piper has always called the tune."

Television coverage has introduced another disruptive factor. For one thing, it is unbelievably expensive. For another, it is shifting the whole direction of campaign strategy. The candidate appeals directly to the individual in his living room, using all the techniques of the advertising industry. Slick packaging replaces serious debate. Whatever sells Alka-Seltzer will sell a President (He too will relieve your present distress). This whole procedure filters out a great percentage of potential leaders. Many fall short of the financial requirement. And, many are repelled by the distasteful public relations gimmicks that win elections. As one recent author has written: "For the most part, our ablest men and women simply do not enter public life today . . . [If] we want to bring about a renaissance in politics . . . we [must] make it possible for our most gifted men and women to be active in that part of our national life."

THE EDUCATORS LOBBY
ON CAPITOL HILL *
NORMAN C. MILLER

Educators for decades were a badly fragmented, amateur Washington pressure group who were viewed lightly by Congressmen. In the past ten years they have been transformed into a tightly-organized professional coalition with considerable political clout. The bill described in this article was passed by the Congress and vetoed by the President. In the face of renewed pressure by education lobbyists the Congress overrode the President's veto.

What groups did the National Education Association bring together to develop broad-based support for its bill? Why were certain Congressmen identified for special "treatment"? What was the "treatment"? How was the Nixon Administration's opposition undercut by one of its own executive agencies? Where was the true public interest in this issue? Was the Congress or President best able to judge? Does this system of legislation by pressure provide for the poorly organized—the poor, the blacks, the elderly?

---

* Reprinted from Norman C. Miller, "The Educators Lobby on Capitol Hill," Wall Street Journal, January 20, 1970, by permission of The Wall Street Journal.

At 7:30 a.m. tomorrow, 40 or more persons will gather for a breakfast meeting in the National Education Association building cafeteria here. In this unpretentious setting, they will plot final tactics for an extraordinary campaign to bend the President of the United States to their will.

The men are lobbyists for education groups that are applying intense pressure on Congress to add nearly $1.3 billion to the budget of the Department of Health, Education and Welfare. Disregarding President Nixon's unqualified promise of a veto, the Senate seems certain to give final Congressional approval, probably today, to a $19.7 billion appropriations bill containing the extra school-aid money the education lobby demands.

The subsequent veto will provoke a dramatic battle, probably next week when the Democratic-controled Congress attempts to override the President. Education lobbyists already have opened a high-pressure drive to corral the necessary two-thirds vote.

"The kind of pressure I'm getting from Illinois is absolutely fantastic," says GOP Sen. Charles Percy of that state. "I think I've heard from every school board and school district in the state."

Well-Organized and Powerful

Still, Sen. Percy says he intends to vote to sustain a veto, because he agrees with the President's argument that inflation is an overwhelming threat. As the Percy intention indicates, the odds favor the White House. But Nixon lieutenants say they have no easy job. "We are facing a superbly organized and very powerful lobbying group," says Bryce Harlow, chief White House lobbyist.

The immediate battle centers on the House because it will act first on the veto. Whatever the outcome, Congress and the Nixon Administration seem headed for continuing combat over the school-aid issue. It is a prime symbol in the increasingly partisan debate about "reordering priorities," with Democrats charging the President with skimping on education while Republicans retort that the need to control inflation is paramount. The pivotal role of education lobbyists and their union allies in this struggle—from its little-noted inception nine months ago to its blossoming as a major national issue—is a classic example of how a well-organized lobby influences legislative policy.

Key education lobbyists have done everything from drafting the controversial money bill to hauling some Congressmen out of their offices and delivering them to the House floor to cast crucial votes for the educators' package.

In the first place, the lobbyists shrewdly concocted a package that added a sort of pork-barrel allure to the general Congressional interest in education. In the basic package, which has since been expanded, the lobbyists tied together $895 million for several education programs to be added to the Nixon Administration budget request. They thereby dangled a promise of more money for schools in almost every Congressional district even though almost half the total was allotted to one long-entrenched program that even some of the lobbyists admit has doubtful merit—special aid to school districts with large concentrations of Federal employees.

Forming a Coalition

Over 80 education groups and allied organizations, including the AFL-CIO, formed a coalition to push the package through Congress. The cause even brought peaceful cooperation between the oft-warring National Education Association and the American Federation of Teachers. The coalition's success in organizing intense pressure from teachers, school administrators, librarians and college trustees was the key to this campaign.

In the current confrontation, which was signaled just before Christmas when President Nixon announced his veto plan, each group in the coalition urged its state and local units to begin prodding lawmakers while they were home for the recent three-week recess. A memo circulated by August Steinhilber, lobbyist for the National School Board Association, was typical:

"Remind your Congressman the veto-override vote is a record vote which will be circulated in the state. . . . Send out press releases on what Federal cuts will mean in terms of increased local property taxes, the dropping of programs etc. . . . Send me a list of school board members or association staff members who can be wired if there is a need to flood Washington with people in favor of education."

Picking the Targets

Washington will indeed be flooded with school people from around the country to pressure House members before the showdown vote on the veto. They'll descend on the Senate too, if the bill gets through the House.

At tomorrow morning's meeting, the coalition's professional lobbyists will swap reports from the field on what lawmakers have told educators who have contacted them back home. Then they'll decide which Congressmen need further pressure. The 86 Republicans who voted for the bill in December are sure to be targets. Among these are men who have been close to school organizations: John Dellenback of Oregon, William Steiger of Wisconsin, Marvin Esch of Michigan and Albert Quie of Minnesota.

Special effort will be made to import educators from the districts or the states of shaky Congressmen. William Simmons, assistant superintendent of the Detroit school system, is organizing a contingent of big-city educators to come to Washington. The total goal is to bring in at least 435 educators, one for each House member. In antici-

pation of a House vote next week, the plan is to have the out-of-town group assembled here by Sunday.

Specific assignments will be handed out at a briefing session planned for Sunday night at the Congressional Hotel near the Capitol. The big group will be split into lobbying teams of a half-dozen persons, each including representatives of key parts of the coalition, such as teachers, librarians, college and school administrators. The teams will begin calling on Congressmen Monday.

The professional lobbyists will brief the amateurs on how to make their pitch. One pro's advice, boiled down, goes like this: "Stick to facts. Show him the importance of the funds in specific cases back home. Ask for a specific commitment, but don't threaten him. If you get nasty, you'll only make him mad. But impress on him that this is one vote that is going to be remembered back home."

The lobbying teams will give written reports on lawmaker's positions to coalition headquarters in the Congressional Hotel. Ken Young, one of the savvy lobbyists on the AFL-CIO's staff, will analyze the reports, deciding which Congressmen seem firmly committed for or against and which might be won over with further persuasion.

Charles Lee, a specialist in education legislation who's the coalition committee's only full-time staffer, will supply data aimed at swaying hesitant Congressmen. A lawmaker particularly concerned about higher education, for example, will almost surely hear a Lee-inspired claim that "over 135,000 students won't be able to get loans they need to return to college for the spring semester unless the bill passes." (The measure includes an unbudgeted $40.8 million for student loans.)

Showing Up to Vote

Mr. Young will head the effort to make sure that all lawmakers who say they support the bill show up to vote. But since it will be a roll call vote, on a heavily publicized issue, most members doubtless will show up without urging. Thus, Mr. Young doesn't plan to set up an elaborate "whip system" like the one that helped give the education coalition its first major victory in the House last July. (Actually, he will be trying to deter some lawmakers from voting, sounding out sympathetic conservatives who feel they can't vote against the President to see if they can arrange to be absent.)

Then, as frequently happens in the House, the problem for the educators was that the crucial votes were non-roll call votes occurring on short notice in a confusing parliamentary situation. Senior members of the powerful Appropriations Committee strongly opposed the $895 million package amendment.

To avoid antagonizing powerful committeemen, it's common for House members who ostensibly support a higher appropriation to miss non-roll call votes or even vote the other way. Consequently it's extremely difficult to defeat the committee during the often lightly attended amendment process.

But Mr. Young organized an operation that left Congressmen who had promised to support the educators little excuse to miss important votes. He stationed one or two men in a friendly lawmaker's office on each floor of the three House office buildings. Each agent had a list of the nearby lawmakers who had promised to vote the educators' way.

Passing the Word

Mr. Young, keeping tabs on housefloor action from a corridor outside the House chamber, had an aide in a nearby telephone booth holding open a line to coalition headquarters. When a vote neared, Mr. Young passed the word to headquarters aides, who in turn phoned the agents in the House office buildings. Then these people dashed into offices to urge the Congressmen to rush to the House chamber to vote.

Arriving on the floor, any of these lawmakers who might have been tempted to vote with the Appropriations Committee, against the education coalition, were quickly discouraged by a glance at the galleries. There the coalition had stationed many of the 300 educators who had come to Washington. Thus, the lawmakers had to line up for "teller" votes, for or against extra school money, under the scrutiny of educators from home.

"We made some eleventh-hour conversions to the cause right there," says Mr. Lee.

By comfortable margins, a series of votes nailed the $895 million package into the bill in a victory that astonished veteran House members. "Our committee on appropriations has been rolled for more money than I can recall in my 14 years as a member," lamented GOP Rep. Robert Michel of Illinois, a leader of the forces opposed to the package.

After that, it was easy to persuade the more liberal Senate to approve extra school money. Indeed, Senators voted still more increases for education and health. In the final bill, the $4.2 billion allotment for education went nearly $1.1 billion above the Nixon budget and health programs got an extra $200 million.

The education coalition's success to date guarantees that it will continue pressing for higher appropriations no matter what the outcome of the immediate battle. "We look upon this as a long-range project," says Stanley McFarland, a National Education Association lobbyist who's the chairman of the coalition committee.

Few thought the coalition could quickly become powerful when it was organized just last April. It was born out of the dismay of several education groups when the relatively austere education budget proposed by the Johnson Administration was cut by the Nixon team.

Hiring an Executive Secretary

Many lawmakers in both parties also considered the $3.2 billion Nixon budget too low. But there was little agreement on which programs should be increased. A half-dozen lobbyists for major education organizations, together with Mr. Young of the AFL-CIO, decided it was imperative to unite. They found widespread agreement when they broached the idea to other education groups. The coalition was dubbed the Emergency Campaign for Full Funding of Education Programs.

A key decision was hiring the affable Mr. Lee as executive secretary. A former staffer on the Senate Education subcommittee, "Charlie had worked with everyone without cutting anyone's throat," says one education lobbyist.

Working through friendly lawmakers Mr. Lee got the U.S. Office of Education to supply much of the data supporting the coalition's case for higher appropriations. At the request of Texas Democratic Sen. Ralph Yarborough, for example, the Office of Education compiled figures on certain actual and potential Federal education allotments in each Congressional district.

To emphasize its "nonpartisan" character, the coalition committee enlisted Arthur Flemming, HEW Secretary in the Eisenhower Administration, to testify before the House Appropriations Committee.

Officially, the coalition asked for $4.6 billion for education, almost $1.4 billion more than the Administration had proposed.

Unofficially, coalition lobbyists were willing to settle for a good deal less. After consulting with key Congressional allies, they reached a political decision to reduce the proposed increase to below $1 billion. "When you go over $1 billion you're just asking for trouble," counselled Mr. Young of the AFL-CIO.

The elements of the package were put together with surprisingly little dispute. The biggest share, representing a $398 million increase over the Nixon budget, was assigned to the program providing aid to school districts "impacted" by high concentrations of Federal employees. Successive Administrations, Democratic and Republican alike, have attacked this program as a boondoggle, but it has irresistible appeal to lawmakers because it provides funds to schools in no less than 355 Congressional districts.

"We beefed up impacted aid for an entirely pragmatic reason," says Mr. Lee. "This is where you can get the votes."

A $131.5 million increase was alloted to vocational education, which has particularly strong backing among Republican Congressmen. Another $110.4 million went to various equipment and library programs commanding broad support. Higher education got $73.8 million for construction and student loans. Finally, $180.8 million was assigned to the aid program for school districts with large numbers of pupils from poor families.

After the $895 million package was ready, the lobbyists faced a crisis finding an Appropriations Committee member to manage it on the floor. They had been relying on Democratic Rep. Jeffery Cohelan of California, an Appropriations Committee member who had worked closely with them. But Mr. Cohelan was needed to lead a separate fight on a civil rights issue that had become entangled in the HEW money bill.

Paying a Price

Democratic Rep. Charles Joelson of New Jersey was pressed into service, even though his contributions to floor fights had previously been limited to tension-easing quips. A few lobbyists spent all day Sunday briefing Mr. Joelson, and he managed well enough during the three-day tussle over the bill. The fight provided a grand finale to the Congressional career of the New Jerseyan, who retired recently to become a state judge.

The education lobby has paid a price for its success by antagonizing some powerful Congressional figures, including at least one who has a strategic position in all school legislation. Democratic Rep. Edith Green of Oregon, chairman of the House Education subcommittee, has deplored the rise of what she calls an "educational-industrial complex" to pressure Congress.

Mrs. Green charges that corporations and consulting groups with a stake in the school market are the real powers behind the education lobby. "There is an inherent danger if we allow decisions to be made on the educational priorities of this country by the pressures of lobby groups that have a personal financial stake in the outcome," she maintains.

Mr. Lee of the coalition committee strongly denies Mrs. Green's charge. Less than 15% of the $53,-000 the committee received in 1969 came from profit-making publishers or equipment makers, he says.

All the committee's $75,000 budget for 1970 will come from non-commercial education interests, adds Mr. Steinhilber of the National School Boards Association, who serves as treasurer of the emergency committee. This will cover Mr. Lee's $100-a-day fee and routine office expenses, he says.

A PRESSURE GROUP FOR THE PUBLIC INTEREST *

DAVID C. ANDERSON

"Common Cause" is a new organization designed to attack the

* Reprinted from David C. Anderson, "A Pressure Group for the Public Interest," Wall Street Journal, August 31, 1970, by permission.

dual problems of institutional decay and the lack of organized pressure for the public interest. As an interest group it is truly unique in that its avowed goals are the public welfare rather than self-advancement. Although over 100,000 people were enlisted during the first six months, can such an organization recruit the membership (1,000,000) it needs to be effective? Is institutional decay really a basic cause of America's troubles? Can anything short of disaster reform institutions? How would you rate the chances of Common Cause's success?

When John Gardner, the former Secretary of Health, Education and Welfare and current chairman of the Urban Coalition, recently announced a plan to launch a broad based "citizens lobby" to press for reform of social and political institutions, response from the press was hardly enthusiastic.

In major newspapers, stories about the project, to be known as "Common Cause," were stashed deep in the inside pages. When Mr. Gardner went on Face the Nation, cynical interviewers tried to get him to say that he is actually trying to get himself elected President by setting up what looks like a fourth party. And when a reporter mentioned his interest in the subject to a Washington-wise colleague, he drew a testy response: "You'll find there's not much substance to what he has in mind; so far as I can tell, it's nothing but a jellyfish."

Disheartening Thoughts

An hour or so spent discussing the plan with Mr. Gardner is enough to persuade a skeptical interviewer that Common Cause is, in concept at least, something more than a jellyfish, and probably deserving of more attention than it has received. At the same time, the discussion leads to some disheartening thoughts about the problem of social change in America.

Admittedly, there is a certain vagueness to Mr. Gardner's plan, which he describes as a lobbying organization to engage in letter writing campaigns and other still undeveloped programs aimed at the somewhat fuzzy goal of institutional reform. The group's efforts would presumably involve such public issues as crime, racial tension, poverty and ending the Vietnam war.

Mr. Gardner contends the need for a group like Common Cause arises from what he sees as the widespread failure of government at all levels to solve problems. "Almost everywhere you touch the public process in this country, you find a failure of performances," he says.

Indeed, he explains, American society seems to suffer generally from a widespread case of institutional decay. Such a "phase of diminished vitality" in social and governmental institutions is hardly a new development, Mr. Gardner says, adding that for the past two decades his career has led him to think about the process of decline and renewal in social institutions.

Such a situation is hardly hopeless, however, Mr. Gardner contends. Indeed, if history has shown that institutions decay nearly inevitably, it has also shown that they can renew themselves. "The disease is curable," he asserts. Furthermore, he believes, it may be possible for enlightened people in a modern democratic society to set in motion such a process of renewal. This, he says, is what Common Cause is all about.

The reform of institutional structure, he contends, is largely impeded by the fact that no pressure group exists to make the case for such general reform to the public and to support public officials who try to enact it.

For, he explains, inefficient institutions have a way of protecting themselves, even to the point of their collapse. "Almost everyone in the system is a prisoner of it," Mr. Gardner says. "I've been thinking about the decay of human institutions for nearly 20 years now, but when I was Secretary of HEW, I thought less about the subject than at any time before or afterward. I was a player in the game, then, and I had to work according to the rules."

"Every modern President has had a backlog of reorganization and reform proposals on his desk," he goes on, "but he's always faced a hornets' nest of opposition in trying to implement them, and he's never had any backing for implementation."

Both the publicity and the popular support necessary to the success of reform efforts, Mr. Gardner believes, might be created by establishment of an "outside constituency," a pressure group with no special interest but the better functioning of the system as a whole.

Mr. Gardner readily concedes that the reform of social and political institutions still is not a subject likely to generate massive popular feeling. But he points out that a relatively small group with an idea whose time may be coming can have great influence. "It doesn't need to be an enormous number," he says. For the United States, "a million people are enough."

And he firmly believes at least this many can be reached. "In every field of special interest there is a percentage of people who understand that if the nation fails, their special interest fails too. You find this at all levels; in unions, in minority communities, as well as in the professions. I don't think of it in liberal-conservative terms so much as in practical terms. These are the people who want to get going and solve our problems."

Mr. Gardner emphasizes that he senses in the nation a depth of such concern that goes beyond empty idealistic posturing. "There is a restlessness over this," he says of the disillusionment with government. "For many people," acting on the feeling that something needs to be done about government failures "is not only moral, but a temperamental imperative."

To gather support, Common Cause recently sent out a test mailing of 200,000 letters to citizens of all social levels in all parts of the country. "Most parts of the system have grown so rigid that they cannot respond to impending disaster," the letter says. "They are so ill designed for contemporary purposes that they waste taxpayers' money, mangle good programs and frustrate every good man who enters the system."

The letter warns that "no particular interest group can prosper for long if the nation is disintegrating. Every group must have an overriding interest in the well-being of the whole society." And it calls for an "active, powerful, hard-hitting contituency" to fight for reforms necessary to protect that interest. The letter asks an enrollment fee of $15.

Though it's too early to gauge response to the mailing, Mr. Gardner's associates say they have been pleased with the popular response to initial publicity for Common Cause. One Gardner spokesman reports that his office currently is receiving about 200 letters a day from people wanting more information about Common Cause. "And it's a fascinating mix of mail," he says. "It isn't predominantly professional or intellectual as you might expect," he says. Rather, the letters seem to come mainly from middle-class people in all parts of the country.

If this looks encouraging, the project as outlined by Mr. Gardner still leaves room for at least three questions.

First, if the feeling of restlessness

for constructive change may exist in some quarters, there is also much popular feeling in the country that would tend to undermine attempts to organize a broad citizens' lobby for the general goal of institutional reform.

Mr. Gardner says the polls show a rising number of people who shun affiliation with traditional political parties. He also says there are statistics to show a surprisingly widespread degree of public agreement in desires for certain changes in areas like housing, employment, education and the administration of justice. Thus, he suggests, Common Cause might be able to link its non-aligned "outside constituency" stance to plans for improvement in these substantive areas, developing political muscle for the overall purpose of institutional reform in the process.

But if there are areas of unanimity, there are also great areas of division. The conflicts between black and white, between people alienated from American life and people defensive about it, and between old and young, are growing more virulent as the months pass, and they may not be separable from the substantive issues Mr. Gardner cites as grounds for new unity. For example, it's hard to see how destructive divisiveness over racial integration could be kept apart from any Common Cause-backed scheme to do something about the shortage of middle-income housing, however widely the housing may be desired.

Catching the Mood

Second, the fact that the need for institutional reform is real and even widely perceived does not necessarily mean that reform on any meaningful scale may be easily generated or controlled.

Mr. Gardner speaks hopefully of the fact that relatively small groups advocating such causes as family planning and environmental conservation have come to have tremendous impact on government policy and on all of society in recent years because they happened to catch a receptive public mood.

But he also admits that historically the process of institutional decay and renewal has not been affected much by rational human activity. Rather, major institutional reforms have usually been forced by such events as wars, plagues or other catastrophes. And his assertion that "we need to produce renewal short of such disasters" seems as obviously lame for any practical purpose as it is obviously true.

Third, even if institutional reform could be realized, there is some reason to question whether the rather diffuse notion of institutional decay is as basic a source of American troubles as Mr. Gardner and many others like to think it is.

There can be no question that institutions of government often seem unresponsive and inefficient, and that there is room not only to improve specific governmental mechanisms but also, as Mr. Gardner suggests, to encourage the feeling both in and out of government that social institutions should continually renew themselves to keep abreast of change.

At the same time, the evidence has begun to grow recently that some of the most serious problems of modern America involve unprecedented changes that bring social strains down to a personal level.

The problem of pollution won't be solved entirely until every American understands, and accepts the fact that a clean environment isn't compatible with all the comforts and conveniences he may take for granted. The agonies of Vietnam might have been avoided had every American understood and accepted the uncomfortable ambiguities of the U.S. role as a superpower. Increasingly bitter cultural factionalism may not come under control completely until people learn to treat what the media show them with a bit of perspective.

And while more responsive social institutions might help, it is hard to see how they can do more than ease the strains a bit. If the idea that institutional reforms won't make things much better, but only less worse, begins to gain acceptance—as it must—how much support can a Common Cause organization hope to retain?

No Startling Answer

Mr. Gardner has no startling answers to these questions. "You can't let yourself be paralyzed by the complexities of the problem," he says. And he adds: "I don't want to rule out the possibility that we're head-over-heels into something we can't control. But if you look at the current situation, you see that we've left some of our most important institutions untouched for many years. We haven't done all we can."

Indeed, he goes on, the most important thing is to try. And he quotes some lines from T. S. Eliot: "For us there is only the trying. The rest is not our business./Home is where one starts from. As we grow older./The world becomes stranger, the pattern more complicated."

All of which leads to the conclusion that perhaps Common Cause is for Mr. Gardner mainly a matter of temperamental imperative more than the result of an absolutely hard headed assessment of current troubles. And if one may wish him well, it is only with a feeling of depression over his chances for success.

THE HIDDEN CRISIS
IN AMERICAN POLITICS *
SAMUEL LUBELL

Mr. Lubell has been a long-time commentator on the American political scene. In his most recent book he suggests that the United States is today plagued with a whole train of unresolved crises: white-black hostility, pollution, crime, the generation gap, inflation, an unpopular war. These issues have tended to polarize Americans, shattering the old politics of reconciliation. Why have so many current conflicts reached a crisis stage? What reaction does the use of violence and raw power provoke? Why have the universities been a focal point of current unrest? Why doesn't prosperity ease social tensions? How does the protest march fit into political bargaining? Have we lost our ability to compromise conflicts?

The compulsive force twisting our political insides and restructuring both parties is the fact that rapid change has become the prime political disturber of our time.

* Reprinted from The Hidden Crisis In American Politics *by* Samuel Lubell *by permission of* W. W. Norton & Co., Inc. Copyright © 1970 by W. W. Norton & Co. Inc. Used by permission.

In its first turbulent stage the reeling impacts of uncontrolled change pushed us off balance as a nation wrenching much of society out of control and leaving us more divided than we dared admit. During the last years of the Johnson Administration we were making decisions like a giant Gulliver hopping on one foot.

In struggling to regain our national balance we naturally tend to pull back toward more "normal" times. But we are carried into the 1970's on a whole train of unresolved crises which we have been unable—or unwilling—to reconcile. Much of our society is being reshaped to continue battling these conflicts indefinitely.

It is these unresolved conflicts which President Richard Nixon is trying to ride and guide so they will bring into existence a new Republican majority.

Virtually the whole of our society is caught up in the "crises"—the deepening hostilities between whites and blacks; air-polluted, crime-stalked cities; the "generation gap" which has been transformed into a crisis of our universities; the resistances to the Vietnam war and how they have projected into a new isolation which pressures for far-reaching changes in foreign policy; the battle to reorder our priorities and to reallocate our economic resources, a struggle made all the more bitter by the slowness in checking inflation.

Each of these conflicts has been headlined repeatedly. Still, what remains elusive is a sense of their lasting impacts, how they have locked together to form what might be termed the politics of a polarized nation . . . that has chopped away so much of the past, now irrevocably gone, has shaken psychological attitudes through the country and still runs on uncontrolled. It is our inability to reconcile these conflicts that divide us that I see as the hidden crisis in American politics today.

Eight points of departure from the old politics of stability stand out:

I

How quickly an unresolved crisis becomes a conflict on the run which can hardly be caught up with.

All the conflicts share a common proliferating quality, generating their own momentum and taking on new forms as they rush along. In the process, old choices of action that are being debated get foreclosed, usually leaving only harsher options.

With our racial crisis most of us can still remember when gradual desegregation would have been acceptable to Negroes generally. Currently, though, a new form of territorial racial conflict is taking over our cities, with whites and blacks separated into expanses of "turf" so large that effective school and residential integration is pushed out of reach. Gary, Cleveland and Newark have already been split into polarized halves, with more such polarization on the way.

We often argue as if prejudice and bigotry were the only enemies. Yet the main force structuring this new racial crisis is residential mobility, which continues unchecked.

When the white exodus to the suburbs began after World War II, it had little to do with race. But the suburban migration soon found itself linked up with two other happenings of the 1950's—the northward drift of Negroes displaced by the mechanization of cotton, and the surging racial militancy stirred by the Supreme Court's desegregation decision. All three time-locked together to transform our cities, break down urban government, and now threaten to nullify the Supreme Court's school-desegregation decision.

Other conflicts of more recent origin display the same proliferating quality. The youth crisis, which might have been eased by sensible draft reform, radicalized much of a whole student generation, pushing our universities into deeper turmoil that became further aggravated by black-studies agitation.

The Vietnam battling between "doves" and "hawks" is also being perpetuated, as colleges and universities are turned into antiwar shelters and opposition to military spending is pressed as a crusade to "regain civilian control of our society" and release funds for social spending.

II

These conflicts on the run have plunged us into zealous combat to remake American thinking, pressed with an intensity not known in this nation since the pre-Civil War period.

Reasoned argument and orderly debate have been shoved aside by efforts to impose beliefs through force, by violence, control of government, and other uses of power.

Black power, student power, George Wallace power—all the varied demands for power—seek to rearrange other people. In fighting back, many of the people who were being rearranged have dug in to resist all change.

That may be the real meaning of "polarization"—to take shelter in hardened silos, to create a situation that others will be forced to accept because they cannot change it.

III

This battling has been targeted largely at our institutions, with the public schools, universities, the draft, the police, churches, the welfare system, perhaps in the future whole cities serving as successive staging areas.

Partly this reflects the fact that these agitations have sought lasting changes in basic social relationships; in our zeal to get at each other, we have been ready to break down institutions that stood in the way.

But rapid change also turns society's points of entry into special fronts of vulnerability, and at least two of the raging conflicts have been basically entry assaults.

Negroes, banging at every door

they can reach, are demanding entry en masse in place of the old pattern of each individual making it on his own.

Less clearly recognized, the so-called "generation gap" has been primarily concerned with how to find a meaningful place in society for greatly enlarged numbers of young people.

In a single year—1965—the count of young people reaching eighteen leaped from 2,769,000 to 3,739,000. By 1970 the number between eighteen and twenty-four was half again as high as in the 1950's.

Certainly, from at least 1965 on, every policy of government should have sought to speed the absorption into society of these youthful millions. Instead, the escalation of the Vietnam war and a failure to change the draft caged these millions back onto the campuses.

Revealingly, some students in our highest institutions of learning and blacks on the streets reacted with similar, near-revolutionary violences. Both tried to seize and transform whatever part of society they could reach, the blacks by asserting "black nationalism" in the ghettos, the college students by occupying buildings and demanding that universities be "restructured."

It may be one of the "laws" of unreconciled conflict that it lunges at whatever can be reached, without plan or rationality.

IV

No longer can we be sure which of the self-correcting strengths of

American democracy still prevail.

We have been accustomed to believe that economic progress overcomes or eases social ills. The unprecedented boom of recent years has yielded remarkable benefits, quadrupling in a single decade the number of families with incomes over $10,000 and reducing by nearly half the proportion of families at the statistical "poverty" level. However, this prosperity has also quickened racial frictions in our cities and is eroding the effective power of all government, aggravating political conflict generally.

In the process, loyalty to all political parties has been loosened, which in turn is changing voter psychology.

Virtually all elements in society appear to have been strengthened so they are better able to fight one another politically, to be more assertive of their rights and self-interests, readier to press their claims upon each other and against the government. It is as much our strengths as our weaknesses that divide the nation.

V

The crisis has been one of management, that is, of a managed society —call it mismanaged if the results seem displeasing.

Through its 1954 desegregation decision, the Supreme Court, without quite realizing it, put the Government into the business of managing racial relations in much of the country. The enterprise brought the most dramatic racial advances in our history, but it also backlogged desires for political revenge that are now being cashed in.

With the tax reduction of 1964, the nation moved officially into a managed economy. For one spectacular year, the performance of the "Keynesian revolution" seemed miraculous, as economic growth soared and tax revenues increased even though Federal tax rates had been lowered. Economists became the newest of our high priests.

But the "model" by which the economy was being managed proved inadequate. It never was programed for the pressures of even a limited war. Booming the economy also unloosed great economic and social demands too costly for local governments to support. Burdening local government further were inflationary rises in costs and the high interest rates used to curb inflation.

"Economic stability" was the ideal talked of by both the new economists and the old money managers, but structural changes in our economy seem to be transforming us into a claimant society in which we fight one another for tax cuts and favored government programs, over what share of the tax dollars are to go to missiles, schools, space, or the wider distribution of food stamps.

VI

A new structure of political bargaining has come into being in the struggle for political visibility, to make oneself seen and heard.

The great peace and civil rights marches on Washington have been the TV spectaculars which illustrates the huge scale on which attention-getting is being organized.

But the proddings for voter recognition also come from how our society is being reorganized. The greater the powers exercised by government the harsher become the costs of being neglected or overlooked.

VII

We seem to be losing the ability to moderate and compromise the conflicts that divide us.

The question must be asked whether we really want to come to terms among ourselves? Certainly during the Johnson and Nixon years dissension has been pushed to the surface and made more visible than areas of agreement.

What has happened to the fabled "middle ground" in American politics? Is it still there?

President Nixon has pictured himself as a "centrist" politically; yet the near-fatal weakness that almost lost him the 1968 election lay in his effort to hold the middle ground without any policies or programs that could bring compromise. The same riddle dominates his Presidency. Can he really "bring us together again" or is he improvising his own partisan patch-work of disunity?

VIII

For the first time since the Civil War the effectiveness of our foreign policy has come to hinge on domestic conciliation.

In his Guam doctrine, Nixon began the hazardous process of reducing our military commitments abroad to use more of our resources at home. Done well, this process could prove highly beneficial, but how long will it take? And while we turn inward, what will happen in the rest of the world? How long can we stay divided without inviting troubles abroad and without impairing our ability to act on behalf of peace?

Taken together, these eight departures add up to a drastically different kind of politics than we have ever known. My emphasis on conflict should not be interpreted as meaning that it is bad in itself. Quite the opposite. Conflict is indispensable for needed change and for continued progress.

What is deeply troubling is that we seem simultaneously to be intensifying conflict and to be weakening our powers of reconciliation. Unless this spiral is broken we risk being torn apart as a nation, with catastrophic consequences for the whole world.

ARE PARTIES RELEVANT? *

ALAN L. OTTEN

American political parties are finished. Voters no longer heed party labels. They elect political personalities.

This analysis is a popular one that consigns our parties to history's dust bin. Why have parties declined in popularity? Are there legitimate grounds for complaint? What functions have parties traditionally performed? Are there real differences between our major parties? Why can it be argued that parties should be made stronger? If our present parties fail, what alternatives exist?

More and more voters, particularly younger ones, proclaim themselves "independents" and proudly split their tickets. New "non-political" personalities prove particularly appealing. Party organizations lose their clout.

There's talk of third and fourth parties nationally, like the four in New York. Divided government—Executive of one party, Legislature of another—becomes common.

The traditional American two-

* *Reprinted from Alan L. Otten, "Are Parties Relevant?"* Wall Street Journal, *March 4, 1971 by permission.*

party system is finished, many analysts now assert, and many citizens probably think that's just fine. Yet the two-party system performs some valid and vital functions, and its demise could be painful and perilous for the country.

The reasons for the parties' decline are numerous and, for the most part, obvious. Increased mobility—from one place to another, from one economic bracket to another—weakens old party loyalties. New generations, better educated and less tradition-tied, break ethnic and racial allegiances to one party or the other. Government welfare and civil service jobs replace the favors and patronage that nourished the old machines. High-impact television far outweighs traditional party vote-getting techniques.

New issues—race, the war—strain the old system. Some citizens turn away in disgust, charging that the two parties are too much alike, or not bold or imaginative enough.

And there is indeed ample cause for complaint. Weak central direction and discipline mean frequent failure to carry out platform commitments. Frequently both parties seem readier to respond to pressure groups or local interests than broad national needs. The parties can be conservative forces, resisting new ideas; party battling slows government response to crisis. Unimaginative hacks climb the party ladder far too often.

Yet on balance the two-party system has served well—peculiarly suited to the independence and diversity of our people and our system of checks and balances. "*These* parties were designed to serve the purpose of *this* people under *this* Constitution," wrote the late Clinton Rossiter, the noted historian.

. . .

One party organizes and administers the government; the other challenges, investigates, counterproposes. Two national parties, however decentralized and formless, certainly can still perform these functions, and serve to check each other, better than a number of smaller, weaker parties—or no parties at all.

True, the parties often appear to be similar, almost indistinguishable, anything but ideologically precise. But that's because each national party must, in order to win, extend its umbrella widely over a broad and diverse constituency, nominating men of wide appeal, avoiding any image of narrowness or extremism. Inevitably they end up resembling and overlapping each other.

And yet, to this extent, they also serve as unifying forces, working against regional or class or racial divisions. Broad national parties tend to reduce the intensity of ideological conflict, and therefore make political life more stable. The alternative—narrow parties appealing to narrow groups on narrow issues, or non-party candidates appealing on personality or one major issue—would almost inevitably produce more factionalism, more disorder, more stalemate. When sharp

ideological issues move to the front, public debate becomes more explosive and more dangerous.

(And while differences between the parties may not be as great as some would like, they certainly exist. The Democrats move right on law and order, but they're still well to the left of the GOP. The Republicans embrace deficit financing, but they're still not ready to spend quite as freely as the Democrats are. Consider the current debate over revenue sharing; the GOP is overwhelmingly committed to giving more policy control to state and local governments, the Democrats are bent on retaining major direction from Washington.)

Parties serve as a necessary recruiting agency for top elective and appointive posts, advancing experienced men of more or less like views. The idea of the citizen-politician is ever appealing—the businessman or college president moving directly into high office—but good intentions rarely can substitute for actual experience. Party service—in the precinct, in a campaign, in the legislature—provides valuable understanding of how to deal with interest groups, how to shape and enact a program, how to run a government.

Parties are valuable think tanks. To be sure, new ideas well up from public groups, academicians and many other sources, yet broad national parties are particularly likely to keep coming up with a varied diet of practical new approaches. Third or fourth parties are apt to focus on just one issue—the Wallaceites, for example, on race, or a liberal 1972 party on Southeast Asia.

. . .

Above all, however, the parties permit the voters to fix some degree of responsibility for the way the country is being run. If the voters don't like the way things are going and want a change, they can dump the incumbent party; if they're satisfied, they can continue it in office. A splintering of parties or an end to parties would make this sort of responsibility-fixing far more difficult.

In fact, it is precisely here that many political scientists fault the American system—holding that the parties are too weak. With so many legislators attuned to local or private interests, leaders can't enforce discipline and keep them in line behind the party's program. The leaders must compromise, deal with interest groups, try to make up for the deserters from their own followers by converts from the other party. All this makes it difficult for the public to fix credit or blame as neatly as might be desirable.

Naturally, there's a danger of going too far to strengthening party leadership. All-powerful or too-powerful leaders could be far more of a problem than too weak ones. The British experience shows that there's no guarantee that strong leadership, with tight party discipline, necessarily produces better answers.

At the moment, however, this worry seems remote. Despite a few minor steps toward greater party responsiveness, most of the movement is in the opposite direction— toward less responsive and weaker party organizations. And this is worrisome. "Parties and democracies arose together," Prof. Rossiter declared. "They have lived and prospered in a closely symbiotic relationship; and if one of them should ever weaken and die, the other would die with it."

THE MANDATE FOR PARTY REFORM *
GEORGE S. McGOVERN

In 1968, the flaws of the presidential convention system were put on display before millions of TV viewers. The Democratic Party, meeting in Chicago, was a particularly uninspiring sight. While thousands of young supporters of Senator Eugene McCarthy surged through the streets, the aging party leaders, protected by a tight security system and barbed wire, made their decisions. In the aftermath of this fracas,

* The Commission on Party Structure and Delegate Selection, Democratic National Committee, Mandate For Reform (Washington, D.C., 1970).

the party appointed a national committee to open the party councils to rank and file members. The committee (chaired by Senator McGovern) made its report in 1970, and the reforms it recommended will be first tested in 1972.

Who selected the convention delegates of 1968 in at least 20 states? What kind of representation was given to blacks, women and young people? Why did the Commission decide to keep the convention system? What dangers do they anticipate if party reforms are not made? What reforms have the states made?

The 1968 Democratic National Convention in Chicago exposed profound flaws in the presidential nominating process; but in so doing it gave our Party an excellent opportunity to reform its ways and to prepare for the problems of a new decade.

The delegates to the Convention, concerned by the chaos and divisiveness, shared a belief that the image of an organization impervious to the will of its rank and file threatened the future of the Party. Therefore, they took up the challenge of reform with a mandate requiring State Parties to give "all Democratic voters . . . a full, meaningful and timely opportunity to participate" in the selection of delegates, and, thereby, in the decisions of the Convention itself.

In order to ensure that this mandate would be implemented, the Convention directed the Demo-cratic National Committee to establish a Commission to aid state Parties in meeting the Convention requirement.

In February 1969, Senator Fred Harris, Chairman of the Democratic National Committee, appointed us to that body mandated by the Convention—*The Commission on Party Structure and Delegate Selection.* We are Democrats who represent every segment of our Party. We find common cause in our Party's history of fair play and equal opportunity. We believe that the continuing vitality of the Democratic Party depends upon its adherence to this heritage.

Since its inception, our Party has been an open party—open to new ideas and new people. From the days of Jefferson and Jackson, the Democratic Party has been committed to the broad participation of rank-and-file members in all of its major decision-making.

In the American two-party system no decision is more important to the rank-and-file member than the choice of the party's presidential nominee. For this reason, popular control over the nominating process has been a principle of the Democratic Party since the birth of the National Convention 140 years ago.

This tradition for participation and popular control, however, has not always been adequately expressed. After a lengthy examination of the structures and processes used to select delegates to the National Convention in 1968, this is our basic conclusion: meaningful participation of Democratic voters in the choice of their presidential nominee was often difficult or costly, sometimes completely illusory, and, in not a few instances, impossible.

Among the findings the Commission has made about delegate selection in 1968 are the following:

• In at least twenty states, there were no (or inadequate) rules for the selection of Convention delegates, leaving the entire process to the discretion of a handful of party leaders.

• More than a third of the Convention delegates had, in effect, already been selected prior to 1968 —before either the major issues or the possible presidential candidates were known. By the time President Johnson announced his withdrawal from the nominating contest, the delegate selection process had begun in all but twelve states.

. . .

• In many states, the costs of participation in the process of delegate selection were clearly discriminatory; in others, they were prohibitive. Filing fees for entering primaries were often excessive, reaching $14,000 in one state, if a complete slate of candidates had been filed. "Hospitality" fees were often imposed on delegates to the convention, reaching $500 in one delegation. Not surprisingly, only 13% of the delegates to the National Convention had incomes of under $10,000 (whereas 70% of the population have annual incomes under that amount).

• Representation of blacks, women and youth at the Convention was substantially below the proportion of each group in the population. Blacks comprised about five percent of the voting delegates, well above their numbers in 1964; since blacks make up 11% of the population and supplied at least 20% of the total vote for the Democratic presidential candidate, however, they were still underrepresented at the Convention. Women comprised only 13% of the delegates with only one of 55 delegations having a woman chairman. In a majority of delegations there was no more than a single delegate under 30 years of age, and in two delegations the average age was 54. The delegates to the 1968 Democratic National Convention, in short, were predominantly white, male, middle-aged, and at least middle-class.

As this information emerged, we recognized that two alternative courses of action were available to us. First, we could suggest that the institution of the National Convention had outlived its usefulness and should be discarded. To be sure, at our public hearings several Democrats gave testimony expressing the judgment that the convention system did not deserve to be saved. There was a substantial body of feeling, in fact, that a national primary within each Party would be the most democratic means of selecting presidential candidates.

Second, we could conclude that there was nothing inherently undemocratic about a National Convention; that 1968 was a culmination of years of indifference to the nominating process, rather than a startling aberration from previous years; that purged of its structural and procedural inadequacies, the National Convention was an institution well worth preserving. The Commission has taken this second course. The following are some of our reasons:

• In view of the stringent demands made upon a President of the United States, the challenge imposed upon any contender for the nomination in seeking support in a wide variety of delegates selection systems should be maintained.

• The face-to-face confrontation of Democrats of every persuasion in a periodic mass meeting is productive of healthy debate, important policy decisions (usually in the form of platform planks), reconciliation of differences, and realistic preparation for the fall presidential campaign.

• The Convention provides a mechanism for party self-government through the election and instruction of a National Committee.

While endorsing the institution, the Commission believes that if delegates are not chosen in a democratic manner, the National Convention cannot perform its functions adequately. In order to ensure the democratic selection of delegates, the Commission has adopted 18 Guidelines binding on all state Parties. . . .

The Guidelines that we have adopted are designed to open the door to all Democrats who seek a voice in their Party's most important decision: the choice of its presidential nominee. . . .

We believe that popular participation is more than a proud heritage of our party, more even than a first principle. We believe that popular control of the Democratic Party is necessary for its survival.

We do not believe this is an idle threat. When we view our past history and present policies alongside that of the Republican Party, we are struck by one unavoidable fact: our Party is the only major vehicle for peaceful, progressive change in the United States.

If we are not an open party; if we do not represent the demands of change, then the danger is not that people will go to the Republican Party; it is that there will no longer be a way for people committed to orderly change to fulfill their needs and desires within our traditional political system. It is that they will turn to third and fourth party politics of the anti-politics or the street.

We believe that our Guidelines offer an alternative for these people. We believe that the Democratic Party can meet the demands for participation with their adoption. We trust that all Democrats will give the Guidelines their careful consideration.

We are encouraged by the response of state Parties to date. In 40 states and territories the Democratic Party has appointed reform commissions (or subcommittees of the state committee) to investigate ways of modernizing party procedures. Of these, 17 have already issued reports and recommendations. In a number of states, party rules and state laws have already been revised, newly written or amended to ensure the opportunity for participation in Party matters by all Democrats.

. . .

In several states there has been substantial reform of party rules governing delegate selection and party structure. In Minnesota, a new party constitution has been adopted that provides for proportional representation and modified "one Democrat—one vote." In Michigan, a meeting of 2,000 Democrats convened in January and adopted the broad recommendations of the Haber Reform Commission. In North Carolina, the State Party has adopted comprehensive reforms of its party structure, including one provision for 18-year-old participation in all party affairs and another for reasonable representation on all party committees and delegations of women, minority racial groups and young people. In Colorado, the State Committee has adopted a proposal that will ensure proportional representation for all presidential candidates at the next convention. In Oklahoma, rules have been proposed which will assure that not more than 60% of the membership of any committee or convention will be the same sex, and will eliminate the role of untimely committees in the delegate selection process. In Missouri, statewide public hearings have been

held to discuss proposals for party rules.

. . .

All of these efforts lead us to the conclusion that the Democratic Party is bent on meaningful change. A great European statesman once said, "All things are possible, even the fact that an action in accord with honor and honesty ultimately appears to be a prudent political investment." We share this sentiment. We are confident that party reform, dictated by our Party's heritage and principles, will insure a strong, winning and united Party.

A FINANCIAL LANDSLIDE FOR THE G.O.P.*

HERBERT E. ALEXANDER AND HAROLD B. MEYERS

The cost of operating our election system has now passed $300,000,000, on its way to the stratosphere. To win elections, parties must have money. This article gives an

* Reprinted from Herbert E. Alexander and Harold B. Meyers, "A Financial Landslide For the G.O.P.," Fortune (March, 1970) by permission.

up-to-date report on the sources of funds and party spending in recent elections.

What and who are the fat cats? What is a typical contribution from the top echelon? Who finances the Republicans? The Democrats? How did AT&T inadvertently make a political contribution? Where does campaign money go? Should TV provide free time for the major parties? How does this overriding concern with campaign costs distort the democratic process?

In terms of votes, Richard Nixon's margin of victory in 1968 was narrow. Financially, however, it was a Republican sweep. The G.O.P. raised and spent more money than any party in history, and emerged from the election campaign solvent and with its fund-raising machinery functioning smoothly. By contrast, 1968 was a year of financial as well as electoral disaster for the Democratic party. The Democrats spent less than half as much as the Republicans, but had unprecedented trouble in raising cash. The party was forced to scrape through to defeat on borrowed money. . . .

· · ·

Where the money came from—and went—in 1968 can now be traced out in considerable detail on the basis of figures painstakingly gathered by the Citizens' Research Foundation of Princeton, New Jersey. Nonprofit and carefully nonpartisan, the foundation collects information on political finance from many sources, including official records in Washington and various state capitals and scores of interviews with candidates' financial backers and managers. Since federal and state laws require only certain types of information on candidates' fund raising and spending, the data on money in politics is fragmentary. For example, reports filed with the House and Senate in Washington by candidates for national office, including the presidency, need not cover the prenomination period, though primary races often involve huge sums. Nevertheless, by analyzing this data and by supplementing it with information from its own investigators, the foundation has been able to put together the most comprehensive body of information available.

As the foundation's estimates make clear, the 1968 election was fabulously expensive. Spending in campaigns for all offices at stake in 1968, from county commissioner to the presidency, totaled at least $300 million. That was a 50 percent increase over the $200 million spent in 1964, which was itself a record breaker. About a third of the 1968 total, or $100 million, was spent on presidential campaigns, a good part of it in expensive drives by unsuccessful candidates—Nelson Rockefeller, George Romney, Eugene McCarthy, Robert Kennedy—for the Republican or Democratic nomination. After Nixon's nomination, national-level Republican committees spent nearly $25 million on the presidential campaign, while comparable post-convention expenditures by the hard-pressed Democrats came to less than half of that—about $10,600,000. Third-party candidate George C. Wallace reported spending $6,985,455.

Return of the Fat Cats

The Republicans were able to spend so lavishly, virtually on a pay-as-you-go basis, because the party's fortunes got a double boost in 1968. The small contributions that had kept Barry Goldwater afloat in 1964 continued to pour in to the party in response to fund-raising letters and television appeals (see "The Switch in Campaign Giving," FORTUNE, November, 1965). In 1968, Republican fund drives produced $6,600,000 in gifts averaging almost $15 each from 450,000 individual contributors. But it was the Republican revival among large contributors, especially businessmen, that really paid the G.O.P.'s way in 1968. Large contributors, traditionally Republican, who had deserted Goldwater to support Lyndon Johnson returned to the fold more open-handed than ever before.

Nowhere is the return to the Republicans more apparent than in the pattern of contributions by members of the Business Council, an elite group of men who own, finance, or manage the country's major enterprises. The Business Council contributions, predominantly Democratic in 1964, were once again overwhelmingly Repub-

lican in 1968, by better than three to one. One Business Council member who went full circle was C. Douglas Dillon, Under Secretary of State in the Eisenhower Administration and Secretary of the Treasury under Presidents Kennedy and Johnson. In 1960, Dillon gave $26,550 to Republicans and nothing to Democrats. Four years later he put up $42,000 for Johnson, nothing for Goldwater. But in 1968, Dillon contributed only to Republicans ($9,-000). One famous 1964 convert, Henry Ford II, stayed largely in the Democratic fold. Ford donated only to Republican committees in 1960 ($7,000), and more heavily to Democrats than to Republicans in 1964 ($40,000 to $4,100). In 1968, Ford gave $30,000 to Hubert Humphrey and $7,250 to various Republicans, including $2,200 to Nixon.

. . .

Campaign donations by the very rich, another special study shows, were much larger than those made by most business executives, but were just as one-sided. Forty-six of the nation's wealthiest individuals—those with fortunes of $150 million or more (FORTUNE, May, 1968)—gave a total of $1,105,000 in 1968. Most of the money—$984,-000—went to Republicans. Democratic candidates got $121,000, miscellaneous groups $11,000, and Wallace nothing. Five of these centimillionaires gave to both major parties.

Centimillionaires who gave only to Republicans included Chicago insurance executive W. Clement

Stone ($200,000); John Hay Whitney ($57,000); Lammot du Pont Copeland ($14,000); and David Packard, now Under Secretary of Defense ($11,000). Democratic contributors included former Senator William Benton ($12,538), oilman Leon Hess ($3,000), and Edwin H. Land, president and chairman of Polaroid ($15,000). One centimillionaire who split her gifts was Mrs. Marjorie Merriweather Post ($2,500 for Democrats, $600 to Republicans).

Debts for Democrats

The Democratic financial collapse in 1968 was the penalty for years of party neglect and mismanagement. After John Kennedy entered the White House, he formed the President's Club to tap large contributors systematically. Members paid $1,000 a year or more and were rewarded with invitations to affairs, such as White House receptions, where they could clink glasses with the mighty. Under Lyndon Johnson, the President's Club flourished almost too well. It became the chief Democratic vehicle for fund raising, to the detriment of broad-based drives like "Dollars for Democrats." The strategy worked well in 1964, when membership in the President's Club reached 4,000. But as L.B.J.'s popularity declined, membership dropped, to only 2,000 by 1966. At the same time, the party machinery —the Democratic National Committee in particular—fell into disrepair. His energies absorbed in

larger issues, including the Vietnam war, President Johnson gave little attention to his role as party leader.

By the time Hubert Humphrey won the Democratic nomination, he had already spent at least $4 million on his candidacy, and his committees still owed more than $1 million of that amount. The Democratic National Committee was in poor shape to finance a presidential campaign. It had just about ceased fund raising after Johnson announced in March that he would not seek another term, and the National Committee itself had outstanding bills of $419,000 before the candidate was nominated. The bitter splits that remained after the violence-marred Chicago convention made Humphrey's financial plight desperate. The party and its financial supporters did not draw together in the post-convention period as they had done in past campaigns.

In the September–December period, the Democratic national campaign received only 93,195 individual gifts—a fifth of the number recorded for Nixon committees. Most donations to Humphrey—88,-596 of them—were for $100 or less, but he actually got more very large contributions than the records show for Johnson in 1964 or Kennedy in 1960. Thirty-two individual contributors gave Humphrey more than $10,000 apiece. Apparently, the Democratic nominee was forced to tap his best supporters more vigorously than had his better-financed predecessors.

Hubert Humphrey's largest

single cash contributor, official records show, was neither a corporation executive nor a centimillionaire. Rather, it was the wife, since deceased, of John (Jake the Barber) Factor, a wealthy California real-estate investor. Factor, now seventy-eight, was the victim of a lurid gangland kidnap plot in 1933. His name first appeared as a political contributor in 1960, when he and his wife gave $20,000 to John Kennedy's campaign and a lesser amount to Nixon's. Two years later Factor was able to become a U.S. citizen after a presidential pardon cleared his record of a 1943 mail-fraud conviction. In 1968, Factor's wife gave Humphrey committees $100,000 in cash, and Factor provided an additional $240,000 in unsecured loans.

Loans proved to be Humphrey's chief financial resource. The party received only $4,869,000 in cash gifts between September and December, and the Democratic National Committee reported at the end of 1968 that it had debts of $6,-155,000. Because of deficiencies in the records, it has not been possible to trace all the loans made to Democratic committees to their source. But available records indicate that Factor and Lew Wasserman, president of Music Corp. of America, were the two largest lenders, at $240,000 each. (Wasserman's cash donations totaled $35,-000.) Nineteen other individuals loaned $100,000 each. Among these lenders were Leon Hess, New York investment banker John Loeb, Manhattan lawyer Edwin Weisl, and Arthur Houghton, a director of Corning Glass. Because of legal restrictions, no single loan to any one committee could exceed $5,000. The Wasserman and Factor loans, for example, had to be divided up among at least forty-eight different campaign committees.

In mid-1969, the Democratic National Committee took over $1 million worth of debts remaining from Humphrey's preconvention campaign and another $1 million in unpaid bills remaining from the campaign of Robert Kennedy, which was ended by his death. The assumption of these debts left the committee owing about $8 million in all. Behind the consolidation of debts was the thought that it would be well for the party to free Humphrey and Senator Edward Kennedy of their individual burdens so that they could devote themselves to fund raising for the party as a whole. The plan has not worked as well as had been hoped. Humphrey has not proved to be much of an attraction at fund-raising events, and Teddy Kennedy's drawing power was reduced by the tragedy at Chappaquiddick. The Democratic National Committee has found it impossible to reduce the party's indebtedness significantly or prepare adequately for this fall's congressional elections. In the end, the committee may be forced to default on its debts—or, at best, negotiate settlements.

A.T. & T.'s $230,000 "Contribution"

True to the old political saying—that winners pay their bills, and losers negotiate—several of 1968's losers settled their debts by negotiation rather than by full payment. Politicians are generally close-mouthed about such intimate matters, but some unusual information has come to light about the Kennedy and McCarthy campaigns, which ended with large deficits.

Robert Kennedy's campaign left debts of $3,500,000, including $550,000 in bills for the California primary campaign. These California bills were not finally cleared up until last June. Bills for less than $100 were paid in full while larger ones were settled by negotiation— it took just $180,000 in cash to pay off the $550,000 worth of California debts. One bill, for $85,000, was from the Ambassador Hotel in Los Angeles where Kennedy was shot. The Kennedy forces first proposed to settle for $28,000, but the Ambassador refused to go along and obtained a writ to attach a Kennedy bank account (which, as it turned out, held only $395). In the end, the hotel agreed to accept $33,500.

The McCarthy campaign was about $1,300,000 in the hole by the time it ended. McCarthy's financial managers paid all bills of $400 or less in full, and negotiated settlement of larger debts—a step that created an awkward situation for some creditors. Many of these large bills—for hotel rooms, car rental, telephone service, and air travel— were tendered by publicly owned corporations, some of them in regulated industries. When a corporation agrees to settle a politician's bill for less than full value, it is in effect making an indirect campaign contribution. Even when the company is forced to take what it can get in order to avoid a larger loss, the settlement can be difficult to explain to stockholders or the various regulatory bodies. Some substantial amounts were involved in the McCarthy settlements. Various McCarthy committees owed A.T. & T. $305,000 for telephone service, but wound up paying only $75,000. American Airlines, which was owed $285,459, got $141,903.

The Biggest Contributors of All

In the preconvention campaigns for the presidential nominations, both winners and losers received some huge gifts from individual supporters. Most of these contributions escaped notice, since federal law, as noted, does not require reporting of preconvention finances. It is perfectly legal—and simple—for candidates to channel funds through committees set up in states that have no reporting laws, such as Delaware and Illinois.

Some of the large prenomination contributions made in 1968 have come to light. The biggest was made by Mrs. John D. Rockefeller Jr. on behalf of her stepson Nelson's bid for the Republican nomination. From June to September, Mrs. Rockefeller made eight gifts to the Rockefeller for President (New York) Committee, in amounts ranging from $10,000 to $425,000, for a total of $1,482,625. Since a federal gift tax applies to contributions of more than $3,000 to a single candidate or committee, Mrs. Rockefeller presumably was subject to taxes—of as much as $900,000—of the money she gave. Nelson Rockefeller himself gave $350,000 to this same committee; but his contribution represented an out-of-pocket expenditure by the candidate in his own behalf, and so probably was not subject to a gift tax.

Centimillionaire W. Clement Stone appears to have been one of the chief financial backers of Richard Nixon's campaign in the months before Nixon sewed up the Republican nomination. Stone acknowledges giving $200,000 to Republican candidates in 1968, most of it after the nomination. But at the time of the Miami convention, press reports credited Stone with having already donated $500,000 to the Nixon treasury, and one of Stone's close associates confirmed the accuracy of the figure. Since then Stone has quit publicizing his prenomination gifts, but it seems likely that the total of his contributions to Nixon and other Republican candidates in 1968 was in the neighborhood of $700,000.

Perhaps the most unorthodox political contributor in 1968 was Stewart R. Mott, thirty-two. He is the son and heir of Charles S. Mott, ninety-four, who has been a director of General Motors since 1913 and controls a fortune of at least $500 million. Stewart Mott lists himself in the New York City telephone directory as "philanthropist" and oversees his investments and good works from a Madison Avenue office. A dedicated opponent of the Vietnam war, Mott set up an organization early in 1968 called "A Coalition for a Republican Alterna-

tive." The coalition's aim was to induce Nelson Rockefeller to come out against the war and enter the presidential campaign.

Mott spent about $140,000—at least $100,000 of it out of his own pocket—on his effort to arouse support for Rockefeller; much of the money went for newspaper ads. But Mott subsequently turned to Eugene McCarthy, whose views on Vietnam were more in line with his own. Mott says that he spent $210,000 in support of McCarthy—as well as an additional $54,000 in backing other dovish candidates and organizations. All together, Mott spent $365,000 on political causes in 1968—an amount that he calculated as being three times his annual after-tax income and equivalent to 7 percent of his total assets. Some of Mott's acquaintances think he may have been poor-mouthing a bit, particularly in view of what he may someday inherit, but in a post-election summary of his political gifts, Mott declared: "I have not yet met anyone who has contributed an equivalent proportion of his assets or income."

Hubert Humphrey was not among the candidates that Mott supported—before or after the Democratic convention. But in October, when Humphrey's campaign was desperately short of cash, Mott arranged for himself and other former McCarthy supporters to meet with the Democratic nominee. Before the scheduled meeting, Mott wrote Humphrey a letter in which he made it clear that the presidential candidate would have to modify his views on Vietnam before he could expect any financial support from this group.

Mott wrote, somewhat imperiously, that he and his friends would "give you a hearing—a personal private interview of an hour's length." He added: "We realize that you would like to have us become contributors toward your campaign, but you should not expect an immediate decision from any of us, checkbook-in-hand. If we become 'turned on' . . . we have the capacity to give $1 million or more to your campaign—and raise twice or three times that amount. But we will each make our own individual judgments on the basis of how you answer our several questions and how you conduct your campaign in the coming weeks." Others of Mott's group later repudiated his letter, and the meeting never took place.

The High Cost of Media

Despite the Mott incident, public disclosure of big contributions tends to discourage rich contributors from demanding that candidates modify their views or promise specific favors. If any reform is needed, it is not to restrict large gifts—which candidates so obviously need—but to make disclosure more complete than it is now. Another desirable reform would be to make more television and radio time available to candidates at free or reduced rates.

An immense and rapidly increasing share of the money that candidates raise goes into broadcasting. About half of Humphrey's post-convention budget went for "media"—$4,400,000 for time and space charges, and more than $1 million for agency and production costs. Nixon's media costs were more than twice as much in the same period, while George Wallace spent about $1,300,000. Figures compiled by the Federal Communications Commission show that all candidates and parties spent $59,200,000 on radio and television broadcasting in 1968, a sharp increase from the $34,600,-000 spent in 1964. If production and other costs are added, the total bill for putting political messages on the air in 1968 was about $90 million—nearly a third of all the money spent on all campaigning that year.

Unfortunately for underfinanced candidates, television and radio time has to be paid for in advance. This means that a politician needs ready cash if he is to get his message across in this age of electronic campaigning. All indications are that television will become even more important in the future, and numerous proposals have been advanced that would reduce the cost of campaigning and equalize the opportunities open to candidates.

A Preference for Paying

Broadcasters generally argue that the most needed reform is repeal of Section 315 of the Communications Act of 1934. This "equal time" section of the law says that any television or radio station which gives or sells time to one candidate must provide equivalent time at comparable rates for all other candidates for the office or nomination. The broadcasters declare that repeal of Section 315 would let them provide more free time for serious political candidates and for discussion. But the free time that they have in mind would be under their control, not the control of the candidates—and the interests of the office seeker and the broadcaster do not always coincide. Networks like freewheeling drama, confrontation, debate—politics as news or entertainment—while candidates, understandably, often prefer careful staging that will let them make the best possible impression. From early 1967 until just before the election, Richard Nixon turned down all invitations to be interviewed on "free" programs like *Meet the Press* or *Face the Nation*. He preferred to pay for his time so that he could control content and format in his television appearances.

Even if ways can be devised to provide candidates with free time that they will use, they will probably continue to want paid time as well. That means there is little chance that political campaigns in this country will become any less expensive in the years ahead. The immediate prospect is that the Republicans, thanks to their 1968 financial triumph, will be in a far better position to play the costly game of politics than the debt-ridden Democrats.

THE SELLING OF THE PRESIDENT, 1968 *
JOE McGINNISS

In traditional democratic theory the political campaign was to be an educational process in which voters learned about the issues and reached rational decisions. With the advent of TV *this concept has been replaced by the candidate's expertise as a performer who appears to be frankly wrestling with the issues, but who is adroitly sidestepping them. The article that follows is a highly irreverent, behind-the-scenes description of the Nixon presidential campaign of 1968.*

Why did Nixon decide to wage a campaign centered around TV *when he found it so distasteful? What relationship exists between political and media experts in waging such a campaign? Where did the press fit into Nixon's campaign strategy? Why? What was the central* TV *strategy? If you "take a cold guy and stage him warm, can you get away with it?"*

* *Reprinted from THE SELLING OF THE PRESIDENT by Joe McGinniss by permission of Trident Press, a Division of Simon & Schuster, Inc. Copyright © 1969 by Joemac, Incorporated.*

He was afraid of television. He knew his soul was hard to find. Beyond that, he considered it a gimmick; its use in politics offended him. It had not been part of the game when he had learned to play, he could see no reason to bring it in now. He half-suspected it was an Eastern liberal trick; one more way to make him look silly. It offended his sense of dignity, one of the truest senses he had.

So his decision to use it to become President in 1968 was not easy. So much of him argued against it. But in his Wall Street years, Richard Nixon had traveled to the darkest places inside himself and come back numbed. He was, as in the Graham Greene title, a burnt-out case. All feeling was behind him; the machine inside had proved his hardiest part. He would run for President again and if he would have to learn television to run well, then he would learn it.

Nixon gathered about himself a group of young men attuned to the political uses of television. They arrived at his side by different routes. One, William Gavin, was a thirty-one-year-old English teacher in a suburban high school outside Philadelphia in 1967 when he wrote Richard Nixon a letter urging him to run for President and base his campaign on TV. Gavin wrote the letter on stationery borrowed from the University of Pennsylvania because he thought Nixon would pay more attention if the letter seemed to be from a college professor.

Dear Mr. Nixon:

May I offer two suggestions concerning your plans for 1968?

1. Run. You can win. Nothing can happen to you, politically speaking, that is worse than what has happened to you. Ortega y Gasset in his *The Revolt of the Masses* says: "These ideas are the only genuine ideas; the ideas of the shipwrecked. All the rest is rhetoric, posturing, farce. He who does not really feel himself lost, is lost without remission. . . ." You, in effect, are "lost"; that is why you are the only political figure with the vision to see things the way they are and not as Leftist or Rightist kooks would have them be. Run. You will win.

2. A tip for television: instead of those wooden performances beloved by politicians, instead of a glamor boy technique, instead of safety, be bold. Why not have live press conferences as your campaign on television? People will see you daring all, asking and answering questions from reporters, and not simply answering phony "questions" made up by your staff. This would be dynamic; it would be daring. Instead of the medium using you, you would be using the medium. . . . Television hurt you because you were not yourself; it didn't hurt the "real" Nixon. The real Nixon can revolutionize the use of television by dynamically going "live" and answering everything, the loaded and the unloaded question. Invite your opponents to this kind of debate.

Good luck, and I know you can win if you see yourself for what you are; a man who has been beaten, humiliated, hated, but who can still see the truth.

A Nixon staff member had lunch with Gavin a couple of times after the letter was received and hired him. Gavin began churning out long, stream-of-consciousness memos which dealt mostly with the importance of image, and ways in which Richard Nixon, through television, could acquire a good one: "Voters are basically lazy, basically uninterested in making an *effort* to understand what we're talking about," Gavin wrote. "Reason requires a high degree of discipline, of concentration; impression is easier. Reason pushes the viewer back, it assaults him. . . . The emotions are more easily roused, closer to the surface, more malleable. . . ."

So, for the New Hampshire primary, Gavin recommended "saturation with a film, in which the candidate can be shown better than he can be shown in person because it can be edited, so only the best moments are shown. . . . [Nixon] has to come across as a person larger than life, the stuff of legend. People are stirred by legend, including the living legend, not by the man himself. It's the aura that surrounds the charismatic figure more than it is the figure itself that draws the followers. Our task is to build that aura. . . ."

William Gavin was brought to the White House as a speechwriter in January of 1969.

Harry Treleaven, hired as creative director of advertising in the fall of 1967, immediately went to work on the more serious of Nixon's personality problems. One was his lack of humor: "Can be corrected to a degree," Treleaven wrote, "but let's not be too obvious about it. Romney's cornball attempts have hurt him. If we're going to be witty, let a pro write the words."

Treleaven also worried about Nixon's lack of warmth, but decided: "He can be helped greatly in this respect by how he is handled. . . . Give him words to say that will show his *emotional* involvement in the issues. . . . He should be presented in some kind of 'situation' rather than cold in a studio. The situation should look unstaged even if it's not."

Some of the most effective ideas belonged to Raymond K. Price, a former editorial writer for the New York *Herald Tribune*, who became Nixon's best and most prominent speechwriter in the campaign. Price later composed much of the Inaugural Address. In 1967, he concluded that rational arguments would "only be effective if we can get the people to make the *emotional* leap, or what theologians call 'leap of faith.' "

To do this, Price suggested attacking the "personal factors" rather than the "historical factors" which were the basis of the low opinion so many people had of Richard Nixon. "These tend to be more a gut reaction," he wrote, "unarticulated, nonanalytical, a product of the particular chemistry between the voter and the *image* of the candidate.

We have to be very clear on this point: that the response is to the image, not to the man. . . ."

So there would not have to be a "new Nixon." Simply a new approach to television.

This was how they went into it. Trying, with one hand, to build the illusion that Richard Nixon, in addition to his attributes of mind and heart, considered "communicating with the people . . . one of the great joys of seeking the Presidency," while with the other they shielded him, controlled him, and controlled the atmosphere around him. It was as if they were building not a President but an Astrodome, where the wind would never blow, the temperature never rise or fall, and the ball never bounce erratically on the artificial grass.

And it worked. As he moved serenely through his primary campaign, there was new cadence to Richard Nixon's speech and motion; new confidence in his heart. And, a new image of him on the television screen, on live, but controlled, TV. . . .

[The Nixon mass media advertising team was expanded by a Nixon law partner, Len Garment, who recruited Frank Shakespeare (a CBS official) and Roger Ailes (producer of The Mike Douglas Show).]

"I am not going to barricade myself into a television studio and make this an antiseptic campaign," Richard Nixon said at a press conference a few days after his nomination. Then he went to Chicago to open his fall campaign. The whole day was built around a television show. Even when ten thousand people stood in front of his hotel and screamed for him to greet them he stayed locked up in his room, resting for the show.

Chicago was the site for the first of ten programs that Nixon would do in states ranging from Massachusetts to Texas. The idea was to have him in the middle of a group of people, answering questions live. Shakespeare and Treleaven had developed the idea through the primaries and now had it sharpened to a point. Each show would run for one hour. It would be live to provide suspense; there would be a studio audience to cheer Nixon's answers and make it seem to home viewers that enthusiasm for his candidacy was all but uncontrollable; and there would be an effort to achieve a conversational tone that would penetrate Nixon's stuffiness and drive out the displeasure he often seemed to feel when surrounded by other human beings instead of Bureau of the Budget reports.

One of the valuable things about this idea, from a political standpoint, was that each show would be seen only by the people who lived in that particular state or region. This meant it made no difference if Nixon's statements—for they were not really answers—were exactly the same, phrase for phrase, gesture for gesture, from state to state. Only the press would be bored and the press had been written off already. So Nixon could get through the campaign with a dozen or so carefully worded responses that would cover all the problems of America in 1968.

. . .

The fourth of the ten scheduled panel shows was done in Philadelphia. It was televised across Pennsylvania and into Delaware and New Jersey. Roger Ailes arrived in Philadelphia on Wednesday, September 18, two days before the show was to go on the air. "We're doing all right," he said. "If we could only get someone to play Hide the Greek." He did not like Spiro Agnew either.

The production meeting for the Philadelphia show was held at ten o'clock Thursday morning in the office of Al Hollender, program director of WCAU. The purpose was to acquaint the local staff with what Roger Ailes wanted to do and to acquaint Roger Ailes with the limitations of the local staff. Ailes came in ten minutes late, dressed in sweat shirt and sneakers, coffee cup in hand. He had a room at the Marriott Motor Hotel across the street.

"One problem you're going to have here, Roger," a local man said, "is the size of the studio. You've been working with an audience of three hundred, I understand, but we can only fit 240."

"That's all right. I can get as much applause out of 240 as three hundred, if it's done right, and that's all they are—an applause machine." He paused. "That and a couple of reaction shots."

"I'm more concerned," Ailes said,

"about where camera one is. I've talked to Nixon twice about playing to it and I can't seem to get through to him. So I think this time we're going to play it to him."

"You ought to talk to him about saying, 'Let me make one thing very clear,' ten times every show," someone said. "It's driving people nuts."

"I have, and Shakespeare told me not to mention it again. It bugs Nixon. Apparently everybody has been telling him about it but he can't stop."

After half an hour, Roger Ailes left the meeting. "Those things bore me," he said. "I'll leave Rourke to walk around and kick the tires." He went across the street to the motel. The morning was clear and hot.

"The problem with the panels is that we need variety," Ailes said. "Nixon gets bored with the same kind of people. We've got to screw around with this one a little bit."

"You still want seven?" an assistant, supplied by the local Republicans, asked.

"Yes, and on this one we definitely need a Negro. I don't think it's necessary to have one in every group of six people, no matter what our ethnic experts say, but in Philadelphia it is. *U.S. News and World Report* this week says that one of every three votes cast in Philadelphia will be Negro."

"I know one in Philadelphia," the local man, whose name was Dan Boozer, said. "He's a dynamic type, the head of a self-help organization, that kind of thing. And he is black."

"What do you mean he's black?"

"I mean he's dark. It will be obvious on television that he's not white."

"You mean we won't have to put a sign around him that says, 'This is our Negro'?"

"Absolutely not."

"Fine. Call him. Let's get this thing going."

"Nixon is better if the panel is offbeat," Ailes was saying. "It's tough to get an articulate ditch-digger, but I'd like to."

"I have one name here," Boozer said. "Might be offbeat. A Pennsylvania Dutch farmer."

"No! No more farmers. They all ask the same dull questions."

The morning produced an Italian lawyer from Pittsburgh, a liberal housewife from the Main Line, and a Young Republican from the Wharton School of Finance and Commerce.

"Now we need a newsman," Roger Ailes said.

I suggested the name of an articulate reporter from the *Evening Bulletin* in Philadelphia.

"Fine. Why don't you call him?"

"He's a Negro."

"Oh shit, we can't have two. Even in Philadelphia. Wait a minute—call him, and if he'll do it we can drop the self-help guy."

But the reporter was unavailable. Then I suggested Jack McKinney, a radio talk-show host from WCAU. Ailes called him and after half an hour on the phone, McKinney, who found it hard to believe the show would not be rigged, agreed to go on. Then I suggested a psychiatrist I knew: the head of a group

that brought Vietnamese children wounded in the war to the United States for treatment and artificial limbs.

"What's his name?"

"Herb Needleman."

Roger Ailes called him. Herb Needleman agreed to do the show. Roger Ailes was pleased. "The guy sounded tough but not hysterical. This is shaping up as a very interesting show."

A newsman from Camden, New Jersey, was added, and, at four o'clock, Ailes called Len Garment in New York to tell him the panel was complete.

". . . That's six," he was saying, "and then we've got a Jewish doctor from Philadelphia, a psychiatrist, who—wait a minute, Len, relax . . . I—yes, he's already accepted, he . . . Well, why not? . . . Are you serious? . . . Honest to God, Len? . . . Oh, no, I can get out of it, it'll just be a little embarrassing . . . No, you're right, if he feels that strongly about it. . . ."

Roger Ailes hung up.

"Jesus Christ," he said. "You're not going to believe this but Nixon hates psychiatrists."

"What?"

"Nixon hates psychiatrists. He's got this thing, apparently. They make him very nervous. You should have heard Len on the phone when I told him I had one on the panel. Did you hear him? If I ever heard a guy's voice turn white, that was it."

"Why?"

"He said he didn't want to go into it. But apparently Nixon won't even let one in the same room. Jesus Christ, could you picture him on a live TV show finding out he's being questioned by a shrink?"

There was another reason, too, why Herb Needleman was unacceptable. "Len says they want to go easy on Jews for a while. I guess Nixon's tired of saying 'balance of power' about the goddam Middle East."

So, at 4:15 P.M., Roger Ailes made another call to Dr. Needleman, to tell him that this terribly embarrassing thing had happened, that the show had been overbooked. Something about having to add a panelist from New Jersey because the show would be televised into the southern part of the state.

"You know what I'd like?" Ailes said later. "As long as we've got this extra spot open. A good, mean, Wallaceite cab driver. Wouldn't that be great? Some guy to sit there and say, 'Awright Mac, what about these niggers?' "

It was five o'clock in the afternoon. The day still was hot but Roger Ailes had not been outside since morning. Air conditioning, iced tea, and the telephone.

"Come on," Roger Ailes said. "Let's go find a cab driver." He stepped out to the motel parking lot and walked through the sun to the main entrance. The Marriott was the best place they had in Philadelphia. Eight cabs were lined up in the driveway. The third driver Roger Ailes talked to said that he was not really for Wallace, but that he wasn't really against him either.

"What's your name?" Roger Ailes said.

"Frank Kornsey."

"You want to go on television tomorrow night? Right across the street there, and ask Mr. Nixon some questions. Any questions you want."

"I've got to work tomorrow night."

"Take it off. Tell them why. We'll pay you for the hours you miss, plus your expenses to and from the studio."

"My wife will think I'm nuts."

"Your wife will love you. When did she ever think she'd be married to a guy who conversed with the next President of the United States?"

"I'll let you know in the morning," Frank Kornsey said.

Back in the motel room, the talk drifted to some of the curious associations into which Nixon seemed to fall. People he sought to align himself with, whose endorsement he was so pleased to accept, when even in political terms they probably did him more harm than good.

"That Wilkinson, for Christ's sake, he's like a marionette with the strings broken," Ailes's director said. The director had come over from the studio in midafternoon, after working on final placement of the cameras.

"Oh, Wilkinson's a sweet guy," Ailes said, "but he's got absolutely no sense of humor."

"If you're going to keep using him as a moderator, you should tell him to stop applauding all the answers."

"He's been told," Ailes said, "he's been told. He just can't help it."

Ailes got up from the table. "Let's face it, a lot of people think Nixon is dull. Think he's a bore, a pain in the ass. They look at him as the kind of kid who always carried a book bag. Who was forty-two years old the day he was born. They figure other kids got footballs for Christmas, Nixon got briefcases and he loved it. He'd always have his homework done and he'd never let you copy. Now you put him on television, you've got a problem right away. He's a funny-looking guy. He looks like somebody hung him in a closet overnight and he jumps out in the morning with his suit all bunched up and starts running around saying, 'I want to be President.' I mean this is how he strikes some people. That's why these shows are important. To make them forget all that."

Richard Nixon came to Philadelphia the next day: Friday. There was the standard downtown motorcade at noon. Frank Kornsey took the whole day off to stay home and write questions. "I got some beauties," he told Roger Ailes on the phone.

Ailes went to the studio at two o'clock in the afternoon. "I'm going to fire this director," he said. "I'm going to fire the son of a bitch right after the show. Look at this. Look at the positioning of these cameras. I've told him fifty times I want closeups. Closeups! This is a close-up medium. It's dull to shoot chest shots. I want to see pores. That's

what people are. That's what television is."

He walked through the studio, shaking his head. "We won't get a shot better than waist-high from these cameras all night. That's 1948 direction. When you had four people in every shot and figured you were lucky you had any shot at all."

The audience filled the studio at seven o'clock. The panel was brought in at 7:15. Frank Kornsey was nervous. Roger Ailes offered him a shot of bourbon. "No thanks," he said. "I'll be all right." He tried to grin.

At 7:22 Jack Rourke stepped onto the riser. He was a heavy Irishman with a red face and gray hair. "Hello," he said to the audience. "I'm Frank Sinatra."

The Nixon family, David Eisenhower, and the Governor of Pennsylvania came in. The audience applauded. This audience, like the others, had been carefully recruited by the local Republican organization. "That's the glee club," Jack Rourke said, pointing to the Nixons.

The director walked into the control booth at 7:24. "He's crazy," the director said, meaning Roger Ailes. "He has no conception of the mechanical limitations involved in a show like this. He says he wants closeups, it's like saying he wants to go to the moon." The director took his seat at the control panel and spoke to a cameraman on the floor. "Make sure you know where Mrs. Nixon is and what she looks like."

A member of the Nixon staff ran into the booth. "Cut the sound in that studio next door. We've got the press in there and we don't want them to hear the warm-up."

"Now when Mr. Nixon comes in," Jack Rourke was saying, "I want you to tear the place apart. Sound like ten thousand people. I'm sure, of course, that you'll also want to stand up at that point. So what do you say we try it now. Come on, stand up. And let me hear it."

"One forty-five to air," the director said in the control booth.

"Tell Rourke to check the sound level on the panel."

Jack Rourke turned to Frank Kornsey: "Ask a question, please. We'd like to check your microphone."

Frank Kornsey leaned forward and spoke, barely above a whisper. His list of "beauties" lay on a desk before him. He was still pale, even through his makeup.

"I was just wondering how Mr. and Mrs. Nixon are enjoying our wonderful city of Philadelphia," he said.

Pat Nixon, in a first row seat, gave her tight, closemouthed smile.

"No, they don't care for it," Jack Rourke said.

"Thirty seconds," came a voice from the control room. "Clear the decks, please, thirty seconds."

Then, at exactly 7:30, while a tape of Richard Nixon's motorcade was being played for the viewers at home, the director said, "Okay, cue the applause, move back camera one, move back one," and Richard Nixon stepped through a crack in a curtain, hunched his shoulders, raised his arms, wiggled his wrists, made V-signs with his fingers and switched on his grin.

Jack McKinney, the talk-show host, was wearing his hairpiece for the occasion. Nixon turned to him first, still with the grin, hands clasped before him, into his fourth show now and over the jitters. Maybe, in fact, ready to show off just a bit. A few new combinations, if the proper moment came, to please the crowd.

"Yes, Mr. McKinney," he said.

Jack McKinney did not lead with his right but he threw a much stiffer jab than Nixon had been expecting: "Why are you so reluctant to comment on Vietnam this year when in 1952, faced with a similar issue in Korea, you were so free with your partisan remarks?"

Not a crippling question but there was an undertone of unfriendliness to it. Worse, it had been put to him in professional form. Nixon stepped back, a bit off balance. This sort of thing threatened the stability of the whole format; the basis being the hypothesis that Nixon could appear to risk all by going live while in fact risking nothing by facing the loose syntax and predictable, sloppy thrusts of amateurs. He threw up an evasive flurry. But the grin was gone from his face. Not only did he know now that he would have to be careful of McKinney, he was forced to wonder, for the first time, what he might encounter from the others.

The Negro was next. Warily: "Yes, Mr. Burress." And Burress laid Black Capitalism right down the middle, straight and soft. Nixon had it memorized. He took a long time on the answer, though, savoring its clichés, making sure his wind had come back all the way.

Then Frank Kornsey, who studied his list and asked, "What are you going to do about the *Pueblo?*" Beautiful. Nixon was honing this one to perfection. He had taken 1:22 with it in California, according to Roger Ailes's chart, but had brought it down to 1:05 in Ohio. Now he delivered it in less than a minute. He was smooth again, and grinning, as he turned to the liberal housewife, Mrs. Mather.

Was civil disobedience *ever* justified, she wondered. Nixon took a quick step backwards on the riser. His face fell into the solemnity mask. There were philosophic implications there he did not like. He could understand the impatience of those less fortunate than ourselves, he assured her, and their demand for immediate improvement was, indeed, healthy for our society in many ways. But—as long as change could be brought about within the system—and no, he was not like some who claimed it could not— then there was no cause, repeat, *no* cause that justified the breaking of a law.

But he knew he would have to watch her, too. The first line of sweat broke out across his upper lip.

The Young Republican from Wharton wanted to know how to bring the McCarthy supporters back into the mainstream, which was fine, but then the newsman from Camden asked if Nixon agreed with Spiro Agnew's charge that Hubert Humphrey was "soft on Communism."

He knew how to handle that one, but while sidestepping, he noted that this fellow, too, seemed unawed. That made three out of seven who were ready, it appeared, to mix it up. And one of them a good-looking articulate woman. And another, McKinney, who seemed truly mean.

It was McKinney's turn again: Why was Nixon refusing to appear on any of the news confrontation shows such as *Meet the Press?* Why would he face the public only in staged settings such as this, where the questions were almost certain to be worded generally enough to allow him any vague sort of answer he wanted to give? Where the presence of the cheering studio audience was sure to intimidate any questioner who contemplated true engagement? Where Nixon moved so quickly from one questioner to the next that he eliminated any possibility of follow-up, any chance for true discussion . . .?

"The guy's making a speech!" Frank Shakespeare shouted in the control booth. Roger Ailes jumped for the phone to Wilkinson on stage. But McKinney was finished, for the moment. The question was, had he finished Nixon, too?

"I've done those quiz shows, Mr. McKinney. I've done them until they were running out of my ears." There was no question on one point: Richard Nixon was upset. Staring hard at McKinney he grumbled something about why there ought to be more fuss about Hubert Humphrey not having press conferences and less about him and *Meet the Press*.

It did not seem much of a recovery but in the control room Frank Shakespeare punched the palm of one hand with the fist of the other and said, "That socks it to him, Dickie Baby!" The audience cheered. Suddenly, Nixon, perhaps sensing a weakness in McKinney where he had feared that none existed, perhaps realizing he had no choice, surely buoyed by the cheers, decided to slug it out.

"Go ahead," he said, gesturing. "I want you to follow up."

McKinney came back creditably, using the word "amorphous" and complaining that viewers were being asked to support Nixon for President on the basis of "nothing but a wink and a smile" particularly in regard to Vietnam.

"Now, Mr. McKinney, maybe I haven't been as specific . . ." and Nixon was off on a thorough rephrasing of his Vietnam non-position, which, while it contained no substance—hence, could not accommodate anything new— sounded, to uninitiates, like a public step forward. The audience was ecstatic. Outnumbered, two hundred forty-one to one, McKinney could do nothing but smile and shake his head.

"Be very careful with McKinney," Shakespeare said, bending over Roger Ailes. "I want to give him a chance but I don't want him to hog the show."

"Yeah, if he starts making another speech I'll call Bud and—"

But Shakespeare was no longer listening. He was grappling with a cameraman who had come into the control booth and began to take pictures of the production staff at work.

"No press," Shakespeare said, and when the man continued shooting his film, Shakespeare began to push. The cameraman pushed back as well as he could, but Shakespeare, leaning hard, edged him toward the door.

Meanwhile, Frank Kornsey, consulting his written list again, had asked, "What do you intend to do about the gun-control law?" Then, quickly, the others: Are you writing off the black vote? What about federal tax credits . . . water and air pollution? And then the Camden newsman, whose name was Flynn, asking about Nixon's action in 1965 when he had called for the removal of a Rutgers history professor who had spoken kindly of the Vietcong —on campus.

Nixon assured Mr. Flynn that academic freedom remained high on his personal list of privileges which all Americans should enjoy, but added, "There is one place where I would draw the line. And that is, I do not believe that anyone who is paid by the government and who is using governmental facilities—and Rutgers, as I'm sure you are aware, Mr. Flynn, is a state institution—has the right to call for the victory of the enemy over American boys—while he is on the campus."

But now McKinney gathered himself for a final try: "You said that the Rutgers professor 'called for' the victory of the Vietcong, but as I recall he didn't say that at all. This is what I mean about your being able, on this kind of show, to slide off the questions. Now the facts were—"

"Oh, I know the facts, Mr. McKinney. I know the facts."

Nixon was grinning. The audience poured forth its loudest applause of the night. Bud Wilkinson joined in, full of righteous fervor. Of course Mr. Nixon knew the facts.

McKinney was beaten but would not quit: "The facts were that the professor did not 'call for' the victory—"

"No, what he said, Mr. McKinney, and I believe I am quoting him *exactly*, was that he would 'welcome the impending victory of the Vietcong.' "

"Which is not the same thing."

"Well, Mr. McKinney, you can make that distinction if you wish, but what I'll do is I'll turn it over to the television audience right now and let them decide for themselves about the semantics. About the difference between 'calling for' and 'welcoming' a victory of the Vietcong."

He was angry but he had it under control and he talked fast and hard and when he was finished he swung immediately to the next questioner. The show was almost over. McKinney was through for the night.

"Boy, is he going to be pissed," Roger Ailes said as he hurried down from the control room. "He'll think we really tried to screw him. But critically it was the best show he's done."

Roger Ailes went looking for Nixon. He wound up in an elevator with Nixon's wife. She was wearing a green dress and she did not smile. One thought of the remark a member of the Nixon staff had made: "Next to her, RN looks like Mary Poppins."

"Hello, Mrs. Nixon," Roger Ailes said. She nodded. She had known him for months. "How did you like the show?" She nodded very slowly, her mouth was drawn in a thin, straight line.

"Everyone seems to think it was by far the best," Ailes said. "Especially the way he took care of that McKinney."

Pat Nixon stared at the elevator door. The car stopped. She got off and moved down a hallway with the Secret Service men around her.

. . .

"This is the beginning of a whole new concept," Ailes said. "This is it. That is the way they'll be elected forevermore. The next guys up will have to be performers. The interesting question is, how sincere is a TV set? If you take a cold guy and stage him warm, can you get away with it? I don't know." . . .

5. Formal Political Institutions (President, Bureaucracy, Congress, Supreme Court) Cumulative Obsolescence Amidst Accelerated Change

As the title suggests, we are concerned in this chapter with the obsolescence of formal political institutions. This formal machinery —the Congress, the Presidency, the Courts, and the Bureaucracy— is used to establish and execute public policy. Each of these institutions is now steeped in its own hoary traditions and procedures and resists renovation. Thus far as a nation we have "muddled through," despite any thorough-going institutional revision.

Institutional Machinery: The Need For Reform

A clear distinction should be made between the reform of institutions and their abolition. Most critics do not suggest that we abolish the Presidency or the Congress. Such basic ideas as the separation of powers, limited government and civil liberties seem as valid today as they did in 1787; but the institutional machinery does not. In fact, one critic has made the sweeping charge that:

City government, state government, the Congress of the United States, the federal agencies, the courts, the political process are so ill designed for contemporary purposes that they cannot serve us adequately.

Often the machinery of government seems antiquated and inappropriate for a technological society faced with massive social change. The formal institutions in many ways are like an old-fashioned parlor

filled with the memorabilia of generations—stereopticon slides, a
wind-up Victrola, faded wedding pictures, a stack of 1927 *National
Geographics,* and brass baby booties atop a color TV.

Our government institutions add, but seldom throw away. Their
accumulated operating procedures are frequently used to create a
stalemate rather than to react to change. The work schedule of the
Senate can be halted for days by a single Senator speaking on creole
cooking *a la filibuster;* some sharp-tongued critics note that it is more
than happenstance that the Department of Agriculture and the Smith-
sonian Museum flourish side by side, while the farm population declines
precipitously. What are some of the more glaring deficiencies in our
formal institutions?

The American Presidency

That power is equally shared by our political Trinity—President,
Congress, Supreme Court—is an obsolete concept, according to those
commentators who describe our system as "Presidential Government."
Following this line of reasoning, national power is concentrated in the
presidential office. A modern president can wage an undeclared war;
he can manipulate the economy; he is the policymaker at home and
abroad.

In its simplest form this "job description" creates a Superman
president with no limits on what he can achieve. If he pushes the right
button, he brings victory on the battlefield; another presidential button
gives us prosperity and full employment; still another causes everyone
to love and admire him. In practice, of course, this theory is nonsense.
Our president is all too human. Although his office confers tremendous
powers, he is faced with overwhelming problems. The critical issue
of the '70's is how to grant the president sufficient power to do his
job without paving the way toward dictatorial rule.

The Bureaucracy

Presidents come, Presidents go, but government flows into the next
administration—and the next. Great power is lodged in bureaucratic
hands, but that power is fragmented into uncoordinated spheres of
influence. Decisions may even be made at the departmental or
bureau level that conflict with presidential goals. Despite conservationists,
the Army Corps of Engineers doggedly drains swamps and builds
dams "come hell or high water." Employees of Health, Education and
Welfare boo the new Secretary and stage a sitdown against a change
in welfare rules. While the Interstate Commerce Commission encourages
mergers, the Justice Department prepares to prosecute under anti-trust

laws. The whole bureaucratic operation is cumbersome, overlapping and bound in red tape. Successful chief executives (presidents) are those who overcome the obstacles, give central focus to the operation, and prune away the dead wood.

The Congress

The American Congress shares some defects with the bureaucracy. It too is a victim of its procedures. In fact its machinery seems best designed to prevent action. Its two Houses seldom work in harmony. Although Congress and the President are jointly charged with law making, there is every possibility that one or both Houses of Congress may have a majority from the opposition party. President Eisenhower faced such a Congress for six of his eight years; President Nixon has faced one for four years.

In many respects Congress is an unrepresentative body where majority rule does not prevail. The key to its operation is the committee system. The committees are in turn dominated by their chairmen, who in turn are selected on the basis of seniority. And seniority is determined by political survival rather than by ability. The Senate preserves its own special device for blocking majority rule. Using the filibuster, a small group of Senators can tie up all business for weeks and avoid a vote.

The archaic machinery of the Congress is under increasing attack and some small changes have been made. A much larger problem is that posed by the narrow state or district view of its members. Someone in Congress most assuredly speaks for Idaho or Florida Fifth district interests. But who speaks for the United States people as a whole?

The Courts: High and Low

In plain truth the Supreme Court of the United States is an aristocratic institution that functions within a democratic political system. The selection of justices is outside the normal election process. No citizen has ever had an opportunity to choose between rival candidates for this office. Beyond this, justices hold their seats for indefinite terms, and as a practical matter are directly responsible only to their individual consciences. This arrangement, on the surface at least, is at complete variance with democratic theory under which leaders are chosen by the people and must regularly submit their records to the general public for endorsement.

In the course of our history six justices have served on the Bench for 32 years or longer. In fact, two consecutive Chief Justices (Marshall and Taney) served a combined total of sixty-two years. These longevity records are surpassed by one present and one deceased member of the Court: William O. Douglas (appointed, 1939) and Hugo L. Black (appointed, 1937).

In a society where two-thirds of the population is under 40 years of age and where early retirement (60) is becoming more fashionable, critics of the Court are fond of quoting these vital statistics on Supreme Court justices. Roughly half of the justices (49) have died in office. Twenty-six of the 99 have served past age 75. The championship is still held by Oliver Wendell Holmes, Jr., who *retired* at age 90, after serving 29 years on the Court (Holmes, by the way, is frequently ranked among the top dozen men who have served on the Bench). The example of Holmes is cited by Court defenders as evidence that long terms and longevity can be assets, when wisdom rather than a bubbling enthusiasm are job criteria.

The role of the Court in a democratic society is a more critical issue than its composition. Should it play a "self restraining" role and accept as constitutional the actions of state legislatures, the Congress and the President unless precedent is clearly violated? Or should it play an "activist" role, insisting on its coequal status and its right to freely employ judicial review.

Both conservatives and liberals in this century have challenged the Court when it assumed an activist role. During the early 1930's the Court found much New Deal legislation unconstitutional. After an overwhelming victory at the polls in 1936, President Roosevelt proposed that the Court membership be enlarged to 15 judges who could then reverse the minority economic doctrine of *laissez faire* held by the Court. Although Roosevelt's grand strategy was blocked, the Court in several significant cases reversed its position and resignations paved the way for a new Court that reflected current economic philosophy. One wit of the period said, "A switch in time, saved nine."

Twenty years later conservative critics (who had offered an unqualified defense of the court against Roosevelt's attacks) were its most outspoken critics. A liberal Court, under the leadership of Chief Justice Earl Warren (1953–1969) became the champion of civil liberties for many minorities. These minorities—blacks, criminals, Communists, atheists, urban voters—could not have secured this protection through majority legislation. The frustrated conservatives, feeling that they spoke for the majority, proposed a series of legal devices to override the liberal Court. Billboards appeared that said simply "Impeach Earl Warren." Once again, some unexpected resignations gave President Nixon an opportunity to change the Court's direction. Under the new Chief Justice, Warren Burger, the Court has given some evidence of retreat toward the conservative position.

The two cases cited above are examples of how close we have come to a "high noon" confrontation between the Court and its critics. In each case a certain amount of political luck involving resignations and appointments spelled the difference. But in a broader view these confrontations have not answered the basic question: For how long in a democratic society can an aristocratic body support minorities against majority opinion?

THE TEXTBOOK PRESIDENCY *

THOMAS E. CRONIN

The American President in this century has emerged as "chief among equals" in the Federal Triangle—President, Congress, Supreme Court. Other institutions are subordinated to the chief executive, who is identified as the major unifying force in American life. This concept is now being challenged.

Why did journalists and textbook writers create a "superman" president? How did Franklin Roosevelt help to create the legend? Should moral and political leadership be intermingled? Why are contemporary Presidents tempted to overstate their capacity to change things? Why is it easy to identify the president as the cause of all our problems? Realistically, to what degree can modern presidents effect new policies or dismantle old ones?

Franklin D. Roosevelt personally rescued the nation from the depths of the great Depression. Roosevelt, together with Harry Truman,

* Reprinted from Thomas E. Cronin, "Superman: Our Textbook President," Washington Monthly, October, 1970, by permission of the author.

brought World War II to a proud conclusion. Courageous Truman personally committed us to resist communist aggression around the globe. General Eisenhower pledged that as president he would "go to Korea" and end that war—and he did. These are prevailing idealized images that most American students read and remember. For convenience, if not for simplicity, textbooks divide our past into the "Wilson years," the "Hoover depression," the "Roosevelt revolution," the "Eisenhower period" and so forth.

Presidents are expected to perform as purposeful activists, who know what they want to accomplish and relish the challenges of the office. The student learns that the presidency is "the great engine of democracy," the "American people's one authentic trumpet," "the central instrument of democracy," and "probably the most important governmental institution in the world." With the New Deal presidency in mind the textbook portrait states that presidents must instruct the nation as national teacher and guide the nation as national preacher. Presidents should be decidedly in favor of expanding the federal government's role in order to cope with increasing nationwide demands for social justice and a prosperous economy. The performances of Harding, Coolidge, and Hoover, lumped together as largely similar, are rejected as antique. The Eisenhower record of retiring reluctance elicits more ambiguous appraisal; after brief tribute to him as a wonderful man and a superior military leader, he gets categorized as an amateur who lacked both a sense of direction and a progressive and positive conception of the presidential role. What is needed, most texts imply, is a man with foresight to anticipate the future and the personal strength to unite us, to steel our moral will, to move the country forward, and to make the country governable. The vision, and perhaps the illusion, is that, if only we can identify and elect *the right man,* our loftiest aspirations can and will be accomplished.

With little variation, the college text includes two chapters on the presidency. Invariably, these stress that the contemporary presidency is growing dramatically larger in size, gaining measurably more responsibilities (often referred to as more hats) and greater resources. Students read that more authority and policy discretion devolve to the president during war and crises; and since our country is now engaged in sustained international conflict and acute domestic problems, presidents are constantly becoming more powerful. One text points out that "as the world grows smaller, he will grow bigger."

Then, too, writers tend to underline the vast resources available for presidential decision-making—the array of experts, including White House strategic support staffs, intelligence systems, the National Security Council, the Cabinet, an Office of Science and Technology, the Council of Economic Advisers, and countless high-powered study commissions. To the student, it must appear that a president must have just about all the inside information and sage advice possible for human comprehension. A casual reading of the chapters on the presidency fosters the belief that contemporary presidents can both make and shape public policy and can see to it that these policies *work as intended.* Textbooks encourage the belief that the "president knows best" and that his advisory and information systems are unparalleled in history. The capacity of the presidency for systematic thinking and planning is similarly described as awesome and powerful suited to the challenges of the day.

Clinton Rossiter wrote one of the most lucid venerations of the chief executive. In the *American Presidency,* he views the office as a priceless American invention which has not only worked extremely well but is also a symbol of our continuity and destiny as a people:

Few nations have solved so simply and yet grandly the problem of finding and maintaining an office or state that embodies their majesty and reflects their character. . . .

There is virtually no limit to what the President can do if he does it for democratic ends and by democratic means. . . .

He is, rather, a kind of magnificent lion who can roam widely and do great deeds so long as he does not try to break loose from his broad reservation. . . .

He reigns, but he also rules; he

symbolizes the people, but he also runs their government. . . .

Recently written or revised government textbooks emphasize the importance of personal attributes, and there is little doubt that dwellings on the president's personal qualities helps to capture the attention of student learners. Not surprisingly, this personalization of the presidency also is reflected in a great deal of campaign rhetoric. Presidential candidates go to a considerable length to stress how personally courageous and virtuous a president must be. Nelson Rockefeller's (1968) litany of necessary qualities is as exaggerated as anyone else's:

The modern Presidency of the United States, as distinct from the traditional concepts of our highest office, is bound up with the survival not only of freedom but of mankind. . . .
The President is the unifying force in our lives. . . .
The President must possess a wide range of abilities: to lead, to persuade, to inspire trust, to attract men of talent, to unite. These abilities must reflect a wide range of characteristics: courage, vision, integrity, intelligence, sense of responsibility, sense of history, sense of humor, warmth, openness, personality, tenacity, energy, determination, drive, perspicacity, idealism, thirst for information, penchant for fact, presence of conscience, comprehension of people and enjoyment of life—plus all the other, nobler virtues

ascribed to George Washington under God.

The Lion's Transformation

The personalized presidency is also a central feature of contemporary political journalism, and no journalist does more to embellish this perspective than Theodore White. His "Making of the President" series not only enjoys frequent university use but additionally serves as presidency textbooks for millions of adults who savor his "insider" explanations of presidential election campaigns.

White's unidimensional concentration on the presidential candidates, their styles, and personalities promotes a benevolent if not reverential orientation toward the American presidency. His narrative histories of American political campaigns have an uncanny way of uplifting and seducing the reader to watch and wait an election's outcome with intense concern—even though the books are published almost a year after the event. His style ferments great expectations and a heightened sense of reverence for the eventual victor. At first there are seven or eight competing hopefuls, then four or five, penultimately narrowed down to two or three nationally legitimized candidates and finally—there remains just one man. Clearly the victor in such a drawn-out and thoroughly patriotic ritual deserves our deepest respect and approval. White subtly succeeds in purifying the victorious candidate: in what must be a classic metamorphosis at the root of the textbook presidency image, the men who assume the presidency seem physically (and implicitly almost spiritually) to undergo an alteration of personal traits.

On JFK's first days in the White House, 1961:

It was as if there were an echo, here on another level, in the quiet Oval Office, of all the speeches he had made in all the squares and super-markets of the country. . . . He had won this office and this power by promising such movement to the American people. Now he had to keep the promise. He seemed very little changed in movement or in gracefulness from the candidate—only his eyes had changed—very dark now, very grave, markedly more sunken and lined at the corners than those of the candidate.

On Richard Nixon soon after his ascendency, 1969:

He seemed, as he waved me into the Oval Office, suddenly on first glance a more stocky man than I had known on the campaign rounds. There was a minute of adjustment as he waved me to a sofa in the barren office, poured coffee, put me at ease; then, watching him, I realized that he was not stockier, but, on the contrary, slimmer. What was different was the movement of the body, the sound of the voice, the manner of speaking— for he was calm as I had never seen him before, as if peace had settled on him. In the past, Nixon's restless body had been in constant movement as he rose, walked about, hitched a leg over the arm of a chair or gestured sharply with his hands. Now he was in repose; and the repose was in his speech also—more slow, studied, with none of the gear-slippages of name or reference which used to come when he was weary; his hands still moved as he spoke, but the fingers spread gracefully, not punchily or sharply as they used to.

What, then, constitutes the recent textbook version of the American presidency? As always, any facile generalization of such a hydra-like institution is susceptible to over-simplification, but, on balance, more consensus than contention characterizes literature on the American presidency. Four sum-mary statements may be singled out without doing great violence to the text literature. Two of these ac-centuate a dimension of presiden-tial omnipotence, and two others emphasize an expectation of moral-istic-benevolence. Taken together, this admixture of legend and reality comprise the textbook presidency of the last 15 years.

Omnipotence:

1. The president is the strategic catalyst in the American political system and the central figure in the international system as well.

2. Only the president is or can be the genuine architect of United States public policy, and only he, by attacking problems frontally and aggressively and interpreting his power expansively, can be the en-

gine of change to move this nation forward.

Moralistic-Benevolence:

3. The president must be the nation's personal and moral leader; by symbolizing the past and future greatness of America and radiating inspirational confidence, a president can pull the nation together while directing us toward the fulfillment of the American Dream.

4. If, and only if, the right man is placed in the White House, all will be well, and, somehow, whoever is in the White House is the right man.

The "Selling of a Textbook"

Radio, television, and the emergence of the United States as a strategic nuclear power have converged to make the presidency a job of far greater prominence than it was in the days of Coolidge and before. While this is readily understood, there are other factors which contribute to runaway inflation in the attributed capabilities of White House leadership.

A first explanation for the textbook presidency is derived from the basic human tendency toward belief in great men. Most people grow up with the expectation that someone somewhere can and will cope with the major crises of the present and future. Since the New Deal, most Americans have grown accustomed to expect their president to serve this role. Who, if not the president, is going to prevent the communists from burying us, pollu-

tion from choking us, crime and conflict from destroying our cities, moral degradation from slipping into our neighborhood theaters? Within the complexity of political life today the president provides a visible national symbol to which we can attach our hopes. Something akin to presidential cults exists in the United States today just as hero-worship, gerontocracy reverence, and other forms of authority-fixation have flourished in most, if not all, larger societies. Portraits of Washington, Lincoln, the Roosevelts, and Kennedy paper many a classroom wall alongside of the American flag. While deification is presumably discouraged, something similar is a common side product during the early years of schooling.

On all but two occasions during the past 17 years, the president of this nation has won the Most Admired Man contest conducted annually by the Gallup polls. The exceptions in 1967 and 1968 saw President Johnson lose out to former President Eisenhower. Mentioning this pattern of popular response to a recent conversation partner, I was informed that "If they were not the most admired men in the country they wouldn't have been elected president!" And his response is, I believe, a widely respected point of view in America. On the one hand we are always looking for reassurance that things will work out satisfactorily. On the other hand, we admire the dramatic actions of men in high places who are willing to take action, willing to cope with the exigencies of crisis and perplexity. Political scientist Murray Edelman writes quite lucidly about this problem:

And what symbol can be more reassuring than the incumbent of a high position who knows what to do and is willing to act, especially when others are bewildered and alone? Because such a symbol is so intensely sought, it will predictably be found in the person of any incumbent whose actions *can* be interpreted as beneficent.

A second explanation of recent textbook orthodoxy is unmistakenly related to the commercial and political values of most text writers. Market considerations are hard to ignore and several text authors unabashedly cite commercial remuneration as a major incentive. The "selling of a textbook" may not be unrelated to a book's function and ideological orientation.

Most textbook authors are motivated by the goal of training "good" citizens just as much as by the goal of instructing people about the realities of the highly competitive and often cruel world of national party and policy politics. But the training of citizens often seems to require a glossy, harmonious picture of national politics, which inspires loyalty but conflicts with reality. When this occurs, as one text writer told me, "the author almost invariably emphasizes citizen training, usually at the expense of instruction."

Building the Great Cathedral

A Franklin Roosevelt halo-effect characterizes most of the recent treatments of the presidency. Writers during the 1950's and well into the '60's were children or young adults during the Depression years. Not infrequently, they became enlisted in one way or another in executive branch service to help fight or manage World War II. These times were unusual in many ways—including an extraordinary amount of attention paid to the way in which President Roosevelt employed the powers of the presidency. Moreover, in the arena of national and international leadership, FDR upstaged all comers as he magnified the personal role and heroic style of a confident, competent leader in the context of tumultuous times. The mantle of world leadership was passing to the U.S., beginning what some writers refer to as the American Era. Understandably these developments, especially the dramaturgy of the New Deal presidency, affected soon-to-be written interpretations as well as popular images of the presidency.

A final reason for the textbook presidency lies in the very nature of the American political and electoral system. We elect a president by a small margin, but after election he is supposed to speak for *all* the people. Textbook and school norms suggest that one can vigorously question a presidential candidate, but after the election it is one's duty to be united behind the winner. It is as though the new president were the pilot of an aircraft with all of us as passengers, whether we like it or not. Hence, we all have a stake in his success.

To be sure, this institution of ritualistic unification serves a need: it absorbs much of the discontinuity and tension promoted in our often hectic and combative electoral campaigns. Then there is the typical first-year grace period in which serious criticism is generally considered off limits. This presidential honeymoon is characterized by an elaborate press build-up in which it appears as though we are trying to transform and elevate the quite mortal candidate into a textbook president.

Other methodological factors also contribute to idealized versions of presidential leadership. Overreliance on case studies of presidential behavior in relatively unique crises is part of the problem. Textbook compartmentalization of problems and institutions is yet another. Both the student and the average citizen may quite reasonably get the impression that national policy is almost entirely the product of a president and a few of his intimates, or alternately of a few select national officials along with the president's consent. Only the presidents can slay the dragons of crisis. And only Lincoln, the Roosevelts, Wilson, or men of that caliber can seize the chalice of opportunity, create the vision, and rally the American public around that vision. The end result may leave the student quite confused, if not ignorant, about the complex transactions, interrelationships, and ambiguities that more correctly characterize most national policy developments.

In all probability we pay a price, however unwittingly, for the way we have over-idealized the presidency. Although this price is difficult to calculate, I shall suggest some of the probable consequences of the textbook presidency—beginning with the dangers of our unwarranted expectations of the president's power and of his capacities as a spiritual reservoir.

Most Americans now believe, along with Theodore and Franklin Roosevelt's celebrated assertions, that the presidency is a "bully pulpit" and preeminently a place for moral leadership. Few of our citizenry wince at James Reston's observation that "the White House is the pulpit of the nation and the president is its chaplain." British Prime Minister Harold Macmillan, on the other hand, could quip, "If people want a sense of purpose, they should get it from their archbishops."

We are accustomed to regarding our "sense of purpose" and pious presidential pronouncements as nearly one and the same. Accordingly, Richard Nixon invoked God five times in his presidential inaugural and talked often of spirit and the nation's destiny: "To a crisis of the spirit, we need an answer of the spirit. . . . We can build a great cathedral of the spirit. . . . We have endured a long night of the American spirit. But as our eyes catch the dimness of the first rays of dawn, let us not curse the remaining dark, let us gather the light. . . . Our destiny offers not the cup of despair, but the chalice of opportunity."

But the trappings of religiosity, while temporarily ennobling the presidential personage, may run the risk of triggering unanticipated and undesirable consequences. Some presidents apparently feel the need to justify a particular strategy on the grounds that it is the moral and righteous course of action. But this moral emphasis can become elevated to overblown courses of behavior. For example, Wilson's attempts to help set up the League of Nations became imbued with a highly moralistic fervor, but the moral environment that generated the commitment was allowed to expand, as Wilson's own role as the nation's preacher expanded, until there was virtually no room for a political negotiator, a non-moralist Wilson to transform the idea into a reality. Perhaps Herbert Hoover's apolitical moral and ideological commitment to rugged individualism similarly inhibited alternative approaches in response to the Depression. Similarly, President Johnson's drumming up of moral and patriotic support for our Vietnam commitment probably weakened his subsequent efforts at negotiations in the languishing days of his Administration.

Part of the problem is related to the way campaigns are conducted and to the intensive hard sell—or at least "oversell"—seemingly demanded of candidates. Necessarily adopting the language of promise and sloganism, candidates and their publicists frequently pledge that they will accomplish objectives that are either near impossible or unlikely. Recall the early declaratory intentions of the War on Poverty, Model Cities, the Alliance for Progress, the war on behalf of safe streets, and an ambitious Nixon promise to underwrite "black capitalism."

The Cost of Elevation

The textbook presidency image may also influence the quality of civic participation. The moral-leader-to-layman relationship is quite often viewed as a one-way street. If the president is our national chaplain, how do we cultivate a democratic citizenry that is active and not passive, that may, on selective occasions, responsibly dispute this national moral eminence? Having been nurtured in the belief that presidents are not only benevolent but also personally powerful enough to end war, depression, and corruption, it is difficult for most average citizens to disagree strongly with their president, no matter what the circumstances. Students are instructed that it is proper to state one's differences in a letter to congressmen or even to the White House. But beyond these rather limited resources, the citizen-student is left alone and without a sense of personal efficacy. Due to the almost assured deference and relative lack of opposition, American presidents can expect at least a five-to-one favorable ratio in their telegram and mail response, and usually a three- or two-to-one ratio in national opinion poll responses about their handling of the presidency.

Most popular is the choice of quietly (if not silently) rallying around the president and offering him permissive support, hoping by such action to strengthen his and the nation's resolve against whatever real or apparent challenges confront the nation. Another pattern of behavior, that of apathy and indifference, is selected by sober citizens who feel secure in the belief that "presidents know best." Thus, a president can usually take it for granted that when major difficulties are faced, most Americans will support and trust him, at least for a while, often tendering him even increased support. It is difficult sometimes for Americans to differentiate between loyalty to president and loyalty to nation. As a result, presidential public support comes not only from those who feel the president is right, but is measurably inflated by those who, regardless of policy or situation, render support to their president merely because he is their president, or because he is the only president they have.

Few people are inclined to protest the actions of their president, but for those selecting to dissent, the textbook wisdom seems to encourage a direct personal confrontation with the president. If he alone is so powerful and independent, it appears logical to march on the White House, and, if necessary, "break" or "dump" the president in order to change policy. But this may be one of the least economical strategies, for, as we have seen, breaking or changing presidents does not ensure any major shift in the execution of national policies.

The point here is that on both sides of the presidential popularity equation his importance is inflated beyond reasonable bounds. On one side, there is a nearly blind faith that the president embodies national virtue and that any detractor must be an effete snob or a nervous nellie. On the other side, the president becomes the cause of all personal maladies, the originator of poverty and racism, inventor of the establishment, and the party responsible for a choleric national disposition.

If the textbook presidency image has costs for the quality of citizen relationships with the presidency, so also it can affect the way presidents conceive of themselves and their job. To be sure, the reverence and loyalty rendered to a new president are a rich resource and no doubt are somewhat commensurate with tough responsibilities that come along with the job. But, at the same time, an overly indulgent citizenry can psychologically distort the personal perspective and sense of balance. Former presidential press secretary George Reedy's acrimonious criticisms of the monarchial trapping of the contemporary White House deserve attention:

The atmosphere of the White House is calculated to instill in any man a sense of destiny. He literally walks in the footsteps of hallowed figures— of Jefferson, of Jackson, of Lincoln. . . . From the moment he enters the halls he is made aware that he has become enshrined in a pantheon of semi-divine mortals who have shaken the world, and that he has taken from their hands the heritage of American dreams and aspirations.

Unfortunately for him, divinity is a better basis for inspiration than it is for government.

The quality of advice, intelligence, and critical evaluation necessary to balanced presidential decision-making can also be adversely affected by too respectful an attitude towards the chief executive. If presidents become unduly protected or insulated, and if White House aides and Cabinet members tender appreciation and deference in exchange for status and accommodation, then the president's decision-making ability is clearly harmed.

The relatively sustained 15-year ascendency of the textbook presidency's idealized image of presidential leadership may be coming to an end. The general American public probably still believes in a version of the New Deal presidency caricature, but the near monopoly of this view is under challenge from a growing list of critiques of liberal presidential government. We are currently witnessing an apparent recrudescence of an interpretation of the presidency, which holds that no one national political leader can galvanize our political system toward the easy accomplishment of sustained policy change or altruistic goals.

Toward Revision

Contemporary policy studies suggest that the more we learn about presidential policy performance, the more it appears that presidents (in both domestic and foreign policy) only rarely accomplish policy "outcomes" that can be credited as distinct personal achievements. More realistically, the presidency serves as a broker for a few party priorities and as a strategically situated and important participant among vast numbers of policy entrepreneurs and policy-bearing bureaucrats. More often than not a president's personal policy views are essentially moderate and only vaguely refined. When in office, however, he finds himself constantly surrounded by people who have "high-energy" interest and investments in specific policy options. Both the president and these elites, however, are in turn surrounded by what Scammon and Wattenberg call the real majority—the large majority of American voters in the center.

In a sample of recent in-depth interviews with 30 White House staffers who served Presidents Kennedy and Johnson, I found that a majority of these presidential advisers feel that the president exercises selective or relatively little power over policy matters. There are some who say that "he [the president] has a lot of influence on those problems he is willing to spend time on," but more responded that "he has far less than people think he has, he is far more constrained than popularly thought." In fact, many even express the somewhat restrained and almost anti-textbook presidency view that presidents can accomplish a limited number of projects and hence should carefully measure their requests and energies. Emphasizing this point were the following two respondents:

I think the White House under Johnson was excessively activist—there was an impulsive need to do something about everything RIGHT NOW! There was always the feeling [given by the president] that we should fix this and fix that and do it now! Overall I think it went too far—there are definite costs and liabilities in that type of excessive aggressive activism. . . .

And a second staffer:

Except in times of emergencies, presidents cannot get much accomplished. . . . In some areas a president can have a psychological influence, a psychological effect on the nation, for example by speaking out on crime concerns. And in an eight-year period a president can start a shift of the budget and of the political system, but it takes a lot of pressure and a lot of time. Basically, the thing to remember is that a presidential intention takes a very long time to get implemented.

On balance, of course, it is true that under certain circumstances a president can ignite the nuclear destruction of a substantial portion of the world or commit U.S. troops into internationally troubled crisis zones. But the American president is in no better position to control Bolivan instability, Chilean Marxism, or Vietcong penetration into Cambodia than he can make the stock market rise or medical costs decline. It is misleading to infer from a president's capacity to drop an A-bomb that he is similarly powerful in most other international or domestic policy areas. The more we learn about the processes of government, the more it becomes apparent that presidents are rarely free agents when it comes to effecting new policies—or dismantling policies which they have inherited.

BRINGING ORDER OUT OF CHAOS *
JOHN FISCHER

The growth of the national government has taken place in piecemeal

* John Fischer, "Can the Nixon Administration Be Doing Anything Right?," Harper's Magazine, November, 1970, pp. 22–24, 30, 32, 34, 35, 37. Copyright © 1970 by Minneapolis Star and Tribune Co., Inc. Reprinted from the November, 1970 issue of Harper's Magazine by permission of the author.

fashion, with agencies and programs being added by fits and starts. The result is a sprawling bureaucracy with little coordination at the top. This bewildering assortment of agencies, rules, forms, and requirements has unnecessarily delayed worthy projects.

To cut through some of this red tape President Johnson established the Heineman task force to reorganize the government. Its recommendations have been implemented by President Nixon.

What evidence is advanced to prove that government is not working? What conflicting explanations for the failure are offered? Why does Fischer say that a corporation organized like the national government "would go bankrupt in a week"? Why have most city officials found it so difficult to get funds for urban projects? How did the Heineman group propose to decentralize and consolidate major programs? In what sense is Nixon carrying out the traditional conservative task?

The one thing that practically everybody in this fretfully divided country seems to agree on is that government isn't working very well. That probably is the only proposition which could gain the assent of William Buckley, John W. Gardner, and Mark Rudd. For at all levels, from city hall to the White House, government evidently is incapable of doing the things its citizens expect. It can't educate the kids who

need it most. It can't clean up the water we drink and the air we breathe. It can't solve the housing shortage. It can't keep the railroads running, or unsnarl our traffic jams, or stop the migration of poor people from farms to overcrowded cities. It can't train them for jobs once they get there. It can't stop the crime rate from climbing like an Apollo rocket, or even build decent jails to lock up the criminals when it catches them. It can't—oh, well, you know the litany, too.

Every day we get plenty of explanations for these failures. Mark Rudd, before he disappeared underground, proclaimed that we were witnessing the final collapse of a corrupt imperialist-fascist system. Buckley blames the feckless incompetence of the Liberal Establishment which has been running things (even if it doesn't realize it) for far too long. Nearly everyone, except Spiro and the shrinking remnants of his Noisy Minority, believes we are spending too much money on a hateful war, and not enough on the troubles in our own kitchen. Edward Banfield of Harvard in his brilliantly unfashionable book, *The Unheavenly City,* argues that we have come to expect government to do far more than *any* government actually can do—and the fact that England, Russia, China, and Cuba are plagued by much the same array of woes, from smog to juvenile delinquency, seems to bear him out.

Granted that the human condition is less than heavenly, and always has been, our government doesn't really have to be as cope-less as it is now. One of its faults is that it was not designed to do the things we demand of it—so a careful job of redesigning, such as Nixon seems to be attempting, quite possibly could make it work a good deal better. Another problem is the difficulty of getting first-rate men to work in the middle ranks of government. When they can be recruited, they seldom stay long—not simply because the pay is not competitive with executive salaries on the outside, but because of frustration. If the management structure can be redesigned so that they waste less time struggling with red tape and bickering with other agencies, then good people should be more willing to enlist for public service.

To one who inspects the working machinery of government closely, as I have been doing for the past few years, it sometimes is hard to believe that it was ever designed at all. If a corporation were organized like the federal Establishment, it would go bankrupt in a week.

During the past two decades, and especially during the Johnson Administration, hundreds of new programs were created to help cure a wide variety of social problems. Nobody knows precisely how many such programs there are, but the number certainly is more than a thousand. All of them were well-intentioned. They were meant to feed hungry people, to clear slums, build sewage plants, retrain un-skilled workers, upgrade police de-

partments, improve highways, finance better schools, and scores of other nice things.

To accomplish all this, the federal government usually offered money ($27 billion this fiscal year) to the states and their local communities, which were then expected to do the actual work. Each offer had a lot of strings attached—and these too were well-intentioned. To get money for housing, for example, or an industrial park or a new water system, a town had to come up with a comprehensive plan, and a sheaf of documents showing just how each project fitted into this plan. It also had to make frequent reports, so Washington could see how the money was being spent, and make sure that not too much of it was being wasted or stolen.

. . .

But things did not, to put it gently, work out exactly as intended. For each of these programs had been enacted piecemeal, with no relation to any of the others, and they were administered by scores of different agencies, most of them hardly on speaking terms. Each of these tied a separate set of strings on the money it was handing out, and demanded different kinds of reports on a bewildering assortment of forms. Often, too, they insisted on different sorts of "comprehensive plans," covering different geographic areas.

To make matters worse, few communities had anybody on the payroll capable of understanding all these federal requirements—much less the trained planners needed to carry them out. One result was a great scramble to hire planners, or consultants who claimed they knew how to deal with the feds. Anybody with the flimsiest credentials in the planning field could, and can still today, take his pick of jobs all over the country at remarkably good salaries.

Once a town laid its hands on a planner, of sorts, he usually found that the data needed to make a sound plan simply did not exist. Nobody had any figures, for instance, on local population trends, or job opportunities over the next ten years, or housing vacancies, or the probable demand for water in 1980. And it was likely that nobody had the remotest idea how to round up such figures. Consequently, many plans, applications for funds, and project justifications which went to Washington were highly imaginative. ("Great works of fiction," was the way Bob Weaver, former Secretary of Housing and Urban Development, described them to me, a little bitterly.) If a mayor couldn't find the numbers that those nuts in Washington demanded, he naturally made some up and hoped that the nuts would never notice.

But they did notice, usually, and sent the proposals back for revision. The upshot was that an urban-renewal project, for example, might take not months but years to wend its way back and forth through the dim corridors of bureaucracy. And by the time it finally got approved,

all too often, the federal money had run out.

When Lyndon Johnson began to understand the mess his Administration was in, he appointed a secret task force to tell him how to reorganize the government from top to bottom. Its leader was Ben W. Heineman, one of the country's most successful railway executives, and its membership included such high-powered characters as McGeorge Bundy, Robert McNamara, Mayor Richard C. Lee, Kermit Gordon, and several noted academic experts on administration.

On September 15, 1967, the Heineman group turned in its final report, stamped "Administratively Confidential." (It has never been released, but I managed to get hold of a copy—not, I would like to emphasize, from any member of the group.) It was crammed with shrewd analysis of the country's woes, and recommended bold surgery to cure them. It told the President how to reorganize his Cabinet and the White House staff, how to get a grip on the runaway bureaucracy. Among other things, it urged him to divide the country into ten federal regions, each with a single headquarters, to replace the "haphazard location of regional boundaries and offices."

The Heineman report also urged "far more decentralization of operational program decisions." Washington should concentrate on making policy, and the President's office should be beefed up so it could make sure that the big policies all pointed in the same direction. But the day-to-day responsibilities for carrying out these policies, through the states and local communities, ought to be handled in the field by "responsible federal officials—men who can make decisions and make them stick." When hassles arise among agencies, they should be settled on the spot—that is, within the ten regions—by "field representatives of the President's Office of Program Coordination." Caesar would have called them proconsuls.

All this, and much more in the Heineman report, made eminent sense. It followed the principles of organization used for decades by most successful big businesses. It also incorporated ideas which had been argued—futilely—by generations of management experts in the Budget Bureau, notably Sam Hughes and Dwight Ink. Johnson, I am told, recognized its merits— but in the end, he sent the report off to the archives and forgot about it. He was preoccupied with Vietnam and with rising unrest at home. Perhaps he was already thinking about his abdication. He also—according to pretty reliable White House gossip—didn't like the recommendation that some federal employees should be moved from Austin to a new regional headquarters in Dallas.

When Nixon took office, one of the few things to which he was clearly committed was more effective management of the govern-ment. He resurrected the Heineman report, and had it restudied by task forces of his own. Much of the recent reorganization of the White House staff and of key federal agencies shows a strong family resemblance to the changes originally suggested by the Heineman group.

And on May 21, 1969, he announced the establishment of ten federal regions. Their boundaries are not precisely the same as those recommended in the Heineman report, but the idea is identical. To the astonishment of many of his aides, and some key permanent civil servants, this order provoked little political flak—presumably because he made his move so soon after taking office, and so quietly that the opposition never got organized.

.   .   .

To begin with, the new regional system will apply only to three departments—HEW, HUD, and Labor—and two agencies—the Office of Economic Opportunity and the Small Business Administration. These are the outfits responsible for nearly all of the welfare and social programs, and they handle by far the biggest chunk of the federal budget, after the Department of Defense. Eventually other agencies dealing with economic and development problems —the Farmers Home Administration, for instance, and the Economic Development Administration—are expected to rearrange their field operations to conform. It is unlikely, however, that the provincial scheme will ever embrace all federal operations; there is no logical reason why the Coast Guard or the Forest Service, to name only a couple, need be fitted into the pattern.

Thanks to careful planning, the scheme was put into operation this fall with a minimum of commotion. Only about 2,300 federal employees had to move to the new headquarters cities. The most painful shift was that of some 420 HEW people from Charlottesville, Virginia, to Philadelphia; but the trauma was eased by compensating Charlottesville with a military installation. To my surprise, I found that it has not been necessary to put up new federal buildings in the provincial capitals; the new concentrations of staff have been accommodated by reshuffling existing offices and renting some space in privately owned buildings. I was also surprised to discover that all this regrouping is being carried through on schedule and should be virtually complete by the end of the year.

Already a regional council, made up of the ranking field officers of each of the agencies, is in operation in every one of the regional headquarters. It selects its own chairman, and meets as often as necessary to thrash out mutual problems. If Ned Breathitt were Governor of Kentucky today, he could meet all those people he needed to see in one place: Atlanta, Georgia.

. . .

Even at this early date the regional councils and a few other closely linked changes in management are beginning to show results. The most spectacular has been to cut in half the time it takes to process a local application for federal money. In some cases, the speedup has been even greater; HUD used to take an average of 96 days to produce a "yes" or "no" to a mayor's request for a rehabilitation loan—but now it is able to make up its collective mind in an average of five days.

Bales of red tape also have been shorn away, though not yet nearly enough. HUD used to require a city seeking urban-renewal money to submit 286 specific items of information, many of which it didn't really need and which the city often could not honestly provide. By cutting out 137 of these items, it has relieved its local applicants of nearly 800,000 pages a year of useless paperwork. HEW has dropped 14 of its required reports and simplified 18 more, thus saving 351 man-years of work annually. And so on through a long list of agencies.

Such achievements may sound picayune to a college militant; but in fact they are significant steps toward one of his proclaimed goals —to make government more responsive and less inhuman. To a harried mayor, trying desperately to hold his city together, it is a great boon to be able to go to his regional council and get a quick answer to his problems—not merely from one federal agency, but from all of them which might be able to help.

Both in this country and in England the traditional job of governments of the left—Liberal, Labor, or Democratic—has been to make innovations. Governments of the right—Tory or Republican—have then come along and tidied up. However bitterly they may despise the latest innovations, whether the income tax or social security, the conservative regimes almost never repeal them. Instead they usually make them work better. They find the flaws which the liberals, in their headlong enthusiasm for change, inevitably overlooked; they patch and tinker and overhaul the clanking machinery of government.

This is natural, for conservatives by temperament are concerned with the arts of management—which the liberals and radicals usually hold in contempt. The managerial reforms which the Nixon Administration is now attempting will never stir up excitement on the campus; indeed, I know of very few professors of government, much less students, who have any interest in them. But they may be about the best we can expect from this Administration. And in the end, they may be far from negligible.

REFORMING THE REGULATORY AGENCIES *

PHILIP ELMAN

Regulatory agencies were originally created to handle problems that seemed to be beyond the grasp of either Congress or the President —policing the securities markets, determining airline routes, fixing rail rates.

In this capacity they were given legislative, executive and judicial powers. Eighty years of experience has shown that the underlying theory justifying such agencies needs to be reexamined.

What would Mr. Elman recommend concerning the judicial powers of such bodies? How would he streamline agency membership? How could a commissioner be removed? What functions would the agency retain? What advantages does Mr. Elman claim for the one man commission?

Today, when all institutions of government are being found wanting, none has been more criticized—and less responsive to such criticism— than the independent regulatory

* Philip Elman, "The Need For Reform of the Regulatory Agencies," Washington Post, August 15, 1970. Reprinted by permission of the author.

commission. With monotonous regularity, studies and reports appear in an unending procession, all saying essentially the same things. While the criticisms cover a very broad ground, the most fundamental deficiency has been found to be the agencies' chronic failure to fulfill their unique quasi-legislative function of developing and implementing regulatory policies responsive to public needs and the public interest. With each new study and report, there is the same ritual call for better appointments and improved administration. Yet the agencies go on essentially unchanged and seemingly undisturbed, with little evidence of basic improvement in performance.

Without a doubt, the theory underlying the independent regulatory commission was original and brilliant. It emphasized the agency's independence; its ability to bring expert judgment to bear upon technical and complex economic issues; its insulation from political partisan control; its capacity to provide both continuity and flexibility of policy; and its blending in a single tribunal of a wide range of powers and functions, from general rule-making to case-by-case adjudication, permitting the agency to exercise broad discretion in choosing the best tool for dealing with a particular problem.

It is almost a century, however, since the Interstate Commerce Commission, the grandfather of the federal agencies, was created in 1887. We must now look to experience more than theory.

Experience shows, I believe, that the independent multimember regulatory commission suffers from the defects of its virtues. Independence, collective deliberation and decision-making, and fusion of powers and functions in a single agency, are all useful values in the administrative process; but we have pushed them too far, relying too much on the pure simplicities of the original theory and neglecting the lessons of actual experience. It is time for radical structural reform. . .

The context of agency deliberation and decision-making differs markedly from court adjudication. But the solution is not to judicialize the administrative process further, or to seek the appointment of "better" commissioners who will make better agency judges. Agency members are not, and should not be, selected for their judicial qualities; and the institutional environment in which they work does not nourish the development of such qualities . . .

In short, agency members will become better regulators if we no longer expect them to act as judges as well as administrators. We should not require conscientious agency members to shoulder the irreconcilable burdens of both vigorously prosecuting and fairly judging in the same case. Those suspected of violating the law should indeed be proceeded against with vigor and dispatch; but the agency should prosecute its cases in an impartial and disinterested judicial tribunal . . .

Thus, while I have long held to the opposite view, I am now convinced that we will lose nothing, and gain much, by eliminating from agencies like the Federal Trade Commission the function of case-by-case adjudication of alleged violations of law. This function should be transferred either to the district courts or, preferably, to a new trade court which is decentralized and holds hearings in every state, thus bringing the judicial phase of the regulatory process much closer to the people . . .

Relieved of its adjudicative responsibilities, the agency's remaining functions should be vested in a single commissioner serving at the pleasure of *both* the President and Congress, and removable by either. This would permit the public to hold both the President and Congress accountable for an agency's continued failures or poor performance.

I do not offer this proposal as a panacea for all agency ills. Nor do I suggest that it is without risks and dangers. On the positive side, however, elimination of the adjudicative function will enable an agency to concentrate its resources on a single central objective; the development and enforcement of regulatory policies carrying out the statutory mandate . . .

Centralizing full authority and responsibility for an agency's activities in a single administrator will unquestionably facilitate the development and formulation of regulatory policy. It will also lighten the burden of fashioning comprehensive and coordinated national policies in those areas where other government agencies or departments have overlapping responsibilities.

Moreover, an agency should be no less independent, in the best sense of the term, because it is under the leadership of a single man. The agency should be required to develop regulatory policies that are truly non-partisan and responsive to public and consumer needs, and not to those of special interest pleaders. By increasing its visibility and accountability to the public, the proposed change in structure should result in a far greater degree of agency responsiveness than now exists.

Admittedly, having only one man in charge may make it easier to exert political pressures on him, bad as well as good. I do not wish to overstate the case, but it seems clear that the present structure of the agencies has failed to insulate them from improper influences, while the proposed change at least offers the hope of increased responsiveness to consumer needs and the broad public interest. Nor do I see any reason why a policy-making government regulator should be appointed for a long term of years, and not be removable from office despite continued public dissatisfaction with his performance . . .

If Congress, the President, or the public is disappointed with an agency's performance, there should be one man upon whom attention can focus and from whom immediate improvement can be sought. We cannot do that with the independent regulatory commissions today; and both they and the public suffer from it.

With a single man given full authority and responsibility for an agency's activities, it should be easier to attract "better" men. A President will be more reluctant to appoint incompetent commissioners for their failure will be his failure; their incompetence will be his embarrassment; continuing them in office, despite poor performance, will be his responsibility . . .

It is perhaps unnecessary to say, in conclusion, that no reforms in the structure of the regulatory agencies will succeed unless there also are radical changes in the climate of government and the political processes. As John W. Gardner has said, "Our political and governmental processes have grown so unresponsive, so ill-designed for contemporary purposes, that they waste the taxpayers' money, mangle good programs, and smother every good man who comes into the system . . . Sooner or later, someone is going to have to tackle the central structures of our society or it isn't going to work." We must institutionalize the means whereby the public may become aware of, and participate in, political and governmental processes that affect the quality of all our lives. We must open wide the doors and windows of government agencies, so that the public may see for itself what is or is not being done, and demand an accounting from those in charge.

THE LEGISLATOR
AS ERRAND BOY *
RICHARD A. SNYDER

All legislators play a variety of roles. In one sense they are law-makers, converting the will of the people into statutes. In another sense they are reduced to errand boys, at the beck and call of every district voter. In fact some senior legislators owe their survival to their zealous concern for the personal needs of constituents.

Why do so many citizens need help? What ceremonial role does the legislator play? How can he "go to bat" for his district? In what sense is he an official "greeter"? A party promoter? Is

* Reprinted from Richard A. Snyder, "The Legislator As Errand Boy," Wall Street Journal, December 23, 1970, by permission.

*a legislative service office desirable?
Could the errand boy role be
replaced by an ombudsman? How
would smaller legislatures and
bigger staffs decrease pressures?
How realistic is it to propose that
constituents make fewer requests
of legislators?*

"Dear Senator: We are working on
a class project and would appreciate your views on all issues. Sincerely. . . ."

Few requests to state lawmakers
are as all-embracing as the student's
letter quoted above, but the appeals flowing into state capitols are
mounting in number, variety and
complexity. A legislator traditionally runs errands for constituents,
but now errands threaten to crowd
out of his day the constitutional
duty that should come first: Making
laws.

As bureaucracy in the state government grows, the number of mis-
handled matters increases, sending
more frustrated citizens to their
lawmaker to unsnarl their problems. While no constitution places
this duty upon him, he does not
turn his back for two reasons: He
may indeed be the only person in
a position to help, and his own re-
election may depend upon those
who remember him kindly.

This rising tide puts the 6,398
state legislators elected in 1970 on
a collision course, for these personal missions come at the time
when the state itself is expanding
into more areas, and legislatures
have more bills and longer sessions.

It poses a hard choice between the
sworn duty to legislate and the
political need to run errands.

The impending crunch points up
the contrast between the civics text
legislator and the flesh-and-blood
legislator. In the textbook, he
studies bills and resolutions in soli-
tude (Sunday afternoons are best);
scans promotional material and
then seeks the Best Judgment
Available from experts, scientists
and even a few professors. The pros
and cons are weighed. Prayerful
contemplation precedes the decision. A position once decided upon,
the advocacy phase follows. In
Walter Mitty manner, the lawmaker
argues before committee and caucus, and finally on the floor of the
Senate or House itself.

In real life it is somewhat different. More likely, the lawmaker
sleeps Sunday afternoon, exhausted
by the previous evening spent
judging a Halloween parade in the
rain or dedicating new bowling
alleys. He doubles as Santa Claus
by passing out state highway maps
(popular with service stations),
commissioning notaries public, dispensing copies of game laws to
sportsmen, and the like.

The ceremonies and give-aways
are the icing on the cake, pleasant
and comforting, despite the danger
that the icing will engulf the cake
and the table and floor as well. Less
appealing is the train of complaints
and pleas for help: A lost paycheck,
an unexplained cut in pension, delay in sending a birth certificate,
admission to a state hospital, or a
parole for a prisoner.

Going to Bat and Bandwagons

The lawmaker gets to more substantive matters when he "goes to bat for the district"—plugging for a new highway; a dining hall for a state college, upgrading a park, attracting an industry. These matters affect whole communities or the economy of the area, and time is well spent. His weapon is the power to appropriate funds, and to a degree this is lawmaking, or state management. For the same reason, he has a sort of "overseer" duty on administration of the state's affairs, and sounds forth boldly on malfeasance.

Promotional activity for himself or party chews further into his time. A great deal is spent climbing onto bandwagons or quietly abandoning them. Then too, women's groups and pupils visit the capital; it would be churlish not to greet them. His political party enjoys a priority on his time, and if it wants a job for old Joe Faithful, the lawmaker tries to accommodate.

A day's mail is varied: "Please get the Governor to greet our convention." (Relayed, without hope.) Copy of beauty culture law wanted. (Sent.) "Please fix driver's license suspension." (Tactfully declined.) Complaint of sharp business practice. (Referred to Consumer Protection Bureau.) Plea regarding mental patient. (Inquiry made.) Passport request. (Federal matter— referred to Congressman.) Invitation to ground-breaking. (Accepted.) Vietnam GI asking for state flag. (Sent.)

Missions are as varied as the constituency. On behalf of a gifted artist who lives in his district, the legislator urges the state museum to display the artist's abstract paintings. Later he seeks more commercial space at the state farm show for an implement dealer's manure-spreaders. All in one day.

Many requests are quasi-legal. Can "they" cancel my auto insurance? Can I get a sales tax refund? Must our little town chlorinate its water? Can you get me excused from jury duty? They want us to widen the doors of our nursing home by six inches; must we? German lady wants to take hairdressing course; is an alien eligible for license?

Indulgences from regulations are asked, and there is no end of "hard cases." One tall young man sought to be a state police recruit, but exceeded the standard by a half-inch. (Exception granted.) A public swimming pool was built in error, being several inches too shallow. (Exception denied.) "If you can help my constituent, I'd appreciate it," the legislator pleads to the bureaucrat almost automatically, but it is wise to add: "Provided you feel it isn't contrary to public policy."

Correspondence concerning pending bills is wholly different and should be encouraged. Every citizen can help his government by expressing his views, preferably without profanity, promises or threats, and especially with information the legislator might otherwise lack. Many a slick trick has been foiled by discovery of a "sleeper" in pending bills after a concerned citizen sounded the alarm.

A letter is indeed the most artful way to get a point of view stated to a public official. It does not require him to scribble notes. It gives him time to weigh his answer if one is needed. It helps build his file on the subject. Some writers have the gift of coupling their advice with kindly words, and the recipient, like Mark Twain, can live two months on a good compliment.

There is a school of thought that contends the lawmakers bring errands on themselves. One rural representative in an Eastern state has made a specialty of delivering his voters' auto license plates, even though procurement would be more efficient by mail. Each week he arrives at the capitol with sheafs of applications and checks; he trudges home weighed down with stacks of metal tags. In adjoining counties the legislators do none of this, never having encouraged the custom.

One device of legislators is to open a "service office" in the home district and formalize the routine. In best professional manner the lawmaker advises on fractured pocketbook, sprained vanity or other "illness" that plague the caller. In the process the consultant absorbs some of his constituents' thinking. Cost prevents much of this, since few states supply funds for home offices. Too, some visitors have no sense of time when provided with a free listener and make a prisoner of the legislator, thereby discouraging others who are waiting.

The service-office device has a more fundamental weakness. A lawmaker's primary duty is still to make laws and, while it entrenches his security by doing favors, it necessarily subtracts from the time spent on the issues. By stressing personal service rather than public interest, it depreciates the fact that what matters in a legislator is judgment, and the hope of our system still lies in those who have it.

Whether the lawmakers invite extra burdens or find them thrust upon them, the state suffers because proposed laws are not scrutinized as they should be. Many a quick decision is made in committee, with members comfortably assuming that someone else has done the homework. Speaker Sam Rayburn is reputed to have said: "When two people agree, one of them isn't thinking." Slipshod laws bring the matter into the courts, with innocent litigants paying the costs. In other instances, policy is developed by default; it is always easier to do nothing.

Four Suggestions

What would get lawmakers back to lawmaking? Four possibilities present themselves:

1. A state ombudsman. This novelty from Scandinavia is being tried in Hawaii, founded on the theory that the public would have a friend on a formalized basis. The hazard is that it would merely create a new layer of bureaucracy,

and the legislators would soon be importuned to ride herd on the ombudsman.

2. Smaller legislatures, with longer terms and higher pay. Greater prestige would discourage the citizenry from seeking trivial favors. Solons might even wear togas again, in the classic Roman tradition. (Judges wear robes, don't they?) The public would be giving up its tether, however, since an official is less responsive to his public if his re-election year is remote.

3. Bigger staff. Except for committee chairmen in larger states, legislators have pitifully little research and administrative help. Many even lack secretaries, and some pen out their correspondence by hand. Congress has solved this with more office help, including human bulldogs and bloodhounds who know how to chase down evasive bureaucrats. Sophisticated and resourceful, these aides know the government and get results.

4. Help from the political structure. This would reverse the maxim about coming to the aid of the party. If the party of the lawmaker maintained a year-round headquarters, staffed and able, it could take the burden of many non-legislative errands. Tammany furnished a ton of coal or a bail bond in the old days. The trouble with that was that the followers of the opposition party had no place to go. If each party kept a "service office" for advice, help and errands, it would serve most of the voting population, but the impoverished party treasuries

at the local level would preclude this in the foreseeable future.

Until a utopian society becomes a reality, constituents could help by addressing fewer requests to their lawmakers, and the lawmakers could help by not encouraging requests that will take them away from their most important work.

THE GREENING OF CONGRESS *

WES BARTHELMES

Optimists are inclined to believe that it is always darkest just before the dawn. The case against Congress is so massive that one can easily conclude that it is a lost cause. But Mr. Barthelmes believes that a tide of reform is running.

What hope does he find in the present membership of the House? What reforms are contained in the recently-enacted "legislative reorganization" bill? What new attitudes exist toward seniority? Why is it unrealistic to expect Congress to

* Reprinted from Wes Barthelmes, "The Greening of Congress," Nation, November 30, 1970, by permission.

reform itself? What role can the average citizen play?

Institutionally, Congress appears to be an incurable mess. Its committees grind out piecemeal or contradictory legislation dealing with festering domestic problems. The rules and procedures of the Senate and the House exacerbate the problem by fragmenting the legislative agendas. There are other handicaps, the most notorious of which is seniority. Unlike any other public or private institution, the House, and to a lesser degree the Senate, cling to the custom of seniority as the exclusive factor in determining the distribution of committee assignments and promotions to chairmanships. They behave as though they thought seniority were written into the Bill of Rights, though in fact it first afflicted the Congress only at the beginning of this century. . . .

These disabilities have generated a set of power relationships that has debilitated the Congress and increased the susceptibility of the Presidency to "Caesarism." However, there's some hope to be found in this deplorable situation. Congress, in respect to its guardianship of the commonweal, may indeed resemble a Tower of Putty, but an extraordinary number of capable legislators have been elected by both major parties to the Senate and the House in recent years— and the trend was continued in this month's general election. That

much scorned body, the House, may now contain more able and conscientious members than it has ever before numbered in its uneven history. This heartening condition is a consequence of the elections of the 1960's, especially those of 1964 and 1966. Sixty percent of the 435 members of the House were elected for the first time within the last ten years—a hopeful portent for a national legislature that knows how to legislate and for what, and when *not* to legislate.

The new members are not exactly exponents of Theodore Roszak's "counter-culture," but they do represent a marked generational break with the waxwork political traditions that hold the House in bondage to the plunderers. Moreover, the new members arrive as needed reinforcements to the lonely Luthers, such as Richard Bolling of Missouri, who for years have publicly denounced unseemly emoluments, the sale of political indulgences and benefices, and the spread of institutional corruption.

One tangible result of this influx of newcomers has been the passage of a "legislative reorganization" bill —the first in twenty-five years. The House labored for months and finally delivered the bill in late September. The Senate approved it in early October. It is a modest accomplishment, but the word "modest" takes on a brighter meaning in an institution that has come to welcome inertia as a virtue.

The bill does not remedy inadequacies, such as the loophole-ridden lobbying registration act and other grimy aspects of money-and-politics. Nor does it authorize the tools, such as computers, needed to examine effectively the Presidential budgets. And, particularly, it does not offer a basis for unifying the badly fragmented appropriation process. But the bill does provide fairer committee representation and discussion time for members of the minority party, a slightly better public view into the interior of the legislative star chambers where the national interest is salvaged, and an end to the unrecorded "teller vote," behind which members have been able to hide from their constituents.

Nevertheless, despite better members and the new bill, the Congressional whole is less, not greater, than the sum of its parts. One major reason is that new members and their senior allies are enveloped in a fog of rules, procedures and folkways that permits a handful of outdated oligarchs—committee chairmen and politically appointed staff members—to determine Congressional priorities and schedules. Is a draft-repeal measure to be discussed on the House floor? No, for Rep. L. Mendel Rivers, Armed Services Committee chairman, is opposed. Is the SST appropriation to be submitted to thorough scrutiny? No, for the aerospace bloc won't permit it. Etc., etc. The committee chairmen, whom seniority has boosted into their safe perches, are seldom accountable to any one as they decide which bills to schedule for hearings, which witnesses to

summon, and how long to continue the hearings. In addition, new members and their senior allies find themselves elected to an institution still laboring under a stifling "go-along to get-along" life style imposed by the late Sam Rayburn of Texas, longest reigning Speaker in the history of the House. Distributive politics, which flourished under Rayburn, gave obedient members access to the annual public-works pork barrel and thus reduced the likelihood of mutiny. This onerous atmosphere has been slightly dissipated because Rayburn's successor, John McCormack of Massachusetts, does not possess the habit of command that would have enabled him to perpetuate the repressive Rayburn style. Now McCormack's retirement in January, after nine years as Speaker, is opening a brutal struggle to fill key Democratic leadership positions. The outcome will fix the pattern of the House for the 1970's.

. . .

Seniority is not a way of life its beneficiaries would relinquish without a struggle. The historian C. Vann Woodward has suggested that acceptance of reform by incumbents in key positions would require the "greatest wholesale forswearing of privilege and prerogative since the Tennis Court Oath during the French Revolution."

Yet the proposal to lessen the grip of seniority is not without support. An authoritative publication, *Congressional Quarterly*, recently reported that among incumbent

House members 73 percent of Republicans and 58 percent of Democrats indicate a willingness to modify the custom. Republicans are more receptive and may actually modify seniority as it applies to themselves in their own caucus next January. Democrats, having become entrenched in the seats of power as members of the majority party in the House for thirty-six of the last forty years, are obviously less enthusiastic.

But those working for reform within the House need help from outside. The earlier reference to Luther is not irrelevant. Just as the medieval Papacy, caught in its own bureaucratic and financial machinery, could not be reformed from within, so the Congress can reform itself only with outside assistance and support. Friends of popular government, battered by assaults from Left and Right, should rally in Nader-like numbers.

The commonality of Americans has rested on a belief in popular government. This has enabled them to carry the functions of government beyond the classic ones of preventing crime and enforcing contracts to those urgent tasks of cushioning or eliminating the brutal aspects of industrialization in a mass democracy. During 180 years of nationhood, this core belief has survived episodic political corruption, economic devastations, a civil war, and even the disenfranchisement of minority groups. But in the mid-20th century, the national legislature, within which popular government is thought to function, is not working. The procedural and power deformations of the Congress produce an inability to solve or make manageable our crisis of unresolved neglects. As the new Congress now stands, each new legislative output merely compounds the problems, making each increasingly intractable.

As a result, the faith in popular government, as measured by the effectiveness of ameliorative legislation, is being undermined. The next phase, as Charles Reich points out in *The Greening of America*, is for Americans to dismiss politics as a way of changing "the system." The country churns with change, but the Congress, protected by custom, privilege and institutional malfunctioning, has been the last to acknowledge the tumult. It risks becoming a marginal institution in American life.

Yet a fundamental reform of this flawed and faded institution is not beyond reasonable expectations. The House is a logical and necessary place to begin. The Senate has its problems, but its relatively loosely woven procedures and rules, administered by a more modern leadership, enable a Church-Cooper amendment or a poverty amendment to be discussed on the floor and voted on, despite recalcitrant chairmen. In the House, this possibility is almost extinguished.

However, reform cannot be accomplished without a broad aggressive alliance of supportive House members and organizations such as the student-based Movement for a

New Congress, the National Committee for an Effective Congress, and John Gardner's Common Cause. . . .

. . .

Americans have organized "strikes for peace" and "walks from hunger." Now we should organize a "run for reform." Reform of the Congress is too important to be left to its members.

SEEKING QUALITY
ON THE HIGH COURT *
EDWARD F. CUMMERFORD

Who should serve on the Supreme Court? What criteria should be used in selection? Since judges are appointed for life and their decisions may have far-reaching effects, these are vital questions. In recent years the prestige of the Court has suffered. The selection process has become a partisan political donneybrook. President Johnson withdrew two nominations in the face of Senate hostility: two

* Reprinted from Edward F. Cummerford, "Seeking Quality On the High Court," Wall Street Journal, January 13, 1971, by permission.

of President Nixon's nominees were rejected. One justice resigned under a cloud of charges; the activities of another prompted a House investigation.

What qualities have the great justices had? Can we expect to secure many such justices when the recruitment process is steeped in partisan politics? What alternate process does Mr. Cummerford propose? Would his suggestion further divorce the Court from the democratic process?

On June 2, 1941, Charles Evans Hughes sent a brief note to the White House, advising President Roosevelt that he was about to retire as Chief Justice of the United States. Thus was brought to a close one of the most distinguished careers in public life that this country has yet known—Governor of New York, Associate Justice of the Supreme Court, Republican candidate for President in the cliffhanger election of 1916, Secretary of State and, finally, Chief Justice. From the standpoint of efficient and harmonious administration of the High Court, Hughes has never been equalled. He left the bench a few weeks later and, from that day to this, no one of his stature as a jurist has sat upon the Supreme Court.

While there have been able men on the Court in late years, it seems clear that the Supreme Court has been steadily sliding downhill in the esteem of the American people.

Its prestige at present is at a low ebb indeed. Recently one Justice was virtually forced to resign after disclosures reflecting upon his ethics, while impeachment action against another was initiated in the House of Representatives. The quality of judges in our highest court is a topic of vital current interest.

Power of the Judges

And well it should be, when we reflect upon the great power possessed by these judges. Having the final say on what the Constitution means, they can nullify Federal, state and local laws. They can override actions of high government officials, even thwart the President himself. They sit for life, or until they choose to retire, and only they make that decision. True, they can be impeached, but as a practical matter this is next to impossible. They answer to no constituents and run in no elections. Public opinion polls trouble them not.

Should not men in whom such awesome powers repose represent the very finest judicial talent obtainable? We may shout a resounding "yes," but the sad fact is that top quality judges have been rare on the Supreme Court, and great ones even rarer. The mediocrities have predominated.

How shall we recruit the ablest jurists for the High Court and strain out mediocrities and second-raters? First of all, we must have criteria of general validity for recognizing top quality. Even lawyers do not always agree on the ability of judges. It is all too human to look favorably upon the judge who shares your views or decides in your favor. One man's distinguished jurist may be another's political hack.

I believe it is possible to isolate and identify some elements of greatness. The best way to start is to study the great judges. Probably the three ablest men who have sat upon the Supreme Court in this century were Chief Justice Hughes, who has already been mentioned, Justice Oliver Wendell Holmes, who served from 1902 to 1932, and Justice Benjamin N. Cardozo, who sat from 1932 until 1938. I have noted at least five distinct qualities in each man, although of course each had his own special method and individual style.

First, each had an unusually brilliant intellect, which is fine equipment to start off with in any calling.

Second, they were all profound scholars—men who loved learning and pursued it all through their lives. Hughes was said to have read all of Shakespeare at a tender age, while Holmes at 90 was studying Thucydides. They were thoroughly versed in history, literature, philosophy and the other disciplines that make for a truly cultured person. They were scholars in an age when "scholar" meant more than being able to toss around words like "dichotomy" and "vis-à-vis."

Third, they really understood law in all of its practical and theoretical aspects. They comprehended its origins, history and development. As one of my law professors observed years ago, before one proclaims what the law ought to be, he should first know what it is. All three produced scholarly works on various phases of law. Holmes is probably the most frequently quoted judge of all time. Cardozo elevated legal writing to a level of quality and style never surpassed. Lawyers have an adjective, "Cardozoesque," to describe especially fine legal writing. All three were realists, not ivory tower dreamers.

Fourth, they were proven successes before they went on the Supreme Court. Hughes, in addition to his public career, was one of the most successful lawyers of his time, as brilliant in front of the bench as he was upon it. Holmes had been Chief Justice of Massachusetts, where his outstanding opinions attracted national attention. Cardozo was Chief Judge of New York's top tribunal, the Court of Appeals, where he wrote many landmark decisions.

Fifth, they kept politics and ideology out of the judicial process. Holmes and Cardozo were never active in politics to any extent. Hughes, while very much in politics at some periods of his life, absolutely barred political considerations from his work as a judge.

While they had well defined philosophies of their own about law, government and life in general, they did not assume that the law must conform to their personal viewpoints, as do the contemporary "judicial activists." They developed and shaped law, but did not try to make it over in their own images. (The five elements were also to be found in the greatest non-Supreme Court judge, Learned Hand, who sat in the Federal Appeals Court in New York for many years and was called "the Tenth Supreme Court Justice."

On the surface, great judges and mediocre ones function very much alike. Any judge can say "affirmed" or "reversed" and write a few paragraphs to justify his position. He can even have his law clerk, who may be a summa cum laude graduate, write for him, with sparkling phrases and clever quotations.

A Link to the Future

But the window-dressing is soon revealed for what it is. The great judges are discovered and appreciated. The great judge understands all the elements in a case and places them in proper perspective. In well reasoned opinions, he analyzes the law, past and present, and forges a link to the future. Styles may differ, but the substance is basically the same. He may be forceful and direct like Hughes, terse and epigrammatic like Holmes or lofty and eloquent like Cardozo. The mediocre judge merely decides cases in exchange for a paycheck; the great judge develops and shapes the law. One plods along in the valley; the other climbs the mountain and sees the broadest possible panorama.

I turn now to the problem of recruiting the superior man (or woman) for the Supreme Court. The existing method, by which the

President selects the nominee, subject to Senate confirmation, is wretchedly unsatisfactory. When the nation was young, the Founding Fathers viewed the Senate as a body of elder statesmen, acting always wisely, with the highest interests of the nation in mind. They did not foresee that someday Senators would be elected by direct popular vote and thus subject to all the pressures and exigencies of partisan politics. Nor, perhaps, did they foresee that Presidents might not always choose the best men but might place their cronies on the High Court, or use such appointments to repay political debts.

The recent Haynesworth and Carswell debacles point up the problem vividly. These men were involved in a swirl of ideological controversy in a debate that went well beyond considerations of their ability. The reasons proferred by some Senators for voting as they did were not the real reasons.

Few people realize that such bitter episodes have happened before. Even Charles Evans Hughes was subjected to venomous attacks in the Senate as a "tool of big business" when he was nominated for Chief Justice in 1930. The charge was ludicrous, but Senate "giants" like Carter Glass, William E. Borah, George W. Norris and Burton K. Wheeler joined in the attack. Despite the man's overwhelming qualifications and magnificent record, 26 votes were cast against him.

The same year, Federal Appeals Court Judge John J. Parker, of South Carolina, was rejected for the Supreme Court after labor and civil rights groups mounted a tremendous campaign against him. Judge Parker, who died in 1958, was considered one of the most outstanding jurists ever to sit on the Federal bench.

A Nerve-Racking Ordeal

When able jurists must undergo scurrilous attacks on the Senate floor, when their every written or spoken word is challenged in a brutal inquisition, when their integrity is impugned, when they are viciously assailed in editorials and cruelly caricatured in cartoons and when they and their families are made to endure a nerve-racking ordeal lasting weeks or months, they may conclude it is just not worth it—and leave the Supreme Court to mediocrities.

The Constitution should be amended to eliminate politics from Supreme Court appointments. Instead of Senate confirmation, there should be a Council on Judicial Appointments. This brief article does not permit much detail on how it would work, but in essence it would be a body composed of the leaders of the legal profession, including eminent retired judges, the president of the American Bar Association, deans of leading law schools and attorneys of outstanding repute. This council would furnish the President a list of, say, a dozen names of the best qualified potential justices, based on ability and experience, with politics kept out so far as is humanly possible. For obvious reasons, the list would be kept secret.

The President would choose from that list. The final choice would be his, but we would be assured that it would be a top-quality legal mind. Mediocrities and second-rates would be effectively strained out.

In a few years we would see a dramatic improvement in the quality of the Supreme Court.

JUDICIAL SELF-RESTRAINT AND THE BURGER COURT *
JULIUS DUSCHA

The history of the Supreme Court can be told in capsule fashion by reviewing the philosophies of a half dozen Chief Justices. The appointment of Chief Justice Burger in 1969 marked the end of judicial activism under Chief Justice Earl Warren. The new Chief Justice publicly announced his support of judicial self-restraint, with a de-emphasis on political innovation.

* *Reprinted from Julius Duscha, "If It Doesn't Make Good Sense, How Can It Make Good Law?" New York Times Magazine, October 5, 1969 by permission. Copyright © 1969 by The New York Times Company.*

How can the Chief Justice (with a single vote) give direction to the Court? What kind of a person is Burger? How does he interpret "judicial self-restraint"? Why would he have questioned the reapportionment decision? What reservations does he have over the Warren decisions on criminal law? Who are Burger's most vocal critics?

Like his eight colleagues on the Supreme Court, the Chief Justice has only one vote, but, as Earl Warren and other strong Chief Justices have demonstrated, the Chief Justice can be far more than the first among equals. The Chief Justice leads the discussions at the weekly meetings where the Justices decide what cases to consider and vote on cases that have been argued, and the way the Chief Justice handles these sessions can have an effect on their outcome. When the Chief Justice is in the majority, he can decide who should write the Court's opinion. The Chief Justice is also the principal administrative officer of the entire Federal Court system.

The Supreme Court cannot be led by even a strong Chief Justice, of course, unless there are at least four Justices ready to go along with him, but Burger ought to have such a following on many key issues. He is an advocate of judicial restraint who believes that the Supreme Court should choose cautiously the issues it will deal with, and that most controversial political, social and economic issues should be handled by Congress and by the President. (Earl Warren, on the other hand, looked on the Court as an activist institution that should be part of the progressive, reformist tradition of American life.)

. . .

During the campaign last year, Nixon said that the Supreme Court ought to interpret existing laws rather than "breaking through into new areas that are really the prerogative of the Congress." He also said that he would appoint to the Court men who believed in a strict interpretation of the Court's role and who were thoroughly conversant with the problems of criminal law and would strengthen "the peace forces as against the crime forces in this country."

In Burger, the President seems to have got the kind of man he wanted. During his years on the Court of Appeals, Burger took a judicial-restraint or strict-constructionist view of the role of the courts. ("There is no reason why we as judges should regard ourselves as some kind of Guardian Elders ordained to revise the political judgments of elected representatives of the people.") Burger also is on the side of "the peace forces." ("Guilt or innocence becomes irrelevant in the criminal trial as we flounder in a morass of artificial rules poorly conceived and often impossible of application.")

. . .

Although he is an advocate of judicial restraint, Burger comes to the Supreme Court out of the same progressive Midwestern political atmosphere that produced Hubert Humphrey, Eugene McCarthy and Harold Stassen as well as Robert M. LaFollette Sr. and George Norris of another generation. Burger is no reformer in the tradition of a Humphrey or a LaFollette, but as a young lawyer in St. Paul he was an early supporter of Harold Stassen, who was elected Governor of Minnesota as a Republican Young Turk in the late nineteen-thirties. During the 1948 campaign, Burger was Stassen's chief of staff when Stassen was the liberal contesting the middle-of-the-road Dewey for the Republican Presidential nomination.

There are, of course, degrees of prairie progressivism. Burger is not the innovator the elder LaFollette and Norris were, but 30 years ago he was a leader of committees in St. Paul seeking to upgrade police training and trying to settle racial disputes. Nor is Burger the philosopher that McCarthy is or the dreamer that Stassen was and Humphrey is, but he is a practical man with an acute sense of justice. A favorite question of his is: "If it doesn't make good sense, how can it make good law?"

Burger is nearly 6 feet tall and overweight at 200 pounds. He wears his white hair fairly long and combs it in a pompadour that peaks at the top and helps to give him the distinguished look a Chief Justice is supposed to have. His complexion is still fair and his face is hardly wrinkled. He has clear blue eyes and bushy eyebrows that underscore the warmth of the man. His voice is deep and strong and retains a Midwestern clarity despite his years in Washington. A friendly, open man who always seems to be of good cheer, Burger is a fine conversationalist—politics is one of his favorite topics—who draws people to him. He is the kind of man who is noticed when he enters a room.

There is nothing stuffy about him, and he has a sense of humor he often turns on himself. Last year he sent a copy of the decision he wrote for the Court of Appeals in the Adam Clayton Powell case, a decision later reversed by the Supreme Court, to Warren B. (Pat) King, a Minneapolis lawyer and law-school classmate. Across the top of the opinion he wrote: "Use at bedtime in place of Seconal."

When King noticed earlier this year a poll of the Chief Judges of the 11 U.S. Courts of Appeals which said they were evenly divided between Burger and Judge Henry Friendly, Jr. of New York as their choice for a Supreme Court vacancy, he wrote to Burger asking him how 11 judges were able to divide evenly on a question.

"Evenly dividing 11 is easy," Burger replied. "Five to five and one man voted for himself! Actually the report was not accurate, but I can hardly object to being elevated into Henry Friendly's class. I'm going to get that photo as soon as I drop

five pounds. [King had asked for an autographed picture.] You'd better not wait until any 'elevation' occurs. It is likely you've a long, long wait. The support of my peers is flattering but one might inquire: 'How many votes do the judges have?' "

The doctrine of judicial restraint which Burger advocates is an old and honored one in American jurisprudence. It means that generally courts, and particularly the Supreme Court, ought to be interpreters of the laws passed by Congress and of the legal basis for actions taken by the executive branch rather than innovators of legal, social or economic change. The foremost proponent of this doctrine in the 20th century was the late Justice Felix Frankfurter, whose political, economic and social views were decidedly on the liberal side. So an advocate of judicial restraint need not necessarily be a conservative in the political spectrum. In fact, liberals who now support the idea of an activist Supreme Court were calling for judicial restraint in the nineteen-thirties when a conservative Court was overturning New Deal legislation.

"I'm for a lot of new things," Burger has said, "but I don't want to do them without linking them with the continuity of the past, and I find it paradoxical that my liberal colleagues often want to short-change procedure for a cause they consider noble. We simply can't have *ad-hoc* procedures."

But it is easy to say in the abstract that the Supreme Court ought to interpret rather than innovate and difficult to follow this doctrine as cases come before the Supreme Court. Burger recognizes this and has been doing a lot of thinking about the role of the Court since his nomination was approved by the Senate. He has not changed his mind about the basic, strict-constructionist approach he will take to most issues, but he realizes that the questions that come before the Court generally do not lend themselves to simple answers easily fitted into categories like judicial restraint and activism.

"Six months ago," Burger told a friend recently, "if you had asked me what the Supreme Court should and should not do, I probably could have given you a quick answer. But now I'm not so sure. New problems arise that the authors of the Constitution did not anticipate. But the answers to the problems ought to be made to fit an existing pattern; a new pattern should not be made. The hardest question though is always: 'When should the Court step in?' "

Burger, for example, has no argument with the Supreme Court's civil-rights decisions over the past 15 years, yet many advocates of judicial restraint have said that the Court should not have gotten into these issues. The reapportionment decisions, which have been as controversial as the civil-rights cases, cause Burger, however, to raise the question of judicial restraint. He has said that he does not know how he would have voted on reappor-

tionment, but that he has found "quite persuasive" Frankfurter's dissent warning the Court against entering "the legislative thicket."

Burger does not take the view that the Court should necessarily furnish answers for all problems that come before it. When he wrote the Court of Appeals decision holding that the courts had no jurisdiction over the question of whether the House should have seated Powell, he said: "That each branch may occasionally make errors for which there may be no effective remedy is one of the prices we pay for this independence, this separateness, of each co-equal branch and for the desired supremacy of each within its own assigned sphere."

Of all the Supreme Court's decisions during the Warren years, several of those involving criminal law remain the most controversial, and it is in this area that Burger finds himself in deepest disagreement with the Warren Court. These decisions affecting the rights of defendants in criminal cases were also the most controversial within the Court itself, which was often divided 5-to-4 on them.

The Warren Court's major criminal-law decisions were *Gideon* (which assured every defendant in a criminal proceeding the right to a lawyer), *Miranda* and *Escobeda* (which were aimed at preventing the extraction of confessions by police by ordering them to tell suspects of their right to a lawyer and their right not to answer questions) and the *Wade* and *Gilbert* cases (which held that the absence of a lawyer at a police line-up confrontation between a suspect and a witness would render the identification inadmissible as evidence).

In its decisions over the past 10 years, the Supreme Court has, in the view of judicial activists, merely reiterated and reinforced the protections guaranteed suspects and the accused by the Bill of Rights. But in the view of the critics, it has revised criminal law on a case-by-case basis and in the process of seeking to protect the rights of individuals has weakened the ability of society as a whole to defend itself against a rising tide of crime.

Burger does not think that the Supreme Court's decisions are responsible for an increase in crime, but he does believe that the case-by-case method used by the Court was not the way to reassert and strengthen the rights of suspects or defendants. In his view, the Supreme Court should have set up a commission made up of lawyers, judges, law-school professors and public officials to revise and update the rules of criminal procedure. A commission of the sort Burger advocates developed new rules for procedures in Federal civil cases 25 years ago. Such a commission, Burger argues, would take into account the entire area of criminal law rather than just the cases which happen to come before the Supreme Court and catch the eye of the Justices. As an example, Burger notes that the Supreme Court has emphasized defendants'

rights while ignoring the lengthy delays in bringing men to trial and the scandalous conditions in prisons, which account in large part for the fact that two-thirds of the men released from prison are back within a few years.

In an extended discussion of his views, Burger told the Ohio Judicial Conference last year:

"Too many law professors for a long time gave uncritical applause to anything and everything they could identify as an expansion of individual 'rights,' even when that expansion was at the expense of the rights of other human beings—the innocent citizens—presumably protected by the same Constitution. . . .

"In the last 10 years, more or less, we have witnessed what many scholars describe as a 'revolution in criminal law.' Today, we have the most complicated system of criminal justice and the most difficult system to administer of any country in the world. To a large extent, this is a result of judicial decisions which in effect made drastic revisions in the code of criminal procedure and evidence and to a substantial extent imposed these new proceedings on the states.

"This was indeed a revolution and some of these changes made were long overdue. All lawyers take pride, for example, in a case like *Gideon v. Wainwright*. . . .The holdings of the Supreme Court on right to counsel, on trial by jury instead of trial by press, and on coerced confession will always stand out. . . .

"I question . . . not the Court or the last decade's holdings of the Court but its methodology and the loose ends, confusion and bitterness that methodology has left in its wake. . . . Rarely can one case or even a dozen cases . . . supply an adequate factual foundation for building a structure of rules or procedure. . . .

"We must constantly recognize that the constitutional concepts 'tacked on' in these dozen years or so may not be as permanent as they appear when they are consistently arrived at by the margin of one vote with four Justices sharply suggesting that the cake which the Court was baking did not have all the essential ingredients for a good cake and that it has not been in the oven long enough. To paraphrase one of the felicitous lines of Elizabeth Barrett Browning, consequences 'so wrought may be unwrought so.' Thus, the constitutional result so wrought against the protest of four may be 'unwrought' by so simple a happening as the advent of one or two new Justices. . . . Even those who do not admire some of these rulings do not want to see constitutional doctrine rise and fall like Governments under the Fourth Republic of France.

"Looking back over the past dozen years, one is left to wonder what has become of the Court's firm policy never to decide a case on a constitutional ground if any other plausible ground was available. The doctrine of judicial supremacy is firmly established in this country, but we have never accepted a concept of judicial infallibility. Herein lies much that would suggest cogent reasons for a belief that several hundred well-trained and sophisticated legal minds functioning within the rule-making process free from the pressures of an appealing case might well do a more comprehensive job of drafting a workable set of rules than nine extraordinarily busy men with no more than a short time to devote to any one case. . . ."

. . .

Most of the criticism of Burger comes from law professors, lawyers and other judges who advocate judicial activism and are in basic disagreement with his concept of a limited role for the Supreme Court. Some of his critics also maintain that he is not enough of an intellectual for the Supreme Court, and one Court of Appeals colleague has said privately that Burger is a man who "sways with the wind."

Typical of the criticism of Burger is a comment made by Monroe H. Freedman, a professor of law at George Washington University and a long-time antagonist. He says: "The trouble with Burger is that he is a fundamentalist. He sees things in terms of fundamental principles. He doesn't recognize that fundamental principles can come into conflict. It's a 19th-century intertwining of moral and legal fundamentalism. Find the right principle and line it up with the case. Burger believes that certain principles are clear and immutable and not subject to modification, much less contradiction. But this is a simplistic approach to a terribly complicated world, and it doesn't work any longer."

6. The Federal Triangle: Mismatched Authority, Money and Problems

The American federal system distributes authority between the national and state-local governments. The present-day crisis in the federal system is caused by the fact that the distribution of authority and money is not equal to the responsibility for domestic problems.

Not too many years ago the whole subject of federalism seemed a rather shop-worn topic for debating teams. The balance between nation and state seemed permanently tilted in favor of Washington. Only dyed-in-the-wool conservatives doubted that the central government could best solve all political problems. During the past decade this rather bland assumption has come under increasing attack as Washington has demonstrated its ineptness in coping with the problems of education, race relations, poverty and pollution. As a result, the issue of federalism has been revived and today it is a pressing issue on Capitol Hill, in state houses, and city halls. This revived federalism, however, is different from the old. What had formerly been a two-level structure (nation-state) has become a triangle, with megalopolis as the third point. This evolution stems from the fact that as our population has become urbanized, most domestic problems have become metropolitan problems.

Big city mayors, faced with insurmountable questions, appealed to both state legislatures and the national Congress for help. A response pattern was quickly established. The mayor of Philadelphia found little sympathy in Harrisburg; the mayor of Chicago had few friends in Springfield. However, both found aid and comfort in Washington. In exchange for favors granted, Presidents and Senators were elected by big city voters. This national-city alliance bypassed the state governments, which were dominated by rural legislators. The formula (national money to the cities in exchange for votes) was used with great success by a generation of Democratic presidents. But the migration into the central cities continued: special federal programs were piled on top of each other without coordination (400 at last count); urban problems remained unsolved. The three-faceted, triangular concept of federalism—national, urban, state—was well-established, although this approach obviously needed to be restudied.

The New Federalism

President Johnson initiated the search for a new relationship, using such terms as "cooperative" or "creative" federalism. Rather than assuming a "big brother" attitude, the national government would plan and carry out programs in concert with state and urban governments. All overlapping grants would be merged into a few multi-purpose programs. Johnson was aware that the grant-in-aid program had grown at a phenomenal rate—from $147 million in 1930 to $25 billion in 1970— and that the national government lacked the expertise to administer these vast programs.

It was at this critical juncture that President Nixon took office. Just as big city mayors were Democratic allies, state governors were apt to be Republican friends. In recasting federalism in the Republican mold the states were slated for a starring role. The balance between Washington and the state capitals was to be shifted to restore state power, forcing big city mayors to function within the older two-dimensional federalism. As might be expected, the mayors protested; the Democratic Congress refused to act and the "new federalism" remained a discussion piece.

The central issue in the "new federalism" is not power but money. Revenue-sharing has captured the headlines and become equated in the public mind with the "new federalism." Existing grants-in-aid give cities and states matching funds for specific programs, under national supervision. President Nixon urged that some of this money be given as an outright grant to the states, without detailed restrictions on its use. By shifting such decisions to the state-local level the President foresaw a wider public involvement in planning and supervision. His critics, however, decried the blurring of national goals. They foresaw the pauperization of the states, which, they said, would become pensioners of the national government; they were especially critical of a weakening of the direct link between national government and the cities.

Something of a stalemate has been reached in the effort to redefine federalism. The national government continues to give money to both states and cities. The relationship between the state governments and cities remains as an ill-defined segment of the triangle. States and cities (those governments that lie closest to the people) are definitely junior partners in the federal triangle. Meanwhile cities struggle with little success to meet their problems, with the limited authority and money available.

The Metropolitan Crisis

Two-thirds of the American people live in slightly over 200 metropolitan areas. Most of these metropolitan areas (core cities and their suburbs) are further concentrated into a dozen megalopolises. In the 1970's we have no political unit that matches the realities of our population concentration. Government is fragmented into hundreds of pieces between core cities and suburbs. Poverty and its accompanying problems snowball in the core city; wealth and the tax base seek refuge in the suburbs. "Can big cities be governed"? is more than a rhetorical question.

To answer this question affirmatively two major steps are needed: (1) the creation of some sort of political unit that will square with realities of the metropolitan area: (2) a comparable area-wide tax base to meet the demand for services.

In searching for solutions a distinction should be made between the ideal and the possible. Habit and custom will block the use of idealistic political blueprints. But a number of alternatives do exist. Perhaps the state should become the governing body that copes with the general problems of megalopolis. Perhaps an expansion and consolidation of federal grants-in-aid is the answer. Perhaps some variant of Nixon's revenue sharing proposal (either directly or through the states) is the solution. Or, perhaps the national government should assume full responsibility for such programs as welfare. All honest observers believe that the crisis is real. The impotence of the cities in the face of their problems is everywhere recognized. Their regeneration will require both self-medication and help from other facets of the federal triangle.

THE CASE FOR
THE NEW FEDERALISM *

RICHARD M. NIXON

*President Nixon bases his case
for the "New Federalism" on the
contention that too much power has
been concentrated in Washington.
He urges that the flow of power
be reversed from Washington to the
states, thereby striking a new
balance. More decisions would be
made at the state-local level, with
funds supplied by the national
government.*

*Why does he believe that most
Americans are "fed up" with all
governments? Why would decentralization encourage creativity?
How would federal funds be
distributed? What programs would
the national government retain?
How would present frustrations be
reduced by the "New Federalism"?*

. . .

As we approach our 200th anniver-
sary in 1976, we remember that
this Nation launched itself as a
loose confederation of separate
States, without a workable central
government. At that time, the mark

* Richard M. Nixon, "State of the Union
Message," January, 1971, Weekly Com-
pilation of Presidential Documents (U.S.
Government Printing Office, January 25,
1971).

of its leaders' vision was that they
quickly saw the need to balance
the separate powers of the States
with a government of central powers.

And so they gave us a Constitution of balanced powers, of unity
with diversity—and so clear was
their vision that it survives today
as the oldest written Constitution
still in force in the world.

For almost two centuries since—
and dramatically in the 1930's—at
those great turning points when
the question has been between the
States and the Federal Government,
that question has been resolved in
favor of a stronger central Federal
Government.

During this time the Nation grew
and the Nation prospered. But one
thing history tells us is that no great
movement goes in the same direction forever. Nations change, they
adapt, or they slowly die.

The time has now come in America to reverse the flow of power
and resources from the States and
communities to Washington, and
start power and resources flowing
back from Washington to the States
and communities and, more important, to the people all across America.

The time has come for a new
partnership between the Federal
Government and the States and localities—a partnership in which we
entrust the States and localities with
a larger share of the Nation's responsibilities, and in which we
share our Federal revenues with
them so that they can meet those
responsibilities.

To achieve this goal, I propose to the Congress tonight that we enact a plan of revenue sharing historic in scope and bold in concept.

All across America today, States and cities are confronted with a financial crisis. Some have already been cutting back on essential services—for example, just recently San Diego and Cleveland cut back on trash collections. Most are caught between the prospects of bankruptcy on the one hand and adding to an already crushing tax burden on the other.

As one indication of the rising costs of local government, I discovered the other day that my home town of Whittier, California—which has a population of 67,000—has a larger budget for 1971 than the entire Federal budget was in 1791.

Now the time has come to take a new direction, and once again to introduce a new and more creative balance to our approach to government.

So let us put the money where the needs are. And let us put the power to spend it where the people are.

I propose that the Congress make a $16 billion investment in renewing State and local government. $5 billion of this will be in new and unrestricted funds to be used as the States and localities see fit. The other $11 billion will be provided by allocating $1 billion of new funds and converting one-third of the money going to the present narrow-purpose aid programs into Federal revenue-sharing funds for six broad purposes—for urban development, rural development, education, transportation, job training and law enforcement—but with the States and localities making their own decisions on how it should be spent within each category.

For the next fiscal year, this would increase total Federal aid to the States and localities more than 25 percent over the present level.

The revenue-sharing proposals I send to the Congress will include the safeguards against discrimination that accompany all other Federal funds allocated to the States. Neither the President nor the Congress nor the conscience of this Nation can permit money which comes from *all* the people to be used in a way which discriminates against *some* of the people.

The Federal Government will still have a large and vital role to play in achieving our national progress. Established functions that are clearly and essentially Federal in nature will still be performed by the Federal Government. New functions that need to be sponsored or performed by the Federal Government—such as those I have urged tonight in welfare and health—will be added to the Federal agenda. Whenever it makes the best sense for us to act as a whole nation, the Federal Government should and will lead the way. But where States or local governments can better do what needs to be done, let us see that they have the resources to do it there.

Under this plan, the Federal

Government will provide the States and localities with more money and less interference—and by cutting down the interference the same amount of money will go a lot further.

Let us share our resources.

Let us share them to rescue the States and localities from the brink of financial crisis.

Let us share them to give homeowners and wage earners a chance to escape from ever-higher property taxes and sales taxes.

Let us share our resources for two other reasons as well.

The first of these reasons has to do with government itself, and the second has to do with each of us, with the individual.

Let's face it. Most Americans today are simply fed up with government at all levels. They will not —and they should not—continue to tolerate the gap between promise and performance in government.

The fact is that we have made the Federal Government so strong it grows muscle-bound and the States and localities so weak they approach impotence.

If we put more power in more places, we can make government more creative in more places. That way we multiply the number of people with the ability to make things happen—and we can open the way to a new burst of creative energy throughout America.

The final reason I urge this historic shift is much more personal, for each and for every one of us.

As everything seems to have grown bigger and more complex in America, as the forces that shape our lives seem to have grown more distant and more impersonal, a great feeling of frustration has crept across this land.

Whether it is the workingman who feels neglected, the black man who feels oppressed, or the mother concerned about her children, there has been a growing feeling that "things are in the saddle, and ride mankind."

Millions of frustrated young Americans today are crying out— asking not what will government do for me, but what can *I* do, how can *I* contribute, how can *I* matter?

And so let us answer them. Let us say to them and let us say to all Americans: "We hear you. We will give you a chance. We are going to give you a new chance to have more to say about the decisions that affect your future—a chance to participate in government—because we are going to provide more centers of power where what you do can make a difference that you can see and feel in your own life and the life of your whole community."

The further away government is from the people, the stronger government becomes and the weaker people become. And a nation with a strong government and a weak people is an empty shell.

I reject the patronizing idea that government in Washington, D.C., is inevitably more wise, more honest and more efficient than government at the local or State level. The honesty and efficiency of government depends on people. Government at all levels has good people and bad people. And the way to get more good people into government is to give them more opportunity to do good things.

The idea that a bureaucratic elite in Washington knows best what is best for people everywhere and that you cannot trust local government is really a contention that you cannot trust people to govern themselves. This notion is completely foreign to the American experience. Local government is the government closest to the *people,* it is more responsive to the individual *person.* It is people's government in a far more intimate way than the government in Washington can ever be.

People came to America because they wanted to determine their own future rather than to live in a country where others determined their future for them.

What this change means is that once again in America we are placing our trust in people.

I have faith in people. I trust the judgment of people. Let us give the people of America a chance, a bigger voice in deciding for themselves those questions that so greatly affect their lives.

. . .

For all Americans, with these changes I have proposed tonight we can open the door to a new era of opportunity. We can open the door to full and effective participation in the decisions that affect their lives. We can open the door to a new partnership among governments at all levels, between those governments and the people themselves. And by so doing, we can open wide the doors of human fulfillment for millions of people here in America now and in the years to come. . . .

A CAUTIONARY WORD: FEDERAL REVENUE SHARING *

LOUIS FISHER

Federal revenue sharing is viewed in some quarters as a panacea for all the financial ills of state and urban governments. In exchange, critics of the program point out that no magic is involved—that in any case the money must be collected from the American people. These critics insist that if existing funds are diverted in this way, present aid programs must be cut.

Is it wise to distribute federal money with no strings attached?

* Louis Fisher, "A Cautionary Word on Federal Revenue Sharing," The New Republic, October 4, 1969. Reprinted by permission of The New Republic, © 1969, Harrison Blaine of New Jersey, Inc.

Can individual states and cities really cope with many of their problems? Why are big city mayors concerned over fund distribution through state governments? Will the money get to where the need is greatest? What is "fiscal drag"? What does Fisher urge as a substitute for revenue sharing?

When congressmen ask their constituents, "Do you think the federal government should return a portion of its revenue to the states to enable them to solve more of their own problems?" 70 to 80 percent say yes. This response rests on a misconception: that revenue sharing will provide a painless source of funds. When the question is worded more honestly, the results are a little different. "Should federal income taxes be increased over federal needs to provide for tax sharing with states?" one legislator asked. 93 percent answered no.

It is a curious notion that the federal government should *begin* sharing some of its revenue with the states. Where do we suppose the money goes now—to the District of Columbia? Guam, perhaps? Of course the government shares its revenue with the states. Grants-in-aid tripled during the Eisenhower years, and tripled again under the Kennedy-Johnson Administrations. Every congressional district benefits from some kind of military installation or defense contract, or public works project. It is facile to argue that "cities need financial relief; revenue sharing provides financial relief; therefore, cities need revenue sharing." The merits of revenue sharing have to be compared with other forms of financial relief: expanded grant-in-aid programs, federal assumption of welfare costs, or direct federal subsidies for municipal bonds.

What distinguishes revenue sharing is not tax relief or "sharing," which is so much flim-flam, but the distribution of federal funds without federal controls. Here are the thorns: local autonomy versus national goals, decentralization versus federal responsibility. In his proposal to share federal dollars with state and local governments (beginning with a modest $500 million in fiscal '71 but holding out the promise of $5 billion a year by fiscal 1976), Mr. Nixon has opted for local autonomy and decentralization; no strings attached. Funds would be allocated on the basis of population with an adjustment for local tax effort.

Previous advocates of revenue sharing will not be entirely happy with this plan. Walter Heller has urged controls to make sure, for example, that states abide by the antidiscrimination provisions of the 1964 Civil Rights Act; he would also prohibit use of revenue-sharing funds for highways, already financed by a separate trust fund. Rep. Henry Reuss (D. Wis.) would make revenue sharing conditional on federal approval of modernization plans for state governments. Other legislators have suggested limiting revenue-sharing funds to health education and welfare or giving special supplements to poorer states.

On the third of last month, the National Governors Conference proposed two more qualifications: taking account of the difficulty Western states have in increasing their tax effort, because of the large amount of nontaxable federal property in their states; and, using some of the revenue-sharing funds expected by local governments for regional projects. Thus even if a majority of congressmen favored revenue sharing, they might remain sharply divided over a concrete proposal.

It is argued that states invigorated by revenue sharing can function once again as "little laboratories" of social and economic innovation notwithstanding their irresponsibility in matters of personal liberties, reapportionment, procedural safeguards and racial discrimination. I find it hard to imagine a renaissance of responsibility in state legislatures, though I know the President believes his plan will help "to restore strength and vigor to local and state governments; to shift the balance of political power from Washington and back to the country and the people." This "back to the people" nostrum is one means of sidestepping federal responsibilities, asking the state to do what they can not or will not. How can New York unsnarl its transportation system, on the ground and in the air, without federally-supported mass transit along the Eastern seaboard? What can one state, say Ohio, do about the fouling and slow death of Lake Erie?

If revenue sharing survives these conceptual infirmities, it must then tangle with Wilbur Mills, chairman of the House Ways and Means Committee, who objects to the federal government collecting money and not supervising how it is spent. For those who want a share in federal revenue, he offers matching responsibility for sharing the federal debt, a bargain the states find unappealing.

Cities have been particularly apprehensive about revenue sharing. It is said that state insensitivity to urban problems is being overcome as a result of reapportionment decisions, but the anti-city bias of state legislatures isn't dead yet. And if seniority and committee chairmanships go on being pocketed by state legislatures from rural areas, it may never be. Moreover, reapportionment is likely to shift power not to central cities but to suburbs. John Lindsay's criticism of his state's budget as "anti-urban" suggests it is premature to say that state government, even in progressive New York, is sympathetic to big-city problems.

To allay the fears of mayors, it is pointed out that states now set aside the bulk of their revenue for education, health, and welfare, and that this would continue under revenue sharing, to the cities' benefit. Mr. Nixon says, "one can reasonably expect that education, which consistently takes over two-fifths of all state and local general revenues, will be the major beneficiary" of revenue-sharing funds. What I want to know is not whether states support education, but how they support it. In rejecting, this past January, a proposal to shift from specific support of compensatory education to general block grants for education, the National Advisory Council on the Education of Disadvantaged Children concluded that "any changes that would further shift the responsibility to the states for distributing education funds would —in many states and possibly in all —diminish the impact of this necessary investment in the education of disadvantaged children." State distribution of funds, it said, "rarely, if ever, favors those sections of the state with the greatest concentration and number of educationally deprived children—the central cities."

Since we can't trust the states to distribute funds on the basis of need, it has been suggested that a certain portion of revenue-sharing funds be given directly to local governments. Mayors feel more comfortable with this "pass through" approach, but it still would not guarantee that federal funds will go where they should. Take Wisconsin. The pass-through formula is generous here (half of state revenue earmarked for municipalities). Nevertheless, Senator William Proxmire points out that it's the prosperous cities that make out best: "They get the share of the income tax they pay, and cities like Milwaukee that earnestly, desperately need it, do not get it." What we need is not funds distributed on the basis of population and tax effort, but a formula that recognizes the cities' special financial problem, a problem due partly to a concentration of the aged and poor who require expensive services, and to the large number of nonresidents who rely on urban services.

The executive director of the U.S. Conference of Mayors, John Gunther has expressed dismay over the lack of city representation throughout the Nixon Administration. His suspicions were reinforced by the handling of federal funds for law enforcement assistance. Planning grants were released by the Justice Department to the states, with the understanding that priority would be given to major urban and metropolitan areas with high crime rates. But a study by the National League of Cities revealed that funds were being used to create "third levels of bureaucracy as a matter of state administrative convenience." Philadelphia, which accounted for almost 25 percent of the serious crimes in the state, got less than 10 percent of Pennsylvania's planning grants. Other mayors have complained that states are distributing funds to rural, urban and suburban areas on a per capita basis, regardless of crime rates.

Naturally then, large cities should find it more to their advantage to press Congress for an expansion of direct federal grants. Federal aid to New York City climbed from $578 million in 1967 to $768 million last year, and passed the $1 billion mark in fiscal 1969. This is the kind of revenue sharing that helps. Federal grants to all metropolitan areas rose from $5.6 billion in 1964 to $16.7 billion scheduled for fiscal 1970, an increase from 55 to 57 percent of total federal grants. In his April budget review, Mr. Nixon noted that federal aid to state and local governments will increase by $3.5 billion in fiscal 1970, of which the urban share is $2.8 billion, a hefty 80 percent.

One of the earlier rationales for revenue sharing was the idea of "fiscal drag." It was predicted that federal receipts would eventually outpace federal spending and produce an annual "fiscal dividend" of some $6 to $7 billion. If left unspent and used to retire the national debt, economic growth would be retarded. The remedy: distribute the dividends among the states.

. . .

Certainly there is no reason to worry about "fiscal drag." Shortly before leaving office, President Johnson received a special cabinet report on post-Vietnam investment possibilities. Full funding of existing domestic programs would cost $6 billion more a year than we're spending. Expansion of existing programs and new programs would run another $40 billion, while "more ambitious, new proposals" (such as negative income tax and guaranteed jobs) push spending even higher.

Studies of the past eight months suggest that these projections may be on the low side. The Budget Bureau recently estimated that an adequate diet for the poor would require an additional $2.9 billion a year. Senator Charles Goodell and others have proposed that the federal government assume the entire cost of welfare, adding $10 to $15 billion to federal spending. The 1970 budget for compensatory education was almost $2 billion below authorized levels and $3 and $4 billion less than recommended by private studies. Mr. Nixon's "commitment to the first five years of life" requires more generous funding for hunger, welfare and education than he has recommended thus far.

Rep. Edward Koch (D. N.Y.) has attracted over a hundred co-sponsors for his mass transit bill, calling for a $10 billion expenditure over the next four years. That's minimum. Federal contributions to the expanded rapid transit system in Washington, D.C. alone will run about $1.3 billion; costs of the high-speed trains between Boston and Washington are far higher. Mass transit in New York City and Chicago over the next decade may cost in excess of $4 billion. At the present rate of production Secretary Romney predicts that over the next decade we will fall more than 10 million units short of our 1968 commitment of 26 million housing units. Municipal hospitals are threatening to close because of too lean budgets and the backlog of present needs in hospital modernization stands at more than $10.7 billion. Mr. Nixon acknowledged July 10 that unless federal action is taken within the next two to three years, "we will have a breakdown in our medical care system which could have consequences affecting millions of people throughout this country."

Estimates of what it will take to cleanse the nation's waters over the next five years go as high as $29 billion. The cost of containing air pollution is put at another $16 billion. A recent federal study on thermal pollution estimates at $1.8 billion the effort needed in this area over the next five years.

Instead of dabbling with revenue sharing, Congress should assist state and local governments in a more forthright manner: assume the entire cost of welfare, increase aid to education, and bring grant in aid programs up to authorized levels. This would take the strain off state and city budgets, releasing more funds for problems of a local nature. It is time to commit the funds needed for our undernourished public sector and ignore the siren call of revenue sharing.

CAN BIG CITIES BE GOVERNED? *

JEROME P. CAVANAGH

Mr. Cavanagh is representative of a generation of mayors who attempted to cope with complex urban problems during the 1960's. By the end of that decade many of these men had concluded that the odds were too great and that big cities could not be governed successfully, Mr. Cavanagh had originally been hailed as an imaginative, progressive leader. In the article that follows he outlines the enormous difficulties that caused him to retire to private life.

Why have American cities been so poorly planned? What is the relationship between poverty and the urban crisis? What is wrong with the tax base of core cities? What psychological differences exist between city and national tax policy? What conflict exists between public and private goods? Is the present college generation more idealistic and socially responsible than their parents?

* A speech delivered at the 11th Annual Public Affairs Forum, Indiana University of Pennsylvania, February 10, 1969. Reprinted by permission of the author.

. . . The situation in America's great cities has reached the alarming proportions of a national crisis and in some ways a national scandal. When we speak of the "Urban Crisis," remember that we are talking about conditions that immediately affect three-quarters of the citizens of this country. For that is the extent to which the United States has become urbanized. Moreover, the number of city dwellers and their proportion relative to the total population will continue to increase in the years ahead. So the problem of the cities is of special concern to the young people, because we are talking about the environment in which they will live out their adult years and rear their children.

The crisis is not that large numbers of people are living and more will gather in giant metropolitan concentrations. There is nothing repellent or even inherently unmanageable about that. Urbanization is a function of technological advance, and it ought to be regarded as an opportunity for developing new and better forms of living. But the crisis we face is that the conditions of urban life are getting worse instead of better.

Let me take a moment to review in broad strokes some of the more salient and perhaps familiar ingredients of the urban crisis.

From earliest times it was commerce and crafts that brought people together in cities and towns. Cities are synonymous with advanced civilization. Only a sophisti-

cated economy, which imposes a complex division of function, provides the conditions for a dynamic culture.

But it was the Industrial Revolution, with its need for a larger, concentrated labor force, that created the cities of today.

In the United States, this need coincided with the great waves of European immigration at the turn of the century. Thus it happened that the population of American cities not only increased substantially but also acquired its distinctive ethnic diversity.

The seeds of many of our present discontents were planted in that period some fifty to seventy-five year ago.

Despite, or perhaps because of, the influx of immigrant labor to the cities, the rest of the nation continued to think of rural and small town America as the authentic America—the land of their forebears, the self-reliant, self-sufficient America of the Puritan tradition. From this perspective the city was seen as something incongruous, even alien.

Since the cities were neither the emotional nor the political center of gravity in American society, it is not surprising that the state and federal governments displayed little understanding and even less concern for urban problems. To a considerable degree this attitude still persists. Even today it is conventional to think of financial aid to the cities as government hand-outs, while the enormous sums of federal money paid to farmers or to the aerospace industry are treated as fair-and-square subsidies in the national interest.

At the same time, it must be acknowledged that until very recently local government itself failed to recognize or respond to the needs of a burgeoning urban society. There was, for example, virtually no planning for orderly growth. Zoning laws and other land use restrictions came rather late in the day, largely because of an exaggerated reverence for unlimited rights of private ownership—an understandable feeling in a rural, pioneer country, but sheer madness in large and expanding population centers.

And so the cities were allowed to grow like Topsy. Most large cities are really an incoherent grab-bag rather than a planned and sensible collocation of districts and neighborhoods.

Both World Wars brought in-migration largely from the rural South. This was especially true in Detroit. As the nation's "arsenal of democracy," Detroit was the center of much of the war production industry, whose need for manpower was nearly insatiable.

Tired of the cycle of rural poverty and attracted by the employment opportunities available in Detroit and other Northern cities, they came in an endless stream—white and black.

But these newcomers to the city encountered enormous problems of adjustment. Wartime restrictions made it impossible to provide enough housing for them, and so a compression into ghettos added to their difficulties. Almost predictably the social pressures exploded in Detroit's tragic race riot of 1943.

The postwar years did not see a reversal of the in-migration of which I speak. On the contrary, the population shift—from farm to city, from South to North—continued unabated.

Municipal boundaries no longer contain the population of today's city. The actual city is an expanding creature which spills across city, township, and county lines— indeed often across state lines, and in Detroit, across international boundaries. While the actual city is economically integrated, it has become a governmental crazy-quilt. Literally hundreds of separate jurisdictions exist side by side, and these are overlapped by still other governmental agencies and subdivisions.

None alone can begin to meet the problems of the total urban community. To the extent that each individual jurisdiction does anything at all beyond sustaining the minimum housekeeping functions of government, it is to safeguard the special interests—real or imagined —of its own constituents, and thus contribute to social fragmentation and irresponsibility.

If one deliberately applied himself to the task of devising the least practical and most inefficient way to organize the government of a metropolitan area, he could not invent a worse system than that which events and inaction have combined to produce.

The movement to the suburbs has drained the central city of much of its economic substance and civic solidarity. In the opinion of many, the central city is on the way toward becoming a ghetto of the poor, and more specifically the black poor.

On the other hand, the outer suburbs—not all of which, by the way, are affluent communities—are barren of the amenities of the central city: the civic and cultural life, the hotels, restaurants, theatres, specialty shops, and all the excitement and hurly-burly of the downtown.

There used to be a mythology holding that life is sweet in suburbia—that taxes are lower and schools are better, that neighbors are friends and streets are safe, that the greatest menace life poses to comfortable householders is crabgrass. When people moved to the suburbs, they used to say that they wanted to get away from the noise and congestion of the city and enjoy a more tranquil, bucolic environment.

But now the mythology is gone and the avowed motivations have changed. Suburbanites miss the services which are a matter of course to city dwellers: paved streets, public lighting, snow removal, trash collection, adequate sewage systems. They find that rapidly growing communities must raise taxes to provide even a semblance of these municipal services. They find, too, that transportation is abominable, whether it is getting around the suburbs or getting into the city.

Yet more and more people move out of the city—not in search of idyllic surroundings, but because they find the city even less congenial than the bland, jerry-built suburbs. There are many factors contributing to this exodus. Some have a basis in fact, others are emotionally exaggerated. One factor is the declining quality of the public schools in the city. Another is the fear of crime. Added to that is anxiety about renewed urban riots, of the kind that have swept across the nation in the past three years. Higher taxation is sometimes given as a reason for flight from the city, although I am convinced that it is rarely a self-sufficient cause and often a rationalization for less creditable motives.

Running through all these concerns is a racial factor which cannot be ignored or denied.

As much as we hate to admit it, the races are moving apart. Despite all the civil rights legislation enacted in this decade, the urban North is more segregated than the South. As an example: according to a recent demographic study of the Detroit metropolitan area, 30 percent of all households in the city are non-white, as contrasted to 4 percent elsewhere in Wayne County, 2.4 percent in adjacent Oakland County, and 1.2 percent in Macomb County. These figures are as much the product of active discrimination in housing as they are a reflection of economic disparities.

There is in Detroit a sizeable Negro middle class, who for all practical purposes are locked into the city not because they cannot afford homes in the suburbs but because of discriminatory real estate practices and white hostility in communities surrounding Detroit. The black citizens, the poor as well as the prosperous, of Detroit are every bit as concerned about the quality of their schools and the problem of street crime as are white citizens. Indeed for them, these are matters which are much less abstract and of far greater personal urgency, because they lack the means of suburban escape—dubious though that is as a solution.

What has happened, in short, is that the newcomers to the city are poor and mostly black, and the people foresaking the city for the suburbs are middle-class and white. Still remaining in the city, are middle-class blacks and low-income whites, particularly elderly people on modest fixed incomes.

The central cities are the inheritors of the problems of rural poverty and discrimination. Hard-core poverty has always existed in this nation, unaffected by decades of general prosperity. Some of that poverty has always been centered in the cities, but much more of it until now was scattered and isolated in the rural South. That poverty never forced itself on the national consciousness nor did it present an immediate threat of social explosion. But transferred to the cities, poverty and its related maladies spell urban and therefore national crisis.

When John Kennedy took office as President, it was conventional to think of poverty as an ugly but relatively minor aberration from a general condition of national affluence. To eliminate it was only to finish the business of the New Deal of Franklin Roosevelt. But now we are wiser and sadder. We know that poverty is not the unfinished business of this nation but the untouched problem. What the experience of the poverty program in Detroit and elsewhere has shown is that neither government nor the public had any idea how deep and difficult, how complex and intractable, are the problems of the poor. The poverty programs have scarcely been able to touch the lives of many of the poor, let alone to lift them out of poverty. But we have at least begun to define the true dimensions of poverty, and it is a sobering discovery.

City government, however, has all it can do just providing the basic public services. Without help from the state and federal government, and from the private sector as well, local officials cannot begin to cope with the more profound human needs of the urban poor.

Historically, the cornerstone of municipal finance has been the property tax. Aside from its inherent inequity, this form of taxation no longer is capable of producing the revenue needed to support the kind of government services required today. In Detroit, as in most major cities, the tax base is eroding while the cost of government is soaring.

One of the factors contributing to the higher cost of government is the militancy of public employees in wage negotiations. The day has long passed when job security is a substitute for better wages. Government must compete with private industry. And public employees have an appealing case when they argue that the payment of noncompetitive wages forces them, rather than the general taxpaying public, to subsidize the operation of government. But unlike private industry, which can pass its increased labor costs on to the consumer in the form of higher prices, municipal government has no way unilaterally to conjure up more revenue.

Even with a local income tax in Detroit as well as a property tax, the city is currently running a deficit of about $17 million. Yet we are now facing a new round of negotiations with the public employee unions.

In addition, our city, by common agreement, needs to expand its police force. On a nationwide basis crime has been rising since 1960 at a rate seven times faster than the population increase. But Detroit's police force today is only 13 percent larger than it was twenty years ago. So we are asking the legislature this year for authority to boost our resident and commuter income tax by another one-half percent solely for this public safety purpose.

Our other municipal needs may compel us to seek a further increase in property taxes. I am painfully aware that the prospects for financing the city's governmental requirements are, at best, uncertain. The mood of the taxpayers is ambivalent. On the one hand they demand and deserve adequate public services. On the other hand, they feel—rightly or wrongly—oppressed by rising taxation.

As a Mayor for seven years, I have learned some interesting things about public psychology. One is that taxpayers tend to expect from local government a return benefit on a ratio of 1 to 1. Curiously, there is less expectation of direct personal return from state taxation, and almost none where federal taxes are concerned.

Thus I have found enormous resistance in the suburbs to the concept of commuter taxes—which do in fact support services for the welfare of the daytime citizen as well as the 24 hour resident. On the other hand, there is less vocal opposition to state taxes, although they often finance activities—worthwhile activities, I might add—having little or no direct impact on many individual taxpayers.

And I cannot help but think that if a city administration proposed a municipal project as dubious in value and priority as is the thin-shield antimissile system, there would be an instant full-scale rebellion of taxpayers. But somehow the federal government is spared that kind of public sensitivity.

Of course, I would be unfair and ungrateful if I did not acknowledge the aid which has been extended to the cities by the federal government. It should be obvious that the cities cannot go it alone. Our local resources are diminishing as our needs are mounting. The city-federal relationship which blossomed in the Kennedy-Johnson years came about in part because of the indifference of state government to the plight of the cities, and partly because the help needed was so enormous that only the federal government could effectively supply it.

In my perception, these conditions have not changed. That is why most mayors are disturbed by talk of bloc grants to states as an approach to the solution of urban problems. Even with legislatures reapportioned on a one-man, one-vote basis, there has been little indication of state compassion for the central city. It is the suburban legislator who holds the key to effective state action. Too often he is an adversary rather than an ally of the city. On some issues I have actually found more understanding from rural legislators than from representatives of adjacent communities.

And as I suggested before, the polarity of city and suburbs is worsening. We seem to be experiencing within our country a kind of local isolationism, a withdrawal of concern for the needs of our own neighbors. But just as a foreign policy of isolationism could not shield America from crisis abroad, there can be turning away from the agony of our central cities.

For too many years urban problems have been allowed to accumulate by neglect. But because the problems have reached an acute stage does not mean that they are insoluble. To despair of their solution would be to commit suicide as a nation.

The question now is not whether government or the private sector is responsible for correcting these problems, because both are. The question is not which unit of government is responsible, because every unit of government has that responsibility—to the maximum of its resources. And if government resources are not now sufficient, then Americans have a critical decision to make. They must decide, while the options are still available, whether they prefer owning a second or third automobile to having adequate public services . . . whether buying a color television set is more gratifying than the improvement of public education.

This nation invests proportionately less in the public domain than any other urban society. The results are as obvious as they are appalling. Almost all Americans—whether white suburbanites or black ghetto dwellers—are unhappy with their environment and growing more distressed every day.

I am saying only what John Kenneth Galbraith said ten years ago in "The Affluent Society." Let me quote just one prophetic passage from Professor Galbraith:

"It is scarcely sensible that we should satisfy our wants in private goods with reckless abundance, while in the case of public goods, on the evidence of the eye, we practice extreme self-denial. So, far from systematically exploiting the opportunities to use and derive pleasure from these services, we do not supply what would keep us out of trouble."

We are today in very deep trouble. I pray that we will act now . . . that the recommendations of the Kerner Commission rather than a posture of quietude will be the policy of the national administration.

And I look with hope to the young people, the college generation. What they are telling us is that the values and priorities of their elders are leading the society to disaster. It is not naive idealism but selfishness in the most rational sense which animates the sons and daughters of America's middle class. They seem to understand far better than their parents that a rich nation which tolerates hunger, which ignores squalor, which wastes human resources and neglects vital public services is a nation in which they can be neither happy nor secure. I hope their clear vision and good sense will prevail.

LOCAL GOVERNMENT IS A FARCE *
FRANKLIN H. ORNSTEIN

The absurdities of local government are documented in the article that follows. As Mr. Ornstein notes, we are in many ways a captive of our history, entangled in a maze of local government— electing such obsolete officials as coal weighers, tree wardens and fence viewers. How would the author create a rational system? What action would he take on federal aid programs? From what source would he recruit local officials?

A ruffian punches the desk sergeant on the nose in police headquarters and the sergeant cries, "Call the police!" It happens in Three Stooges films, but it also can happen in the headquarters of the Nassau County police, in New York City's suburbs. Legally, the county's 2,700-man force should summon a Garden City policeman to make the arrest because the police headquarters is located in Garden City. As the clerk of Nassau County, I have

---

* From Franklin Ornstein, "Local Government Is A Farce," The Saturday Evening Post, December 2, 1967, pp. 10, 16. Reprinted with permission of The Saturday Evening Post. Copyright © 1967 The Curtis Publishing Company.

actually seen such absurdities. I have seen a village policeman rush to the County Building to aid a heart-attack victim while a county cop was tagging a parking violator outside my office window.

The governmental farce played in my county is far from unusual. Indeed, it illustrates the comical crisis which pervades local government. In Park Forest, Ill., for instance, a citizen might well be forgiven if he were not sure what to do about *any* local problem. After all, he is governed by two counties, three townships, five school districts, a forest preserve district a mosquito-abatement district and, oh yes, his own village board of trustees. In Fridley, Minn. (population 25,000), the taxpayer votes in 10 different governmental units —federal, state, county, and city, along with school, sewer, sanitary, hospital, airport, and mosquito-control districts. In the Philadelphia suburbs—a patchwork quilt of communities ranging from Ivyland (population 490) to Upper Darby (93,158)—the path of a state-police car was traced by a newspaper reporter. Within eight miles of the Philadelphia boundary the trooper passed through seven boroughs and three townships. Similarly, Nassau County's Route 1 changes name 19 times as it sweeps through 15 communities, three towns and one city.

Anyone who takes a look at his own municipal backyard is likely to find an equally silly scene. Across the nation we elect more than 500,-000 local officials—who appoint hundreds of thousands of others—

to run some 80,000 fragmented, overlapping governments. The voters in Maine, for example, are still electing "fence viewers" to settle property-line disputes. If there is any underlying principle in the labyrinth of American local government, it is confusion. In July, 1966, the Committee for Economic Development stated accurately: "Most American communities lack any instrumentality of government with legal powers, geographic jurisdiction and independent revenue sources necessary to conduct local self-government in any valid sense." With local government in such a condition—and this is what bothers me most of all—is it any surprise that popular participation is on the wane? Seventy-six percent of those queried in a Gallup poll said they could name only the top-level candidates for whom they had voted.

The plain fact is that we are trying to operate local government in the jet age with horse-and-buggy methods. The results—and I see them every day in my own county —are costly, inefficient and inequitable.

A man who can testify to all three results is the Levittown, N.Y., plumber who paid $1,100 in fees to obtain licenses from 60 different Long Island towns and villages last year. In a typical suburban area it would take a computer to produce all the facts on which village permits a driver to make a "right turn on red," and which one expects him to observe the traffic signal one block ahead. There are 1,400 signals in my county: 675 are owned by county government, 345 by the state, 340 by the cities or villages and, what's more, 40 private signals.

I shake my head in disbelief when I drive across the New York City line at night and plunge into the darkness of the Long Island Expressway, the county's most heavily traveled highway. It is a state road, and the state makes no provision for lights. The expressway runs through four villages and two towns, all of which have decided that lighting a state road wouldn't help locally. So there are no lights.

The confused motorist is lucky, however, compared to the one who is injured or killed. It took a number of accidents to get a traffic light installed at one of my county's busiest intersections—right outside the courthouse. A village boundary runs through the intersection and officials of Garden City, Mineola and Nassau wrangled for years before the county installed the signal. Pedestrians can also be the victims of government confusion. Los Angeles's control of its own pedestrian crosswalks was challenged—and the city lost! A judge set aside the city crosswalk ordinance because it conflicted with the state vehicle code.

Los Angeles is a splendid example of why local government desperately needs reform. A major problem is the special district—and Los Angeles County has some 350 of them, along with is 76 cities and 100 school districts. A special district is an area in which the residents receive a specific service—street lights, for instance—and are taxed specially to pay for it. Unfortunately, such districts multiply like people, although people may not know which districts are supposed to be doing what for them. I can't help wondering what happens to representative government when only a handful of voters in the 300-odd special districts in my county bother to vote for the commissioners who give them water, sewers, parks, libraries, garbage collection or fire or police protection. In May, 1966, for instance, a $130,000 firehouse addition was approved by a vote of 75 to 17 in the 15,000-voter Levittown fire district.

Few people who walk into my office can tell me what districts they live in. Indeed, many know only that they send a check to the bank once a month and somehow their taxes get paid.

Special districts have been created for almost everything imaginable, building a war veterans' memorial, operating an escalator at a railroad station. A sewer-pipe manufacturer got a contract to lay more pipes than the community could ever use—after he had managed to organize a "citizens' committee," and thus got a special sewer district created.

Cities have also been "invented" for objectionable reasons. Levittown is Nassau's largest community (population 66,800), but has no government while Long Beach (population 29,000), where I grew up (a great place to live), was incorporated in 1922 under the aegis of a developer who laid out the streets, dug the canals, set up his own water company and raked in the profits.

Perhaps the ultimate joke of local government is what the officials actually *do*. I felt like Alice in Wonderland recently when, on the same day, both Nassau County and a town government in Nassau announced plans to hire people to screen all narcotic-education programs—presumably including each others' programs. For the 822,000 people in Hempstead, the town board must hold a public hearing on every no-parking sign, marshland lease renewal or hydrant location.

I think M.I.T. Prof. Robert C. Wood, now on leave as Under Secretary of Housing and Urban Development, put it nicely when he labeled the New York metropolitan area "one of the great unnatural wonders of the world. . . . A vigorous metropolitan area, the economic capital of the nation, governs itself by means of 1,467 distinct political entities (at latest count), each having its own power to raise and spend the public treasure. . . ." Prof James C. Charlesworth of the University of Pennsylvania reported from the Midwest: "In a chaotic mélange like metropolitan Chicago the voter has long since abandoned attempts to know where he stands vis-à-vis the multitudes of wraithlike officials who serve him." Americans tramp to the polls to elect coal weighers, tree wardens and lumber inspectors. Such is the apathy of American local government that there are incorporated municipalities with zero popula-

tion; there are no people to vote for dissolution.

There is one subject about which voters would not be apathetic if they knew the facts. The subject is taxes, and where the money goes. The cost of local government in the United States has jumped from $20.1 billion in 1952 to $60 billion in 1967. It's still rising, and no leveling-off is in sight. Waste, according to experts not given to exaggeration, is about 25 percent.

Alarmed local officials are turning more and more to Washington. Instead of looking to the Federal Government, I believe they should be turning their eyes upon the inadequacies of their own regimes. Above all, they should review their chief source of funds, the property tax, which still provides more than $58 of every $100 raised by local government. This tax is unfair; it takes no account of income. Moreover, it can be unequal. In a Pennsylvania study the ratio of assessed valuation to full value ranged across the state from 20 to 78 percent and in New Jersey from 16 to 56 percent. The New Jersey Commission on State Tax Policy freely uses the term "tax lightning" to describe an assessor's sudden strike for tax gold.

Our real need today is for new kinds of government. The outlook for any real change, however, will remain bleak as long as the public doesn't care. And it doesn't. I know I can get a rise out of a friend or neighbor by saying the right (or wrong) thing about Vietnam or Medicare, but when I turn to local government, I know I am losing his interest. The New England town meeting has been sentimentalized as "pure democracy," but a study of Winchester, Mass., revealed that nearly half of those attending town meetings were public officials. Another New England town-meeting study found only one out of 13 registered voters in attendance. And apathy toward government isn't the only obstacle. Any change inevitably upsets well-greased working arrangements involving contracts between government and industry. The very politician who should lead the fight for reform may be anxious to keep his corner of profit or prestige, and he has a ready-made weapon: He poses as a defender of "home rule."

The home-rule battle cry has been raised not to preserve local freedom but to keep the dogcatcher on the ballot. In my supposedly sophisticated county, I was pleased to see the Town of Hempstead drop its cemetery trustees from the ballot, but winced when town officials decided to keep their array of sanitation district commissioners, receiver of taxes and town clerk.

I propose that we bring about a total reorganization of American local government. The minimum electorate for a government providing health services might be fixed at 75,000. For a government operating schools, the figure might be set at 25,000 to 40,000. We should also have limits—both maximum and minimum—on electorates seeking to provide themselves with all the other local services: recreation,

garbage collection, and even sidewalks.

In this way, we could eliminate the enormous leakage of local money—the duplicate spending about which the public seldom knows or seems to care. The number of local communities could profitably be reduced from 80,000 to a maximum of between 15,000 and 20,000 by consolidating small municipalities and uniting the county-town functions, eliminating the duplicating services and abolishing all special districts and phantom townships.

Any new federal-aid programs to local government should be ruled out, and the existing ones should be cut back. Federal officials are all too eager to grant aid to local government, knowing that another tentacle of power is attached to every dollar. In state capitals, just as in Washington, one finds the same reluctance to relinquish power that plagues the city and town halls.

In Nassau this year, counting federal and state aid as well as local taxes, the average taxpayer is paying nearly $2,000 a year on local government, almost one third the country's median annual family income. In all, we're spending close to a billion dollars a year on local government for Nassau County's 1.4 million people—and comparable amounts are being spent everywhere, most noticeably in suburbia. The cost of local government in the United States is expected to soar to $90 billion by 1972. I urge that we set up a Local Government Improvement Corporation (LOGIC), perhaps financed by a foundation and not beholden to government or industry. LOGIC would train people for careers in local government and help community leaders who seek to modernize their government. We must act now, with LOGIC, before town hall becomes just another federal agency.

NEW FORMS OF METROPOLITAN GOVERNMENT *

RICHARD F. HEIGES

Urban government today is an irrational maze of authorities, districts, and independent governments for the central city and each of its suburbs. Modern metropolitan problems demand metropolitan answers. But no unit of government is prepared to give such an answer! This vacuum must be filled in some manner if an urban society is to cope with its problems.

* *Reprinted from Richard F. Heiges, "Fragmentation, The Band-Aid, and Creeping Metropolitanism," The Pennsylvanian, April, 1971, by permission of the author.*

Why did we create so many special districts? Why does the author label this a band-aid approach? Why does he label other solutions as improbable? Why does he reject a single, all-powerful metropolitan government? Why do both blacks and whites resist metropolitan federation? What advantages does it offer? What reforms of county government are needed if it is to fill the void? What factor is apt to be the compelling force in overcoming fragmentation?

The problems of the metropolis are, of course, complex; their study is interdisciplinary; and their solutions are interdependent. The political scientist can easily identify one problem as political. The name of the game is "fragmentation" of government or the overabundance of governing units in these areas. Over 18,000 local governments exist in the metropolitan areas. Thus one-fifth of local government units occupy one-twelfth of the land. The Chicago area leads with over 1000 local governments, double that of New York. Almost two-thirds of these units are school districts and special districts.

The Fragmentation Problem

Fragmentation of government in metropolitan areas, it has been charged, leads to: (1) disparity of tax bases and thus services among wealthy and poorer areas; (2) inefficiency and duplication of services; (3) high overhead operating costs; (4) imposition of a multitude of taxes as layer after layer of government is piled upon the taxpayer; (5) lack of coordination and planning in coping with regional problems such as air and water pollution control, mass transit, recreational facilities, and law enforcement.

While one finds no single government in a metropolitan area, political scientists can identify and in general terms describe a political system in such an area. The system consists of competing governmental units as well as the usual conflicts of economic interest groups, parties, races, and ethnic groups. The system is non-rational, non-directed, and indeed, political scientists are not agreed even as to a technique to be used to discover the real decision-makers in the system.

Proposed solutions to fragmentations are numerous and have been categorized in many ways. For convenience here, we will develop three such categories: (1) the "band-aid" approach, (2) the improbable, (3) and the possible.

The Band-Aid Approach

In most metropolitan areas where it has been realized that fragmentation of government impedes the solution of any problem, ad hoc or band-aid solutions have been applied to meet near-crisis situations.

First, the most common attempt to overcome fragmentation is co-operation. Cooperation may be (1) informal agreements between governing authorities, such as a city police department which will agree to provide emergency help to a surrounding rural area with little or no law enforcement personnel; (2) formal contracts, usually a year in length and renewable, under which one unit may sell services to another. In Los Angeles county, for example, under a device known as the "Lakewood Plan," the county sells dozens of services to other units of government. Some local governments purchase virtually all services from the county. Formal contracts may also be used to develop shared facilities, such as a sewage treatment plant for two or more governments. And contracts are utilized for joint purchasing by several units. The problem with contracts is that they may be terminated and thus void long-range plans, and one unit may not be able or willing to provide services to another; (3) metropolitan or regional councils of government (known as the COG movement) is coming into favor. Under this arrangement, the governments of an area support financially a small agency which is limited to planning, data collecting and exchange, and a forum for developing formal agreements. Such councils have no governmental powers and are often ignored by some governments in the area. The work of such councils can, of course, lead to some tangible solutions to the fragmentation problem and can be viewed as a desirable first step.

A second type of band-aid approach is the creation of single-purpose and multi-purpose special districts. Here a single problem, such as obtaining adequate water supply and treatment, is met with several local governing authorities creating a special district for this purpose. Under state legislation in some states the district may enjoy such governing powers as taxing, assessing, selling rates, eminent domain proceedings, and investigations. With the exception of school boards, the special districts are usually governed by boards appointed by the member local governments. Thus, we have created a layer of units which are not directly responsible to voters and taxpayers. The alternative of electing such boards is viewed with disfavor in light of already too lengthy ballots. The use of single-purpose special districts tends to distort the use of financial resources, already limited, in the metropolitan area. The districts, created as a result of the area's more powerful interest groups, are likely to enjoy reasonable financial resources, while other legitimate functions of local governments are underfinanced or ignored. Since single-purpose districts are often successful in coping with a particular problem, other functions may be added. A water resource district may eventually also be authorized to develop sewage treatment facilities. As functions are added, we see the growth of a multi-purpose spe-cial district. Eventually, as in the Seattle area, we may see develop what is at least a primitive metropolitan government for the entire area. This form of "creeping metropolitanism" unfortunately leads to a governing body that is not directly dependent upon the citizens of the region.

Improbable Solutions

The most unlikely of the "improbable" solutions to fragmentation is annexation and consolidation. Annexation is the taking over by a municipality of a surrounding unincorporated area; consolidation is the merger of two or more incorporated municipalities. Except in some western states and in Virginia, annexation and consolidation are extremely difficult to accomplish because of state laws requiring approval of a majority of voters of each unit. Furthermore, social scientists today are usually as much opposed as are the local politicians to the creation of one super government for the metropolitan area. The potential if questionable savings to be realized by a single gargantuan local government are considered too high a price to pay when metropolitan man needs a sense of identity, a concept of community, a pride in neighborhood, and a sense of participation in decision-making. That is, psychology and sociology are more relevant in developing guide-lines for size of units than are principles of public administration.

Two other proposed solutions to fragmentation of limited usefulness are city-county consolidation and city-county separation. Where an entire county is highly urbanized, it is, of course, desirable and practical to combine city and county offices into one government, such as Philadelphia. Often, however, parts of a highly urban county may be quite rural. And more importantly, urbanization does not stop at a county line (or even a state boundary), so consolidation does not substantially attack the problem of fragmentation throughout a metropolitan area. In city-county separation a city is removed from the jurisdiction of county government, leaving the less urbanized area as a rump county with insufficient resources. Actually the result is less coordination of governments in the metropolitan area.

Possible Solutions

Politics is said to be the art of the possible. Some approaches to fragmentation can be overcome through two approaches: (1) federation and (2) the urban county plan.

Toronto is the classic example of metropolitan federation. The area consists of the city of Toronto and 12 suburban municipalities. These units retain important responsibilities, while a metropolitan governing board exercises powers in assessing property, water supply, sewage disposal, arterial roads, transit, health and welfare, admin-

istration of justice, housing, and planning. The board consists of 32 members (12 from city; 20 from suburbs, and a chairman appointed by the board). These members are mayors and councilmen, and thus as board members are not directly elected. The federation plan has the advantages of retaining local governments while meeting metropolitan-wide problems with an area government. The disadvantages are that (1) still another layer of local government has been created—and one somewhat removed from the people; (2) there is no objective criteria for establishing which functions remain under local control, which are delegated to the federation government, and which are to be shared; (3) it is difficult to arrange for a governing board that fairly represents the central city and its suburbs. Each area is afraid of losing control to the other. In the United States these fears may be emphasized by the tendency of cities to be Democratic and suburbs Republican. Making federation still more difficult is the schism between the races, with black population growing in the central cities to the point of political control and the suburbs remaining and even increasing their white middle class homogeneity. The black man in the city is likely to view federation proposals as an attempt to cancel out his political gains, while the white suburbanite, a recent emigrant from the decaying city, has no desire to become a part of the city again politically. Socially and economically, the fate of the central city and suburb is intertwined.

Another approach, with enough appeal to have been adopted in several metropolitan areas (Dade County—Miami, Florida), is the urban county plan. In this arrangement the existing county government unit is used as the building block for metropolitan government. Usually through the adoption of a charter, requiring state legislation, voter approval, and perhaps even state constitutional revision, a county assumes functions deemed to be of an area-wide nature, while other local governments remain in existence performing purely local services. The major advantage to this approach is, of course, that no new unit of government need be created and voters may feel fairly comfortable with a minimum of structural change in local government (functional change may be great, of course). The disadvantages are similar to those of the federation plan. The most obvious impediment to the urban county plan is the generally sorry state of county government. County government has been labeled the dark continent of American politics. Here the spoils system holds out (except where the strings attached to federal and state grants impose a merit system). Structurally, the county government is of 18th century English origin (long since abandoned by the British), further distorted by Andrew Jackson democracy which made dozens of offices elective. The long ballot produces voter apathy if not cynicism, inefficient and mischievous decentralization of executive responsibilities, and occasionally a leadership or power vacuum which must be and is filled by the county political organization of the majority party. Before county government can function as a metropolitan government it must be organized, borrowing structural concepts from council-manager and strong-mayor-council plans of city government.

Prospects for Reform

As for most contemporary problems, one cannot be optimistic about the prospects for overcoming fragmentation of government in the metropolis. The obstacles to such reform include (1) public apathy, (2) entrenched interests and politicians who fear change would harm them, (3) restrictive state constitutions, (4) unresponsive state legislatures, (5) an American value system emphasizing "home rule" at the most basic level, and (6) racial antagonism between city and suburb. Yet Seattle, Minneapolis, and Miami are examples of where the metropolis is becoming governable. As local taxes mount, public apathy wanes; grass roots movements supported by such powerful interest groups as big business's Committee for Economic Development challenge the traditional vested interests; restrictive state constitutions are revised, as in Pennsylvania where all units of local government are now empowered to adopt home rule charters, and optional forms of government, to enter into cooperative arrangements, to exercise all powers not expressly forbidden by the state, and to experiment with new "area" governments; state legislatures now apportioned by court order on the basis of population become more responsive to metropolitan (not necessarily central city) pressures.

Conservatives and liberals can unite in a common cause to modify metropolitan government fragmentation: the conservative because he believes in effective local government to resist trends toward dependence on the national government; the liberal because he believes that there are problems that can be met only by government and that the present local government system is a failure.

While principles and rational arguments will be important, it is likely that the prime motivation for reducing fragmentation will be the federal government grant. It is clear that from now on the federal agencies will favor those metropolitan communities where there exists an apparatus for metropolitan-wide planning, control, and implementation of programs.

RECASTING STATE GOVERNMENT INTO METROPOLITAN GOVERNMENT *

ALAN K. CAMPBELL

Most discussions of the urban tax crisis assume that the solution lies either in consolidating the central city and its suburbs into a single tax unit or pinning our hopes on federal revenue sharing. Mr. Campbell suggests that we have overlooked a much more likely way of preventing urban bankruptcy by converting state governments into metropolitan governments.

Why can't central cities create an adequate tax base? How does their present tax effort compare with suburbs? Why can't we assume that the restructuring of urban government into metropolitan units will take place? Why can it be argued that state governments today should be the super-government for metropolitan areas? What city functions might the state assume directly? How

* "*Metropolitan Organization, Politics, and Taxation*" by Alan K. Campbell, reprinted from Proceedings of the Academy of Political Science, "*Municipal Income Taxes*," 28 (January, 1968), 138–41, 144–49 by permission.

might it become involved in revenue sharing?

. . . Composed of numerous small jurisdictions, the local-government system possesses boundaries that do not coincide with any meaningful economic areas. Taxes imposed on only a part of an interrelated economic area cause a variety of difficulties. The imposition of a sales tax in a small part of such an area may cause customers to cross invisible governmental boundaries to do their shopping. Equally, a local income tax may cause residents to change home as well as job location. Obviously, the larger the local jurisdiction, or rather the closer it approximates a meaningful economic area, the less likely these consequences will follow.

More important, however, than these difficulties are those associated with the present distribution of revenue bases and service needs. More and more people and economic activities are concentrated within the country's metropolitan areas. Each of these areas consists of a central city or cities and their surrounding suburban hinterland, and the 228 areas, as defined by the Census Bureau, contain approximately 67 percent of the country's population. Because of the sorting-out process taking place, more and more people with the greatest needs for public services are concentrated in the central cities, while the superior revenue base is concentrated in the areas outside these cities.

There is, therefore, a mismatch between service needs and tax base. In this situation the need for increased revenue is greatest in the central city, and yet the likelihood of inequity and of serious economic consequences is greatest if taxes to produce that revenue are imposed in these areas.

These differences between central cities and their suburbs have resulted in considerably greater local tax effort being made in the cities than outside them. For the twenty-two largest metropolitan areas in the United States tax effort, as measured by taxes as a proportion of personal income, is 33 percent higher in central cities than in their suburbs.

This difference in tax effort between central cities and their economically related outlying areas is a result of the need for greater services in cities, while these areas receive, in general, less external aid than do their suburban counterparts. In fact, the difference in revenue needed between city and suburb for traditional municipal services (such as police, fire protection, and sanitation) and poverty-related services (welfare, health, hospital and educational services for the disadvantaged) account for most of the differences between city and suburban tax effort.

If non-property taxes are to be used, it would appear that some form of regional jurisdiction is necessary. Only through such a device would many of the competitive disadvantages of such taxes be overcome, and, more important, the tax base and service needs could be better matched. These arguments, of course, constitute only part of the rationalization often used for some form of metropolitan government.

In fact, the major push for metropolitan government has been based primarily on the need for increased effectiveness in performing governmental services. Great stress has been placed on the lack of correspondence between jurisdictional boundaries and public needs. Automobiles, goods, and people flow back and forth across the boundaries as if they did not exist. To solve the problems emerging from such movement requires, it is argued, governmental jurisdictions which encompass the areas of such movement—metropolitan areas are the usual candidates.

Arguments for metropolitan government, which have been made by good government, business, and civic groups since at least the 1920's, have had very little impact on the actual governmental reorganization that has taken place in metropolitan areas. The reorganizations which have occurred, except for the occasional use of the county as a metropolitan governmental unit (Dade County, Florida, and Davidson County, Tennessee) have resulted in the establishment of special one-function jurisdictions. The functions selected are usually related more to the hardware than the software services of government—transportation, water supply, and sewage disposal, rather

than education, health, or welfare. It appears that the necessity for this movement's making a fundamental contribution to present inequities is not great since the greatest needs are concentrated in central cities. Such schemes as multi-jurisdiction imposition of the same tax, or even the imposition of a surtax on a state tax, may contribute to solving the competitive problem of non-property taxes imposed differentially, if at all, by many small jurisdictions, but they do not make any contribution to offsetting the present differences in tax effort between cities and their surrounding areas. Such joint agreements among jurisdictions for the imposition of a tax would probably not result in any one of them providing aid to another jurisdiction by granting a part of the revenue collected within one jurisdiction to another possessing greater need. Nor is it likely that a state surtax would be distributed to the jurisdictions on any basis other than where it is collected.

State Government as Metropolitan Government

If local government reorganization is not likely to create a unit capable of supporting equitable non-property taxes, what is the alternative? It has been suggested that the logical alternative is state government. For example, Professors Martin Meyerson and Edward C. Banfield, writing specifically about Massachusetts, said, "When one remembers that four-fifths of the

Massachusetts people live in metropolitan areas already, and that the proportion who live in them is bound to increase, it is hard to see how the state can fail to become the equivalent, for all practical purposes, of eight or more metropolitan governments." [1]

There are at least two ways in which the state governments may make a contribution to solving the fiscal problems of local governments. One is through the direct assumption of functions that are now performed at the local level and the other is by the provision of increased aid.

There are reasons, of course, other than fiscal, to transfer functions from the local to state government. Efficiency, effectiveness, and policy innovation may be added. The concern here, however, is primarily with the contribution functional transfers and increased state aid may make to the fundamental fiscal problems of local jurisdictions and, more significantly, of the nation's cities.

A function which in some states is now performed at the state level, but in many industrial states is not, is welfare. This function, already highly aided by both state and federal governments, is also tightly controlled in its administration by the higher levels of government.

If welfare in New York state were transferred from the units which presently administer it—New York

City and outside of New York City, mostly counties—the disparity in fiscal effort (local taxes as a proportion of income) between New York City and its suburbs would be reduced from the present 28 percent difference to 11 percent. In other words, in the case of New York City the result would still leave the city with a higher fiscal effort than its surrounding suburbs but would reduce the gap considerably—for the country's twenty-two largest metropolitan areas the gap would be decreased from 33 to 18 percent.

Another, or possibly concurrent, route which the states could follow is the provision of greater state aid. The significant need here, however, is not just to add to the present aid systems but rather to direct the aid to those jurisdictions that have the greatest needs and are making the greatest fiscal effort. Such redirection would cause more aid to flow to central cities and to those suburban jurisdictions with neither a strong residential nor industrial-commercial tax base.

In general, state-aid systems tend to aid suburban and rural areas more heavily than urban areas. The reason for this situation is both historical and political. For many years the wealth of American society was concentrated in its cities and appropriately it was tapped by state legislatures to improve the level of public services in the country's rural areas. Further, this pattern of taxing city residents to aid non-city areas reflected the representation pattern of state legisla-

---

[1] Martin Meyerson and Edward C. Banfield, *Boston: The Job Ahead*, (Cambridge, 1966), 23.

tures. The aid system in most states reflected the vast over-representation of rural areas.

Perhaps the inequities in the aid system can be most readily seen by examining the pattern of state aid for education in New York state. The difference in the amount of aid received by the five largest cities of New York state, between city and suburb, is least for Buffalo, $74, and highest for Albany, $186. The other cities all have differences of similar magnitude—Syracuse, $175; Rochester, $176; and New York City, $134. Total aid averages around $500.

. . .

Quite apart from reapportionment the state must overcome a long history of nonattention to city problems. Further, many states possess constitutions that stand in the way of an effective response to any problems—urban or other kinds. Nevertheless, the state alternative seems more feasible, politically, than any of the others —particularly more so than local government reorganization.

If this analysis is correct, it does not seem that non-property taxes are economically, administratively, or politically wise within the present local-government jurisdictional system. It is possible that arrangements could be worked out through local agreements or through a state-designed plan of either locally imposed non-property taxes or surtaxes on state taxes which could provide an economically viable tax base. However, it appears unlikely, politically, that either local jurisdictional agreement or state arranged-for taxes would move resources in the quantities needed into those areas of greatest social need. These areas are primarily, although not exclusively, located in cities.

Another alternative, and one more likely to fit administrative and economic criteria, is for the state to play a larger role. Such a role would require both the direct assumption of responsibility for certain functions and the provision of greater state aid to those areas of greatest need. The political likelihood of the states' moving in this direction is uncertain. It is certain that the creation of general metropolitan government, the best candidate for the operation of an equitable system of non-property taxes, is at best politically unlikely.

Whichever route is taken will require political talent and courage. The political implications of any tax increase, and especially state and local ones, will necessitate such courage. The talented politician, however, is the successful translator of policy necessities into politically acceptable programs.

PART TWO

The Policy Crisis: Problems, Resources and Political Realities

To this point we have concentrated on the crisis within the political system. That crisis is very real. Unless the system is rejuvenated, we cannot effectively cope with our multiple political problems. Even if the system is reformed, however, the problems of our urban society and the international order are of such a magnitude that they may not respond to medication, given our limited resources and the existing political realities. These problems are so complex, and the proposed policies so unpalatable politically, that we face a policy crisis at least as challenging as the crisis in the political system.

The Crisis in Urban America

Most Americans now live in an urban society. It follows that most of our domestic crises are urban-centered. In the chapters that follow, we have identified several of these problems and examined them individually. In the real world, of course, problems are interrelated, and politically leaders must look at the total urban scene. City blight, pollution, poverty and crime are intertwined, with each reacting on the other. Start at any point! A rising crime rate promotes urban decay because more middle-class whites tend to move to the suburbs, and that brings on a lower tax base, that produces inferior ghetto schools, that perpetuates poverty. Or begin with poverty as the first cause, and run through the problems in some other pattern. Arrange them as you will, they are variations on a central theme—the crisis of urban America.

How seriously should we view this complex crisis? Is it a matter of life or death or is it merely a chronic irritant? To probe this question, it may be useful to assume that all of the dire predictions about the fate of the city come true. What if the central city continues to crumble and becomes a vast slum? What if air, water and noise pollution double and redouble, while mounds of uncollected garbage and discarded cars fill the alleys and streets? What if violence and theft become so commonplace that no man travels unarmed? What if poverty is accepted as only the just due of the ghetto resident, ill-educated as he is by his slum school? What if the good life is regarded as beyond the aspirations of these subhuman city folk? What real difference would this scenario make to the comfortable suburban majority and their small town friends?

These are legitimate questions that deserve honest answers. If the march of events during the last decade is any indicator of the future, this scenario is more realistic than is one predicting reforms that will save the city. In a sentence, collapse of our central cities would destroy the American dream. We will have created two nations: one superior; the other inferior. We will be well on our way toward a caste system, with the path of upward mobility permanently blocked. Democratic idealism will be forever tarnished.

The scenario also assumes that the crisis can be confined to the inner city and that its residents will accept their fate without protest. Violent riots of recent years should dampen this optimism. The fire next time may see the suburbs ablaze from coast to coast. Nor can pollution be confined to the city limits. The costs of containment may well run higher than those for city rejuvenation. If the right of the majority to rule is challenged by any sizeable minority that feels exploited, our national political stability will be permanently impaired.

There are also compelling economic reasons for saving the city. It has for centuries been the crossroads of trade, business and culture. Can any industrial society function if this point of focus is erased? And what of the city as a cultural center? Can anyone seriously visualize the suburbs creating substitutions for the Buhl Planetarium, the Metropolitan Museum of Art, the Shedd Aquarium, the St. Louis Zoo, The New York City Public Library, or the Franklin Institute?

The Crisis in World Order

Our concern for the future of American cities should not blind us to the global crisis in world order. Today the world has become a global village that lives under a sketchy political framework. Our concern for poverty in the United States is a relative matter when compared to the poverty of New Delhi or Rio de Janeiro. The resources available for our domestic urban crisis are severely restricted by our search for security in a world where each nation "goes it alone."

As a nation we have lived under the shadow of nuclear warfare for a generation. In our race with the Soviet Union for military superiority, we have achieved an uneasy balance of terror. Our long-range chances of survival are dependent on some mutual agreement with the USSR that will permit both nations to retreat from the edge of the abyss.

On the international scene, we have played the role of world policeman for a quarter century, to the neglect of our domestic problems. Now we are in the unenviable position of making hard choices between national and international priorities. Much to the distress of suburbanites who have the good life at their fingertips, they cannot become isolationist and disregard either the city or international crisis. If these crises are to be met adequately, more of our resources must be diverted from private consumption. The overriding political question becomes: Will the American people, having grasped the seriousness of the crisis, rise to the challenge?

7. The Crumbling City: Blight and Decay

Most of our cities are old and sick, abandoned by the people who built them. Evidence of this illness is everywhere apparent. Unlike the popular song's lyrics, "Nothing is happening, Downtown." The central business district is no longer the agreed-upon center of the metropolitan area. Established department stores have closed their doors or are fading while they build million dollar branches in the suburbs. In most cities, there are many vacancies in downtown office buildings.

In the old entertainment district, the theater marquees are blanked out: night club life is fading: prestige restaurants languish. In downtown Cleveland, for instance, four first-run movie houses have closed their doors (one carries an advertisement for "Love Story" —playing in the suburbs).

The degradation of the business-entertainment area is matched by the decline of the older manufacturing districts, "done in" by ancient plants, high taxes, difficult transportation, and obsolete machinery. International Business Machines pulls up its roots in Manhattan; Squibb Drug Company (a century-old firm) follows. The Terminal Tower looms over central Cleveland as a monument to a bye-gone age—there is no inter-state passenger rail service out of Cleveland. Residential areas are similarly afflicted, as the whole central city takes on the characteristics of a super-ghetto, swarming with the new migration.

This slum-ghetto is a hallmark of Big City, U.S.A. It is characterized by its black, chicano, or Puerto Rican residents; its cramming of several families into former one-family dwellings; its prevailing atmosphere of violence; its all-inclusive poverty; its drugs, alcohol, and general vice, and its dirt and stench. In simplified form the total picture is one of a dying core surrounded by youthful, vibrant satellites who have no concern for the welfare of the old town.

This cancerous development is not yet terminal. In fact, at high noon, the central city is still filled with suburbanites who work there. But when the nightly exodus is complete, the streets are left to the permanent residents with their permanent problems.

Causes of Decay

The decline of the city is easier to describe than to analyze. Why have millions of white Americans rejected urban for suburban living? Why do other millions who still work in the central city endure the strife of daily commuting? For many the suburb represents the best of two worlds—a blending of open-country living and contact with the heart of the American economy. But increasingly, the negative aspects of city life have become the overriding factors. Outward migration rates have doubled in the past five years. The central city has become the center of pollution; it is the focus point of delinquency, crime and vice; its educational system is substandard; its tax rates are high, reflecting the need for greater public services, and it is the poverty nucleus. In summary, the central city is viewed by suburbanites as the antithesis of "the good life."

Can We Save the City?

Reforms such as urban political reorganization and a revision of the tax base have been explored in a previous chapter. In this section we concentrate on the reversal of physical decay. Most of the government's earlier attempts at physical rebirth emphasized urban redevelopment projects and public housing. Dilapidated sections of the city were leveled by bulldozers to gain a fresh start. Unfortunately, the chief beneficiaries of urban renewal turned out to be real estate interests, while housing for the poor was destroyed. President Johnson tried to revitalize this program by a "model cities" approach that required a master plan for the whole community. Although this approach was not rejected by President Nixon, he has given it a low budget priority. Another, more drastic proposal, would be to concentrate public and private spending on completely new towns, such as Reston, Virginia or Columbia, Maryland.

No clear-cut, obvious answer to urban blight is at hand, and it seems highly improbable that modern America, with its wealth and ingenuity, will abandon its central cities to permanent blight. However, the possibility exists. One wry wit, a victim of rising unemployment in Seattle, posted the following notice in the airport: "Will the last one out, please turn off the lights?" Another commentator foresees a future sign at the tip of Manhattan:

Sale! Originally $24!
Marked down to $3.98!
Exact change required!

A NEW YORK GHETTO:
THE KELLY STREET BLUES *
DONALD MOFFITT AND
ART SEARS, JR.

In an abstract sense, life in the ghetto may be hard to visualize. In this article it is fleshed out with real people, who live in one block of one ghetto. Where do the people come from? Why do they stay? What vices are commonplace? Does the area have any middle-class attitudes? Why are so many of the residents children? Is there any reason to believe that these children are "locked into" the Kelly Street environment? Who has the better chance to escape—Butch or his pigeons?

Sitting in the crowded kitchen of her apartment, Mrs. Betty Alston, 31, cracks open a bottle of Ballantine's Ale and offers it to a visitor. Then she wets a piece of brown paper with her tongue and presses the paper to the forehead of 5-month-old Kwame Kenyatta Wray Jackson, the baby of a neighborhood friend. "My father's from the

* Reprinted from Donald Moffitt and Art Sears, Jr., "Kelly Street Blues," Wall Street Journal, January 6, 1969, by permission.

West Indies, and he says that stops the hiccups," she explains.

Betty Alston is a black slum-dweller. A portly, amiable young woman, she is one of some 900 people who live on the west side of the 800 block of Kelly Street in New York City's borough of the Bronx. Until a few months ago, she supported herself and her three sons by working for the Post Office. Now, like most of her neighbors, she lives on public assistance. She is proud of other members of her family, most of whom live in New Jersey. "Grandpa had about 50 grandchildren," she says. "There's an airplane pilot and a policeman in the family. Everybody but me turned out to be something."

In disgust, Betty Alston quit her job after burglars broke into her apartment while she was at work and "robbed me blind." She would like to move away from Kelly Street and get back to work, but she is afraid to leave her apartment untended to look for a new place to live and a job. Kwame Jackson's father was shot five times while standing in the street last Labor Day, and the next day Betty's own son Kevin, 11, playing in the street, was shot seriously in the abdomen. "When you're black and you live in this place, or any place like this," she says, "it's not by choice."

Kelly Street is a ghetto within a ghetto. For blocks around the neighborhood is predominantly Puerto Rican. Kelly Street is more than 90% Negro. The other residents are Puerto Ricans.

Roughly 600 of the 900 residents

in 204 apartments on the west side of the block are children, and more than 200 of the others are women. Many fathers of children in the block cannot appear to live there without jeopardizing the welfare assistance that supports fatherless families. Fewer than 100 men live "officially" on the block.

Kelly Street is a mixture of four-story and five-story buildings with as many as 20 walk-up apartments in each. The buildings are 40 to 60 years old. Despite six-day-a-week pickups of trash, gutters, sidewalks and stoops by evening are littered with wrapping paper, cartons and beer and soft-drink cans.

A layer of fine broken glass is dusted over the sidewalk and street. Kelly Street residents consume large quantities of soft drinks, and the wide use of nonreturn bottles means that children no longer save them for small change. Instead, they enjoy breaking them.

Jews Who Are Black

Kelly Street has long been a ghetto of sorts. Raleigh Lay, 38, a Negro who works as a city garbage truck driver, says that when he moved into the block with his parents in 1942, the neighborhood was largely Jewish with a sprinkling of families newly arrived from Puerto Rico. There still is one synagogue in the neighborhood, the red-brick Congregation Mount Horeb, a few blocks away. But there are few white Jews any more. "Are you Jewish Negroes?" a passerby asks a bearded black rabbi unlocking the building. "We are not Negroes, sir," he answers with testy dignity. "We are Jews who happen to be black."

Another old-time black resident, Mrs. Eleanor Richardson, also remembers when Kelly Street was different. When she moved into the block in 1943, she recalls, "my next-door neighbor was a Jewish hardware merchant. There were fewer kids. There was a Puerto Rican family of eight kids upstairs, but you didn't see those kids till they was going to Mass on Sunday."

Then the poorer Negroes "started moving in and the others started moving out," says Mrs. Richardson. "After that, the landlords didn't care who they were taking in. Soon as a Negro would move in, a white would move out."

Hope in Harlem

Kelly Street today is comparable, in its physical decay and high crime rates, to other New York ghettos like the Bedford-Stuyvesant area of Brooklyn or Harlem, situated on Manhattan some 40 blocks from Kelly Street. However, part of Harlem is anticipating something of a renaissance. The state plans to build a huge office building complex there, and efforts to improve maintenance on Harlem's apartment buildings are beginning to show results. Across the Harlem River in the south Bronx, though, the relative optimism of Harlem gives way to an attitude that's close to despair.

A long stroll through the south

Bronx around Kelly Street shows why. Two visiting reporters pass abandoned automobiles, stripped, gutted and crammed with garbage. The foyer and first-floor apartments of a condemned building are filthy with garbage and rank with the odor of human excrement. The building is a hangout for narcotic addicts, one of many such buildings in the Kelly Street area.

A woman and her small children peer down from a window on the second floor. Only six families are left in the building, she says in response to a question, and none have been able to find other housing. "We're just going to stay here until the city finds us something," she says. "I don't know why they haven't yet."

The strollers happen onto two fires being fought by city firemen. "You keep walking through here," says a fireman manning a hose at an apartment building, "and it will tell you more than I can."

At a nearby corner "bodega," or Puerto Rican grocery-delicatessen, a crowd has gathered. Two policemen are investigating a quarrel. "Take a walk," a ruddy-faced white policeman orders a surly Puerto Rican.

"Why should I take a walk? I don't wanna take a walk," the Puerto Rican snaps back.

"You take a walk now," the policeman answers, "or I'll fix you so you can't walk."

A woman involved in the quarrel shouts at one of the policemen, "Take your damned hands off me! How do I know what you've been doing with your damned hands?"

Outside a corner bar, several junkies — narcotics addicts — and pushers loiter. One of them is a black youth called Chico, dressed in a bright red sweater, who supports his $60-a-day habit by dealing in heroin. Nodding toward the reporters, he asks a man with them, "What are they doing around here?" Their companion, a recent Columbia University graduate, is a resident of a public-housing project in the Bronx and a former drug-rehabilitation worker who has tried unsuccessfully to get Chico off narcotics. "Don't worry, they're not interested in narcotics," he says. Chico shakes hands with the visitors, and they move off.

A Fight Over Customers

Further along, there's a fight in a sandwich shop. A prostitute has accused a competitor of luring away a "John," or customer, whom she had been trying to "hustle." She is especially angry because the second prostitute bragged that the John subsequently paid $15, compared with the going rate of $5. A patrol car pulls up and two policemen walk into the shop, only half a block from the 41st Precinct station. Meanwhile, a dozen or so other prostitutes loiter in nearby doorways, waiting for potential customers. Most of the women are heroin users.

In a bar, a Puerto Rican called Benito comes in, greets an acquaintance and buys a round of beers. Benito doesn't use drugs himself, but he is well-known in the neighborhood as a dealer. He has just been released from prison in California. His acquaintance tries to buy some "reefers," or marijuana cigarettes, from Benito, but Benito says no.

This kind of environment frightens and offends many of the people on Kelly Street. "So much goes on around here that you wouldn't believe it," said a 30-year-old woman named Elizabeth. "There was one fellow shot. You're scared to say anything to anybody around here because of what the junkies will do to you." (Actually, there were four shootings on the block last summer.)

Elizabeth lived in Harlem until last December. She moved to Kelly Street so her husband couldn't find her. He was released from prison last December after serving a seven-year term for armed robbery. When he got home, out of resentment over her refusal to give him $50 a week from her welfare payments and anger over her year-old child fathered by another man, he cut her with a razor blade. She bears a long scar down the side of her face. The wound required 27 sutures to close. "He's been calling my aunt," Elizabeth says, "and telling her he's gonna kill me. But she won't tell him where I am."

Makeshift Playground

Pressed to tell what's *good* about Kelly Street, most residents are hard put to answer. "In the summer, they (the police) close up the street so the kids can play," says Mrs. Shirley Mayo, a youngish-looking mother of five. Her oldest offspring is 17, her youngest three weeks. She is separated from her husband, and she lives on welfare.

People live on Kelly Street not because they like it but because it offers rents they can afford to pay and, for many, rents the welfare department will permit. For their rent money they get more room than is available in Harlem. Many of the women in the block, in fact, moved from Harlem when the birth of another child sent them looking for larger quarters.

Mrs. Christine Small, 40, had lived in a three-room apartment in another neighborhood in the Bronx. She moved to Kelly Street because she found a four-room apartment for only $92.51 a month, which her $360-a-month income from public assistance permits. She is separated from her husband. She has five children ranging in age from five to 15.

Most of Mrs. Small's neighbors were born in Georgia, South Carolina or, like Mrs. Small herself, in North Carolina. She comes from the small town of Richmond Square, where she worked occasionally as a maid, for $2 a day, and as a field hand, for $3 a day. "I couldn't make it down home, with my children," she says.

A Broken Mirror

Mrs. Small chats with visitors while she sits in her kitchen, combing her hair before a triangular piece from a broken mirror propped on a chair.

In her living room, a chest of drawers lies on its side next to a wall. Two of its legs are broken; the upright side is used as a table. Her youngest son, a five-year-old with club feet, drags himself over the floor.

Beulah Hunter, 16, lived in Harlem with her mother, Ella, 33, until a year ago. Then Beulah became pregnant, and Mrs. Hunter found a larger apartment for them on Kelly Street. Her pregnancy forced Beulah to quit high school, where she was taking a commercial course —typing, shorthand and the like.

Beulah's baby was born last summer, and she returned to high school in the fall. She dislikes Kelly Street. "It's too bad around the block—people getting shot and all," she says.

"Being on welfare and trying to get out of the neighborhood is hard," says a 20-year-old woman named Gail, who has children aged six, four and three years. "The landlords don't want welfare, and they don't want kids." Gail is separated from her husband. "He wasn't my type," she says. "He came from down South, he believed in keeping a woman barefoot and pregnant and he would roam the streets at night then come home and beat you up. He didn't want to better himself. He used to take my little girl out to bars with him."

A Small Boy's Plan

Gail is worried about Kelly Street's influence on her children. Her two young sons each have seen two of the recent shootings on the block, and her six-year-old daughter has seen three. "My three-year-old boy said, 'If somebody bothers me, I'll put firecrackers in my (toy) rifle and shoot 'em,'" she says. "He's only three; he thinks gunshots are just firecrackers, but that's nothing a three-year-old boy should be thinking about.

"One day he was lying in bed, and he called his sister a dirty name. I told him never to use that kind of language, and he said, 'Well, a *lady* said it.'"

Not all Kelly Street tenants are husbandless mothers living on welfare. Jerome Poage, 28, works for the city's Department of Social Services—the "welfare department"— carrying case records of transient "clients" from one welfare center in the city to another. He earns $154.30 a week, relatively high for Kelly Street, and he's a bachelor.

Mr. Poage complains about the street's crime and narcotics. Recently, he says, he found three "trays"—glassine envelops of adulterated heroin costing $3 each—on the sidewalk, apparently dropped there by an addict fearing arrest.

40 Quarts of Ale

Marijuana and "hard" narcotics, especially cocaine and heroin, are used on the block, but alcohol is far more obvious. As Betty Alston puts it, "A lot of people around here smoke reefers—we just drink." On weekends, she and her boyfriend often get together with an upstairs neighbor and her friend to drink ale and Scotch. "We drink about 40 quarts of ale on a weekend," she says. On another woman's bureau, there are a dozen bottles that might well be found in a fashionable East Side apartment—Beefeaters gin, Smirnoff vodka, Bacardi rum, among others.

The desire for middle-class possessions and furnishings on Kelly Street appears as strong as in any white middle-class suburb. There are exceptions, but Kelly Streeters in general do not live in the total squalor that might be imagined by looking at the façades of the buildings. Nearly all the apartments have a television set, and some have two. One mother on welfare has a color set, the gift of a friend. She also has a black-and-white TV-phonograph console that her son bought on the street for $35; the young man doesn't care to speculate on how the seller came by it.

One apartment, typical of many, is clean and bright except that lights are usually not turned on during the daytime in order to save on utility bills. The wall-to-wall carpeting is red, with bright blue throw rugs. In front of a new corner sofa, covered with protective plastic, is a coffee table decorated with artificial flowers. On a wall hangs a framed photograph of the late Martin Luther King, Jr.

Another apartment has linoleum floors and a stuffed armchair covered with an old blanket. On the walls hang a large print of a flock of flamingos, a gilded plate with a design showing an 18th century French couple in powdered wigs

and bearing the legend, "Souvenir of Toledo, Ohio," a brass plate with a medieval scene in relief, a watercolor print depicting a North African village and a color magazine photograph of a European quay in winter.

Soap Opera Fans

A few Kelly Streeters attend church, but organized religion doesn't loom large on the block. Phonograph music and television provide most entertainment; TV soap operas are extremely popular. Many residents lock themselves in their apartments early to avoid being bothered on the street by purse snatchers. In the late afternoon, men wait on street corners to learn whether they've made a "hit" on the numbers, the gang-run gambling game popular in many ghettos.

When they're not in school, younger children play in the street. A favorite game is "skells," played by flicking buttons over a course chalked on the pavement. Older teenagers spend much of their money on clothes and partying. They earn some money by working at part-time jobs, and they also get money from relatives. But the origin of much of their spending money is obscure; authorities say thievery and narcotics peddling are important sources.

Drinking starts at a young age. "If we ain't got money for whiskey, we get a bottle of wine," says a 16-year-old named Butch.

Butch, who has eight brothers and sisters, sits in his mother's living room chatting with several friends and visitors. The boys wear white tennis shoes and bright corduroy trousers—purple, red and green are faddish colors—with black turtleneck sweaters, black windbreakers or sport shirts. The boys all also own silk and mohair trousers that are custom-tailored at $19 a pair; they buy the material a few blocks away for 98 cents a yard. Butch hopes to get his mother to help him buy a $125 leather overcoat with a Persian lamb collar before winter is out. He says he can pay $40 if she will pay the rest.

'A Nice Quiet House'

Butch has just enrolled in Alfred E. Smith High School, a vocational school in the Bronx. He is taking a carpentry course. He says he likes carpentry and intends to continue it when he graduates. One of his mother's brothers is a carpenter.

When he turns 21, Butch, who expects by then to be married, plans to build himself a house in a Long Island or New Jersey suburb —"a nice quiet house in a nice quiet neighborhood," he says. He has $6,000 in a bank trust account, the insurance settlement from an accident several years ago in which he was struck by an automobile on the street.

Butch and his "boys," as he calls the informal clique of youths with whom he spends his spare time, raise pigeons on the roof of his apartment building. They like pigeons partly because of the competition for birds that goes on with other rooftop pigeon raisers nearby. Certain birds in a flock act as herders, rounding up other pigeons and keeping them together. Butch and his friends delight in sending up their birds to intercept other flocks, hoping to lure new birds into their coop. When a pigeon fancier loses a bird to somebody else's flock, he can buy it back for 50 cents.

The boys' flock occasionally brings in relatively valuable homing pigeons banded by members of pigeon fanciers' clubs in the Bronx and elsewhere. Butch also insists that U.S. Government agents have examined his flock looking for Army pigeons. Butch believes that the Army uses pigeons "to, like, fly messages back to the United States from Vietnam."

CITY SERVICES ARE COLLAPSING *
U. S. NEWS & WORLD REPORT

Many of the niceties that make cities habitable are neither mas-

* Reprinted from "Are City Services Breaking Down?" U.S. News & World Report, *May 24, 1971. Copyright 1971 U.S. News & World Report, Inc.*

sive nor mind-boggling. Inefficient garbage collection, building code violations, street pot holes, the lack of extra-curricular school programs, misplaced street signs, sagging city transit, and bumbling fire and police protection are a sample of the irritants. Each year urban taxes creep upward; every year the quality of city services seems to decline. Some of this decline can be explained by red tape and inefficient administration; some can be explained by the steady erosion of tax dollars through inflation.

But the real crisis in city services is yet to come. Heretofore most city workers have been civil service employees, outside the collective bargaining process. We are now caught up in a national movement to unionize city workers. The odds seem very great that union-ization will force up employee wages and that cities with their static tax base will be compelled to cut their work forces—leading to a further deterioration of city services. Chicago has already cut its teaching personnel; Cleveland has cut back on recreation; Pittsburgh has cut its building custodial staffs; dozens of cities have cut their street maintenance programs.

In the face of these develop-ments how long will cities remain habitable? Or are the cities finished?

At a time when cities are crying the financial blues and threatening fur-ther cutbacks in services, many res-idents claim they already are being short-changed on their tax dollars.

Talk with city dwellers around the country and you find it is the lapses in common, everyday public services that seem to irritate them most.

Garbage collection, or the lack of it, is high on any list of com-plaints.

Tempers boil easily in discussions of city-run utilities, such as water departments. But many citizens have despaired of success in battles with public officials and now either acquiesce or sulk silently in frustra-tion.

I. D. Robbins, trustee and past president of the City Club of New York, a citizens' "watchdog" orga-nization, makes this observation:

"I think the average citizen is probably anesthetized by now. He's gotten used to things being rather poorly done."

Gripes in Chicago

Statistics kept by the mayor's office in Chicago show that in March this year the city received nearly three times as many complaints regard-ing building-code violations—not enough heat in apartments, elec-tricity shut off, no water—as it did about police services.

The city of Milwaukee says it receives more gripes about ineffi-cient snow removal than on any other matter.

"People tend to forget that we've got over 1,300 miles of streets," says one Milwaukee official, "and we simply cannot plow them all simultaneously. All the citizens know is that their property taxes keep going up, so they expect better and better service. The fact is, most of the tax money goes for welfare and schools, anyway—not for removing snow."

Mrs. Thelma Miller, a PTA official, complains New York City public schools are not set up to meet the extracurricular needs of her 12-year-old daughter, who is bused to a Queens school.

Mrs. Miller says the Queens school district gets $100 for each bused pupil to pay for special activities scheduled for late afternoon. Her daughter, however, must catch a 3 p.m. bus in order to return home, and misses the after-school sessions.

A former New York City teacher, Mrs. Doris Gordon, calls the schools in her new home town of Silver Spring, Md., "heaven, compared to where I taught." But Mrs. Gordon still has reservations. She feels schools take too much of her tax dollars, "try to fit the children into a mass-production mold," and give parents the brush-off.

"I wrote to the State asking what they proposed to teach in new sex education programs," Mrs. Gordon recalls. "They said they were teaching 'character.' I asked them to define 'character.' They never wrote back."

Oh, That Garbage

An almost universal gripe has something to do with garbage—the way it is collected (messily), what the service costs (more and more), or the frequency of pickups (less and less).

Ralph Hulsey, superintendent of Atlanta's sanitary division, admits: "The biggest problem we have is scattering garbage."

In Sandy Springs, Ga., an Atlanta suburb, Mrs. Perry W. Mullen complains:

"They doubled our taxes and now we get garbage pickups only once a week. It used to be three times a week."

Jon H. Hill, a sales supervisor in Ashland, Va., north of Richmond, receives no public garbage collections and is glad of it. He pays $36 a year for a private service and, he says, "the man will take anything we put out."

But in Hillcrest Heights, Md., says Silvester DeThomasis, a printing-company executive, the area has switched from private collections to a county service and now "we never know whether they're coming or not—we've gone for as much as a week without a pickup, and they never make it in snow."

Businessman John Garner in Atlanta calls the city sanitation service inefficient for lack of competition.

Co-operative Plan

Mr. Garner sought to change things by proposing private garbage collection for apartments through an apartment-owner co-operative. His plan: Collect the garbage, recycle wastes at a profit and then share the profit among co-operative members. "There can be no strikes," read his printed proposal, which promised "great price savings."

Atlanta officials were less enthusiastic, however. The city attorney ruled that even if the city didn't collect the garbage, apartments would still have to pay the city sanitation tax. This killed the private proposal.

Capitalizing on the public's feeling that it can't fight alone, many newspapers have set up special columns or departments to act as ombudsmen.

Thomas Houston, director of one such column, "Action Line," for "The Detroit Free Press," says, "People are getting stoic about the state of services." As far as complaints about local governments are concerned, Mr. Houston observes: "We run into bureaucratic stupidity more than anything else."

Bum Joke

In the San Fernando Valley near Los Angeles, one resident describes spending months trying to get the city to fix a broken sidewalk in front of his home. Inspections were made, reports filed and decisions for action carefully weighed.

When public approval finally was given, the cement was poured. But it was late in the afternoon of Halloween.

By morning, the new sidewalk was covered with initials, mottoes and remarks which the taxpayer felt were hardly things he wanted outside his door forever. So he had to begin his campaign all over.

When Glenn Haschenburger bought a new home in the Shadow Hills area of Los Angeles, he soon discovered that nobody could find the house.

The problem: His street is a short off-shoot from a main street going up a hill. At the bottom of the hill was a sign saying "No Thru Street."

Mr. Haschenburger figured the solution was simple: Move his street sign a short distance so that it could be spotted from the bottom of the hill. He made this suggestion to the Van Nuys office of the Los Angeles department of streets and was treated "most cordially."

But nothing happened.

Weeks later Mr. Haschenburger discovered Los Angeles has a thick set of rules which say street signs must stay where they are put.

Still later, Mr. Haschenburger prevailed upon his city councilman. More time passed, but a service crew finally arrived and moved the sign.

Within two weeks an errant motorist knocked the sign down. Mr. Haschenburger says he hasn't worked up energy enough to renew the battle.

Tree Trouble

In Detroit, Mr. and Mrs. Andrew Shedlock complained last October about a tree in front of their home that leaned into the street. After several tries at getting the tree cut down, they dropped the matter until spring.

Mrs. Shedlock resumed her efforts in March. At one point she told a city employee that in desperation she had hacked some low branches from the tree. She was warned: "You have no right to touch that tree—it's city property."

Many calls later, Mrs. Shedlock gave up on the city's forestry department and called the mayor's office. The tree was removed.

James Kates of Cleveland says he is so worried about danger from a burned-out abandoned house next door to his home that he and his wife take turns standing guard at night.

The hulk is so close to the Kates's home that the eaves touch. The city of Cleveland says it doesn't have the money to tear down the structure. Mr. Kates offered to pay. But first he must obtain clearance from the owner, a widowed Social Security recipient who has moved twice since the January fire. Mr. Kates says city attorneys are trying to help untangle the red tape, but, "they are not trying hard enough."

Mr. Kates says worry and a shortage of sleep have caused him to lose 24 pounds since January. Prior to the fire, Mr. Kates canceled his insurance when his rates doubled. Now, he says, he is unable to get insurance at any price as long as the abandoned house stands.

Daily users of San Francisco's Municipal Railway have all kinds of complaints about the comfort and dependability of the equipment they depend on to get to work.

"I consider the trip downtown and back on the city bus or street car as the hardest part of my working day," says a San Francisco secretary who lives in the Sunset residential section.

"In the morning, my husband drives me several blocks so that I can take a bus, because the street car near me is not dependable. At night, when I do take the street car home, I often am told to get off about halfway there, because they decide to reroute the street car. Sometimes another car comes along soon. Other times I have to wait a long time. One night I had to walk a dozen blocks. The day I can afford a car to use to get to work, I sure won't be riding the city buses."

Also in San Francisco, the public-utilities commission has decided to cut off service in the evening of the California Street cable-car run, despite public outcries.

Mrs. Hans Klussmann, a leader in previous fights to preserve the cable-car service, told the PUC:

"The cable cars are San Francisco. They are the No. 1 attraction of the city and, since tourism is already slipping, you may be killing off the golden goose."

In the mainly Mexican-American and Negro areas of Houston and the predominantly Negro sections of Birmingham, Ala., and Atlanta, you hear concern about police protection.

A black woman who lives in one of the public housing projects in Atlanta, says this:

"There's lots of vandalism. As for police protection, there's really very little of it. Once there was some shooting in an apartment. Children were screaming. We called police and it was pretty near three hours before they got to the scene."

Sometimes there is grousing over fire-fighting.

In the Birmingham, Ala., suburb of Mountain Brook, a resident complained to the city council that it took firemen 15 to 20 minutes to answer a call only five blocks from the fire station. A neighbor said four fire alarms were turned in and finally a boy on a motor scooter was dispatched to the fire station. When firemen finally arrived, the fire hydrant in front of the blazing house didn't work.

All at Once

A Kansas City man gripes about simultaneous repair work on bridges linking Missouri and Kansas and asks:

"Is there no method to the madness of the people who plan such things?"

In Arlington, Va., a mother with four small children waits hours at juvenile court to testify that she saw a teen-ager steal and crash a car. The judge dismisses the case without having the witness called.

Willie Davis, an Atlanta laborer, is confronted with a $1,800 water bill at his rented house because of a leaking underground pipe. The owner disclaims responsibility and the city says it's up to Mr. Davis to pay, although the bill was reduced—to $1,300.

A visitor to the Kansas City zoo complains that the public rest rooms are no cleaner than the animal cages.

There are some kind words, and some obvious efforts by the cities to respond. Examples: "City Hall Central" in Detroit, set up to direct citizens to the proper place for help; a departmental troubleshooter hired by the sanitation department in Charlotte, N.C.

Los Angeles adds new routes and new vehicles to its bus system, and its department of water and power sponsors a nightly television show outlining services and inviting criticisms.

Houston expands trash pickups, switches from private to less expensive public emergency-ambulance service.

Yet if rising costs force cities to cut back further—and this is the threat throughout the nation—even more complaints are certain to be heard.

URBAN RENEWAL:
'DESTRUCTION,'
CONSTRUCTION *
NICHOLAS VON HOFFMAN

Urban renewal is often pictured as a panacea that will erase city blight. But the cure itself may create other problems as in the following case involving Charleston, West Virginia. Who benefits from urban renewal? Who loses? Is the public or private interest being served? What role do urban planners see for the average citizen? Is renewal in itself a part of the urban problem?

The diesel animal with caterpillar feet looked like a famished, steel-toothed hippopotamus. It would lift up its toothy mouth, grab a hunk of wall or a slice of roof, shake it and yank it, pull it off the building, and slam it on the ground, and then run back and forth over it with its metal treads.

The hippo was demolishing buildings to make way for the soon-to-be-built Interstate 77. Its fero-

* Reprinted from Nicholas von Hoffman, "Urban Renewal: 'Destruction,' Construction," The Washington Post, March 11, 1970, by permission.

cious foraging among the small, shingled houses where black people once lived demonstrates how little practical connection the words of national politicians have with the operations they run. On every level the destructive grazing of the hippo should not have been permitted.

I-77 is absorbing valuable flatland, of which there is too little in hilly Charleston. There is no reason for it since the highway could have been built over a railroad right of way. This lack of economy extends to the wasteful hippo discharging gas, noise and energy into the air as it tears and rips, insuring that not one usable piece of wood will be salvageable from the ruin it causes.

I-77 will stand next to an urban renewal project on which there will be housing for low-income and old people and this will breed a new misfortune. Charleston is built in a narrow valley along a river where for 50 miles chemical plants discharge odorous, sulphurous, particulate ordure into the air where, sheltered from winds and strong breezes, it stays, bestowing sinusitis and emphysema on the wheezing populace. The people in the housing projects will be twice blessed for they will not only have the filthy air everyone must breathe, they will also have the fumes from the huge semis dragging their awesome tankards of chemicals out of Kanawha Valley to industrial customers far away.

The renewal plan itself is an assault on all we've learned about cities as well as what we're repeatedly told is public policy. The chosen instrument for carrying it out is total clearance; there are no provisions for the people who live or do business there to fix up their buildings.

. . .

They all must surrender their land, as *Architectural Forum* pointed out in a recent article, to such organizations as the Society of Colonial Dames and Beni Kedem Shrine. One of the original objections to urban renewal, one that was made a generation ago, was that it attacked the integrity of private property by taking a man's house and reselling the land to another man who would use it for another private purpose. As the plan here shows, this attack on the confidence people can have in ownership continues under the conservative George Romney, as it has under his liberal predecessors.

Aside from the favoritism and the unfair enrichment of real-estate racketeers which has been inseparable with urban renewal since its inception, the Charleston program folds back a point of view renewal planners can't rid themselves of; it's a distrust of the small efforts of many individuals. Instead, there is a desire to sweep everything clean.

The idea of using public money and public power to create a framework within which individuals can invest, improvise and build as may suit their needs and fancies is absent. The urban-renewal agency

here pushes ahead with its projects when there are extensive sections of the city without paved streets, parks, sewers or even fire hydrants. The local planners and the people who okay and pay for these things in Washington prefer to use the big muscle, to let the steel hippo loose and proceed in the most wasteful fashion possible.

Everything they do engenders the maximum expenditure of energy. The relocation plans call for moving flatland people up into the hills and hollows, which they dislike and which frightens them. They resist with an angry energy discharge.

This administration has made much noise about bringing government to the people. The President even went yahooing off to Indiana to manifest the carrying out of this principle in his royal person, but read what the Charleston Urban Renewal Agency told HUD would be the nature of citizen participation here:

Such participation can be too extensive resulting in confusion to the administration of a project. On the other hand, too little participation by affected citizens can result in belligerence toward Urban Renewal activities . . . involvement . . . gives residents the opportunity to actually participate in the improvement of their community. An example of resident involvement is a clean-up campaign whereby existing vacant lots can be cleared of dangerous rubbish, rusty nails, glass, etc. Of course, resident involvement in such aspects as planning, and other technical areas is not feasible, although creditable ideas from residents may well be considered and possibly used . . . mass meetings, it is recognized . . . can get out of hand with audience participation. Therefore, these meetings will include panels, speakers, etc. which do not require audience participation. Mass meetings will be infrequent . . .

Under this method the role of the resident is to occupy a seat in the cheering section, a proposition which was proved out when local people hired an out-of-town planner whose technically feasible ideas were ignored. His propositions were of a low energy type, the kind of things that rest on the slow perfection of individual endeavor and the quiet progress of the small neighborhood group.

The low energy, slow yield program that puts its emphasis on the efforts and thoughts of single people is inimical to the kind of administrator spawned by HUD. Yet it is he who must be renewed and made to understand that his kind of program not only doesn't work, as two decades show, but creates waste on a scale the society no longer can tolerate. The politicians would have us think that pollution control is merely a matter of spending money to clean up lakes and forests, a job that can be accomplished by the simple expenditure of money, but this city illustrates that's not so. Our whole way of doing business, of planning, of administration must change to insure that energy expenditure is kept low and that when we do spend our calories, it's done economically, on a one-time-only basis, so that it lasts, so that the product is usable and the hippos are kept quietly in the zoo.

NEW TOWNS:
CAN THEY WORK? *
EDMUND B. LAMBETH

Like Topsy, most metropolitan areas have "just grown." Private developers or individuals purchase plots of land on the city's edge and erect houses, factories, and stores in helter-skelter fashion. With this urban sprawl as an accomplished fact, they then demand such public services as highways, schools, sewers, and the other amenities of urban life.

Is there a better way? Drawing on European experience, some Americans are now urging "New Towns," with all needs anticipated in the planning stages. What has

* Reprinted from Edmund B. Lambeth, "New Towns: Can They Work?" The Washington Monthly (October, 1969), by permission.

*been our experience thus far? Can
private builders put together such
complexes? How can government
encourage and guide such developments? What impact would
new towns have on existing
ghettos? Is the whole concept a
form of escapism? Why do some
big city mayors view such proposals with reservations?*

Writing two and a half years ago
from Tarn House, Norwich, Vermont, H. Wentworth Eldredge, the
Dartmouth urban scholar, looked at
the near future of urban America:

"At the present, there seems little
likelihood, under the American federal governmental system, of making the necessary synthesis of city
development, new towns and comprehensive transportation thinking
in a national planned system, by
regions. . . .

"And yet on the other hand, lacking population control, some form
of ordered expansion of urbanization cannot be far ahead and federal legislation to that effect seems
to be just around the corner, resting
heavily on private experience, as it
should, in our very mixed economy."

Eldredge's forecast was nothing
if not prescient.

Within the Nixon Administration,
and in Congress as well, a "national
urban policy" is increasingly regarded as an idea whose time has
come. More specifically, the new
town is winning favor as a concept
that may do for the urban dilemma
what the moon landing did for

space exploration—supply a needed
focus and furnish a symbol to
stimulate commitment.

The idea of new towns fits well
with what little accepted wisdom
there is in the inchoate field of
urban affairs. Demographers predict a population increase of 100
million by the year 2000, consuming some 18 million acres of land.
The bulk of this growth will occur
on the fringe of some 20 metropolitan areas. The new-town advocates
ask: Need this growth replicate the
urban sprawl of the 1950's, with its
waste of land, diseconomies of
scale, and disregard of social needs?

Within the next 10 years alone, 26
million dwelling units will be
needed. Can planned new towns
help form the large markets required to give birth to a genuine
mass-production housing industry
in the United States? Many new-
town advocates think so.

Politically, the climate for new
towns, linked closely to a national
urban policy, has never been better.
Not the least of the reasons is that
the idea is one of the few that the
Johnson Administration declined to
embrace.

President Nixon, in his population message, called the concept
"stimulating." Vice President Spiro
T. Agnew, unofficial poet laureate
of the new town of Columbia,
Maryland, has presided over a
series of meetings on the subject
attended by businessmen, Congressmen, bankers, labor leaders,
and spokesmen for municipal governments. The President's Urban
Affairs Council, of which Dr.

Daniel Patrick Moynihan is executive secretary, has appointed a cabinet-level subcommittee on land use and new towns. The subcommittee, chaired by Secretary of Transportation John A. Volpe, is expected to confront the issue in depth this fall. A new-towns task force has been formed within Volpe's department, and Sherman Unger, the ambitious and alert general counsel of the Department of Housing and Urban Development, is taking a team of experts to Britain to study new-town financing and building techniques.

HUD's Assistant Secretary for Metropolitan Development, Samuel C. Jackson, has urged that states charter urban development corporations, which would give them the eminent-domain powers needed to assemble land for new communities.

To help assure their success, Jackson held open the possibility of direct loans to pay interest and other carrying charges, loans for capital investment, "and possibly even capital grants." Jackson's view is that the existing, modest program of federal assistance to new communities—which will guarantee debentures issued by builders in such communities—is probably not enough. "It is clear," he said, "that if the full range of potential benefits of new towns is to be realized, something more than the existing program is needed."

The precedent for Jackson's proposed state initiative is New York's Urban Development Corporation, a Rockefeller-created authority with power to override local zoning codes, condemn and assemble land, and sponsor the construction of houses, factories, schools and parks.

Headed by planner Edward J. Logue, late of Boston and New Haven, UDC will break ground next spring on a new town 12 miles northwest of Syracuse. Its population is expected to reach 16,000 in 10 years. A much bigger community will take shape under UDC auspices in Amherst, a Buffalo suburb that is the site of a new state university campus.

Several strategically placed Senators, Congressmen, Governors, and Mayors have put their signatures on a report called "The New City," which urges the creation, with federal assistance, of 100 new towns of 100,000 population and 10 with a population of one million.

The report, which includes several essays financed by the Ford Foundation, was sponsored by Urban America, Inc., and—more significantly—the U.S. Conference of Mayors, the National League of Cities, and the National Association of Counties. The municipal lobbies, adamantly opposed to new towns when the issue first came up in 1964, changed to support in 1967. Their stated reason is that, properly conceived and administered, new towns could relieve existing cities, particularly when it comes to the shortage of decent houses and jobs.

In the House of Representatives, one of the signers of "The New City" report, Thomas Ludlow Ashley (D-Ohio), persuaded Wright

Patman (D-Tex.), chairman of the Banking and Currency Committee, to appoint a special ad hoc subcommittee on urban growth, of which Ashley is chairman. New towns will figure prominently in the hearings, which will attempt to massage the Congressional central nervous system enough to make "urban growth"—and thus new towns—an actionable issue.

But the average member of Congress is like the citizen he represents. Few have visited a new town and those who have would be hard pressed to define what one is.

By HUD's definition—a degree of self-sufficiency and a land area of at least 1,000 acres—there are only 64 new towns in America, 40 of them built in the last decade. They range in projected population from 10,000 (Joppatowne, in Harford County, Maryland) to 600,000 (California City, in Kern County, California). Eighteen states have new towns but most are in the playland states of Arizona, Florida, and California.

By the most generous analysis, however, new towns built so far show little promise of relieving the American city of its unemployed or ill-housed. Even the widely praised Columbia, Maryland, built between Washington and Baltimore by developer James Rouse, makes no pretension of relieving the ghettos of either city. As Morton Hoppenfeld, Columbia's chief planner, candidly explains:

"Columbia was designed to be attractive to that majority segment of the population which is economically viable in the market. As a venture of private capital, Columbia will be unable to reach and affect some of the gut social problems of American urbanization."

Many developers, moreover, do not have the "patient" money available to Rouse. Thus Dale City, Virginia, where 2,500 families have bought homes in a planned "dream community," now finds itself barren of such promised amenities as golf courses, riding trails, and Olympic-sized swimming pools. In the words of Dale City's planner, who had hoped for a city of 80,000, the community now is "just like any other typical real estate development."

The problems facing a private new-town developer are formidable. He must assemble enough land, arrange financing that is patient enough to wait 10 years for a profit, and find management experts who are willing to risk their reputations on one of the most difficult of all real estate ventures.

The American new towns that have been able to meet all these conditions have been "flukes," that is, special exceptions that prove the grim rules.

The 12,000 acres on which Litchfield Park, Arizona (population 100,000), is rising had been owned intact by the Goodyear Tire & Rubber Co. since World War I days. Irvine, California, with 88 acres of debt-free land, is the inheritance of an old southern California ranch family. Few families have acreage on hand covering four times the land area of Manhattan.

Other new towns are built by

big national corporations with ready cash. The Pennsylvania railroad found itself with money aplenty when forced under anti-trust laws to sell the Norfolk & Western Railroad. As a result, it bought Macco Realty—the developer of Porter Ranch in Los Angeles county and the owner of 100,-000 acres in southern California.

Other big corporations enter the new-town business to push the sale of their products. Boise-Cascade, a lumber and timber company, has bought two home-building firms (Perma-Built Enterprises and U.S. Land Corporation) and is building resort communities near Cleveland, Chicago, Gary, Kansas City, and Fredericksburg, Virginia. Westinghouse is building Coral Springs, Florida (population 60,000), as an "urban laboratory" for its products. Walt Disney Productions, Inc., likewise is building a new community near Orlando, Florida, to introduce, test, and show off new technologies. Humble Oil Company had land, investment money as well as a product sales motive in mind when it began building Clear Lake City on 15,000 acres near Houston.

But other large companies, less favorably situated with respect to the key ingredients of the new-town business, have found the entry barriers formidable. General Electric dissolved its Community Systems Development division last February, after a two-year exploration of whether to enter the city-building business. GE concluded that the risk was too high and the profits too slow; it also found that low-cost land and special financing were too difficult to assemble. New communities on a large scale will not flourish, GE decided, until government agrees to help.

In view of the impending policy decisions on new towns in the federal government, GE's recommendations are worth quoting in some detail:

It just makes sense that the power of eminent domain must be granted to private corporations or to state development corporations in order to assemble land in the right location and to take advantage of existing and planned public investment in highways, water works, sewage disposal facilities, airports, and railways.

Perhaps something similar to urban renewal must be created, whereby land is assembled, master planned, zoned, and resold at a write-down to private builders by a local development authority.

Tax restraint must be exercised to relieve the financial burden on the developer in the early stages; taxes can then be raised on a gradual basis after actual improvements are put in place.

At the state level, legislation must be created that will permit the developer to retain a measure of control over planning, zoning, and community services for an agreed-upon development period, so that a dissident group cannot thwart financial planning or the very concept itself.

GE said it would maintain an "avid interest" in the city business and would re-enter it "under the proper combination of conditions" —meaning a federal subsidy similar to that for urban renewal. Its recommendations have the virtue of at least forcing the new-town advocates to face some of the harder questions.

What would the public gain in return for such a subsidy? An adequate supply of low-income housing? Why will new towns allow or encourage this when it has eluded new neighborhoods, city or suburban, for 30 years?

When the state or local development authority begins searching for tracts large enough for new towns, what will govern the price paid for the land? Will the big corporations now buying land as a hedge against inflation be given the benefit of price accrual due to the government's known plans for a new town?

If autonomous new towns are the goal, can it be assumed that industry and business will voluntarily locate there to provide jobs for the new residents? If not, what will have to be done to induce them to a new-town location? Why will a new town make an industrialist more willing to invest in jobless workers than a city location?

Significantly, the report sponsored by the municipal lobbies and Urban America, Inc., called for long-term loans or loan guarantees, rather than outright subsidies. Loans would defer repayment and interest for 15 years—which amounts to a substantial indirect

subsidy. And no one familiar with the way federal "loan programs" begin can have much doubt that direct subsidies would evolve.

John Gunther, executive director of the U.S. Conference of Mayors, said in an interview that the mayors' switch on new towns was merely an attempt to be constructive.

"We kept getting asked about new towns in Congress and we didn't want to be negative. We've studied the matter now and we see positive advantages, provided that it's done right. We *think* the ideas in 'The New City' are the right ones. Our goal is to make existing cities as good an investment as new towns and to use new towns to solve some of our problems."

Although Gunther says that the 1967 riots did not cause the mayors' change of heart, it is clear that the violence made a ghetto-dispersal policy much more attractive to big-city governments. In any event, the advocates of new towns have already begun to anticipate opposition from black-power separatists who claim, or will claim, that new towns are an attempt by the white man to decimate black majorities before they form.

Arithmetic answers the separatists. Even if new towns were to become home for 10 million Negroes in the next 30 years—a prodigious accomplishment—black voting strength in the central cities would not appreciably diminish.

Perhaps more significantly, such influential black militants as Clarence Funnye, director of planning for the National Committee Against Discrimination in Housing, have spoken up forcefully against the separatists. The ghetto, Funnye insists, has the least land available for the kind of large-scale industry which could create new jobs. That land is in outlying areas. He advocates "deghettoization" via new towns and an aggressive open-occupancy program for the suburbs.

But aside from the expected opposition of some black separatists, the policies outlined in "The New City" have a remarkable unifying power. The proposed development corporations would not only be empowered to build new towns in the countryside, but also on the metropolitan fringe, within existing cities and around small rural towns that are either dying or failing in growth.

Even though new towns on the magnitude envisioned in "The New City" would accommodate only one-fifth of the nation's urban growth over the next 30 years, this is a substantial fraction. It is a fraction, moreover, that would drain away a commodity more scarce in America than land or mortgage money—urban management talent.

The excitement of a new town is real. To the urban developer, a new town is what forgiveness is to the sinner or town drunk: a fresh start spiritually, the opportunity to begin from scratch. The old town offers no such respite. As the Rand experts imported by Mayor John Lindsay learned, the cliché "prob-lems of the cities" masks a reality even more severe than they thought.

Nathaniel A. Owings of San Francisco, principal in the architectural firm of Skidmore, Owings and Merrill, told a recent St. Louis symposium on new towns: "To my mind they are even immoral. . . . The new town is one of these illusions used to palliate the issues and get away from the problems."

And Edmund N. Bacon, the respected Philadelphia planner, added that the new town is "representative of the American propensity, when faced with a problem, of changing the subject."

These criticisms are recognized by the more cautious exponents of new towns. Thus Paul Ylvisaker, a founder of the war on poverty and now Commissioner of New Jersey's Department of Community Affairs, told a Congressional committee:

I've considered carefully the subconscious motives behind it (the new town idea). If we are to build new communities, and I hope we will, we ought to be clear about our own motivation, since the possible motives are several. . . .

After all, there is an escapist tendency in new-town thinking which leads people to where there are, or seem to be, no confining parameters and no conventionalism; the politics are new, the land is clear, and even the zoning laws might be changed. The danger here is that needed resources and energies will be diverted from the problems of our cities.

There are some caveats to the building of new towns, but there is more to the idea than escapism and there are ways of nourishing the new without starving the old. The effort to build new towns may be a cathartic in our present system. We may have reached a dead end in evolving an urban culture, at least in some respects.

We must break loose the old and invent the new. We cannot rely entirely on the incremental method to achieve the full measure of progress that is now necessary. Radical departures are called for, both in reshaping our old communities and in designing the new. Certainly the new town in this sense is a healthy concept and I am among those who welcome it.

If Ylvisaker's assessment is near the mark, several overriding questions face the Nixon administration.

Can it find or afford the money to fund a new-towns program on a scale large enough to influence the direction and character of urban growth?

If it can, will the now-fragile "new federalism" become strong enough to overcome the new town's inherent tendency to overpromise and underdeliver?

8. The Sick Environment: Man Fouls His Nest

The American people have recently discovered that great wealth carries a high environmental price tag. Modern man devours resources at an alarming rate; he leaves behind him mountains of discarded materials and waste. The average American, it has been alleged, pollutes his environment at fifty times the rate of the average Indian. Walt Kelly's Pogo underlined the basic issue in his classic remark: "We have met the enemy, and it is us."

The Scope of Pollution

Some of the "early warning" signs of global contamination are found among endangered wild life species. Antarctic penguins, separated by hundreds of miles from man, have DDT in their fatty tissues; swordfish contaminated with mercury are banned from our supermarkets; both Louisiana's state bird (the brown pelican) and the American bald eagle are moving toward extinction because they are unable to reproduce. Only one survivor seems certain —a mutant of the carp has mastered the new world and thrives amidst the poison-laden waters of Lake Erie.

Man, himself, has become an endangered species. His environment has become poisoned with noise, exhaust fumes, sewage, garbage, chemicals. His life is shortened by lung disease; his nerves are shattered by excessive noise.

Consider for a moment the atmosphere. It may be true that on a clear day you can see forever, but in most American cities the ever-present smog limits visibility and causes your eyes to smart. One of New York City's art treasures, Cleopatra's Needle, has deteriorated more in the past 90 years than in the previous 3000. A deadly combination of automobile exhaust fumes and smoke from power plants, home heating, and incineration hangs over Manhattan, causing one hard-bitten New Yorker to say: "Never breathe anything you can't see."

The nation's water supply is equally polluted. Only one major river near a city (Minnesota's St. Croix) remains undefiled; the rest are filled with industrial and human wastes. A new high in pollution was achieved recently when Cleveland's Cuyahoga River caught fire. Tanker spills and oil well blowouts pollute the seas and soil the beaches; heat from nuclear power plants endangers ecological balances and destroys aquatic life.

Americans are a messy people; a trait which is aggravated by sheer abundance. Only in America does a snack at a drive-in (hamburger, french fries, milk shake) create a minor garbage disposal problem— french fry sack, hamburger wrapper, cup and lid for milk shake, packaged straw, a container each for salt, mustard, catsup, two napkins, a sack to hold the lot. The average American throws away nearly 2000 pounds of waste each year, not counting such major items as junked automobiles.

Noise today is a very real pollutant. The entire urban scene is blanketed by a constant roar, rumble, screech and whine. It is no accident that hard rock, with its amplified sound, is regarded as the music of contemporary America. Peace and quiet are nostalgic terms for the United States of long ago.

Curbing Pollution: The Search For A Policy

The pollution problem has captured the attention of Americans. Thus far scare headlines and prophesies of doom have dominated the discussion, with relatively little attention being paid to the big questions and the hard choices. Community drives to recycle tin cans will not solve the solid waste problem, nor will the abandonment of colored Kleenex end water contamination.

No one today favors pollution. But we have not really looked at some of the alternatives. Will we settle for less acceleration in our automobiles? Will we forego our bland assumption that the future holds more and more consumer goods? If we seriously dedicate ourselves to the reduction of pollution, major economic costs are involved. *The Wall Street Journal* recently estimated that the average electric bill would have to be increased annually by $80 to cover anti-pollution measures. How will we foot the bill? By higher consumer prices? By high taxes and subsidies? Can we buy our way out of pollution? If the price tag is a lower standard of living, will we pay it? Have we any choice? Where is the line of compromise between a pollution-free environment and a goods-and-services oriented society of over 200,000,000 people? Thus far the cry of alarm has been raised by the biologists; only a few economists have speculated on the socio-economic costs. Many political leaders have marked time by damning pollution in general terms while they await an aroused public opinion that will support hard-nosed pollution legislation. The laws, if they are forthcoming, will inevitably intrude on time-honored private decisions such as the size of the family, for we can no longer avoid the fact that our pollution is linked to our exploding population.

ECO-CATASTROPHE *

PAUL R. EHRLICH

In the last sentence of this article Dr. Ehrlich, a prominent Stanford biologist, reminds his readers that "nature bats last." If pollution expands at the present rate, what does the future hold? The author presents a doomsday view. Accepting his forecast, how did the oceans end? Why did the "Green Revolution" fail? Why did workers organize into a group called the "Walking Dead." Why did the Indian Ambassador call the birth of an American baby a disaster for the world? Assuming that Ehrlich's predictions have more than a grain of truth, will the American people or nature bat last?

I

The end of the ocean came late in the summer of 1979, and it came even more rapidly than the biologists had expected. There had been signs for more than a decade, commencing with the discovery in 1968 that DDT slows down photosynthesis in marine plant life. It was

announced in a short paper in the technical journal, *Science,* but to ecologists it smacked of doomsday. They knew that all life in the sea depends on photosynthesis, the chemical process by which green plants bind the sun's energy and make it available to living things. And they knew that DDT and similar chlorinated hydrocarbons had polluted the entire surface of the earth, including the sea.

But that was only the first of many signs. There had been the final gasp of the whaling industry in 1973, and the end of the Peruvian anchovy fishery in 1975. Indeed, a score of other fisheries had disappeared quietly from over-exploitation and various eco-catastrophes by 1977. The term "eco-catastrophe" was coined by a California ecologist in 1969 to describe the most spectacular of man's attacks on the systems which sustain his life. He drew his inspiration from the Santa Barbara offshore oil disaster of that year, and from the news which spread among naturalists that virtually all of the Golden State's seashore bird life was doomed because of chlorinated hydrocarbon interference with its reproduction. Eco-catastrophes in the sea became increasingly common in the early 1970's. Mysterious "blooms" of previously rare microorganisms began to appear in offshore waters. Red tides—killer outbreaks of a minute single-celled plant—returned to the Florida Gulf coast and were sometimes accompanied by tides of other exotic hues.

It was clear by 1975 that the entire ecology of the ocean was changing. A few types of phytoplankton were becoming resistant to chlorinated hydrocarbons and were gaining the upper hand. Changes in the phytoplankton community led inevitably to changes in the community of zooplankton, the tiny animals which eat the phytoplankton. These changes were passed on up the chains of life in the ocean to the herring, plaice, cod and tuna. As the diversity of life in the ocean diminished, its stability also decreased.

Other changes had taken place by 1975. Most ocean fishes that returned to fresh water to breed, like the salmon, had become extinct, their breeding streams so dammed up and polluted that their powerful homing instinct only resulted in suicide. Many fishes and shellfishes that bred in restricted areas along the coasts followed them as onshore pollution escalated.

By 1977 the annual yield of fish from the sea was down to 30 million metric tons, less than one-half the per capita catch of a decade earlier. This helped malnutrition to escalate sharply in a world where an estimated 50 million people per year were already dying of starvation. The United Nations attempted to get all chlorinated hydrocarbon insecticides banned on a worldwide basis, but the move was defeated by the United States. This opposition was generated primarily by the American petrochemical industry, operating hand in glove with its subsidiary, the United States Department of Agriculture. Together they persuaded the government to oppose the U.N. move—which was not difficult since most Americans believed that Russia and China were more in need of fish products than was the United States. The United Nations also attempted to get fishing nations to adopt strict and enforced catch limits to preserve dwindling stocks. This move was blocked by Russia, who, with the most modern electronic equipment, was in the best position to glean what was left in the sea. It was, curiously, on the very day in 1977 when the Soviet Union announced its refusal that another ominous article appeared in *Science*. It announced that incident solar radiation had been so reduced by worldwide air pollution that serious effects on the world's vegetation could be expected.

II

Apparently it was a combination of ecosystem destabilization, sunlight reduction, and a rapid escalation in chlorinated hydrocarbon pollution from massive Thanodrin applications which triggered the ultimate catastrophe. Seventeen huge Soviet-financed Thanodrin plants were operating in underdeveloped countries by 1978. They had been part of a massive Russian "aid offensive" designed to fill the gap caused by the collapse of America's ballyhooed "Green Revolution."

It became apparent in the early '70's that the "Green Revolution" was more talk than substance. Distribution of high yield "miracle" grain seeds had caused temporary local spurts in agricultural production. Simultaneously, excellent weather had produced record harvests. The combination permitted bureaucrats, especially in the United States Department of Agriculture and the Agency for International Development (AID), to reverse their previous pessimism and indulge in an outburst of optimistic propaganda about staving off famine. They raved about the approaching transformation of agriculture in the underdeveloped countries (UDCs). The reason for the propaganda reversal was never made clear. Most historians agree that a combination of utter ignorance of ecology, a desire to justify past errors, and pressure from agroindustry (which was eager to sell pesticides, fertilizers, and farm machinery to the UDCs and agencies helping the UDCs) was behind the campaign. Whatever the motivation, the results were clear. Many concerned people, lacking the expertise to see through the Green Revolution drivel, relaxed. The population-food crisis was "solved."

But reality was not long in showing itself. Local famine persisted in northern India even after good weather brought an end to the ghastly Bihar famine of the mid-'60's. East Pakistan was next, followed by a resurgence of general famine in northern India. Other foci of famine rapidly developed in Indonesia, the Philippines, Malawi, the Congo, Egypt, Colombia, Ecuador, Honduras, the Dominican Republic, and Mexico.

Everywhere hard realities destroyed the illusion of the Green Revolution. Yields dropped as the progressive farmers who had first accepted the new seeds found that their higher yields brought lower prices—effective demand (hunger plus cash) was not sufficient in poor countries to keep prices up. Less progressive farmers, observing this, refused to make the extra effort required to cultivate the "miracle" grains. Transport systems proved inadequate to bring the necessary fertilizer to the fields where the new and extremely fertilizer-sensitive grains were being grown. The same systems were also inadequate to move produce to markets. Fertilizer plants were not built fast enough, and most of the underdeveloped countries could not scrape together funds to purchase supplies, even on concessional terms. Finally, the inevitable happened, and pests began to reduce yields in even the most carefully cultivated fields. Among the first were the famous "miracle rats" which invaded Philippine "miracle rice" fields early in 1969. They were quickly followed by many insects and viruses, thriving on the relatively pest-susceptible new grains, encouraged by the vast and dense plantings, and rapidly acquiring resistance to the chemicals used against them. As chaos spread until even the most obtuse agriculturists and economists realized that the Green Revolution had turned brown, the Russians stepped in.

In retrospect it seems incredible that the Russians, with the American mistakes known to them, could launch an even more incompetent program of aid to the underdeveloped world. Indeed, in the early 1970's there were cynics in the United States who claimed that outdoing the stupidity of American foreign aid would be physically impossible. Those critics were, however, obviously unaware that the Russians had been busily destroying their own environment for many years. The virtual disappearance of sturgeon from Russian rivers caused a great shortage of caviar by 1970. A standard joke among Russian scientists at that time was that they had created an artificial caviar which was indistinguishable from the real thing— except by taste. At any rate the Soviet Union, observing with interest the progressive deterioration of relations between the UDCs and the United States, came up with a solution. It had recently developed what it claimed was the ideal insecticide, a highly lethal chlorinated hydrocarbon complexed with a special agent for penetrating the external skeletal armor of insects. Announcing that the new pesticide, called Thanodrin, would truly produce a Green Revolution, the Soviets entered into negotiations with various UDCs for the construction of massive Thanodrin factories. The USSR would bear all the costs; all it wanted in return were certain trade and military concessions.

It is interesting now, with the perspective of years, to examine in some detail the reasons why the UDCs welcomed the Thanodrin plan with such open arms. Governmental officials in these countries ignored the protests of their own scientists that Thanodrin would not solve the problems which plagued them. The governments now knew that the basic cause of their problems was overpopulation, and that these problems had been exacerbated by the dullness, daydreaming, and cupidity endemic to all governments. They knew that only population control and limited development aimed primarily at agriculture could have spared them the horrors they now faced. They knew it, but they were not about to admit it. How much easier it was simply to accuse the Americans of failing to give them proper aid; how much simpler to accept the Russian panacea.

And then there was the general worsening of relations between the United States and the UDCs. Many things had contributed to this. The situation in America in the first half of the 1970's deserves our close scrutiny. Being more dependent on imports for raw materials than the Soviet Union, the United States had, in the early 1970's, adopted more and more heavy-handed policies in order to insure continuing supplies. Military adventures in Asia and Latin America had further lessened the international credibility of the United States as a great defender of freedom—an image which had begun to deteriorate rapidly during the pointless and fruitless Viet-Nam conflict. At home, acceptance of the carefully manufactured image lessened dramatically, as even the more romantic and chauvinistic citizens began to understand the role of the military and the industrial system in what John Kenneth Galbraith had aptly named "The New Industrial State."

At home in the USA the early '70's were traumatic times. Racial violence grew and the habitability of the cities diminished, as nothing substantial was done to ameliorate either racial inequities or urban blight. Welfare rolls grew as automation and general technological progress forced more and more people into the category of "unemployable." Simultaneously a taxpayers' revolt occurred. Although there was not enough money to build the schools, roads, water systems, sewage systems, jails, hospitals, urban transit lines, and all the other amenities needed to support a burgeoning population, Americans refused to tax themselves more heavily. Starting in Youngstown, Ohio in 1969 and followed closely by Richmond, California, community after community was forced to close its schools or curtail educational operations for lack of funds. Water supplies, already marginal in quality and quantity in many places by 1970, deteriorated quickly. Water rationing occurred in 1723 municipalities in the summer of 1974, and hepatitis and epidemic dysentery rates climbed about 500 percent between 1970–1974.

III

Air pollution continued to be the most obvious manifestation of environmental deterioration. It was, by 1972, quite literally in the eyes of all Americans. The year 1973 saw not only the New York and Los Angeles smog disasters, but also the publication of the Surgeon General's massive report on air pollution and health. The public had been partially prepared for the worst by the publicity given to the U.N. pollution conference held in 1972. Deaths in the late '60's caused by smog were well known to scientists, but the public had ignored them because they mostly involved the early demise of the old and sick rather than people dropping dead on the freeways. But suddenly our citizens were faced with nearly 200,000 corpses and massive documentation that they could be the next to die from respiratory disease. They were not ready for that scale of disaster. After all, the U.N. conference had not predicted that accumulated air pollution would make the planet uninhabitable until almost 1990. The population was terrorized as TV screens became filled with scenes of horror from the disaster areas. Especially vivid was NBC's coverage of hundreds of unattended people choking out their lives outside of New York's hospitals. Terms like nitrogen oxide, acute bronchitis and cardiac arrest began to have real meaning for most Americans.

The ultimate horror was the announcement that chlorinated hydrocarbons were now a major constituent of air pollution in all American cities. Autopsies of smog disaster victims revealed an average chlorinated hydrocarbon load in fatty tissue equivalent to 26 parts per million of DDT. In October, 1973, the Department of Health, Education and Welfare announced studies which showed unequivocally that increasing death rates from hypertension, cirrhosis of the liver, liver cancer and a series of other diseases had resulted from the chlorinated hydrocarbon load. They estimated that Americans born since 1946 (when DDT usage began) now had a life expectancy of only 49 years, and predicted that if current patterns continued, this expectancy would reach 42 years by 1980, when it might level out. Plunging insurance stocks triggered a stock market panic. . . . Giants of the petrochemical industry, attempting to dispute the indisputable evidence, launched a massive pressure campaign on Congress to force HEW to "get out of agriculture's business." They were aided by the agro-chemical journals, which had decades of experience in misleading the public about the benefits and dangers of pesticides. But by now the public realized that it had been duped. The Nobel Prize for medicine and physiology was given to Drs. J. L. Radomski and W. B. Deichmann, who in the late 1960's had pioneered in the documentation of the long-term lethal effects of chlorinated hydrocarbons. A Presidential Commission with unimpeachable credentials directly accused the agro-chemical complex of "condemning many millions of Americans to an early death." The year 1973 was the year in which Americans finally came to understand the direct threat to their existence posed by environmental deterioration.

And 1973 was also the year in which most people finally comprehended the indirect threat. Even the president of Union Oil Company and several other industrialists publicly stated their concern over the reduction of bird populations which had resulted from pollution by DDT and other chlorinated hydrocarbons. Insect populations boomed because they were resistant to most pesticides and had been freed, by the incompetent use of those pesticides, from most of their natural enemies. Rodents swarmed over crops, multiplying rapidly in the absence of predatory birds. The effect of pests on the wheat crop was especially disastrous in the summer of 1973, since that was also the year of the great drought. Most of us can remember the shock which greeted the announcement by atmospheric physicists that the shift of the jet stream which had caused the drought was probably permanent. It signalled the birth of the Midwestern desert. Man's air-polluting activities had by then caused gross changes in climatic patterns. The news, of course, played hell with commodity and stock markets. Food prices skyrocketed, as savings were poured into hoarded canned goods. Official assurances that food supplies would remain ample fell on deaf ears, and even the government showed signs of nervousness when California migrant field workers went out on strike again in protest against the continued use of pesticides by growers. The strike burgeoned into farm burning and riots. The workers, calling themselves "The Walking Dead," demanded immediate compensation for their shortened lives, and crash research programs to attempt to lengthen them.

It was in the same speech in which President Edward Kennedy, after much delay, finally declared a national emergency and called out the National Guard to harvest California's crops, that the first mention of population control was made. Kennedy pointed out that the United States would no longer be able to offer any food aid to other nations and was likely to suffer food shortages herself. He suggested that, in view of the manifest failure of the Green Revolution, the only hope of the UDCs lay in population control. His statement, you will recall, created an uproar in the underdeveloped countries. Newspaper editorials accused the United States of wishing to prevent small countries from becoming large nations and thus threatening American hegemony.

Politicians asserted that President Kennedy was a "creature of the giant drug combine" that wished to shove its pills down every woman's throat.

Among Americans, religious opposition to population control was very slight. Industry in general also backed the idea. Increasing poverty in the UDCs was both destroying markets and threatening supplies of raw materials. The seriousness of the raw material situation had been brought home during the Congressional Hard Resources hearings in 1971. The exposure of the ignorance of the cornucopian economists had been quite a spectacle—a spectacle brought into virtually every American's home in living color. Few would forget the distinguished geologist from the University of California who suggested that economists be legally required to learn at least the most elementary facts of geology. Fewer still would forget that an equally distinguished Harvard economist added that they might be required to learn some economics, too. The overall message was clear: America's resource situation was bad and bound to get worse. The hearings had led to a bill requiring the Departments of State, Interior, and Commerce to set up a joint resource procurement council with the express purpose of "insuring that proper consideration of American resource needs be an integral part of American foreign policy."

Suddenly the United States discovered that it had a national consensus: population control was the only possible salvation of the underdeveloped world. But that same consensus led to heated debate. How could the UDCs be persuaded to limit their populations, and should not the United States lead the way by limiting its own? Members of the intellectual community wanted America to set an example. They pointed out that the United States was in the midst of a new baby boom: her birth rate, well over 20 per thousand per year, and her growth rate of over one percent per annum were among the very highest of the developed countries. They detailed the deterioration of the American physical and psychic environments, the growing health threats, the impending food shortages, and the insufficiency of funds for desperately needed public works. They contended that the nation was clearly unable or unwilling to properly care for the people it already had. What possible reason could there be, they queried, for adding any more? Besides, who would listen to requests by the United States for population control when that nation did not control her own profligate reproduction?

Those who opposed population controls for the U.S. were equally vociferous. The military-industrial complex, with its all-too-human mixture of ignorance and avarice, still saw strength and prosperity in numbers. Baby food magnates, already worried by the growing nitrate pollution of their products, saw their market disappearing.

Steel manufacturers saw a decrease in aggregate demand and slippage for that holy of holies, the Gross National Product. And military men saw, in the growing population-food-environment crisis, a serious threat to their carefully nurtured Cold War. In the end, of course, economic arguments held sway, and the "inalienable right of every American couple to determine the size of its family," a freedom invented for the occasion in the early '70's, was not compromised.

The population control bill, which was passed by Congress early in 1974, was quite a document, nevertheless. On the domestic front, it authorized an increase from 100 to 150 million dollars in funds for "family planning" activities. This was made possible by a general feeling in the country that the growing army on welfare needed family planning. But the gist of the bill was a series of measures designed to impress the need for population control on the UDCs. All American aid to countries with overpopulation problems was required by law to consist in part of population control assistance. In order to receive any assistance each nation was required not only to accept the population control aid, but also to match it according to a complex formula. "Overpopulation" itself was defined by a formula based on U.N. statistics, and the UDCs were required not only to accept aid, but also to show progress in reducing birth rates. Every five years the status of the aid program for each nation was to be re-evaluated.

The reaction to the announcement of this program dwarfed the response to President Kennedy's speech. A coalition of UDCs attempted to get the U.N. General Assembly to condemn the United States as a "genetic aggressor." Most damaging of all to the American cause was the famous "25 Indians and a dog" speech by Mr. Shankarnarayan, Indian Ambassador to the U.N. Shankarnarayan pointed out that for several decades the United States, with less than six percent of the people of the world had consumed roughly 50 percent of the raw materials used every year. He described vividly America's contribution to worldwide environmental deterioration, and he scathingly denounced the miserly record of United States foreign aid as "unworthy of a fourth-rate power, let alone the most powerful nation on earth."

It was the climax of his speech, however, which most historians claim once and for all destroyed the image of the United States. Shankaranarayan informed the assembly that the average American family dog was fed more animal protein per week than the average Indian got in a month. "How do you justify taking fish from protein-starved Peruvians and feeding them to your animals?" he asked. "I contend," he concluded, "that the birth of an American baby is a greater disaster for the world than that of 25 Indian babies." When the applause had died away, Mr. Sorensen, the American representative, made a speech which said essentially that "other countries look after their own self-interest, too." When the vote came, the United States was condemned.

IV

This condemnation set the tone of U.S.-UDC relations at the time the Russian Thanodrin proposal was made. The proposal seemed to offer the masses in the UDCs an opportunity to save themselves and humiliate the United States at the same time; and in human affairs, as we all know, biological realities could never interfere with such an opportunity. The scientists were silenced, the politicians said yes, the Thanodrin plants were built, and the results were what any beginning ecology student could have predicted. At first Thanodrin seemed to offer excellent control of many pests. True, there was a rash of human fatalities from improper use of the lethal chemical, but, as Russian technical advisors were prone to note, these were more than compensated for by increased yields. Thanodrin use skyrocketed throughout the underdeveloped world. The Mikoyan design group developed a dependable, cheap agricultural aircraft which the Soviets donated to the effort in large numbers. MIG sprayers became even more common in UDCs than MIG interceptors.

Then the troubles began. Insect strains with cuticles resistant to Thanodrin penetration began to appear. And as streams, rivers, fish culture ponds and onshore waters became rich in Thanodrin, more fisheries began to disappear. Bird populations were decimated. The sequence of events was standard for broadcast use of a synthetic pesticide: great success at first, followed by removal of natural enemies and development of resistance by the pest. Populations of crop-eating insects in areas treated with Thanodrin made steady comebacks and soon became more abundant than ever. Yields plunged, while farmers in their desperation increased the Thanodrin dose and shortened the time between treatments. Death from Thanodrin poisoning became common. The first violent incident occurred in the Canete Valley of Peru, where farmers had suffered a similar chlorinated hydrocarbon disaster in the mid-'50's. A Russian adviser serving as an agricultural pilot was assaulted and killed by a mob of enraged farmers in January, 1978. Trouble spread rapidly during 1978, especially after the word got out that two years earlier Russia herself had banned the use of Thanodrin at home because of its serious effects on ecological systems. Suddenly Russia, and not the United States, was the *bête noir* in the UDCs. "Thanodrin parties" became epidemic, with farmers, in their ignorance, dumping carloads of Thanodrin concentrate into the sea. Russian advisors fled, and four of the Thanodrin plants were leveled to the ground. Destruction of the plants in Rio and Calcutta led to hundreds of thousands of gallons of Thanodrin concentrate being dumped directly into the sea.

Mr. Shankarnarayan again rose to address the U.N., but this time it was Mr. Potemkin, representative of the Soviet Union, who was on the hot seat. Mr. Potemkin heard his nation described as the greatest mass killer of all time as Shankarnarayan predicted at least 30 million deaths from crop failure due to overdependence on Thanodrin. Russia was accused of "chemical aggression," and the General Assembly, after a weak reply by Potemkin, passed a vote of censure.

It was in January, 1979, that huge blooms of a previously unknown variety of diatom were reported off the coast of Peru. The blooms were accompanied by a massive die-off of sea life and of the pathetic remainder of the birds which had once feasted on the anchovies of the area. Almost immediately, another huge bloom was reported in the Indian ocean, centering around the Seychelles, and then a third in the South Atlantic off the African coast. Both of these were accompanied by spectacular die-offs of marine animals. Even more ominous were growing reports of fish and bird kills at oceanic points where there were no spectacular blooms. Biologists were soon able to explain the phenomena: the diatom had evolved an enzyme which broke down Thanodrin; that enzyme also produced a breakdown product which interfered with the transmission of nerve impulses, and was therefore lethal to animals. Unfortunately, the biologists could suggest no way of repressing the poisonous diatom bloom in time. By September, 1979, all important animal life in the sea was extinct. Large areas of coastline had to be evacuated, as windrows of dead fish created a monumental stench.

But stench was the least of man's problems. Japan and China were faced with almost instant starvation from a total loss of the seafood on which they were so dependent. Both blamed Russia for their situation and demanded immediate mass shipments of food. Russia had none to send. On October 13, Chinese armies attacked Russia on a broad front. . . .

V

A pretty grim scenario. Unfortunately, we're a long way into it already. Everything mentioned as happening before 1970 has actually occurred; much of the rest is based on projections of trends already appearing. Evidence that pesticides have long-term lethal effects on human beings has started to accumulate, and recently Robert Finch, Secretary of the Department of Health, Education and Welfare expressed his extreme apprehension about the pesticide situation. Simultaneously the petrochemical industry continues its unconscionable poison-peddling. For instance, Shell Chemical has been carrying on a high-pressure campaign to sell the insecticide Azodrin to farmers as a killer of cotton pests. They continue their program even though they know that Azodrin is not only ineffective, but often *increases* the pest density. They've covered themselves nicely in an advertisement which states, "Even if an overpowering migration [sic] develops, the flexibility of Azodrin lets you regain control fast. Just increase the dosage according to label recommendations." It's a great game—get people to apply the poison and kill the natural enemies of the pests. Then blame the increased pests on "migration" and sell even more pesticide!

Right now fisheries are being wiped out by over-exploitation, made easy by modern electronic equipment. The companies producing the equipment know this. They even boast in advertising that only their equipment will keep fishermen in business until the final kill. Profits must obviously be maximized in the short run. Indeed, Western society is in the process of completing the rape and murder of the planet for economic gain. And, sadly, most of the rest of the world is eager for the opportunity to emulate our behavior. But the underdeveloped peoples will be denied that opportunity—the days of plunder are drawing inexorably to a close.

Most of the people who are going to die in the greatest cataclysm in the history of man have already been born. More than three and a half billion people already populate our moribund globe, and about half of them are hungry. Some 10 to 20 million will starve to death *this year.* In spite of this, the population of the earth will increase by 70 million souls in 1969. For mankind has artificially lowered the death rate of the human population, while in general birth rates have remained high. With the input side of the population system in high gear and the output side slowed down, our fragile planet has filled with people at an incredible rate. It took several million years for the population to reach a total of two billion people in 1930, while a *second two billion will have been added by 1975!* By that time some experts feel that food shortages will have escalated the present level of world hunger and starvation into famines of unbelievable proportions. Other experts, more optimistic, think the ultimate food-population collision will not occur until the decade of the 1980's. Of course more massive famine may be avoided if other events cause a prior rise in the human death rate.

Both worldwide plague and thermonuclear war are made more probable as population growth continues. These, along with famine, make up the trio of potential "death rate solutions" to the population problem—solutions in which the birth rate-death rate imbalance is redressed by a rise in the death rate rather than by a lowering of the birth rate. Make no mistake about it, *the imbalance will be redressed.* The shape of the population growth curve is one familiar to the biologist. It is the outbreak part of an outbreak-crash sequence. A population grows rapidly in the presence of abundant resources, finally runs out of food or some other necessity, and crashes to a low level or extinction. Man is not only running out of food, he is also destroying the life support systems of the Spaceship Earth. The situation was recently summarized very succinctly: "It is the top of the ninth inning. Man, always a threat at the plate, has been hitting Nature hard. It is important to remember, however, that NATURE BATS LAST."

THE UNENDING ROAR:

BANG, CRASH, THUMP *

ALAN L. OTTEN

Modern Americans from cradle to grave are subjected to an unending roar. Young people bathe in an ocean of electronically-amplified hard rock. Nor do their elders escape the noisy environment: 93,000,000 automobile motors; the neighbor's power lawn mower on Sunday morning; the ubiquitous,

* Reprinted from Alan L. Otten, "The Unending Roar: Bang, Crash, Thump," Wall Street Journal, *February 12, 1970, by permission.*

turned-up transistor radio. The list goes on, and on, and on. Topped off with that marvel of American ingenuity—the Boeing 747.

Is this hallmark of American society merely a nuisance? Or does it imperil our national health? Is noise as much of an environmental pollutant as air-borne sulphur dioxide, water-borne sewage, or rusting automobile grave yards?

The environment suddenly becomes the "in" issue. The Republican President and the Democratic leaders talk about it. So do student activists and corporate executives. Even ordinary citizens worry about dirty air, dirty water, mountains of trash.

A surprising orphan in all this current concern is an equally obnoxious form of pollution: Excessive noise. The President, for example, never mentioned it in his 14-page message to Congress Tuesday. And yet in many ways excessive noise is far more intrusive and offensive than dirty water or other environmental hazards. The roar and rumble of modern life, highly mechanized and increasingly urbanized, force themselves on us day and night, at home and at work.

A recent Federal study estimates that noise in the U.S. is doubling every ten years. The big diesel and the unmuffled hot-rod, the angry honking of traffic-snarled cars, pounding presses and other factory machines, jackhammers and other construction equipment, the jet's whine, banging trashcans and buzzing lawn mowers—there's no escape.

Lightweight construction opens apartments and offices to noise from outdoors and next door. Air conditioners, vacuums and other whirring machines build home noise, along with the insistent beat of the teen-ager's record player. The jukebox disrupts restaurant dining, and the turned-up transistor offends on public transport and on the street. Ahead, most traumatic of all: The window-shattering boom of the supersonic transport.

Yet people seem willing to dismiss the noise problem. Perhaps they don't recognize the danger; it's annoying, they figure, but little more, while polluted air or water can make you sick.

But so can noise, it turns out. Researchers are unanimous that prolonged exposure to excessive noise is probably the single most important cause of loss of hearing. It's estimated, for instance, that anywhere from 6 million to 16 million workers suffer hearing damage from on-the-job noise.

Steadily gaining scientific support is the idea that too much noise —by disturbing peace of mind, interfering with rest and sleep— breeds tension and irritability and can lead to ulcers, high blood pressure, heart attacks, nervous breakdowns. One recent research paper said violent noise could permanently damage unborn babies. A British study showed that people living near London's Heathrow Airport had far higher rates of admission to mental hospitals than similar types of people living in nearby quieter areas.

Ordinary conversation runs about 60 decibels; noise experts figure that anything above the 85 to 90 decibel range signals trouble. Heavy city traffic usually checks out around 90 to 95, a food blender at 93, pneumatic hammers and compressors at 95, a loud outboard motor at 102, a power mower around 95, and a low-flying jet at about 115.

Anti-noise action so far has been incredibly weak. A few states have laws regulating truck noise and many cities have anti-noise ordinances, but these are spottily enforced.

Washington is only beginning to act. Empowered back in mid-1968, the Federal Aviation Administration has just gotten around to setting maximum noise standards for new jets; they'll be less uproarious than they might otherwise be, but by no means quiet. "You'll like the sound of the 747," FAA Administrator John Shaffer declares. "It's a very soft—if you'll pardon the expression—roar."

The Department of Transportation has awarded a contract to a Virginia firm, appropriately named Serendipity Inc., to suggest ways of cutting all types of transportation noise, but its report isn't due for another year. The Labor Department last summer proclaimed limits on the number of hours each day that workers on Government contracts could be exposed to high-decibel noises, but again, enforcement is still an unknown quantity.

This general slowness to act is particularly remarkable because most experts agree that noise can be attacked relatively easily. It's simple to detect, simple to measure. Technological solutions—quieter machines, noise absorbers, other devices—are either at hand or, for the most part, promptly obtainable. In some cases, such as quieting engines on existing jets, the cost might be substantial, but in many instances it's low, particularly compared to the huge outlays needed to clean dirty air or dirty water.

Quieter vacuums and other appliances could be turned out almost overnight. A Bethlehem Steel garbage can uses sound-dampening materials so it gives off "a dull thud instead of a reverberating clang." General Motors has a new garbage truck substantially more silent than the old grinders.

More efficient mufflers could readily be installed on trucks and motorbikes, power mowers, major construction equipment. Building codes could require stouter materials in walls and floors. Plane takeoff and landing patterns could be kept farther from residential and commercial areas. Horn-blowing regulations and other anti-noise ordinances can be enforced.

. . .

One solution being seriously advanced now, however, is clearly a step backward: Lessening the impact of high-decibel noise by keeping a low-decibel noise constantly present. The gentle background hum of fan, air conditioner or special noisemaking machine could, some acoustical wizards suggest, make more bearable the neighbor's hi-fi, the garbage truck's grinding, the jet's whine.

As the New Yorker magazine remarked recently, this sort of solution opens an intriguing vista.

"Might not water-supply officials consider introducing vinegar into our city pipes to distract us from the chlorine?" the New Yorker asked. "How about maternity hospitals' packing newborn babies three or four to a crib so they will operate more smoothly in the world in which they will grow up? Why not ease the standards of color-TV-set production to help us accommodate to new levels of radiation? Couldn't the Joint Chiefs base their strategic plans on the theory that a continuum of small wars will ease the shock of transition to the unthinkable?

"There is food for thought here, and it should be taken with plenty of additives."

THE GARBAGE EXPLOSION *
CHARLES A. SCHWEIGHAUSER

Obviously, new answers are needed to the problems of garbage disposal. Land fill, incinerators and dumps are no longer adequate solutions. Two fundamental questions must be answered: Can garbage be reduced to basic chemical elements and reused? Can any such process be made profitable for private industry? Or must garbage disposal be regarded as a social cost and financed with tax dollars?

The accumulation of solid waste in the United States is reaching alarming dimensions. Each person throws away more than half again as much waste as he discarded fifty years ago. A larger and more affluent population, buying an increasing quantity of goods designed to be discarded after temporary use, produces a gigantic disposal problem. Each one of us in a year throws away 188 pounds of paper, 250 metal cans, 135 bottles and jars, 338 caps and crowns, and $2.50 worth of miscellaneous packaging. And every year we amass 2 percent more refuse which, coupled with

* Reprinted from Charles A. Schweig-hauser, "The Garbage Explosion," The Nation, September 22, 1969, by permission.

a 2 percent annual population growth, indicates a 4 percent annual growth in the solid waste disposal problem.

In 1920, the daily per capita disposal was somewhat less than 3 pounds; in 1965 it was 4.5 pounds, not including industrial solid wastes, which account for an equal amount. In 1920 the citizens of this country were throwing away 100 billion pounds per year; today the amount is more than 720 billion pounds per year—not including 6 trillion pounds of mineral and agricultural solid wastes. By 1985, household wastes alone will amount to an estimated 1.25 trillion pounds per year.

The trend is illustrated by the history of glass containers. The first "no deposit, no return" beer bottle was made in 1938; in 1958 more than 1 billion bottles were made, and in 1965, nearly 5 billion bottles were distributed. The throwaway soft-drink bottle production was more than 1 billion. By 1970, the estimated combined beer and soft-drink use will exceed 12 billion nonreturnable bottles. That's 33 million bottles a day.

Nearly all major urban areas have run out of suitably inexpensive land for solid waste disposal, and are forced to dispose of solid waste by either long-distance removal or incineration. Incineration is more expensive than land disposal because of smoke pollution laws, and incinerator residue must be disposed of somewhere on the land.

The traditional method of disposing of solid waste was to put it either on the land, under the land, or down the side of a bank, where it decayed and was covered by vegetation. Very little thought was given to the pollution that resulted from using the land as a dump. Water, air and visual pollution weren't noticeable because their effects weren't very large. With an increasing population producing proportionately more waste, the physical insult to the land and to human sensibilities can no longer be tolerated. Urban areas must look for new methods and procedures to handle solid waste, as traditional techniques become unsatisfactory.

Few successful attempts have been made to re-use the paper, glass, plastics, rubber, rags and garbage that make up most of our domestic solid waste. About 35 percent of total paper production, and about 10 percent of plastics are recycled; glass not at all. The re-use of some metals is higher, as most major nonferrous metals can be economically salvaged. Copper re-use accounted for about 40 percent of the supply in the United States in 1963, discarded lead was recovered at a rate that was more than double that produced from domestic mines, and scrap aluminum accounted for about 25 percent of the total supply in the same year. Recovered scrap iron and steel currently account for about 50 percent of total production. The recovery of rubber for chemicals, rubber and fibers is beginning to increase, and now stands at about 15 percent.

The nearly 180 million tons of

annual municipal refuse are estimated to contain ferrous and nonferrous metals valued at more than $1 billion. Each ton of residue from incineration contains 500 pounds of iron and 50 pounds of aluminum, copper, lead, tin and zinc. Fly ash from incinerators weighs about 20 pounds for every ton of refuse incinerated, and contains enough silver and gold to be comparable to a normal mine assay in the West.

Our solid waste disposal problems would be much worse if some materials were not recycled. A great deal more recycling could be done, but rising labor costs, uncertain markets, synthetics, and the mixing of refuse all make re-use costly and difficult.

Our industry is organized to use continuous input of new, rather than recovered, materials, and is sustained by constantly increasing consumer affluence and demands, built-in obsolescence, self-service merchandising, and competitive enterprise. We collect sometimes widely scattered resources, process and distribute them. But the responsibility of the private enterprise manufacturers stops at the shipping door. Neither distributors nor the retailers ever took responsibility for the disposal of the material they distribute (returnable bottles were an exception). Goods are used and then discarded; there are no consumers in the literal sense of the word. Responsibility thus passes from producer to user to a local government disposal agency.

So far it has been economically more feasible to build a new product out of new resources, because our industrial systems are so constitued, than to recover and re-use old products and their parts. Re-use systems could work in one of two ways: the material to be recycled could be collected by the producer, or the public agency or private individual keeps responsibility for returning the product to the producer/manufacturer (reverse distribution). The former system has worked, but in a rather disorganized and unsystematic manner; missing are economic incentives to encourage an efficient re-use system. Compounding the problem is our resistance to investment of money in an item that we will never use again. Solid waste disposal, therefore, has a low priority status with the general public and its agencies.

Recycling of garbage presents some interesting and difficult situations. Before urbanization, domestic garbage was recycled through pigs, chickens and other farm animals. Piggeries still use domestic garbage, but on a lesser scale. Garbage must be separated from nonorganic solid waste, usually in the home, which causes problems. Most states require domestic garbage to be cooked before it is fed to swine in order to stop the trichinosis cycle, a requirement that is necessary for public health but that is also expensive and time consuming for the piggery operator.

Another recycling method for garbage is composting, a process that involves biochemical degradation of the organic material. This material must be separated from ferrous metal, usually by magnet, and from all other metals, glass, paper, rubber and plastics by hand. The remainder is shredded, put through a short aerobic period to increase bacterial action and to hasten decomposition, and then allowed to cure for several months. The final product is a soil conditioner.

The product is of good quality, but the cost of producing it is greater than that of other types of soil conditioners. The cost of compost material from other sources is higher in Europe than in the United States, and thus composting of solid waste is much more widely practiced there. Contribution to the cost factor is labor (including pickers), rather expensive equipment, time for the product to mature, and the relatively low percentage of organic material in the total refuse. About 30 percent of the original material must still be disposed of by other means. Vermin are also hard to control in a compost operation.

A number of schemes have been proposed, and a few are being developed, using other kinds of technology. For example, containers that dissolve in water or by the action of soil acids and sunlight are being investigated. Organic solid waste, mixed with sewage sludge, may give a high-grade composting material, provided that the pathogens can be removed. This process may also be valuable in curtailing excessive use of nitrogen, and thereby slowing down the tendency toward entropy in lakes and waterways.

Home solid waste grinders, analogous to contemporary garbage grinders, have been proposed. These larger and more rugged units might handle objects of paper, glass, plastics and light metal up to a cubic foot or more in size. After grinding, the material would be disposed of through sewer systems.

The Japanese have built large compactors to reduce solid waste to high-density blocks, which are then encased in an asphalt sealer and used for building foundations and other construction purposes. The city of Cleveland is also experimenting with a similar technique, using a mixture of solid waste, fly ash, dried sewage sludge, river and lake dredgings, and incinerator residue made into small, compact bricks for use as fill material to reclaim submerged lands adjacent to Lake Erie.

Paper products make up the largest percentage of most domestic solid waste. Since paper is nearly all cellulose, and since ruminants (cattle) can digest cellulose and turn it into protein, a number of public and private groups are experimenting with the use of paper products, supplemented with vitamins and minerals, as cattle feed. Today's newspaper may be tomorrow's steak.

Power production from incinerated solid waste has also been proposed. Milan, Italy, will soon be running all of its streetcars and subways by electricity generated by incinerated solid waste. Similar attempts in this country have been less successful, however, because of the inconsistent quality of the refuse to be incinerated and the production of electricity by other, hitherto less expensive means.

Other ideas have been put forward, such as adding hydrogen to wastepaper to make a high-grade fuel. Sanitary land-fill techniques along the sides of highways, power lines, sewer interceptors and other public rights of way have also been suggested. Such innovations have met with little enthusiasm, however, due to economic factors, entrenched procedures and lack of organized promotion campaigns.

The annual sum spent on solid waste collection and disposal in this country is large in comparison with other services. The annual cost of refuse collection and disposal, according to a recent federal document, is estimated at more than $4.5 billion, an amount that is exceeded only by schools and roads among public services. An estimated additional $750 million will have to be spent each year over the next five years to bring the collection and disposal systems of the nation to an acceptable health and aesthetic level.

The figures show only how much we have extracted from our natural environment, used briefly, and discarded permanently. They tell nothing about the supply of metals, pulp and other resources still left in the natural environment that we will use once and discard. Will we run out of resources before we choke on our own midden?

We can no longer treat solid waste as something to be shoved so far away that we'll never see it. There just isn't anywhere left to put it. We must learn to treat solid waste as a fact of life, and learn how to live with it, as we have learned to live with, or at least tolerate, sewers, automobiles, manufacturing plants and all other aspects of our modern age.

It should also be realized that our traditional attitude toward solid waste disposal is untenable in view of further environmental deterioration. This attitude can be characterized by the phrase "symptom-chasing." The disposal problem will not be solved by improving procedural techniques: it can only be postponed for a few years at best. The ultimate goal of refuse disposal —or any pollution control—is 100 percent recycling of materials and energy. Advanced refuse recycling systems for urban areas are in the distant future; for the countryside they are even further away.

The problem can be viewed from another perspective. To control the effluent of our affluent society one must understand and rectify the causes in human behavior, and not just the symptoms. If a man has a brain tumor we would hardly expect his total treatment to be an aspirin. We must somehow convince the refuse makers—both the producers and the consumer-users (that means all of us)—that our overpackaged, overstuffed, throwaway life-style will bring long-term ecological and economic disaster. We probably will not much longer have the luxury of making decisions that will affect the ecosystem, as nearly all decisions ultimately do, based solely on economic and political expediency.

It is comparatively simple to write about solid waste practices and to recommend certain changes and improvements. It would be infinitely more difficult—but much more to the point—to study ways of drastically reducing solid waste effluent. And we must recognize that our solid waste situation, as well as our larger environment, can be improved only by self-imposed restraints.

WHO OWNS THE ENVIRONMENT? *

PETER SCHRAG

The dark side of our affluence is now beginning to show. Instead

* Reprinted from Peter Schrag, "Who Owns the Environment?" Saturday Review, July 4, 1970. Copyright © 1970 Saturday Review, Inc.

of a brighter tomorrow, we may face a future where, as a people, we will never be as rich again. The magic of science shows little promise of solving pollution problems.

If our affluence has indeed peaked, must we find new ways of distributing goods? Why may we get socialism because we are producing too much? Can we justify tax penalties on resource depletion? Should we tax large families? How might we reorient our society to deemphasize production? In what ways does our government presently encourage environmental destruction? Why is much of the present cry meaningless in terms of developing an environmental policy?

It is hard to listen to the accumulating prophecies of environmental apocalypse without the nagging sense that the country is about to stage its greatest and—if the prophets are right—its last revival, a millenarian event unmatched in modern history. In my local bookstore where, six months ago, I could hardly find a volume of Commoner or Ehrlich, there is now a large paperback section marked *Ecology!* —the exclamation point is dark and bold—flanking a smaller shelf labeled *Technology . . . ?* The books in that section, the teach-ins, the platform rhetoric, the magazine pieces, the ecology action groups, and conservation societies, the population planners, and the assorted unclassifiable Cassandras of destruction seem to be telling me —collectively, if not individually— that the end is near. If air pollution and poisoned water don't get us, overpopulation will. I am being prepared for the worst.

And yet—at the same time, I hear something else, polite but determined, comfortable yet anxious. The same issues, but with limited vision, a sort of environmental myopia, reminiscent of a suburban zoning meeting: People who have theirs—nice houses and lawns, nice schools and little shoppes and country clubs—getting together To Do Something about the unsightly litter on the mall—empty beer cans on the grass and four-letter words on the gate of the swimming pool. Moreover, it is said, some real estate operator is getting ready to put up some cheap housing (Negroes?) and a trailer park at the edge of town. Can't have that; have to keep the place up. This is not the time for anyone to ask for more; this is the time to clean up the mess produced by the goods we (or some of us) already enjoy. Fine the polluters. Keep the streams clean. Protect the fish.

You are told that it's all the same thing, that The Environment means everything from the beaches of Santa Barbara to street cleaning in Canarsie and rats in Harlem, everything from the greenhouse effect to famine in India. And so, in a way, it does. If necessary The Environment will envelop every problem of mankind, making it a handy political device to convert explo-

sive social pressures — protest against the Vietnam War, racial friction, youth revolt, hunger, poverty—into an era of good feeling in which we all Work Together to Save the Earth. Unpalatable issues can be deferred or ignored or obfuscated in the larger cause. And yet, in meaning everything, The Environment means nothing because we have not yet devised means to assess the rates of exchange: the necessity to feed growing numbers of people against the measurable depletion of the soil; the jobs of auto workers (or the lack of public transportation) against the frustration of traffic jams and the hazards of air pollution; the civil liberties of people who want large families against the demands of population control; the elimination of crop insects and malaria (DDT?) against the preservation of fish.

Moreover, we do not know—and this is likely to be the most important issue of all—whether the disamenities of increased production (pollution, resource depletion, crowding, waste disposal, noise) have already begun to exceed its benefits, whether we have reached or passed the point where growth as measured by Gross National Product is already inconsistent with what we now call the quality of life. Does every additional automobile create more problems for the society than it solves? Does every skyscraper or every highway in a "growing" city create more difficulties in pollution, crime control, congestion, and frustration than it resolves in taxes, jobs, and other benefits? Is growth itself counterproductive? No economist is prepared to answer the question because disamenities are hard to calculate, yet clearly something is rapidly changing: We are in the early stages of a revolt against "affluence," "growth," and traditional notions of efficiency, but we have not yet decided who the enemy is and who should pay the price. It is, for obvious reasons, the affluent who are most concerned about "growth," not the poor; their problem is food and housing, not clean beaches; "the environment" is still a class issue. And because growth, expansion, and wealth are among the most fundamental articles of solid Americanism, the ultimate conflict is likely to be more divisive than the issues which it has temporarily replaced. "We have met the enemy," said Pogo, "and it is us."

If the environment is everything, there can be no experts; so far, moreover, most instruments of economic measurement—GNP, growth, profits, employment, foreign trade —are calibrated in such a way as to conceal the most fundamental environmental problems. Gross National Product, it has been said, is a misnomer: What it measures is cost—the cost of goods and services from refrigerators and food to the fees paid to doctors for treating the victims of pollution-caused emphysema (which happens to be the most rapidly growing cause of death in America), from electric toothbrushes to mink coats. "What

GNP measures," someone said, "is garbage." But it does not measure all the garbage: the anxiety of crowding, the impersonality of large cities, the time lost in commuting, the destruction of resources, or the general ugliness of the landscape. There have been attempts to measure the price of air and water pollution—the extra cost of laundry, medical care, water treatment—but it is impossible to convert ugliness and discomfort into dollars.

.   .   .

Harvey Wheeler of the Center for the Survey of Democratic Institutions speaks about a revolution of declining expectations. "As a people," he said, "we will never be as rich again." At the same time, the economists point out that they have heard such predictions in the past and that science and technology have always come to the rescue. "The environmentalists," said one, "are making asses of themselves. Certainly there are always possibilities for disaster, but we really don't know where they are." People such as Commoner or Ehrlich answer that this time science isn't likely to rescue anybody, that, in fact, the untested use of scientific "breakthroughs" has helped create the environmental catastrophe we are about to face.

.   .   .

For most of us, "choice" is based not on necessity but on cultural conditioning; people are trained to be consumers, to feel inadequate if they don't buy the best, or get the wash as white as the woman next door, or turn in the car every three years. (If women's liberation really begins to catch on, it may well destroy the economy, not only by teaching women to refuse exploitative jobs but by making it clear that consumption is not the road to fulfillment.) It is hardly news to say that we rarely have wants for goods that do not exist; we *create* wants, through advertising and schooling, for what manufacturers have available. Choice, moreover, is limited not only as to environment and product—you can't get away from the foul air, nor can you buy a discontinued model— but also as to the conditions, hours, and places of employment. People are taught that the price of affluence is a dull job whose nature is dictated by "technology." Freedom is a cart in the supermarket. The choices we have, in other words, are made available through denial of other options whose value never appears in the statistics. And one of those options is the environment itself.

The current campaign against pollution seems—at least at the official levels of government—to be directed primarily toward the most obvious phenomena: waste disposal, sewage treatment, air pollution control, and the protection of wildlife. Its general tendency will be to require polluters either to cease and desist or to pay the price of the damage. A good thing. In the long run, however, the cost of effective waste disposal will simply be built into the price of the goods; in turn, pollution control will also create new economic activity—sewage plants, filters, air cleaners— which will also be part of "growth" in GNP. The environment, in other words, is supposed to be structured into existing economic assumptions and arrangements; it is not, for the moment at least, prompting any fundamental re-examination of "growth," GNP, or the conventional indices of well-being.

At the same time, the government—meaning the public—continues to subsidize environmental destruction in the name of progress. In the current federal budget, which includes $27-million for air pollution research, $275-million was appropriated for the development of the SST, which is likely not only to shatter the landscape with its sonic boom but also to foul the stratosphere—perhaps permanently —with vapors and exhaust materials affecting weather and climate. Instead of encouraging the importation of foreign oil, while we can still get it, we restrict it, allegedly to reduce our dependency on overseas operators but, in fact, to maintain the prices and profits of domestic producers. Moreover— and more important—we continue to subsidize mineral resource depletion through tax allowances, and large families through tax deductions. The President's Coordinating Council on the Environment is supposed to make existing federal agencies aware of environmental considerations, but if you ask about economic planning or the relation of GNP and growth to the environment, they hardly know what you're talking about.

Nonetheless, it is striking how a growing minority is coming to regard the old artifacts of "progress" as symbols of destruction: Although the marriage continues—there are, after all, no existing alternatives—our romance with the automobile is coming to an end; smoking chimneys bring on the pollution inspectors and embarrassment at the Chamber of Commerce, and those nice sudsy detergents elicit uncomfortable apologies from the soap industry. All that may be no more than a set of precious gestures on the part of those who already have theirs—the cars, the houses, the chlorinated private swimming pools —and yet it is clear that "affluence" is producing something more than the old elitist contempt for suburban materialism. Against the once unqualified celebration of production and growth there appears the first awakening of a perception of disamenities and a sense that something is coming to an end.

The students—and many others —who constitute the radical wings of the environmentalist movement are, many of them, more interested in the failures of affluence than they are in the more obvious manifestations of pollution that it produces; the crack in the picture window, relabeled ecology, is becoming a crusade against growth. Which is to say that even if the disamenities can't be measured, they are being felt. Resentment of the business rat race and the well-advertised reluctance of affluent kids to enter high-paying jobs in industry represent not simply a revolt against corporate organizations and org-men, but more fundamentally a reflection of the feeling that what corporations do isn't worth doing even if there were no environmental issues. Production, for them, is no longer an adventure but a travesty; since we discovered the sulphides in the air and the phosphates in the water, their view of that travesty has become respectable.

But there is something else— another set of disamenities—that may generate really violent divisions regarding ecology and growth. The economist Robert Lekachman summarized the question in a recent issue of *Commentary:* "If we are so rich," he asked, "why do we feel so poor?" Part of the reason, as he points out, is inflation, but part also derives from the very lack of basic choice. . . . You have to buy a smelly car that will break down in three years (with luck that is) because no other transportation is available; you can't (usually) buy your way out of pollution; you can't find a competent mechanic to repair the gadgets that are supposed to make your life so rich. "Even if markets were unrigged," he wrote, "and consumers [were] as rational as economists sometimes generously assume them to be, they could not buy appliances that function with reasonable reliability, foods innocent of chemical preservatives, medicines uninflated by the pharmaceutical companies' labeling and marketing maneuvers, or living space securely protected from intolerable environmental noise."

The feeling of being poor cuts across a fairly broad spectrum of class and economic lines; you can win the votes of Buffalo factory workers with attacks on the destruction of the fish in Lake Erie; you can find members of local trade unions opposing industrial expansion because "growth" in jobs and in the membership of the union will be offset by more pollution, and you can hear the presidents of established corporations and foundations questioning "that form of economic growth that simply multiplies production and consumption of material goods." And yet, if the feeling is common, the possible solutions are divisive. *The issue of "environment" brings together those who already consume, not those who aspire to it.* When Ecology Action buried a new automobile in California recently, black militants demanded that the car be turned over to them for the movement; why should anyone destroy $2,000 worth of stuff—however important the symbol—when you can convert it into breakfast for 5,000 hungry kids? The environment, in other words, can become not only a consumer good, but the ultimate item in conspicuous consumption for people who are so classy or affluent that they can bury or otherwise destroy cars that the lower classes are killing themselves to ride.

Some people, in short, feel poor because they are poor, and no set of environmental controls and no restriction of growth is going to do much for them unless we can figure out a way of allocating the goods that are produced to give every person an adequate portion. J. George Harrar, president of the Rockefeller Foundation, recently told a Congressional subcommittee that "our resources are not limitless, and when those that are nonrenewable are consumed or transformed, they can never be replenished. . . . More attention should be devoted to services and to those areas of life that enrich the quality of human existence: cultural activities, the arts, literature, intellectual and scientific pursuits, esthetic improvements, and human relationships." One must assume from the use of the word "should" that Mr. Harrar favors systematic economic planning—socialism by whatever name —to produce such services, control destruction of the environment, and ensure equitable distribution of material production to the poor, the hungry, and to those who enjoy neither the amenities nor the goods which are said to impair them. (The argument that socialist countries have their own environmental problems proves little, since economic planning has, historically, always been employed to maximize production and resource exploitation—including human resources— and not to restrict them. There is no reason why planning can't be directed to other ends.)

So far, however, there has been little talk about such planning, except in the area of population, which happens to be the sector most likely to affect individual freedom and personal choice. The population argument by itself, however stated, always seems to express more contempt for breeding and for bodies than concern about the vulgar affluence of the rich and the despair of the poor. At the moment when we have a plan for the equitable distribution of resources, arguments for population control may sound more democratic and persuasive.

Which brings us back to the basic premises of American life and "affluence." We are out of free land, air, water, and soil. Growth without control—perhaps any growth— is no longer automatically consistent with the "quality of life." GNP does not measure human welfare, and booms in population, industrial expansion, real estate prices—perhaps even in certain areas of education and technical competence —have ceased to be blessings. A half-century ago Frederick Jackson Turner speculated that education and science might replace the frontier as the open territories of American aspiration and development, but even those "frontiers" are now developing technological limitations. What are we going to do with all those aeronautical engineers, the draftsmen, the technicians if we don't build an SST or maintain a growing space program? Do we train technicians to exploit resources or to conserve them? Are we an overdeveloped society, not only in natural resources but in human resources as well? Have we taught people so much about work

and its value that we have forgotten how to do anything but produce?

This country—we thought— escaped the rigid divisions of class and wealth that plagued other nations because we were all incipient liberal capitalists mining unlimited resources. There was enough for everybody. But just as the once invisible under classes tried to get theirs, those who already had it announced that the environment was being destroyed. If we are to resist that destruction, we will be confronted with novel and difficult political choices of economic distribution: It is not that, lacking environmental problems, the poor might eventually have shared in our "affluence," and that our "affluence" ran out at an unfortunate moment. That was probably inevitable; the affluence of the majority created its own disamenities. But now, having discovered the limits of our resources, we are at a point where we must admit that the things we possess must be distributed in a different way, that new promises, new economic and social indicators, and a new ethic must replace those that we are forced to surrender.

The battle to save the environment is just beginning; but until the nation decides which sectors of the environment will get priority, and who will pay the price, ecology is nothing but rhetoric. If we do restrict or eliminate growth, whose goods will be curtailed, and how will we provide for those who have nothing now? There are possible "capitalist" answers to such questions, but they are not likely to prove adequate. We have already established the principle that ownership of a piece of land does not give the proprietor unlimited use: Zoning laws, building codes, air pollution regulations, and other restrictions limit his freedom. If we regulate waste disposal, then should we not also curtail resource depletion by charging for the extraction of every ton of coal and ore, for every barrel of oil, every gallon of water, and for every measurable depreciation in the growing quality of soil? Should we impose tax penalties on families rather than offer them benefits and deductions? The difficulty with most of these solutions is that, in raising the price of goods, they would affect the indigent much more severely than the rich. They will do little to provide alternatives, either in the quality of life or in personal motivation, to the pressure for more private goods and services.

The most likely course of action, therefore, is to reduce the incentive to amass private wealth and to provide adequate social services—medical care, housing, public transportation, recreation—for all, to reduce the private sector and enlarge the public. For years there have been arguments that higher taxes for the wealthy will reduce incentive, but that is now precisely the point. The tax structure is not only inequitable, but it encourages exploitation, not only of resources but of people. We have to reduce that incentive, to control the private sector and to enlarge the public. Galbraith proposed that years ago, and so have others, but the environmental issue gives his argument new urgency. Historically, America rejected general economic planning and broad social welfare systems because there was always the promise of enough for all without them. Now, ironically, we are likely to get socialism, not because, as everywhere else, we couldn't produce enough, but because we may be producing too much—and, by so doing, destroying everything we have.

9. The Lawless Society: Survival In The Urban Jungle

Urban Americans are afraid. No longer do city residents move about freely after dark. A nighttime stroll through Central Park has become a form of Russian roulette. Even patrolmen walk the streets in pairs, backed up by police dogs. Crimes against persons— rape, aggravated assault, homicide, muggings—show a steady increase year after year. Burglary, theft, vandalism and arson follow a similar pattern. The whole tone of urban society is muted by this atmosphere of violence, and urban life styles have been drastically altered.

A direct relationship exists between the decline of downtown life (theaters, restaurants, department stores) and the rising tide of crime. Americans have retreated behind an arsenal of security measures: barred windows, alarms, complicated locks, vicious watch dogs, all forms of rifles, shotguns, and pistols. The open nature of American life is steadily being contracted as we adopt a fortress mentality.

White-Collar Crime

In popular mythology, crime always involves brutality, guns, and the "ten-most-wanted men" on the FBI list. But an amazing number of middle-class Americans are caught up in non-violent "white-collar" crime. In Wall Street offices, securities valued at $400,000,000 "disappear" in six months; the typical expense account is "padded"; shoplifting is a nagging problem across the nation, including bookstores in our "best" universities. Motels assume that their guests will cart off such items as towels by the millions—even bolted-down TV sets are vulnerable. Thousands upon thousands of people stock their homes with supplies brazenly or discreetly carried out of the factories or offices where they work. Top corporation executives quietly break the law by reaching price-fixing agreements in posh restaurants or on the 19th hole. In one sense, at least, Pogo's remark about pollution can be altered to read, "We have met the criminal, and it is us."

Organized Crime

The average American sees little connection between street violence and organized crime. Yet the cost of individual violence is dwarfed by the total amount that organized crime siphons from society. The American genius for business organization has produced an underworld economic empire that reputedly surpasses the efficiency of legitimate business. With the revenues derived from gambling, loan sharking and narcotics, the empire has allegedly been able to "buy" some state and urban political leaders. Although the scope and organization of this underworld is greatly exaggerated, millions of Americans believe this inflated version and view as suspect many local political figures.

Most of this operation is hidden from public view: the average citizen sees only a penny-ante set up. Criticism is also muted because millions of Americans get services from criminal cartels that are unavailable elsewhere. The small businessman, caught in an economic squeeze, can readily get money from the Mafia when his banker says "no." The desperate drug addict has no place else to turn but to organized "loan sharks." Many "average guys" play the numbers, place bets, and shoot crap, in the eternal hope of a big killing; all of these rackets provide millions for the underworld.

Some observers have argued that lower interest rates and legalized gambling would undercut organized crime, although doubt is cast on this theory by the recent invasion of legitimate businesses—such as resort hotels—by racketeers.

Reforming the Criminal Justice System

Any plan to reduce crime and violence must be based on an answer to the questions: What causes crime? Why is the U.S. crime rate steadily escalating? Two widely-divergent theories of the causes of crime are commonly advanced. One theory stresses lax home discipline, poor law enforcement, and court decisions that coddle criminals. Following this analysis, we can curb crime by tossing aside the theories of Dr. Spock, supporting our local police, and reversing Supreme Court decisions that protect the criminal at the expense of his victim. Tough parents, tough laws, tough cops, tough judges, tough sentences (with a dash of capital punishment), and tough prisons will restore a law-abiding America.

The alternate analysis stresses the faults of society, while de–emphasizing individual guilt. Broken homes, slum living, bad schools, high unemployment, degenerate moral values, a dead-end welfare system, grueling poverty, police brutality, and prisons that turn first offenders into professional criminals are among the charges brought against society.

Following this analysis, what must be done? Obviously a far-reaching reform of the environment is needed—better housing, more jobs, better education and health services. The entire criminal justice system should be reformed. Police should be better-educated and have higher salaries. The long gap between arrest and trial should be shortened by expanding the court system. Prisons should be converted from holding pens to rehabilitation centers. We should expand our parole and probation system.

The cleavage between the two theories of social reform is almost total: the "get tough" school wants immediate action based on the existing society. The "reform" school takes a long look, and sees little hope for crime reduction until society is reoriented. Caught in this crossfire, political leaders must soothe both groups while they wrestle with the basic problem.

VIOLENCE IN AMERICA:
TOWARD CITIES
WITH FORTRESSES *
NATIONAL COMMISSION ON
THE CAUSES AND
PREVENTION OF VIOLENCE

In one of its last reports the National Commission on Crime drew a disturbing profile of violent crime in America. In every category—homicide, forcible rape, aggravated assault and robbery—the trend was sharply upward, with robbery doubling in eight years. Obviously, such trends, if not reversed, could reduce urban America to a medieval fortress, with the enemy inside the gates.

Where do crimes of violence most frequently occur? Who commits them? Against whom? How does the U.S. crime rate compare with that of other industrial nations? Why has it been suggested that future American cities will be fortresses? What would a fortress city look like?

Between 1960 and 1968, the national rate of criminal homicide per 100,000 population increased 36

* Reprinted from the National Commission on the Causes and Prevention of Violence, Violent Crime, Homicide, Assault, Rape and Robbery (U.S. Government Printing Office, 1969).

percent, the rate of forcible rape 65 percent, of aggravated assault 67 percent, and of robbery 119 percent. These figures are from the uniform crime reports published by the Federal Bureau of Investigation. These reports are the only national indicators we have of crime in America; but, as the F.B.I. recognizes, they must be used with caution. . . .

Some part of the increase in reported rates of violent crime is no doubt due to a fuller disclosure of the violent crimes actually committed.

Violent crime in the United States is primarily a phenomenon of large cities. This is a fact of central importance. . . .

Violent crime in the city is overwhelmingly committed by males.

Violent crime in the city is concentrated especially among youths between the ages of 15 and 20. . . .

Violent crime in the city is committed primarily by individuals at the lower end of the occupational scale. . . .

Violent crime in the cities stems disproportionately from the ghetto slum where most Negroes live. . . .

The victims of assaultive violence in the cities generally have the same characteristics as the offenders: victimization rates are generally highest for males, youth, poor persons and blacks. Robbery victims, however, are very often older whites. . . .

Unlike robbery the other violent crimes of homicide, assault and rape tend to be acts of passion among intimates and acquaintances. . . .

By far the greatest proportion of all serious violence is committed by repeaters.

While the number of hardcore repeaters is small compared to the number of one-time offenders, the former group has a much higher rate of violence and inflicts considerably more serious injury. In a Philadelphia study, 627 of the 10,000 boys were chronic offenders, having five or more police contacts. Though they represented only 6 percent of the boys in the study, they accounted for 53 percent of the police contacts for personal attacks—homicide, rape and assault —and 71 percent of the contacts for robberies.

Americans generally are no strangers to violent crime.

Although it is impossible to determine accurately how many Americans commit violent crimes each year, the data that are available suggest that the number is substantial, ranging from perhaps 600,000 to 1,200,000—or somewhere between one in every 300 and one in every 150 persons. Undoubtedly, a far greater number commit a serious violent crime at some time in their lives.

A comparison of reported violent crime rates in this country with those in other modern, stable nations shows the United States rape rate clear leader. Our homicide rate is more than twice that of our closest competitor, Finland, and from 4 to 12 times higher than the rates in a dozen other advanced countries, including Japan, Canada, England and Norway.

Similar patterns are found in the rates of other violent crimes; averages computed for the years 1963–1967 show the United States rape rate to be 12 times that of England and Wales and 3 times that of Canada; our robbery rate is 9 times that of England and Wales and double that of Canada, our aggravated assault rate is double that of England and Wales and 18 times that of Canada.

The way in which we have so far chosen to deal with the deepening problem of violent crime begins to revise the future shape of our cities. In a few more years, lacking effective public action, this is how these cities will likely look:

¶ Central business districts in the heart of the city surrounded by mixed areas of accelerating deterioration, will be partially protected by large numbers of people shopping or working in commercial buildings during daytime hours, plus a substantial police presence, and will be largely deserted except for police patrols during nighttime hours.

¶ High rise apartment buildings and residential compounds protected by private guards and security devices will be fortified cells for upper-middle and high-income populations living at prime locations in the city.

¶ Suburban neighborhoods, geographically far removed from the central city, will be protected mainly by economic homogeneity and by distance from population groups with the highest propensities to commit crimes.

¶ Lacking a sharp change in Federal and state policies, ownership of guns will be almost universal in the suburbs; homes will be fortified by an array of devices, from window grills to electronic surveillance equipment; armed citizens in cars will supplement inadequate police patrols in neighborhoods closer to the central city, and extreme left-wing and right-wing groups will have tremendous armories of weapons which could be brought into play with or without any provocation.

¶ High speed, patrolled expressways will be sanitized corridors connecting safe areas, and private automobiles, taxicabs, and commercial vehicles will be routinely equipped with unbreakable glass, light armor and other security features. Inside garages or valet parking will be available at safe buildings in or near the central city. Armed guards will "ride shotgun" on all forms of public transportation.

¶ Streets and residential neighborhoods in the central city will be unsafe in differing degrees and the ghetto slum neighborhoods will be places of terror with widespread crime, perhaps entirely out of police control during nighttime hours. Armed guards will protect all public facilities such as schools, libraries and playgrounds in these areas.

¶ Between the unsafe, deteriorating central city on the one hand and the network of safe, prosperous areas and sanitized corridors on the other, there will be, not unnaturally, intensifying hatred and deepening division. Violence will increase further, and the defensive response of the affluent will become still more elaborate.

Individually and to a considerable extent unintentionally, we are closing ourselves into fortresses when collectively we should be building the great, open humane city-societies of which we are capable.

Public and private action must guarantee safety, security and justice for every citizen in our metropolitan areas without sacrificing the quality of life and other values of free society. If the nation is not in a position to launch a full-scale war on domestic ills, especially urban ills, at this moment, because of the difficulty of freeing ourselves quickly from other obligations, we should now legally make the essential commitments and then carry them out as quickly as funds can be obtained.

LIVING SCARED *

MONROE W. KARMIN

The increase in crime is often reported as a cold statistic: robbery up 27%; murder up 13%. In

* Reprinted from Monroe W. Karmin, "Living Scared," Wall Street Journal, February 12, 1970, by permission.

*the form of statistics, the true
impact of the rising crime rate is
hard to visualize. But in the real
world crime is not abstract. It is
the sudden flash of a gun or a
switchblade; it is a snatched
purse; a mugging or a brutal rape.*

*How does one church protect
its collection plate? Must high-
rise apartments become armed
fortresses? Are we reverting
to the state of medieval European
cities—when no man ventured into
the dark streets unless fully armed?*

John D. Holland is afraid.

For 40 years he has been selling
packaged liquor at his Maryland
Beverage Mart in this city's southeast sector. Four years ago he installed a burglar alarm system.
Three years ago he put iron bars on
his windows. Two years ago he began arming. Now on his desk on a
platform overlooking the sales floor
are a black Italian-made pistol, a
silver German-made pistol, a Winchester rifle and an L. C. Smith
shotgun. "I've never been held up,"
Mr. Holland declares, "and I don't
intend to be." Since mid-1967, intruders have murdered seven local
liquor dealers in the course of an
estimated 700 robberies of such
stores.

Leroy R. Bailey, Jr. is afraid.

He drives a taxi. Last year he
paid $20 to install an emergency
flasher in his cab. If he's threatened, Mr. Bailey steps on a button
that sets off a flashing signal for
police aid in his front grille and

rear bumper. At night, he says,
"nine out of 10 cabs won't pick up
a man alone." The number of
Washington cab drivers has dropped to about 11,000 from 13,000
two years ago. Says James E.
Jewell, president of the Independent Taxi Owners Association:
"This is a very dangerous town to
drive in. Many men won't work
after the sun goes down."

The people at the Mexican embassy are afraid.

Last September, during an independence day celebration, two
guests were robbed. Female employees have been accosted. Vandals have struck repeatedly. Now
all embassy doors are kept locked.
A fence has been erected around
the property, located two miles
north of the White House. "We live
in fear," says a spokesman. So does
much of the crime-plagued diplomatic community. President Nixon
is asking Congress to expand the
250-man White House police force
to offer additional protection for
Embassy Row.

The No. 1 Issue

Most of Washington is afraid of
crime.

Fear has changed the way of life
of residents of the nation's capital
and its environs, affecting everyone from cab-driver to Senator. It
has also changed the way institutions, from schools to embassies,
operate. While race relations continue to be a major problem for
this city, whose 850,000 residents

are more than 70% black, there is no doubt that today's No. 1 public concern is personal safety.

"A couple of years ago the city's tension was seen in terms of white police versus the natives," says an aide to Mayor Walter Washington. "Now it's seen as criminals versus victims. It's more crime and less racial."

Mayor Washington, himself a Negro, says that black as well as white neighborhoods are demanding more foot patrolmen, even though the cop on the beat was viewed as "a Gestapo agent" by many blacks not long ago. The mayor finds ground for optimism in the change. "Never before have I seen such an attitude on the part of the people of the city, both black and white, to work together on a problem," he says.

A "Tragic Example"

The nation's capital is by no means alone in its fear of crime; rather, as Mr. Nixon pointed out in his State of the Union Message, it is a "tragic example" of the way crime and violence "increasingly threaten our cities, our homes and our lives." But Washington is suffering more than most cities. In the nine months through September, according to District of Columbia Police Chief Jerry Wilson, reported crime in Washington jumped 26% over a year earlier, compared with an average national increase of 11%. Cleveland, San Francisco and Balti-more also topped the national average.

Chief Wilson, who was appointed last summer, hopes to come to grips with the rising crime rate here this year, if he gets enough help. President Nixon has proposed a new $12.4 million crime-fighting package for the District to supplement the city's regular budget, which emphasizes public safety measures. And Congress is at work on other anticrime legislation for Washington.

This war on crime focuses on several trouble spots. It aims to break the local court bottleneck (it now takes an average of nine months for a criminal case to go to trial and some wait as long as 20 months); to curb the freedom of those awaiting trial through a controversial preventive detention measure (an estimated 35% of those arrested for armed robbery and released on bail commit another crime before they come to trial); and to crack down on drug traffic and use (50% of those arrested here are drug addicts).

Expanding the Police Force

But this year's main thrust, Mayor Washington says, is to put more policemen on the streets. The mayor hopes to beef up the force to 5,100 men by June 30 from 3,868 on Jan. 1. Also planned are expanded criminal rehabilitation and social-welfare programs that the mayor hopes can be meshed into a comprehensive criminal justice system.

Because Washington is the seat of the Federal Government, the crime surge here is an important stimulus to action on both district and national anticrime legislation. Among the victims of local crime have been Sen. Frank Church of Idaho, White House Press Secretary Ronald Ziegler, Mr. Nixon's personal secretary, Rose Mary Woods and Deputy Defense Secretary David Packard, to name just a few. Political partisanship is diminishing as liberal Democrats feel the impact of crime and join the President in his anticrime crusade.

Senate Majority Leader Mike Mansfield recently expressed outrage over the "senseless" slaying of a fellow-Montanan and friend in the streets of Washington. He took the Senate floor to demand "new and better ways to fight crime, to cut down the inordinate rate of violence." Another liberal Democrat, Rep. Frank Thompson, Jr. of New Jersey, warned the other day that "things may get worse if the Administration and Congress do not put crime control on the front burner."

But until this campaign begins to make headway, life in the District of Columbia will reflect fear, especially after dark.

Cruise through downtown Washington in a police car on a Saturday night and the mood can be felt. On F Street, the main downtown shopping street, merchants lock their doors at 6 p.m. Many put up iron grill-work nightly to protect their windows. Shoppers and employees hurry to the bus stops. Many employees who fear the lonely walk at the end of the bus ride wait in the stores until their spouses drive by to take them home. At 7 p.m. F Street is almost deserted.

The relatively small number of people out for an evening of entertainment arrive a bit later. Some go to the National Theater, which now raises its curtain at 7:30 p.m. instead of 8:30 so patrons can get home early. Some head for downtown movie theaters. The servicemen's crowd patronizes the rock joints along 14th Street. Fashionable Georgetown, more than a mile from downtown, is still lively, as are some of the posh restaurants and clubs. But that's about it. Much of Washington is dark, and scared.

"Watch the people," advises a seasoned policeman. "See how they walk quickly and with a purpose. There's no casual strolling. People don't come into this town at night unless they have a specific destination in mind. They go straight to it and then go home as fast as possible."

Restaurants Close

The effects are evident. The Ceres restaurant next to the National Theater is closed, nearby Caruso's restaurant is gone and neighboring Bassin's has lost 50% of its night business. The Commerce Department, a block away, was robbed recently. Fumes Bassin's angry manager, Ed Hodges:

"There isn't a waitress, cashier, busboy or anyone who works here who hasn't been robbed, mugged or attacked in some way. And there isn't a place in this block that hasn't been robbed, and most have been hit more than once."

A few blocks away, on 9th Street, the Gayety Theater is showing "Man and Wife," an intimate film "for adults over 21." Even an attraction of this nature fails to draw the audience it once did. "Business is very bad, way off," says Robert Morris, the ticket seller. "People are afraid to come downtown. We've had lots of purse-snatchings, pockets cut out and all sorts of other things."

Fear inhibits daytime activity as well. A survey taken last summer by the Metropolitan Washington Council of Governments discovered that 65% of the city's largely white suburban residents visit the downtown area less than once a month, and 15% come downtown less than once a year. Asked their chief worry, the large majority of those surveyed responded: "Crime."

Actually, crime is spreading in the suburbs as well as in the city. Three brutal slayings of young women, one in Alexandria, Va., and two in Bethesda, Md., have occurred within the past few weeks. While these crimes remain unsolved, many suburbanites tend to view crime in their neighborhoods as a spillover from the city, and they still feel downtown is more dangerous.

Crime continues to speed the flight of Washingtonians to the suburbs. Though many single people and childless couples remain in the city, Joseph Murray of the big Shannon & Luchs real estate firm reports: "Families are leaving at an accelerated rate; this includes both black and white." (In neighboring Prince Georges County, Md., Negro arrivals have recently outnumbered white newcomers.)

"No Cash"

Sales of downtown department stores dropped by 4% in the first 11 months of last year from a year earlier, while sales throughout the metropolitan area, including those of suburban stores, were rising 8%. A recent Commerce Department survey of 10 central-city areas showed that the District of Columbia suffered the steepest loss of business of all. Shoppers who do venture downtown are continually reminded of the risk. D.C. Transit bus drivers use scrip instead of cash to make change. Delivery trucks bear signs proclaiming, "This Vehicle Carries No Cash."

There are bright spots. New office buildings are sprouting in some parts of town. Convention business continues to grow, and tourists arrive in record throngs. Lane Bryant has opened a new store on F Street, and the downtown Woodward & Lothrop department store is remodeling. But the merchants know safety must be assured before enough suburban shoppers will come downtown again to make business snap back.

The big department stores are bolstering their protection. Harold

Melnicove, an executive of Hecht's, says his organization now has a security force "big enough to protect some small cities"; he won't give details.

Smaller stores do the best they can. Frank Rich, president of both Rich's shoe stores and the D.C Urban Coalition, is a downtown optimist. But in his F Street store he no longer displays shoes in pairs, just singles; all display cases are locked; key employees carry electronic devices in their pockets to summon help in the event of danger.

High's dairy stores, which stay open nights and Sundays, have been robbed so many times, says General Manager William Darnell, "we don't like to talk about it." The chain's 37 D.C. stores were held up "hundreds of times" last year, Mr. Darnell sighs, and several had to be closed. Money in all stores is kept to a minimum by frequent armored car pickups.

Getting Out

A survey by the mayor's Economic Development Committee of small businessmen found that one out of seven contacted "wanted to close down, relocate or simply stop doing business in the city."

One who wants to get out is E. N. Hampton, president of the Hampton Maintenance Engineering Co. His firm has been robbed, his trucks have been vandalized and his employees have been threatened. "It's disgusting," Mr. Hampton snarls. "Now we ride armed guard in the trucks with shotguns.

As soon as I can find somebody to buy this I'm getting out."

Nor is black business immune. Berkeley Burrell's four dry cleaning stores have suffered 17 holdups in 10 months. Now the front door of each is locked; a customer can't get in "without a ticket or pair of pants in his hand," says Mr. Burrell. Employees are armed, and the proprietor is trying to replace females with males. "I may sound like Barry Goldwater," he says, "but we've got to get the community back to where it's safe to live in."

Banks have been a favorite target for bandits. Though these attacks have slackened lately, Francis Addison, president of the D.C. Bankers Association, says a "very high percentage" of local banks are robbed every year. The National Bank of Washington recently closed one branch because of the danger. All banks have tightened security, but the most extreme case is a Security Bank branch in the northeast section.

In 1968 the branch was held up three times within 55 days. Now the bank has put all employees behind plexiglass.

Tellers receive any payout money through scoops beneath the plexiglass. "The personnel were all shook up and couldn't work," President Frank A. Gunther says, "so we bullet-proofed the whole place." The bank has not been held up since.

Insurance Hard to Get

Faced with the cost of crime in Washington, insurance companies have turned cautious. "Lots of companies have stopped writing fire and casualty insurance," says Thornton W. Owen, president of the Perpetual Building Association, the city's biggest savings and loan outfit. "And lots of investors will abandon properties rather than maintain them." Hilliard Schulberg of the local liquor dealers association says that for his members "the cost of crime insurance is extremely high, and many companies won't write it." Proposed legislation would permit the Government to offer crime insurance where private insurers won't.

Office building managers, both Government and private, are attempting to cope with the danger. James Sykes, manager of the William J. Burns Detective Agency here, reports many buildings have posted guards at their front doors and says, "We're providing lots more escort service for female employees working late at night." The local chapter of the American Federation of Government Employees has advised its members to buy, at $5 apiece, anti-mugger aerosol spray devices.

Security is a prime concern of apartment dwellers. The 670-unit Marberry Plaza, open three years ago in southeast Washington, exemplifies what a new building must offer to reassure nervous tenants. On weekends the project is patrolled by four armed guards with two dogs. All exterior doors are locked. A tenant who has invited a guest for dinner must present an "admit slip" with the guest's name

to the desk clerk during the day. When the guest arrives, he must identify himself to the clerk and sign the register. "All of this is at the request of the tenants," says Sidney Glassman of the Charles E. Smith Property management company.

School Violence

In some neighborhoods, newsboys no longer collect for their papers for fear of being robbed; subscribers must mail in payments. One cabbie drives with self-addressed envelopes; whenever he accumulates $10 he mails it home. Some maids require their employers to drive them home. An outbreak of violence including the shooting of a junior high school student has prompted Mayor Washington to post policemen throughout the city school system. Many schools have stopped dealing in cash, requiring students to pay for supplies and other items costing more than a dollar by check or money order.

"It used to be that holdup students would use their fists; then came knives; now it's guns," says George Rhodes, a member of the D.C. school board. "Not that there have been that many incidents, but it's the fear that parents and teachers must live under that is most troublesome."

School principals, anxious to protect the reputations of their institutions, tend to minimize the problem. William J. Saunders, principal at Eastern High School (2,400 students including just three whites), says violence is "not a major problem" in the school. Yet several thousand dollars worth of football equipment has been stolen, and police officer Sherman Smart says there have been three alleged rapes in and around the school since September. As Officer Smart talks to a reporter, a photographer's agent joins in to complain that he has visited the school twice to take orders for class pictures and has been robbed of his receipts both times.

Not even the churches are spared. At the Vermont Avenue Baptist Church, the collection plate was stolen by intruders in full view of the parishioners. Says Charles Warren, executive director of the Greater Washington Council of Churches:

"Some churches have begun to lock their doors at 11 a.m. on Sundays for the worship service. Some have policemen at the service during the offering. Some have canceled evening activities or rescheduled them for the afternoons."

The National Presbyterian Church has moved from its 60-year location about half a mile from the White House to a new site three miles farther out. The Rev. Edward L. R. Elson calls the new location "the quietest zone in Washington," but vandalism is as bad at the new church as at the old one. According to Mr. Elson, the vandalism has included "obscenity on chapel pillars, destruction in the church hall and lights pilfered and broken."

CLASSIFIED CRIME *

THE WASHINGTON POST

Every day, in brief form, serious crimes are listed in the daily press. The Washington Post *has reserved a special section (next to the classified ads) to report the day's crime, dividing it into major categories. What follows is one day's activity in the capital city. Names of all persons have been omitted to protect the innocent.*

A 17-year-old girl was raped at gunpoint Monday night by a man who approached her as she was returning to her home in Northwest Washington, police reported.

The girl told the police the gunman approached her in the 800 block of N Street NW about 10:55 p.m. and forced her into an alley in the rear of the 1200 block of 8th Street.

The armed man told the girl to enter an abandoned Volkswagen bus in the alley, where the assault occurred.

In other serious crimes reported by area police up to 6 p.m. yesterday:

* Reprinted from "Crime and Justice," The Washington Post, February 12, 1970, with permission.

Robbed

. . . was held up about 9 p.m. Monday while she was sitting in her car near her apartment house by two youths who said to her, "I want to talk to you for a minute," then added, "Give me your money." One of the youths pulled out a gun and opened the door of . . . 's car. When she handed them her pocketbook, the gunman ordered, "Take out the money," and took the bills she offered. Warning her to lie down on the seat, the pair escaped.

American service station, . . . , was held up about 9:15 p.m. Sunday by three youths. One of them asked the attendant, . . . , for change for a quarter and then displayed a pistol. "This is a holdup," he said and took the money . . . handed him. The gunman then grabbed the change carrier from the desk in the office and removed . . . 's wallet. The trio fled on foot north in the 800 block of 21st Street.

. . . was robbed about 9:05 p.m. Monday by two teen-aged girls and a 12-year-old boy who approached her at the bus stop at . . . . One of the girls flashed a razor and ordered . . . to take off her black fur maxi-coat. When her assailants demanded money, . . . replied she had none and showed them her pocketbook. After searching the purse, the trio ran across the street and fled north on 8th Street.

. . . was held up at 7 p.m. Monday by a man brandishing a revolver who stopped her at . . . . The gunman forced her to surrender her pocketbook and fled on foot.

. . . was held up in front of his home Monday night by two men. "Give me your money," one of them ordered and drew a silver pistol. Grabbing . . . 's cash, the pair ran east on Forrester Street.

. . . was held up about 1:05 p.m. Monday by a man who approached him while he was standing beside his truck in the rear of the 2200 block of Georgia Avenue NW. The man pulled out a gun and told . . . , "Give me all your money." The gunman ran west in the 600 block of W Street NW with the bills.

. . . was treated at Sibley Hospital for injuries he suffered when he was beaten and robbed about 9:30 p.m. Monday. . . . said two young men approached him while he was walking in the 3600 block of Chesapeake Street NW with . . . , and pointed a gun at him. "This is a holdup, and don't move," the gunman ordered and removed the wallet from . . . 's pocket. He then struck . . . over the head with the weapon and fled on foot with his companion.

High's dairy store, 6133 Georgia Ave. NW, was robbed about 3:15 Monday by a man with a gun in his pocket who said to the clerk, "Give me all the bills," and escaped with the money from the cash register.

McDonald's Carryout, Georgia Avenue and Peabody Street NW, was held up about 6:15 p.m. Monday by a young man brandishing a revolver who approached the clerk at the counter and said, "Put all the money in a paper bag." Grabbing the sack full of cash, the gunman made his escape.

. . . was beaten and robbed

about 8 p.m. Monday after he answered a knock at his door. A man asked him, "Where is John?" and forced the door open, allowing two youths and two teen-aged girls to enter the room. Three of the intruders beat . . . in the head while a fourth ransacked the premises and removed the cash from a dresser drawer. The youths then fled out the front door.

High's dairy store, 3527 12th St. NE, was robbed about 7:35 p.m. Monday by a man who browsed through the store selecting merchandise, which he piled on the counter. After the clerk had put the items into a bag, the customer told him, "Put the money in the bag," and fled from the front door into the 1200 block of Newton Street, where he entered a white car and drove off.

. . . gas station, 6815 Annapolis Rd., Hyattsville, was held up about 11:45 p.m. Monday by a man brandishing a sawed-off shotgun. The gunman approached the attendant inside the office, held the weapon at his back and demanded money.

. . . was robbed about 6 p.m. Monday by two 13-year-old boys who approached her at 48th Street and Sheriff Road NE. One of them grabbed her purse and the pair fled north on 48th Place.

. . . was robbed, beaten and tied up by two men who forcibly entered his apartment while he was sleeping, about 3:30 a.m. yesterday. . . . told police the two gunmen demanded money and he offered to write them a check. One of them beat him in the head with his weapon, tied him and fled on foot with $2.

. . . 3228 Pennsylvania Ave. SE, was robbed about 1:50 p.m. Monday by two youths who picked up two containers of ice-cream, which they carried to the cash register. When the clerk opened the register, one of the youths pushed her aside and began taking the money from the cash drawer. Warning the clerk, "If you move, I'll blow your brains out," the youths fled from the front door on Branch Avenue SE.

. . . food store, 5010 New Hampshire Ave. NW, was held up about 8:25 p.m. Monday by two young men. One of them drew a handgun and grabbed the security officer on duty around the neck and disarmed him. The other man asked the clerk for the combination to the safe but she replied she did not know it. The gunman then jumped over the counter, opened the safe himself and the pair escaped with the money and the special policeman's revolver.

Gas station, 403 S St. NW, was held up about 4:40 p.m. Monday by a young man who approached the owner, . . . , inside the station and said, "Give it here." Holding a revolver on . . . , the man took the money and fled from a side door across the 400 block of Florida Avenue.

. . . Esso station, 631 Howard Rd. SE, was held up about 3:10 a.m. Monday by a man wielding a shotgun who approached the attendant seated at the desk and said, "I want the key to the drawer." Forcing the employee into the rear room to unlock the cash drawer, the gunman took the money from the drawer and the bills from the pockets of the attendant, ... The armed man escaped in a gray car towards the South Capitol Street Bridge.

. . . was beaten and robbed about 3:45 p.m. Monday by two men who approached him at 8th Street and New York Avenue NW. One of them struck him over the head with a hard object while the other took the bills from his pockets.

. . . was treated at Rogers Memorial Hospital for injuries to his abdomen and lower back he suffered during a robbery. Three men walked up behind . . . in an alley in the rear of the 800 block of H Street NE, and forced him to hand over his bills and papers.

. . . was robbed while she was walking in the 500 block of 15th Street SE, by a youth who grabbed her pocketbook and fled.

. . . was admitted to Freedmen's Hospital with a gunshot wound she suffered about 12:35 a.m. yesterday. Two men drove up to her while she was walking in the 1200 block of 7th Street NW, and asked her to get into the car. When she refused, one of the men drew a gun and fired a shot at her, then drove north on 7th Street.

. . . , a driver and delivery man for the Wometco Coffeetime Co., of Cheverley, was robbed about 6:45 a.m. yesterday. . . . had just serviced the vending machines at the Prince George's County Hospital, on Landover Road in Cheverley, and was returning to his truck in the parking lot when a lone gunman stopped him. Brandishing his revolver, the man forced . . . to open the safe in the truck and removed about $550 in coins. After locking the driver in his truck, the armed man made his escape.

. . . was robbed about 2:05 p.m. yesterday after he made a delivery in the 2000 block of 1st Street SW. A man with a gun in his pocket approached . . . at his truck and demanded all the money in his pockets. Taking the bills that the driver handed him, the gunman made his escape.

. . . was treated at D.C. General Hospital for injuries he suffered when he was beaten and robbed about 10:20 p.m. Monday by a man who placed a gun at his head in front of his home and told him, "This is a holdup. Give me your money." . . . told police he pushed the gunman aside. Then two more young men attacked him, striking him over the head with the handgun. Taking . . . 's wallet, the trio made its escape.

. . . , a newspaper carrier for the Evening Star, was held up about 8:20 p.m. Monday by two men who approached him at Anacostia Avenue and Hayes Street NE. One of them displayed a sawed-off shotgun while the other demanded, "Give me your money." Searching . . . 's pockets, the pair took his wallet and money and fled south on Anacostia Avenue.

. . . and . . . were robbed about 6:50 p.m. Monday by three youths who approached them near their apartment house. One of them held a pistol on the women and ordered, "Give me your money." Grabbing the pocketbooks of both victims, the trio fled west on Jay Street.

. . . was held up about 8:40 p.m. Monday by a youth armed with a sawed-off shotgun who confronted her at 14th Street and Potomac Avenue SE. "Give me your purse," the gunman demanded and snatched the bag containing $2.

. . . was held up in front of his home about 10:30 p.m. Saturday by three teen-agers. One of them wielded a gun and told . . . , "This is it. Put your hands up." Taking the money, the trio ran west in the 1500 block of C Street NE.

. . . was held up by a youth wielding a revolver who approached her at a bus stop near the 2900 block of Birney Place SE, and said "Give me your pocketbook." Taking a wallet containing $5, the youth fled on foot.

Store at 300 8th St. NE was held up about 11:20 a.m. yesterday by three youths, one wielding a gun who told the clerk, "Give me it all." They forced him to enter the manager's office and open the safe from which they removed the money. Holding a gun on another employee, the youths ordered him to open the cash registers and emptied them. The trio fled with the cash east on D Street NE.

. . . was robbed by two men who approached her from the rear while she was walking in the 1600 block of C Street NE. When one of them pointed a revolver at her, she threw up her hands and dropped her pocketbook which contained $5.

Stabbed

. . . was treated at Rogers Memorial Hospital for wounds that he suffered about 6 p.m. Sunday during an attempted robbery in the 600 block of 45th Street NE. Two men approached . . . from the rear demanding money. When he replied he had none, one of the men drew a knife and slashed . . . on the wrist.

. . . was admitted to Washington Hospital Center for shoulder wounds he suffered during a fight inside a barber shop at 4724 14th St. NW, about 9:15 p.m. Monday. During the fight, . . . was cut by a woman armed with a razor.

Stolen

A stereo tape deck, six tapes and a 33,000 megacycle television set, with a total value of $1,050, were stolen from a truck driven by . . . , sometime between 11:40 and 11:55 p.m. Monday when the vent window of the truck was forced while it was parked in the 1800 block of 14th Street NW.

A television set, a man's suit, a tuxedo, a suede coat, a painting and a pair of gold cuff links, with a total value of $839, were stolen from an apartment at . . . , rented by . . . , sometime between 9:30 a.m. and 5:30 p.m. Monday.

Four sports coats, a leather top coat, 12 dress shirts, 12 pairs of men's shoes and three men's suits, with a total value of $714, were taken from . . . when his apartment at . . . , was burglarized between 12:30 a.m. and 2 a.m. Monday.

A green carpet, a bar with two bar stools, a bedroom suite, a dresser set, a chest of drawers and a television set, with a total value of $600, were taken from a storage house at the rear of . . . , sometime before 11:30 a.m. Monday.

A tear gas gun, two shotguns, two pistols, five rifles and four revolvers, with a total value of $515, were stolen from the apartment of . . . , sometime after 7 p.m. Monday.

$800 was stolen between 4 p.m. Monday and 8:45 a.m. Tuesday from the cashier's office at the Washington Daily News . . . .

Fires Set

Three separate fires were set about 5:15 p.m. Monday inside an apartment rented by . . . .

THE WHITE-COLLAR CRIMINAL *

TOM HUTH

The scope of "respectable" white-collar crime is suggested by the fact that the Reader's Guide to Periodical Literature *now carries it as a separate topic. The white-collar variety of crime is genteel. Normally no force or burglary is*

* *Reprinted from Tom Huth, "The Employee As A Thief,"* The Washington Post, *July 11, 1971, by permission.*

involved. The white-collar criminal holds a position that makes it easy for him to appropriate property for his own use. Since undetected criminals do not fill out questionnaires, estimates concerning the amount of such crimes are guesses. Evidence suggests, however, that the volume is rising and that a high percentage of white-collar workers are involved to a greater or lesser degree. The article that follows is an account of how one large, faceless corporation was exploited unmercifully by its own employees. Variations of this story could probably be reported by nearly all major corporations.

Do you think that GEM employees are a typical cross-section of middle-class America? Why did no one report the thefts? What motivated the employees to steal? Poverty? The challenge to their ingenuity? Social climbing? Could a GEM employee have convinced himself that he was not really stealing? Can we ever mobilize enough law enforcement officers to check this kind of crime if it becomes socially respectable?

After months of investigation, a detective hired by a suburban Washington department store chain has uncovered an employee theft ring that illustrates dramatically "how some professional white-collar thieves can rob a retail store blind and cover it up with paperwork."

The ring, known to some of its members as "The Brotherhood," operated in one of the branches of GEM Inc., which has stores in Virginia and Maryland.

"If one was a member of the Brotherhood," the detective said, "anything in the store could be obtained."

The detective estimated that a substantial percentage of the store's employees were engaged in "continual and active theft," either as part of the ring or on their own, and that the company lost half a million dollars over the three years the ring operated.

The investigation of the ring's operation is continuing; but no current employees of GEM are involved.

According to the detective who uncovered the theft ring, the former employees who were involved worked in every one of the store's 15 departments. They manipulated cash registers, swapped merchandise with each other and on at least two occasions drove away with truckloads of furniture.

Other large-scale thefts by employees have also been uncovered in other GEM branches.

The detective who prepared the report on The Brotherhood said employee theft at GEM does not typify the general problem of employee theft because the chain's security policies were not as tight as those in other stores.

Security officers at other department store and drug chains in the area estimate that one-third to two-thirds of their "shrinkage" results from employee theft rather than shoplifting. Dollar amounts are difficult to calculate because the losses from employee theft are lumped together with those from shoplifting, bookkeeping errors and other factors.

A Hecht Co. security official estimates that half of the firm's theft is committed by employees. Kahn's security director says that "losses due to internal theft exceed shoplifting." The Woodward & Lothrop security chief says that internal stealing "has increased tremendously."

Fehmi Zeko, GEM vice president for the Washington-Baltimore area, refused to discuss GEM's security problems or the detective's report on The Brotherhood.

Sales personnel in department stores generally earn from $2 to $3.25 an hour, plus commissions. Department managers may earn $10,000 or $15,000 a year.

One common method of stealing, a detective said, is to manipulate the cash register. A clerk can make a sale, ring up "no sale," and pocket the money. He can ring up a sale correctly, claim that he has rung up too large an amount, and pocket the difference. He can take money out and hand it to a friend who is bringing in stolen goods for a fraudulent refund.

Various Methods

There are also many ways of stealing merchandise. A worker can simply walk out with some goods. He can give them to a friend and ring up "no sale" or stuff added items into a shopping bag during a legitimate sale. He can discount merchandise for friends or fellow employees. He can mark it damaged and give it away at a reduced price or for nothing.

The losses sometimes can be covered by juggling the paperwork, especially if the thief is a department manager. Or they may not be covered at all, in which case the store's annual or biannual inventory shows an unaccountable loss, or shrinkage.

(The "shrinkage" last year in the automotive department in the store where The Brotherhood worked, according to the detective, amounted to 30 percent of gross sales.)

Security officers say that theft in credit departments also is common. A mailed payment may be credited to a friend's account, or a customer's charge plate may be used to buy merchandise.

'King-sized . . . Headache'

The operations and relationships of The Brotherhood were complicated —so complicated, the detective said, that "when we sat down and tried to explain to the police sergeant what we were uncovering and what was involved, I knew just by looking at him that he was getting one king-sized Excedrin headache, just trying to sort it out."

All names used in this account are fictitious, because most of the principals were given immunity from prosecution in return for confessions and promises of restitution.

The detective, who was hired by the company in February specifi-

cally to crack the ring, has obtained about 20 confessions so far.

Persons who did not demand immunity or who failed to live up to agreements under which it was granted may be prosecuted.

This story is put together from the confessions and from the accounts of the detective and other GEM sources.

Brotherhood Set-Up

The Brotherhood included eight or 10 employees working closely and 10 or 20 others working in alliance with them. The ring worked one end of the store, the end that sold drugs, housewares, furniture, gifts, televisions and small appliances.

At the other end were the solo operators, the independents who worked the cash registers and stole a little at a time in other ways.

"If someone wanted something from the other end of the store, it was easy to get," a GEM official said.

A leading member of the ring gave an example in his signed confession:

"Ron came down to the department and asked me if I needed any clocks. And I told him I could use a couple and he asked me to come down to his department and pick out the clocks that I like . . .

"Later on he did ask for things in return. Not in return, but just asked for merchandise. It didn't necessarily have to be 'I give you so much, you give me so much.' Whenever he felt he needed something he would come up and ask for it."

Blackmail Tactic

A store official said, "Once a guy got someone to do something for him, he had him in his power. And after that, it was either do it or else . . . Ron wanted a lawnmower this one particular time, and the salesman turned him down. And Ron said, 'Get the lawnmower or I'm just going to come down and take it. If you try to stop me I'm going to tell on you.' So he took the lawnmower right out."

Workers found it easy to walk out with merchandise because two of the guards were in collusion with them and because at the time, a GEM official admitted, the management "had the lowest regard for security. It was incompetence, if you want to know the truth. They didn't care."

Another former employee said in his confession, "The word was around as far as lack of security, and any darn thing that you wanted to take out of the store could be taken out."

The detective said that one of the store guards "warned them of every move being made by security and he assisted them in removing the merchandise by loaning members of the ring his keys to the store, opening the store early and allowing them to go on 'shopping sprees' prior to the arrival of the cleaning crews and turning his back when they walked past him at the exit door with stolen property."

Some of the managers did not take part in the stealing, but that did not always stop The Brotherhood. One former employee said that one woman took some wall tiles from an uncooperative manager. She explained, "If he won't give it to me, the skinflint, I'll take it."

Lasting Relationship

The swapping sometimes continued after an employee had left to work for another company, as in the case of an ex-worker who had gone to work for a hot dog company and gave a former colleague some hot dogs in return for a toy airplane.

One member of the ring, the detective related, left GEM to work for a furniture company and while he was there gave another member a houseful of rental furniture.

The detective explained, "K— paid the delivery charges, the first month's rent and the security deposit. The papers filtered across R's desk and he ripped them up. And he got approximately $2,000 or $3,000 worth of furniture that way.

"The last time I talked to them (the furniture company) they had about a dozen suites of furniture out that they couldn't account for, but whether R— was doing this or somebody else in their organization who had found the same method, they don't know."

Truck Delivery

In about February of 1970, The Brotherhood took a company truck, drove it to the back doors and loaded on three 9-by-12-foot rugs, six rocker-recliner chairs, two bedroom sets, lamps, end tables, rocking chairs and three dinette sets.

A store guard kept a lookout. The others drove off, made deliveries to each other's homes and brought the truck back empty.

Late last year, on the Sunday before Christmas, the gang did the same thing. The store was closed and only a few workers were there rearranging displays. The guard let five or six employees in the back door. One of them later told a detective, "It was like a lot of hungry mice scrambling around for scraps of cheese."

One department manager recalled that he vaulted over the partition into the jewelry department and scooped up four watches, rings, pen-and-pencil sets and other items.

One excerpt from an employee's confession, dealing only with the goods he got from one other worker, illustrates the scope of the stealing:

"Bill Gave Me . . ."

"Bill gave me an end table that I took home in a car . . . and he gave me a coffee table . . . and he also gave me a 9-by-12 gold rug . . . Also I got a rocker lounge chair, a tan one. I got a three-piece stack table set from Bill. Also I got some cartoon plaques of the Gingerbread Man and such; he gave me three different sets to hang on the wall . . . While I was there he also gave me a high-chair seat that sets on a chair so the kids could set up to the table . . ."

This former employee says he has given GEM two restitution checks totalling $3,000. His list of what he can recall having stolen includes 69 items for 1969 and 1970 alone, ranging from a $3 cutting board to $250 worth of toys and $410 in records.

The ring was uncovered, the detective said, when one employee (not in the ring) told another that he was suspicious about a $77.12 refund that he had given last Feb. 18 for five Hummels, or German figurines. It turned out that the woman receiving the refund was the wife of the man known as Ron.

The store membership card that had been used to get the refund belonged to an old Air Force buddy of Ron's. And the same card was used by his wife to get a $49.65 refund for two lamps on the same day from another one of the chain's stores.

"Relationship . . . Closer"

This second refund was authorized by a female department manager. A background check showed that "her relationship with Ron became much closer than that of supervisor and employee," according to an 18-page report that the detective has written about the Ring.

On Feb. 27, the woman was interrogated in the store and confessed "that a wholesale theft ring had been operating . . . for nearly a year and a half," the report says.

Her confession included the

names of other members of the ring, and one by one they were interrogated by security officials. One former department manager showed up for her interview with a restitution check for $1,111.94.

Today, five months after the ring was discovered, most of its members have resigned or been fired.

The detective blames the GEM management as much as the thieves for the thefts. The company's failure to tighten security procedures "has ruined a lot of people," he said.

"Most of them were just average, middle-class people who got caught up in something that was too big for them . . . Everything in the store is marked 'Take me.'"

ORGANIZED CRIME
IN THE UNITED STATES *
G. ROBERT BLAKEY

Most Americans think of crime only in terms of TV programs that

* Reprinted from G. Robert Blakey, "Organized Crime In the United States," Current History, June, 1967 by permission of Current History, Inc. and the author.

emphasize violence against persons and property. Although this kind of crime is spectacular and merits concern, truly "big time" crime is a multibillion dollar operation that is organized in a fashion highly parallel to that of industrial corporations, headed by authoritarian "robber barons."

Under what conditions did the membership of the Mafia and Camorra migrate to the United States? What ready-made opportunity did they find in national prohibition? How are they organized? In what illegal enterprises are they chiefly concentrated? Would the legalization of gambling destroy their base? What kind of borrower uses the services of loan sharks? Into what legitimate businesses have they infiltrated? What relationship do they have with politicians? Why does organized crime continue to flourish? Realistically, can it be checked?

. . . The late nineteenth and early twentieth century . . . saw the rise of the great city-wide gang combinations, usually in alliance with the *nouveaux riches* and the *nouveaux politiques*. The first gangs of the Little Old New York area were Irish. San Francisco in the gold rush days had its Australians. New York in the mid-1920's saw the embarrassment of the Jewish community at the phenomena of the "Jewish gangster." By the 1930's however, the Italian-Sicilians had gained dominance everywhere.

The Italian-Sicilians were the last of the great immigrant groups. Like the others before them, they came seeking hope in a new country; yet with them came two predatory groups: the Mafia of Sicily and the Camorra of Naples. Largely through the efforts of the Italian government in the 1920's and 1930's, many members of the Mafia and the Camorra found it necessary to seek refuge and victims in a new country. At first, largely during the era of prohibition, these groups warred among themselves and against those who came before them. Like business, industry and finance in the United States at the turn of the century, however, organized crime had its great consolidator—Charles "Lucky" Luciano. It was Luciano who finally brought the various factions together and through the unique strength of the Italian groups' family-like structure was able to forge the confederation that now is dominant in organized crime everywhere.

Structure of the "Families"

Today, the core of organized crime in the United States consists of 24 groups operating as criminal cartels in large cities across the nation. The wealthiest and most influential operate in New York, New Jersey, Illinois, Florida, Louisiana, Nevada, Michigan and Rhode Island. Estimated overall strength of the core groups is put at 5,000, of which 2,000 are thought to be in the New York area alone. These groups, coupled with their allies and em-

ployees, constitute the heart of organized crime in the United States at this time.

Each of the 24 groups is known as a "family." Membership varies from 700 down to 20. Most cities have only one family; New York City has five. Family organization is rationally designed with an integrated set of positions geared "to maximize profits" and to protect its members, particularly its leadership, from law enforcement. Like any large corporation, and unlike the criminal gangs of the past, the organization functions regardless of individual personnel changes, and no one individual is indispensable. The killing of Jesse, for example, ended the James gang; the deportation of Luciano merely resulted in the leadership passing to Frank Costello.

The hierarchical structure of the families closely parallels that of Mafia groups that operated for almost a century on the island of Sicily. Each family is headed by a "boss," whose primary functions are order and profit. Beneath each boss is an "underboss." He collects information for the boss; he relays messages to him and passes his instructions to his underlings. On the same level with the underboss is the *consigliere*, who is often an elder member, partially retired, whose judgment is valued. Below him are the *caporegime*, who serve either as buffers between top men and lower level personnel, or as chiefs of operating units. As buffers, they are used to maintain insulation from the investigative procedures of the police. "To maintain their insulation . . . , the leaders . . . avoid direct communication with the workers."

All commands, information, complaints and money flow back and forth through the buffer. Below the *caporegime* is the *soldati* or the "button" man. He actually operates the particular illicit enterprise, using as his employees the street-level personnel of organized crime. These employees, however, have no insulation from detection by police action. It is they who are most often arrested, for it is they who "take bets, drive trucks, answer telephones, sell narcotics, tend stills, or operate legitimate businesses." And often they are not of Italian extraction. For example, in a major lottery business in a Negro neighborhood in Chicago, the workers were Negro; the bankers, Japanese-Americans; but the operation "was licensed, for a fee, by a family member."

There is a tendency to see organized crime in terms of those groups engaged in gambling, narcotics, loan sharking or other illegal business. This is useful since it distinguishes youth gangs, pickpockets and professional criminals generally, which groups are ad hoc. There are at least two aspects of high level organized crime, however, that "characterize it as a unique form of criminal activity": the "enforcer" and the "corruptor." The duty of the enforcer is to maintain organizational integrity by arranging for the maiming and killing of recalcitrant members. The cor-

ruptor has as his function the establishment of relations with those public officials and other influential persons whose assistance is necessary to achieve the organization's goals. By including these positions, each family becomes not only a business but a government.

The highest ruling body of the 24 families is the "commission." This body serves as a combination legislature, supreme court, board of directors, and arbitration panel. Members look to the commission as the ultimate authority on organizational and jurisdictional disputes. It is composed of the bosses of only the nation's most powerful families, but has authority over all. Its composition has varied from 9 to 12 men. Currently, 9 families are represented; 5 from New York City, 1 each from Philadelphia, Buffalo, Detroit and Chicago. The commission is not a representative or elected body. Members are not equals. Men with long tenure, the heads of large families, those with unusual wealth, all exercise greater authority and command greater respect. The balance of power rests with the New York leaders and New York has always been at least the unofficial headquarters of the entire organization.

Professional Gambling

Organized crime has never limited itself to one particular criminal activity. Law enforcement officials agree today, however, that syndicated gambling is the greatest source of revenue for organized crime. The general prevalence of gambling seems to indicate that gambling is a fundamental human activity that cannot be suppressed. From this, the professional gambler has led the American people unquestionably into the patently false conclusion that gambling must therefore be controlled by the professional. In truth, the operations of the professionals can only be described as parasitic and corruptive. The estimated net take is placed at $7 billion, probably twice that gained from all other crime combined.

Professional gambling activities today range from simple lotteries to bookmaking on horses or sports events. Most of our nation's large slum areas have within them some form of a lottery known as "numbers." Bets are placed on any three digit numbers from 1 to 1,000. The mathematical odds of winning are, therefore, 1,000 to 1. Seldom, however, is the pay-off over 500 to 1, and then, on "cut numbers," it is even less. The "gambler" thus seldom gambles. In addition, he hedges his bet by a complicated "lay-off" system. Even assuming an honest pay-off—an unguaranteed occurrence—the ultimate effect of the racket is to drain the income of slum residents away from food, clothing, shelter, health and education. This says nothing of corruption.

The professional bookmaker, on the other hand, has at least the virtue of exploiting primarily those who can afford it. Yet he seldom "gambles" either. He gives track odds or less without track expenses, is invariably better capitalized or "lays-off," takes credit bets to off-balance the bettor's judgment and stimulate the play and, finally, often as not, fixes the event by corrupting private and professional sports to his own ends. Honest police enforcement of existing laws is widely hampered, inter alia, by the use of modern scientific developments such as flashpaper or telephone and organizational techniques such as street-level expendable personnel.

Narcotics

Next to professional gambling, most law enforcement officials agree that the importation and distribution of narcotics—chiefly heroin—is organized crime's major illegal activity. Its estimated take is $350 million a year. More than one-half of the known heroin users are in New York City. Others are located primarily in the other great metropolitan areas. Within the cities, addiction is largely found in areas with low average income, poor housing and high delinquency rates. The addict himself is likely to be male, between 21 and 30 years old, poorly educated, unskilled, and a member of a disadvantaged minority group.

The destruction of the human personality, the violation of human dignity, even death, associated with addiction need not here be belabored. More, however, is involved. Environment, too, is affected. The cost of narcotics varies, but it is seldom low enough to permit the typical addict to obtain drugs by lawful means. Estimates of the percentage of crime caused by addiction run to 50 percent; although the figure cannot be accurately assessed, it is clear that it is high. Thus, addiction in the ghetto seriously affects the quality of urban life.

The need for action in the direction of medical and psychological treatment of the addict and general improvement of the social environment that produces him seems clear. It is, however, a false dichotomy which sees this and law enforcement as mutually exclusive alternatives. Addiction to narcotics may be a symptom, but their importation and distribution is the vilest sort of exploitative crime.

The opiate traffic on the East coast is run by organized crime and the product is European in origin. Grown in Turkey, diverted from legitimate markets, refined in the Near East and France, the heroin is finally smuggled into the United States. The importers, generally top men in organized crime, do not handle and seldom see a shipment of heroin; their role is strictly supervisory and financial. "Fear of retribution, which can be swift and final, and a code of silence protect them from exposure." Through persons working under their direction, the heroin is distributed to high-level wholesalers; low-level wholesalers are at the next echelon; finally, pushers (often addicts) and the addicts themselves make up the last rung of the ladder.

Primarily because all of the transactions are consensual, law enforcement is at all levels difficult, most difficult at the highest level. Dangerous undercover operations and the use of insider informants are essential. The top men are hard to identify; they always have a shield of people in front of them; and by not handling the drugs, they incur no direct liability for possession, sale, or other prohibited acts. Generally, they are vulnerable only through the conspiracy laws, and this requires live testimony or a substitute. As in gambling operations, low-level personnel are expendable and are most often "stand up guys." Even under present limitations, however, enforcement has been successful in reducing "the incidence of addiction in the general population. . . ." Further reductions seem unlikely without a strengthening of the evidence-gathering process, including the authorization of electronic surveilance techniques.

Loan Sharking

Most law enforcement officials agree that, close to or on an equal level with narcotics, loan sharking is organized crime's next major illegal activity. Its estimated annual take is $350 million. Like narcotics, loan sharking is organized in a hierarchical structure. At the top is the boss, who lends large sums of cash to trusted lieutenants, usually at the rate of one percent per week. Under the lieutenants are street-level loan sharks who deal directly with the debtors. The rate varies, but is normally five percent per week.

Occasionally, the lieutenant will make large loans himself—in the neighborhood of $1 million. The setup also involves "steerers," who will direct possible borrowers to the loan sharks. The steerer can be any individual who comes into contact with large numbers of people. Finally, there is the "enforcer," who sees to it that the debts are paid.

The victims of loan sharks come from all segments of society: the professional man, the industrialist (particularly in areas like the garment industry), contractors, stockbrokers, bar and restaurant owners, dock workers, laborers, narcotic addicts, bettors and the bookmakers themselves. Only two prerequisites are required: a pressing need for ready cash and no access to regular channels of credit—again demonstrating the exploitative character of organized crime. Repayment is everywhere compelled by force. Often debtors in over their heads are pressed into criminal acts to pay off, including embezzlement, or acting as number writers or fingermen for burglary rings.

Law enforcement activity is even more difficult than in gambling and narcotics. Records need not be kept. Nothing is illegally possessed. The standard organized crime insulation shield is made doubly invulnerable when by definition the victims are already in bodily fear.

Legitimate Business

Legitimate business is another area in which organized crime is extending its influence. In many cities, it dominates the fields of juke-box and vending-machine distribution. Laundry-service, liquor and beer distribution, night clubs, food wholesaling, record manufacturing, the garment industry and a host of other legitimate lines of endeavor have been invaded. Control of business concerns has usually been acquired by the subrosa investment of profits acquired from illegal ventures, accepting business interests in payment of gambling or loan shark debts, or using various forms of extortion. After takeover, the defaulted loan is sometimes liquidated by professional arsonists burning the business and then collecting the insurance or by various bankruptcy fraud techniques. Often, however, the organization, using force and fear, will attempt to secure a monopoly in the service or product of the business. When the campaign is successful, the organization begins to extract a premium price from customers. Purchases by infiltrated businesses are always made from specified allied firms.

With its extensive infiltration of legitimate business, organized crime thus poses a new threat to the American economic system. The proper functioning of a free economy requires that economic decisions be made by persons free to exercise their own judgment. Force or fear limits choice, ultimately reduces quality, and increases prices. When organized crime moves into a business, it seems inevitably to bring to that venture all the techniques of violence and intimidation that it used in its illegal businesses. Competitors are thus eliminated and customers are confined to sponsored suppliers. Its effect is even more unwholesome than that of other monopolies because its position does not rest on economic superiority.

Unions

Closely paralleling its takeover of business, organized crime has moved into legitimate unions. Control of labor supply through control of unions prevents the unionization of some industries and guarantees sweetheart contracts in others. It provides the opportunity for theft from union funds, extortion through the threat of economic pressure, and the profit to be gained from the manipulation of welfare and pension funds and insurance contracts. Trucking, construction and waterfront entrepreneurs have been persuaded for the sake of labor peace to countenance gambling, loan sharking and pilferage. All of this, of course, makes a mockery of much of the promise of the social legislation of the last half century.

Much of what has been outlined above could be tolerated within the community within a certain minimum range. First, in order to exist, then to increase its profits, however, organized crime has found it necessary to corrupt the institutions of American democratic processes. Today's corruption is less visible, more subtle and therefore more difficult to detect and assess than the corruption of the prohibition era. Yet everything indicates that organized crime flourishes only in a climate of corruption. And as the scope of organized crime's activities has expanded, its need to corrupt public officials at every level of government has grown. With the expansion of governmental regulation of private and business activity, moreover, the power to corrupt has given organized crime greater control over matters affecting the everyday life of each citizen. "Contrast, for example, the way governmental action in contract procurement or zoning functions today with the way it functioned only a few years ago." The potential for harm today is greater if only because the scope of governmental activity is greater.

Crime and Politics

Organized crime has money and money underwrites politics. The scope of the growing political influence of organized crime is well illustrated by the conservative estimate made by the most comprehensive examination of the relation between crime and politics yet undertaken, which put the level of all political contributions stemming from criminal sources at 15 percent. At various times, organized crime has thus been the dominant political force in such metropolitan centers as New York, Chicago, Miami and New Orleans. Only fortuitous circumstances prevented the take over of Portland, Oregon and Kansas City, Missouri. Smaller communities, such as Cicero, Illinois and Reading, Pennsylvania, have been virtual baronies of organized crime. The parade of horribles could be extended almost indefinitely.

A political leader, legislator, police officer, prosecutor or judge who owes allegiance to organized crime cannot render proper service to the public. When a newly-nominated judge in New York City pledged undying loyalty to a Cosa Nostra boss for procuring his selection to the bench, he perverted his office and all it stood for. When the organization requests it, such a man must protect hoodlums who have committed not only gambling offenses but also murder or other crimes of personal violence. He is no longer a public servant, selected by and accountable to the people, as democracy demands; he is the servant of a small class of professional criminals. Once accustomed to accepting bribes from the criminal organization, many such public servants, moreover, soon begin to expect side payments for acts performed in the usual course of business. Thus the government soon loses any sense of allegiance to the public or to the moral standards that good government demands. Citizens can tolerate, in short, relatively large amounts of vice and street crime, but little governmental corruption.

Organized crime also seriously affects the quality of American life. Mr. Justice Louis D. Brandeis, in his classic dissent in *Olmstead v. United States*, rightly suggested that "our Government is the potent,

the omnipresent teacher. For good or for ill, it teaches the whole people by its example." Mr. Justice Brandeis spoke in the context of lawless law enforcement.

Teaching By Example

There is, however, another way in which government teaches by example. Its failures, too, do not go unnoticed, especially among the young, who see what is done and seldom listen to what is said. Unlike the successful criminal who operates outside of an organization and who requires anonymity for success, the top men in organized crime are well known both to law enforcement agencies and to the public. In earlier stages of their careers, they may have been touched by law enforcement, but once they attain top positions in the rackets, they acquire a high degree of immunity from legal accountability. The statement of a leading worker with gang boys long ago pointed out the effect of this process:

When a noted criminal is caught, the fact is the principal topic of conversation among my boys. They and others lay wagers as to how long it will be before the criminal is free again, how long it will be before his pull gets him away from the law. The youngsters soon learn who are the politicians who can be depended upon to get offenders out of trouble, who are the divekeepers who are protected. The increasing contempt for law is due to the corrupt alliance between crime and politics, protected vice, pull in the administration of justice, unemployment, and a general soreness against the world produced by these conditions.

Within the fold of organized crime, an ambitious young man knows that he can rise from body-guard and hood to pillar of the community, giving to charities, dispensing political favors, sending his boys to West Point and his girls to debutante balls. The President's Commission on Law Enforcement and Administration of Justice summed it up in these terms:

In many ways organized crime is the most sinister kind of crime in America. The men who control it have become rich and powerful by encouraging the needy to gamble, by luring the troubled to destroy themselves with drugs, by extorting the profits of honest and hard-working businessmen, by collecting usury from those in financial plight, by maiming or murdering those who oppose them, by bribing those who are sworn to destroy them. Organized crime is not merely a few preying upon a few. In a very real sense it is dedicated to subverting not only American institutions, but the very decency and integrity that are the most cherished attributes of a free society. As the leaders of Cosa Nostra and their racketeering allies pursue their conspiracy unmolested, in open and continuous defiance of the law, they preach a sermon that all too many Americans heed: The government is for sale; lawlessness is the road to wealth; honesty is a pitfall and morality a trap for suckers.

The extraordinary thing about organized crime is that America has tolerated it for so long.

SOCIAL REFORM AND CRIME PREVENTION *

RAMSEY CLARK

Rather obviously an uncertain connection exists between crime and social conditions. The exact nature of this relationship is debatable, but Ramsey Clark (formerly U.S. Attorney General) here makes an eloquent case for crime prevention through social reform.

Why does Clark argue that fear is destructive? What reaction does

* Reprinted from Ramsey Clark, "Turbulent Times," a speech delivered before the Convention of the Amalgamated Clothing Workers of America, AFL-CIO in 1970. Reprinted from Sidney Hillman Reprint Series No. 35, Sidney Hillman Foundation. Reprinted by permission of the Sidney Hillman Foundation and the author.

*brute force normally breed?
Assume that you arrive in an
unfamiliar city with the intention
of locating its center of concentrated crime: What questions
would you ask about housing?
Unemployment? Poverty? Education? Health? Family structure?
If you identified the areas where
these problems were acute, could
you construct a map of the crime
center without reference to crime
statistics? How would Clark reform
the prisons? What relationship
does he see between law and
moral leadership? Why is dissent
vital in solving our problems?*

. . . If you have not noticed, these
are turbulent times. For those of
you like me, who would prefer some
peace and quiet, I must tell you
that in my judgment we will not
find it. Turbulence will continue
because turbulence is created by
change and change is the fundamental fact of our day.

. . .

In this turbulence it is natural for
mankind to fear. Fear was a good
instinct for the caveman. It saved
his life. It got him out of harm's
way.

Fear today is destructive. We
live in a different time—mass society, urbanized, technologically
advanced, and interdependent—
finally wholly interdependent. Fear
first deprives us of any concern for
others, for those who need our help,
for those who cannot endure without our help.

We are all in this adventure together now. When any suffer, all
suffer. When Watts riots, Beverly
Hills trembles; when Columbia is
in turmoil, Park Avenue watches
anxiously. Without help the very
forces of turbulence increase and
that in turn causes fear itself to
increase.

Fear, second, deprives us of any
concern for justice, for justice itself.

Through fear, we wiretap, knowing it demeans human dignity and
undermines confidence in government.

We are prepared to smash in
doors without knocking, knowing
it creates violence.

We say, "We'll keep people in
jail who have not been convicted of
any crime," though we say we pre-
sume the innocence of every individual, though we know that most
jails manufacture crime.

This is the cost of fear in America
today.

Finally, fear makes brute force
sovereign, and only force can rise
to meet it.

The Real Causes

Let us face it, there are real causes
for our problems. We have to address ourselves to them effectively.
We fail to release half the energies
of our people. We need workers
and builders who can make a better
world. We have a million people on
welfare in New York City alone.
Think what it would mean to this
world where we, six percent of the
people, have half the wealth, if we

could release those energies for the improvement of the human condition, for health, for education, for decent housing, for good jobs, and better jobs constantly for everyone.

We tinker with housing. We need millions of units now. The house is the place for the family. And the family, in America, is in jeopardy because of our failure to build for human dignity. Human dignity is the central issue of our times.

It is in these areas that we can control turbulence and reduce crime in America. We know where crime comes from, if we care to see. Plato told us where crime comes from. "Poverty is the mother of crime," he said.

Map of Crime

You can go to any major city in America, and you can put crime on the map. You know where it is. It is where life expectancy is ten years less than for that same city as a whole. It is in the ghetto where infant mortality is four times more frequent. It is where mental retardation from all its environmental causes, the lack of pregnancy care, malnutrition for several generations, perhaps, or of the mother during pregnancy—mental retardation, with all it means in suffering and the crushing of human hopes, is eight times more frequent per capita. That is where crime comes from. We know that.

That is where families break down. It is where economic conditions are intolerable.

Until recently when it rose, we boasted, and I think wrongly, about an unemployment rate that had been less than four percent for many years now, failing to realize this four percent is the size of the Republic when the Constitution was adopted, millions of lives wasted; opportunities wasted; opportunities for those individuals and for the world.

That fact—the overall unemployment rate—is the enemy of truth, because when you go to the central city you find what unemployment really is. In this great nation, twenty-five percent of the teenage black boys are unemployed, and thirty-three percent of the teenage girls who are black are unemployed.

But when you go where unemployment is highest, among the forty percent of the blacks in this country who live in poverty it is a multiple of twenty-five and thirty-three percent for teenagers.

Half the buildings in the world have been built in the last thirty years. Half the buildings in Harlem were built before 1900, and those buildings are unsafe and unhealthy. Fire alarms are thirteen times more common in Harlem than in the rest of New York City. People die in those fires. Rats have chewed the insulation off the electric wiring. Many tenements are in violation of building codes. Those who want to enforce the law in America ought to enforce the law that gives the opportunity for decent living, too.

Ghetto Education

Education in the ghetto is miserable. Talk about violence in the high schools of the suburbs—go to the high schools of the ghetto. It was that way in the thirties, but nobody cared then because it did not affect the children of power in America.

In law enforcement there are things that must be done, and we had better face up to them.

The average policeman in the United States has a salary that is three-fourths that necessary to support a family of four at a minimum standard of living. Most police officers with a family of that size have to moonlight to make enough to provide for their families, for clothing, food, and shelter.

Is that how much we care about our safety?

We need professional police. Our liberty and safety depend on it.

You cannot get it without paying for it. It will take good salaries; broad recruitment; and high standards to professionalize the police.

In prisons we manufacture crime. We cause crime. Eighty percent of all serious crimes in the United States today are committed by people who have been arrested and convicted before, and brutalized in jail. We beat the last drop of human pity out of some there. They are dangerous when we release them.

Why?

Prison Priorities

We spend ninety-five cents of every dollar for prisons on pure custody; iron bars and stone walls; and they dehumanize. We spend five cents on hope—health, mental health and physical health, education, vocational training, employment services, family guidance, community services. Most of those inmates have never been to a dentist. Psychoses and neuroses among those people —a major cause of crime—are immense.

Alcoholism—there are seven million alcoholics—accounts for one-fourth of all the non-traffic arrests in America.

Do we really feel police can cure alcoholism?

Drug addiction—if we took one-half the cost of a Polaris submarine we could find chemicals that would release individuals from physical dependency on heroin.

What do we do? We send untrained police out to arrest them.

The law itself can only provide moral leadership. Let's face it. You cannot control the conduct of two hundred and ten million Americans by a police force.

Look at *Brown* v. *Board of Education*—moral leadership. We said what we always knew, that segregated schools are inherently unequal and our children have a constitutional right to equal education.

We measured the progress of law enforcement after nine years and found one percent of the black students in the public school of the eleven states that comprised the Confederacy, one percent in desegregated schools. All deliberate speed takes nine centuries at that rate. We will either learn to live together with dignity and respect and love—or we will live with conflict, hatred, fear and violence throughout the history of the nation.

The law must provide moral leadership. It cannot protect the public by mere enforcement. In America today our system of criminal justice does not secure a conviction for one serious crime out of fifty. It will not do much better. Even if performance could be increased tenfold, the odds would be one to five. The law can only provide moral leadership and when the law itself acts immorally, its one chance to serve humanity and achieve justice is lost.

Dissent is Vital

We have to seek to solve our problems. To do so, we have to hear each other. We must seek to hear every idea, viewpoint and need. This is where dissent comes in. It is vital. All through history dissent has been the principal catalyst in the alchemy of truth.

Dissent is a positive force.

. . .

Those who seek to stifle dissent by repression will divide this nation more than it is already divided. Repression is the one clear chance for irreconcilable division in America.

It was St. Mark and not Lincoln who first said, "if a nation be divided against itself, then that nation cannot stand."

There are many divisions in our nation. There are the rich and the poor, the educated and the uneducated; divisions between the people who work and build and create, and the students, young Americans. This is an intolerable division, one that must be bridged now before it is too late.

There is the division between black and white, between brown and white, that must be bridged.

From one side of the house divided we hear the call for order, "there must be order." From the other side the plea for justice— "give us justice," but the long history of mankind says that you will have neither order nor justice unless you have both.

CRIME: THE NEGLECTED BATTLEGROUNDS *
ALAN L. OTTEN

Much of the discussion about crime is one-dimensional, stressing a single cause or solution. Thus we have spokesmen who blame all crime on bad housing, poor education, parental permissiveness, court rulings that restrict the police,

* Reprinted from Alan L. Otten, "Crime: The Neglected Battlegrounds," Wall Street Journal, August 20, 1970, by permission.

or TV violence. The list of solutions is equally long, but they emphasize new and tougher police methods.

Neglected in most discussions are such undramatic proposals as prison reform and streamlining the court system. What is wrong with the present prison system? What does it do to the first-offenders? What are the shortcomings in our present parole, probation and correctional systems? How could the courts use more manpower? In what ways are court procedures antiquated? What specific reforms does Mr. Otten propose?

. . . For many years, the nation simply wasn't very concerned about crime. Then, when crime did become a top concern, it was almost inevitable that officials would try to deal with it by tough new anti-crime laws and by beefing up police departments. Police were, after all, the visible frontline troops in the anti-crime fight, the men to give the most bang for the buck, the ones who had been complaining most vocally of public neglect.

And so the great bulk of anti-crime thought went into new police methods and approaches, and the great bulk of recently rising anti-crime outlays went for more cops, higher pay, special training, new and sophisticated equipment. Corrections and courts got only stray thoughts and odd dollars.

Outdated Prisons

Certainly the neglect is not for want of knowing the problem. Quite clearly, the nation's prison system is hopelessly out of date, both physically and philosophically. Sixty-one of the larger prisons were opened before 1900, and 25 of these are more than 100 years old. Jails and prisons are incredibly overcrowded. Young prisoners and first offenders are often confined with hardened criminals, to be attacked and molested, to be taught more sophisticated crime. Prison staffs are small, poorly paid, inadequately trained. Guidance and counseling are notably inadequate. Vocational training is either non-existent or obsolete, training prisoners for types of jobs no longer there.

In short, instead of rehabilitating criminals, the jails and prisons breed tougher ones. Two-thirds of all released prisoners will commit another crime, usually a more serious one.

Asking Attorney General Mitchell last November to look into 13 specific ways to improve the Federal correctional system, President Nixon noted that repeater rates are even higher for persons under 20 than those over 20, and declared that "there is evidence that our institutions actually compound crime problems by bringing young delinquents into contact with experienced criminals." Asserts Rep. Abner Mikva, a Chicago Democrat deeply interested in the problem, "The way jails today corrupt rather than correct, I'm not sure we wouldn't make more progress against crime by doing away with them completely."

Other correctional activities today are no better. Work-release and school-release programs, group homes, halfway houses and similar efforts are still far too scarce. The *Washington Star* last week reported that 95 District of Columbia convicts were in jail, even though judges had officially assigned them to halfway houses, because there were no houses to take them. Probation and parole systems are similarly spotty across the nation. Caseworkers are ridiculously overloaded, unable to exercise any real supervision over their charges; a brief interview once or twice a month is the best most of them can manage.

The court system is similarly antiquated. Judges are overworked, the job of the good ones made infinitely harder by elderly colleagues who won't retire but don't carry their share of the load. They are buried under mountains of paperwork, the product of administrative procedures still back in the 19th century and of a dreadful dearth of trained court administrators. More significantly, the number of cases steadily soars as drug offenses and other law violations increase, as more cops arrest more people, as new legal aid efforts contest charges.

Dockets become ever more jammed, and the time between arrest and trial and sentencing steadily lengthens. Bail procedures are crazily complex. Rarely does a judge have any pre-trial background information on the accused. Plea bargaining is increasingly common—the prosecutor and defense attorney negotiating on the plea to be entered and the sentence to be passed, with the judge a more or less passive onlooker. New York Mayor John Lindsay told the ABA convention last week that of 18,000 prisoners in his city's jails, 8,000 were awaiting trial; twenty new criminal judges, a 30% increase, had made no appreciable dent in calendar delays.

And with the courts and correctional institutions in such a mess, it's practically inevitable that almost everyone involved with them quickly loses respect for the whole criminal justice system, seriously aggravating the already huge crime problem.

Need for New Facilities

If the problems are relatively clear, so are many of the answers. Federal, state and local governments must engage in a massive construction program of new correctional institutions—up-to-date and specialized facilities, local and regional, for juveniles, alcoholics, drug addicts and other special types of offenders. These new facilities must have first-rate diagnostic services, excellent treatment programs and counseling, relevant job training.

Far more effort must be made to keep prisoners closer to home, to develop open-prison and work-release programs, to operate halfway houses and other highly-supervised alternatives to prison. New efforts are needed to help suspects between arrest and trial—pre-trial counseling, programs for conditional work release without trial. Special attention must be devoted to juvenile offenders, with large specially trained staffs, with the use of foster homes or group homes to remove youths from unfavorable family or neighborhood situations, with community treatment of juveniles and other special rehabilitation programs.

Far more and better trained professionals are needed at every level —from prison guard to prison psychologist to parole worker—and more use of paraprofessionals and volunteers. Better research is needed in dozens of areas.

As Justice Burger said, the courts need more judges, more business-like procedures, specially trained personnel to handle the administrative load. They need more prosecutors and more defense lawyers to get earlier and speedier trials, perhaps night and Saturday sessions.

Judges need other kinds of help, too—to provide detailed information on prisoners coming up for trial, to study sentencing practices in other jurisdictions, to give other helpful background data. Perhaps most importantly, several major types of cases should be completely removed from the criminal courts, switched to administrative or other non-judicial bodies: Routine drunkenness cases (one-third of all arrests are for drunkenness), drug addiction, prostitution, gambling.

Happily, there are finally a few small signs of progress. Mr. Nixon's November directive to his Attorney General, ordering work in 13 specific correctional areas, is one bit of evidence. The American Bar Association, in response to a speech last year by Justice Burger, has set up a special commission to enlist public support for improvements in local correctional systems.

While Federal funds under the so-called Safe Streets Act are still going preponderantly into police work, there has been a significant increase in spending on corrections, both in actual dollars and in the percentage of the total funds—up from 14% in the year ending in June 1969 to about 27% in the year ending June 1970. A recently passed House bill to extend the act would require at least one-fourth of all future outlays to go for correctional facilities and probation work, and would increase to three-fourths from one-half the Federal share of the cost of new facilities.

A number of state and local governments are increasing their own spending on corrections and the courts, and some are carrying on interesting experiments with detoxification centers, special drug treatment programs, pre-trial release without bail, job training for young offenders between arrest and trial, broader community involvement in rehabilitation programs. A new court management institute in Denver will train people to ease the administrative load on judges. There seems to be an initial open-minded reception for Justice Burger's proposal for a special Judicial Council that would study ways to use the courts better, including ideas for removing types of cases from court jurisdiction.

Frightening Costs

Progress still comes far too slowly, though. The costs involved frighten many away from any action at all. A Prisons Bureau study headed for Mr. Nixon's desk, for example, proposes 166 new Federal correctional institutions, at a cost of $700 million, while needed state and local institutions would require billions more. The cost of training thousands of more correctional workers, of more court help, of better-paid prison guards, are all substantial.

Governments at all levels still find it politically more appealing to put scarce tax dollars into more dramatic anti-crime work, such as more cops or fancier equipment. Mr. Nixon, for instance, asked Mr. Mitchell for a progress report on the 13-point program by mid-May; the report still hasn't appeared. The Justice Department has been conspicuously unenthusiastic about the House provision reserving one-fourth of Federal funds for corrections. Any specific proposals to remove certain types of cases from the criminal courts are sure to be highly controversial.

Yet continued delay in dealing with all these problems not only raises questions about likely progress in the entire war against crime but means that even greater outlays of money and far more drastic solutions will likely be needed whenever the nation does finally turn its attention to them. Construction costs rise steadily for prisons or halfway houses just as they do for homes or office buildings. The shortage of trained workers will grow steadily more acute. The research and experimentation questions will multiply.

It should be painfully apparent that arresting more and more people will do little good if they are then committed to an excruciatingly jammed judicial system and a dismally debasing correctional system. The nation cannot be truly considered serious about fighting crime until it devotes dramatically more imagination, effort and dollars to these two neglected battlegrounds.

10. The Lost Fifth:
Poverty In The Ghetto

The average American enjoys a standard of living higher than any in human history. Only in an affluent society, where nearly everyone has "made it," can political leaders be concerned with an impoverished minority—the lost fifth.

Profile of the Poor

Although for the most part they are out of sight, a sizeable minority of Americans are poor. Our rural poor live on rutted, untravelled roads, while our urban poor are huddled together in city ghettos. This bottom fifth of the American people receive only five percent of the national income. Most poor people are children; the second largest group are the elderly. Able-bodied men are few and far between (less than one percent). Many are black, although there are more impoverished whites. They are ill-educated, lack skills, and are often in families headed by a woman. A general air of hopelessness is commonplace.

The Present Welfare System

The present welfare system was glued together for temporary distress during the Great Depression. For the long haul government insurance programs were created to provide for the elderly and the unemployed. We confidently expected that with the return of prosperity very little tax money would be used for welfare. But welfare payments have not disappeared. In the face of general prosperity, some programs such as Aid to Families with Dependent Children (AFDC) have actually increased, until well over half of the total welfare clients now fall under this program. In a recent year, 15 million persons were on welfare rolls: this number represents only one-half of the potential welfare clients. As it totters along today the "system" is tremendously inefficient, contradictory, and expensive.

In Search Of A Welfare Policy

No one defends the present welfare system. Welfare clients, tax-payers, welfare administrators, and political leaders are unanimous in damning the existing monstrosity, although they do not agree on a replacement. The deficiencies are obvious: the system destroys human dignity; it discourages work; it provides a very low standard of living. Eligibility requirements tend to destroy family units; welfare children tend to become welfare parents in an unbroken cycle.

The Nixon administration's Family Assistance Plan represents a complete overhaul of the existing AFDC system. Day-care centers and job training programs would bring welfare mothers into the work force. Welfare families could keep their first earnings without any cutback in payments; larger earnings would result in only a percentage reduction. The working poor would receive a subsidy. Fathers would be encouraged to stay with their families.

An alternate approach to Family Assistance is a family allowance payment to all parents for each of their minor children. Payments to high income families would be recovered through taxation (the conflict between this plan and that urged by Zero Population advocates should be noted in passing).

Another proposal is a negative income tax or guaranteed annual income. Under this arrangement, all families would file an annual W–2 form. Those with incomes above the poverty level would pay a tax; those below the poverty level would receive a compensatory payment.

"Poverty" and "welfare" are bad words in present-day America. Conservatives are prone to picture welfare clients as lazy drones who live off the earnings of others, and who, with any initiative, could escape from poverty and become useful members of society. Conservatives fear that the remaining poor are a special subculture that will not respond to normal, middle-class motivation. This stereotype sees millions of welfare women who spawn illegitimate children to fatten their monthly checks. Welfare men refuse to expend more energy than that required to toss empty beer cans over the porch railing. Only a return to frontier justice—"he who works not, eats not"—will end the sitdown strike of these ne'er-do-wells.

Liberals view the problem from a completely different perspective. The poor are not deliberate loafers. Instead, they are ignorant and not prepared to cope with modern urban life. With a helping hand from the government most of the poor will break out of the poverty pattern.

Both liberals and conservatives agree that welfare rolls can never be reduced to zero. The blind, the disabled, the children, and the elderly will never become self-supporting. One measure of any civilization is the manner in which it cares for its helpless citizens. Without penalizing these groups in any way, we are in search of a national policy that will break the poverty cycle and bring millions of Americans into the economic mainstream.

PROFILE OF THE POOR *

COMMITTEE FOR ECONOMIC DEVELOPMENT

Any consideration of poverty must be prefaced with a statistical analysis. Who are the poor? What yardstick defines poverty? How many Americans are poor by this definition? What groups are most likely to be poor? Why do these statistics lead to the conclusion that our present welfare system has failed?

Poverty in the United States is more prevalent among elderly persons than among any other age group. In 1968, the elderly poor (sixty-five years of age and over) numbered 4.6 million, or 18 percent of the total poor, and they constituted about 25 percent of all aged persons. . . .

The largest group of poor persons consists of children under eighteen. About 10.7 million children are poor, and they constitute 15 percent of all children under eighteen. About 60 percent of all poor live in families headed by a male, the remainder in families headed by a female. . . .

* Reprinted from Committee for Economic Development, Improving the Public Welfare System, 1970, by permission.

Poor children in . . . nonwhite families headed by women rose by more than a half-million (or 35 percent) between 1959 and 1968, despite an overall decline (about 38 percent) in the number of poor children in this period. . . . Poverty among children is also highly correlated with the size of families . . . about 44 percent of all poor children are in families with five or more children. . . .

Of all population groups, households with dependent children that are headed by women have the highest likelihood of being poor. Among whites, 36 percent of all such households were poor in 1968; among nonwhites, 62 percent. . . .

It should also be noted that the number of nonwhite poor in families headed by women increased by about 700,000 (or 24 percent) between 1959 and 1968, despite an overall decline in the number of poor persons. The number of poor white persons in such families, on the other hand, declined by about 16 percent, leaving the total number of persons about the same in 1968 as in 1959. The most obvious cause of poverty among families headed by women is the need of mothers to stay at home. . . .

Of the 39.5 million people who were classified as "poor" in 1959, some 7 million, or about 17 percent, were receiving some form of cash allowances under public assistance. In 1968, of the 25.4 million poor people, some 10 million, or about 40 percent, received such assistance. . . . Over the period from 1960 to 1969, the total amount of cash living allowances under public assistance almost doubled. . . .

Most southern states have had a reduced welfare population, while the northern industrial states have experienced a sharp increase in their rolls. To what degree public assistance payments, which are lower in the South than the North, account for this migratory pull is not known. Many authorities feel that the possibility of jobs at good pay has been a greater factor than welfare assistance in inducing migration. . . .

[An] unpleasant and unpalatable fact about the present welfare system in the United States is that those who must avail themselves of it in order to exist are consigned to a very low level of subsistence— even in states with the highest maximum benefits. . . . About half the states provided an allowance for a family of four of $2,400 or more, while below that the allowance ranged down to $600 a year. . . .

These figures speak eloquently of the real failure of the welfare "system," namely, its reflection of the larger national failure to have a proper regard and concern for the welfare of its less fortunate minority.

WELFARE ON KELLY STREET: A CASE STUDY *
DONALD MOFFITT
AND ART SEARS, JR.

Although statistics are a useful tool in analyzing the nature and scope of poverty, they fail to picture the poor as living, breathing people in an environment complete with street names, broken windows and rats. In the case study that follows, two Wall Street Journal *reporters tell the poverty story in terms of Kelly Street residents caught up in the poverty cycle.*

Why do tenement landlords prefer to rent to welfare clients with large families? Among welfare problems why does housing have priority over narcotics and drugs? Did the reporters find living conditions as Kelly Streeter's had reported them? Are Kelly Street landlords reaping huge profits? Why are there few adult males on Kelly Street? What problems does any Kelly Streeter face who tries to leave the welfare rolls? What are the odds that a "native" will ever leave Kelly Street?

* Reprinted from Donald Moffitt and Art Sears, Jr., "Kelly Street Blues," Wall Street Journal, January 10, 1969, by permission.

To the landlords who own the dilapidated tenements on Kelly Street in the black ghetto of New York's South Bronx, a desirable tenant is a welfare recipient with lots of children.

Unlikely as such a preference may seem, there are logical reasons for it. Having a welfare recipient for a tenant means the landlord can hope to collect his rent regularly, because welfare checks represent a steady if low income. And the more children a welfare recipient has, the more money the welfare department allots the family for rent.

The resultant jamming of big families into shabby buildings scarcely improve the quality of life on Kelly Street. People must live somewhere, of course, and with New York currently suffering from a housing shortage some degree of crowding is inevitable. But on Kelly Street the problems of over-crowding and decay seem at times to be overwhelming. "If I were to list priorities in the problems facing us," says Robert LaForey, assistant director of the Kelly Street Block Association, "I'd say housing comes before narcotics and jobs."

Not all the apartments on Kelly Street are occupied by welfare families, of course. There remains a small number of long-time, middle-class black residents who stay mainly because their rents are kept low by the rent-control laws that have existed in New York City since World War II. Such families may be headed by construction hands, civil servants or employed mothers who have managed to break away from the welfare system.

But Kelly Street's growing economic dependence on the welfare system is undeniable. Most of the middle-class residents have left, upset by crime, tawdriness and the influx of welfare families. As they leave, the rent-control law permits landlords to raise rents on their apartments to levels approaching the maximums the city's Depart-of Social Services—the welfare department—will permit recipients to pay.

Some startling disparities have resulted. Mrs. Madeline Desisso, a mother of three who draws $320.70 a month in welfare checks, pays $96.42 a month for her four-room apartment in the 800 block of Kelly Street. But Raleigh Lay, a city garbage truck driver who makes $678 a month, pays $44.70 for the five-room apartment occupied by him, his wife and their three children.

Rents charged some other welfare recipients have risen a good deal higher than Mrs. Desisso's. Mrs. Margaret Cochran, a 42-year-old mother of 13 children, pays $175 a month for her seven-room apartment.

Like most Kelly Street residents, Mrs. Cochran has numerous complaints about her apartment: The landlord is slow to repair broken windows. Often there's neither hot water nor heat. The hallways are dirty. Neighbors throw garbage into the yard behind the building.

An Occasional Rat

Two reporters living for a few weeks in another apartment on the block find that such complaints are well-founded. It is often impossible to take a hot bath because of a lack of hot water. There is refuse in hallways and in yards, and there often are roaches, silverfish and other insects creeping over walls and floors. An occasional rat also comes to visit.

Many Kelly Streeters are continuously involved in disputes with their landlords. Raleigh Lay filed suit against his landlord when a chunk of plaster fell on him from the ceiling as he lay in bed. Many others have taken advantage of a city ordinance that allows tenants to pay reduced rent until repair plumbing, painting and other work is done.

Landlords, for their part, complain that it's hard to avoid losing money on ghetto apartment buildings even with higher rents. Some details are provided by Gilbert M. Wolkenberg, a real estate and insurance man whose firm manages a 20-unit building that's one of the largest on Kelly Street. The building, Mr. Wolkenberg says, was sold "cheap" to a business associate of his a few months ago, though he won't reveal the price. Two previous landlords, he says, failed to earn a profit on the building.

Profitable in Two Years?

Total rent income from the building should amount to $18,000 a year, Mr. Wolkenberg says. Since the new owner took over, he says, $9,000 has been spent for new window sashes, repainting and other repairs. Taxes are $3,400 a year, the water bill $768 and the superintendent's salary another $1,200. With continuing repair expenses, Mr. Wolkenberg contends it will take at least two years before the building is profitable; rent reductions by tenants claiming building code violations could extend the time.

Like most slum areas that depend heavily on welfare money, Kelly Street is markedly lacking in male heads of households. Swarms of children crowd the street after school and on Saturday, and women are present in practically every household. But there are few men in residence. Many are absent for reasons to be found in any stratum of society—death, divorce, military duty and so forth—but a high percentage have deserted their families after deciding their families could fare better without them. Many of the men possess only minimal job skills, and their wages are low. But when they leave home, their families become eligible for the relatively generous ADC, or aid to dependent children, welfare payments.

Sometimes the men desert permanently. But often, Kelly Streeters admit, the husbands simply move to a rented room in another part of town, continue working and visit their families regularly—but secretly. The man's income combined with welfare payments enables the family to live much better than it could on either the wages or welfare alone.

Another reason for the large proportion of women and children is the high rate of illegitimate births. Though no statistics are available, many women on Kelly Street freely admit they have never been married, though they may have several children. Such women, of course, also qualify for welfare assistance.

Once on welfare, it's difficult—and often highly impractical—for a mother to seek other sustenance. A mother and three children can receive as much as $4,149 a year in ADC payments in New York City. Working for the $1.60-an-hour Federal minimum wage, by contrast, would provide an income of only $3,328 on a 40-hour-a-week basis. Even aside from the lack of financial incentive, the practical difficulties of day-to-day household management facing a husbandless mother who tries to work are formidable.

In theory, a welfare recipient has a duty to work if possible, and the city operates day care centers that are supposed to take care of children whose mothers must work to support them. But there are more than 600,000 children on the city's welfare rolls, and the day care centers can accommodate only about 7,500. Mothers of another 7,500 children are on waiting lists.

Still, there are mothers on Kelly Street who are trying to break away from welfare. Gail Williams, 20, is one. Through a private program called SAVE, she receives $17 a week for expenses involved in attending Monroe Business Institute, where she is learning secretarial skills. When she graduates this year, she hopes to find a job that will enable her to live without public assistance. She has been able to place her two preschool children in a day care center near Kelly Street, and she has friends and family in New York willing to help her with special problems.

Pride obviously plays a major role in Mrs. Williams' determination to get off welfare. "When you tell somebody you're on welfare, they look at you like they think you sit around all day and drink whisky," Mrs. Williams says. "The welfare investigator who used to come here would sit down and look as if she were thinking, 'I've got to be careful not to let any dirt rub off on me.'"

A Self-Supporting Mother

Mrs. Ruth Peterson, in her late 40s, has been supporting herself and her eight children (including triplets) for the past four years. Before that, she had received $44 a month in welfare assistance as a supplement to the income of her husband, serving in the Navy. Then he died. Mrs. Peterson managed to get a job in a department store to become self-supporting.

Mrs. Peterson insists that welfare department caseworkers, presumably trying to perpetuate their own jobs, tried to persuade her not to go off the welfare rolls and actually told her employer to fire her from one job. Jack R. Goldberg, the city's welfare commissioner, says that such persuasion "clearly is not department policy, but it does happen in some instances."

Men on Kelly Street have a profound distrust of employment in private business and industry. Mr. LaForey, a hulking ex-football player who works as a city hospital ambulance attendant at night and serves during the day as assistant director of the Kelly Street Block Association, advises youngsters to try for civil service and other governmental jobs. "Find a job where you won't be laid off, where you know you have a guaranteed income after 20 years, where you really know that you won't have to work all the rest of your life," he says.

Raleigh Lay, 38, says that quitting his well-paying job in private industry to accept a lower-paying job as a city garbage truck driver was "the luckiest thing I ever did." A graduate of a New York vocational school, the School of Aviation Mechanics, he worked at a suburban General Motors Corp. plant for 10 years. As he got older, he says, "I realized I had no security up there. If I got sick, I might lose my job. And they were talking about moving the plant to Ohio. If you didn't want to move, you'd be out of a job."

Wanted to Play Ball

Once a fine athlete—he earned high school letters in baseball, basketball, track and swimming—Mr. Lay says he regrets not having been able to become a professional baseball player. He was the only Negro player on his high school team in 1947, at a time when organized baseball was still all but closed to Negroes. Whether Mr. Lay was good enough for the major leagues is now impossible to say, of course, but several of his white teammates were scouted by major league teams. One of the white players was Whitey Ford, who went on to fame as a New York Yankee pitcher.

Failing to break into baseball, Mr. Lay became a professional boxer. As an amateur, he won a local Amateur Athletic Union middle-weight championship in 1949. As a professional, he won seven fights and lost one before he broke with his manager and quit boxing.

Mr. Lay aims eventually to buy a house on suburban Long Island, where one of his sisters who grew up in the Kelly Street neighborhood now lives. He says he is afraid to move from his low-rent apartment until he is sure he'll be able to afford the payments on a $16,000 or $18,000 home.

But many householders on Kelly Street seem destined to spend much of their lives there or on similar streets, supporting their families through public assistance.

Complication of Welfare

Obtaining welfare assistance is more complicated than one might suppose. Typically, a woman must appear at one of the city's 30-odd local welfare centers, where she receives an application blank and an appointment for an interview. When she shows up for the interview she must bring birth certificates for herself and her children, a marriage certificate if she is married, any insurance policies or bank books and the name and address of her landlord. She must also be prepared to give an account of how she has maintained herself and her family.

In general, during the interview she will also be asked about her relatives, her employment and her marital status. She then sees a welfare "resources consultant" who decides how much if any of the insurance she owns should be retained for funeral costs (usually $250). The rest of the cash value of the policy is supposed to go to the welfare department. If the applicant has been making purchases on installment plans, the consultant tries to determine whether some of the merchandise can be turned back to the seller in order to conserve funds.

Finally, an investigator visits the applicant at her home and then tries to verify her statements by talking to her landlord, building superintendent, minister, neighbors, parents and others. The process may take as long as 30 days.

Meticulous Budget

The amount of regular monthly assistance, which is divided into semimonthly payments, depends on the number and ages of children the mother supports. The "budget" that determines the size of the check is prepared with meticulous detail; a member of the family, for example, is allowed 90 cents a day for food—15 cents for breakfast, 25 cents for lunch, 50 cents for dinner.

Welfare families are also entitled to free monthly rations of Federally supplied surplus commodities that can be picked up at a designated center. The Federal program provides such fare as prune juice, prunes, instant potatoes, cheese, canned tomatoes, powdered eggs, evaporated milk, canned beef, dried beans, split yellow peas, butter, canned chicken, rice and lard.

Not all welfare recipients receive surplus foods; one mother on Kelly Street says she doesn't know how to apply.

Many other mothers on Kelly Street supplement the Federal rations by spending $30 to $60 on groceries from their semimonthly checks to provide more varied meals. They buy bread, cereal, whole milk and additional meat, plus such items as detergents and toilet paper.

Extra Money Plan

Until recently, a mother who needed extra money for major purchases such as winter clothing or furniture had to apply for a special grant from the welfare department. In August, however, the department instituted a "simplified payments" system providing $25 a person for each family four times a year.

The aim, in part, was to eliminate the cost of processing special grant applications. The change also reflected a rising militancy among welfare mothers who were demanding and demonstrating for more liberal grants; in one year, New York City's special grants more than tripled to a level of $13 million a month, yet the money largely was going to the militant, demanding mothers rather than the more passive, and sometimes more needy, ones.

On Kelly Street, the flat payment plan has met a mixed reception. Mrs. Rosita Eady, a mother of nine, likes it. "It leaves it up to you to budget as best you can," she says, "but for some others it's bad." Another Kelly Street woman says, "These mothers who got that money in a lump sum for the first time were all excited. But as soon as they used it up, and they saw they weren't going to get any more money for three months, many of them ran to their neighbors, who are in the same miserable condition, to borrow to feed their children."

Mrs. Peterson, who acts as welfare specialist for the Kelly Street Block Association, says $25 a person every three months is too little. "What are you going to do?" she asks. "Just buy the child a coat, not buy him any underwear?"

Illegal Welfare Supplements

Some Kelly Street mothers manage to supplement their welfare checks by working, despite the rule that any earnings, except from certain job-training programs, are supposed to be deducted from their basic monthly grants. These mothers generally find relatives, neighbors or others—sometimes their older sons and daughters to care for their younger children during the day.

One young mother of two children says she works in a dress factory and earns about $65 a week, which she doesn't report to the welfare department. "You work," she says, "and you just hope that welfare doesn't find out." Another mother who works says, "It makes you feel guilty. That's what I don't like about being on welfare. But you just got to buy your children a few nice things once in a while. I do it for my children, not for myself."

The welfare department recently started an experimental program to permit some mothers to receive welfare assistance legally while working. Under the plan, they will be permitted to keep $85 a month plus a third of any amount over that before earnings are subtracted from their monthly welfare payments. But the experiment is a minuscule one, affecting only 4,500 mothers in the city, and it faces potential resistance from low-income persons who are not receiving welfare assistance.

Drugs for Arthritis

New York State's Medicaid program, in operation almost three years, has sharply raised the standard of medical care on Kelly Street. It provides for essentially all necessary medical care for welfare families and some other low-income groups. Mrs. Eleanor Richardson, a retired garment worker, says she feels considerably better now that she can obtain drugs for relief of her acute arthritis. Mrs. Ernestine Dove, a cheerful welfare mother, is having three missing front teeth replaced.

The neighborhood's Lincoln Hospital is chronically overcrowded. Even on a weekday night visitors find more than 50 persons awaiting treatment in the emergency room. But there are few complaints in the neighborhood about the quality of medical care.

IN THEIR OWN WORDS *

PRESIDENT'S COMMISSION

ON INCOME MAINTENANCE

PROGRAMS

The profile of the poor is perhaps best reported in their own words. Even though this story may lack

* Reprinted from President's Commission on Income Maintenance Programs, Poverty Amid Plenty (U.S. Government Printing Office, 1969), pp. 16–21, 26–27, 30.

polished phrases, it has a genuine ring that proves that the poor too have hopes, aspirations and feelings. If nothing else, this kind of reporting destroys the comfortable belief that the poor are a kind of sub-human species. The following selections are drawn from testimony offered before a Presidential Commission.

How well do the poor budget their money? What dilemmas do they face? Do they get adequate medical care? What sort of housing do they find? Why are present job training programs a source of frustration? Do many of the poor hold full time jobs? How are they isolated by birth from the mainstream of American life?

How the Poor Survive

Technically, an income at the poverty level should enable families to purchase the bare necessities of life. Yet an itemized budget drawn at that level clearly falls short of adequacy. There are many items for which no money is budgeted, although those items may be needed. Funds for them can only come out of sums already allotted to the basic necessities of life. As one witness told the Commission, "I either eat good and smell bad, or smell good and don't eat." When another witness was asked how he made ends meet, he simply replied, "They don't meet."

The fact that low-income households are able to survive at all despite incomes below the subsistence level suggests that many of them possess remarkable skills in stretching their incomes. Means of coping with inadequate incomes that have been cited in Commission field research include: skipping a rent payment or a utility bill— sometimes being evicted saves a month's rent; "borrowing" food from friends and relatives; and reliance on credit. "We don't pay the full price for food," one witness said, explaining, "we get credit on food and pay once a month. But we don't pay all of it, we just pay a portion of it." Who pays the rest? "He (the grocer) just carries it over to the next month." Other witnesses told of disposing of possessions to meet current expenses. "We sold our home and sold everything we had. Had to. I always have to plan it out some way or find something around the place to sell or something."

FOOD

Many poor families are not fed adequately. To keep families from going hungry, poor women often use great ingenuity to reduce their food costs. They may buy at markets where day-old bread and damaged canned foods are sold at discounts. Many use cheaper dried milk despite their preference for liquid milk. They buy large amounts of inexpensive foods, like spaghetti and dried beans, that do not spoil and are nutritious. They use surplus commodities distributed by the Government when these goods are available to them, and Food Stamps when they can afford

them. They may share transportation costs for shopping trips away from small neighborhood stores.

In spite of these efforts, the Department of Agriculture's 1965 Food Consumption Survey showed that 63 percent of households with incomes under $3,000 had inadequate diets. The Commission heard first-hand evidence to this effect throughout the country:

I have to cut corners and now I am cutting down the middle. I don't have any corners left to cut.

Maybe if I have four potatoes I will fry them and give them all to go around. Sometimes we don't eat. When the check comes I don't have maybe $3 left. With those $3 we have to eat. Sometimes we eat and sometimes we look at each other.

I don't have enough to buy food. That is the reason why I am sick today with high blood pressure, heart trouble, because I don't have money to buy the kind of food that I am supposed to have.

MEDICAL CARE

Most of the poor cannot afford private medical care and are not covered by insurance. And many cannot afford the transportation to free medical facilities, which are often miles and hours away. Or, there may be no medical charity— public or private—available to them. Their plight is suggested in incidents related to the Commission:

It took me nine months . . . to get a man in the nursing home. He fell and broke his hip and injured his foot. He was ninety-two years old. When we finally got an opening . . . he (had) died because the foot had already become infected, gangrenous, and it was too late.

I can't get a dentist appointment for my two children anywhere. "We do not take welfare patients"—and these (are) people that the Welfare recommended. As far as eyeglasses, I waited three months to have my son's eyes checked . . .

. . . a couple of weeks ago she (her daughter) fell again . . . I called the doctor and I said as I am holding her, bleeding in my arms, "I's bringing my daughter," and he said, "I'm going home to dinner early this evening. You will have to find somebody else." And I said, "I don't know how to get to find anybody else. I have no way." And he said, "Well, I guess you're just going to have to find a neighbor . . ."

I went in (to the County Hospital) and told the head nurse about it (his son hit by a car), she said, "Well, we can't take him." Of course he was in pain. His leg was just smashed all to pieces where the bumper hit him.

The only place we can refer for charity hospitalization is the University Medical Center in Little Rock (150 miles away). But even then, they are so crowded that the doctors always have to make prior appointments and make sure space is available.

HOUSING

Millions of the poor live in substandard, squalid housing. The shanties and shacks found in rural areas often look like remnants from an earlier era. One rural resident who lives with her daughter and eight grandchildren in a small shack described her housing to the Commission:

It is a four-room house and another little room out the house, and it rains into it. Have to get up at night and put a dishpan to keep the rain off the children. I told the owner. He told me I would have to have the house fixed up myself.

The barrenness of housing of the urban poor sometimes is hidden behind the façade of ordinary looking row houses. Yet the interior may reveal serious decay—falling plaster, holes in the wall, gaps in window frames, rats and roaches, and deteriorated plumbing. One mother told the Commission:

The house is in bad condition and every time it rains the water comes in. I've called public housing many times and they just tell you over the phone, "What am I to do about this?" And the roof leaks, and the water comes through the windows. This is a contaminated condition and a health hazard. My children get sore throats and they are sick all the time.

The physical condition of the homes and neighborhoods in which the poor live and the crowding that often occurs have severe effects on health, as well as on social and behavioral patterns. The struggle to meet basic physical needs under depressing and frustrating living conditions undermines attempts to escape from poverty.

The people have an apathy about cleaning a place that is about to fall down on their heads. Believe me, if you lived in a house that had a leaky roof, and the paper's off the wall, rats, and roaches, no matter how you clean. The front steps fall down; the back steps fall down. Half the steps in the house are broken, the pipes leak, the toilet is broken. Well, I could mention anything else, but you get the general idea. Do you blame a person for not wanting to clean a place like this?

JOB TRAINING

The demand for labor also will affect the outcome of training programs. Many witnesses at Commission hearings expressed frustration at going through training programs which were not geared to jobs currently available or to the skills of the trainees.

The program put me into them (three different types of training for jobs.) What I was wondering is if they could put somebody in there who has been through the mill like I have and talk to the people, tell them what kind of a job they could get and what they would like . . . Because they sent me to Lowrey Field for sheet metal. Well, they say it pays pretty good but it takes four years to learn the trade and then $400 to join the union. And then you have to know too much math and algebra and all that.

I have been trained . . . I was trained with my cane (for the blind). Training people for what, for sitting in the corner? They have given me the training of a king or queen and today I still sit in my corner with my knitting in my hand. . . I have been trained to take dictaphone dictation and I have been trained to do answering services and I have been trained to do sewing . . . And what am I doing today? Sitting in my corner, waiting for the world to call me a leech, I am not willing to give any more time for any more training, thank you.

Well . . . back in 1965, I went to the Bureau of Indian Affairs school . . . and they accepted me and I received my training in Chicago. The trouble was that I went out for welding and somehow when I got up there they had me down as a barber. (After completing barbering courses and finally receiving training as a welder) I tried to get a job and they throw the bit up to me about "Do you have any tools?" or "Do you have any experience?" And I said no. And I can't get no job, they won't hire me. I might as well go out and dig a ditch for Tom or Joe . . . because I am sick and tried of going to trade school.

The whole system is bad . . . you start them on training full of hope and what guarantee? What job is there after the end of that training? Nothing but a waiting list.

People are training for the jobs that they originally were hopeful of getting. But the problem has been that we haven't been able to locate them a job with industry because of the fact, as you probably are aware by now, there are no jobs in Albuquerque, New Mexico.

When there are no jobs for the head of the family, then other members of the family may have to help support the family. One witness told the Commission:

A poor family cannot put his child to work according to age, he puts him to work according to the needs of his family.

In 1966 at least 160,000 male family heads were forced to work less than they desired because of an inability to find more steady employment. More than a million others were working part-time hours at low-paying marginal tasks.

One witness heard by the Commission, for example, spends part of the year raising cotton on a ten-acre plot in return for a share of the product. After paying all the costs associated with raising the crop, his net income from share-cropping is $400 annually. In addition, he earns $5.00 daily as a tractor operator when that work is available. During the winter, he sells firewood to supplement his income. He testified:

Nine people live off it. Just figure how could you do it with nine people; just one biscuit a day. A man with $5.00 can hardly cover that. And I only receive that through the summer. Winter time there ain't nothing to do. They give us a little something to do around and pay up what we owe; you don't get through paying what you owe. And if there were something to do, I would sure appreciate doing it. I wouldn't back off from no work.

Many women heading families with children can work only at the expense of their family responsibilties.

I would like to state . . . that I do have a high school education; I have one year of college. I have ten years working experience behind me. The reason I am not employed at the present and am having to take AFDC is because of inadequate child care for my children.

One witness told the Commission:

I said that I was a New Careerist in the CEP, Concentrated Employment Program. I earn $1.60 an hour and I take home $242.22 every month for the support of myself and three children. My rent is $75 a month. The cost of my being employed far exceeds my income . . . By this I mean that it would be to my advantage to be on welfare. I am one of those people that are motivated, but is it worth it? I sometimes wonder.

THE QUALITY OF LIFE

In poor neighborhoods we have seen overflowing garbage pails resulting in garbage-strewn streets, while in affluent areas of the same city garbage is picked up regularly. Many low-income neighborhoods are poorly protected against crime. There are severe barriers to educational and occupational achievement:

. . . you have the situation where one member of the family is in school today and the other member isn't: and when one asks, "where is your brother today?" (he is told) "It's not his turn to wear the shoes today."

I keep one of them (her six children) to stay home (to babysit while she works). I figure it's bad but it's the only way for me to make a living. I keep one out; that is the only way I have to do it.

It is often difficult even for middle-class residents of middle-class communities to escape the neighborhood's influence on themselves and on their children. How much more difficult it is for the urban poor.

(My daughter asked) "Why is all them doctors out in the hallway?" I said, "Doctors?" She said, "Yeah, they all got needles in their hands." . . . there's junkies, dope addicts, and the rats—don't mention them. They are going hungry now because I ain't got no food.

A recent study of life patterns of welfare recipients pointed out that:

To go to school costs money—books, notebooks, pencils, gym shoes, and ice cream with the other kids. Without these the child begins to be an outcast.

To go to church cost money—some Sunday clothes, carfare to get there,

a little offering. Without these one cannot go.

To belong to the Boy Scouts costs money—uniforms, occasional dues, shared costs of a picnic. Without these, no Scouts.

To have friends into the house costs money—for a bit of food, a drink.

To visit relatives costs money—for travel, a gift for the kids. These people cannot afford to visit their relatives.

For a teen-ager to join his friends on the corner he must have some money—for a coke, a show.

How does a fellow take a girl out on a date without some money? And how does a girl pretty herself for a fellow without some money?

How do you join a club? Buy a book, a magazine, a newspaper?

Poverty settles like an impenetrable cell over the lives of the very poor, shutting them off from every social contract, killing the spirit, casting them out from the community of human life.

THE WELFARE MUDDLE *

EDWARD C. BANFIELD

Criticisms of the welfare system abound. In the article that follows, Professor Banfield identifies four major areas of concern.

What evidence does he present to show that the present system breaks up families? Why does he believe that the system encourages men to "cop out"? Why does the system discourage job hunting and concentrate the poor in areas of little economic growth? Why does he believe that welfare clients are more apt to cheat and be cynical about governmental authority than the general run of taxpayers? How does he dispose of the argument that welfare can be justified because many segments of society receive subsidies?

. . .

There are those who think that what is mainly wrong with the present system is that it does not give large enough benefits to enough people. In 1965 only 20

* Reprinted from Edward C. Banfield, "Welfare: A Crisis Without Solutions," The Public Interest, Summer, 1969, pp. 93–97. Copyright © National Affairs, Inc., 1969. Reprinted by permission of the author.

percent of poor persons received public assistance and, of these, 82 percent remained poor after receiving it. Payment levels are low: the average monthly payment per recipient is only $42.35 (August 1968) and in Mississippi it is a mere $8.50. New York's payment—$69.70—is slightly above the officially defined poverty level, but many people do not consider it enough.

The poor, it is sometimes pointed out, are in a sense less "dependent" than most of the rest of us. In our society almost everybody benefits from some kind of subsidy and the larger the individual's income the larger the subsidy that he is likely to get. No one seems to boggle at subsidies to homeowners, or farmers, or union members, or businessmen or college students. The amounts that the poor get are small in comparison (public assistance payments have always been about 1 percent of gross national product); why, then, so much fuss about rising welfare costs?

I will presently try to show that the welfare system entails large *real* costs to the society as opposed to mere transfer of money within it. But even if this were not the case, it seems to me that the answer to the "everyone's-getting-it-why-shouldn't-the-poor-get-it-too" argument is that *no one* should get it. The government should use its power to take from some and give to others, not for the sake of the others, but only for that of the whole society. Except as there is good reason to believe that the whole society is somewhat improved by subsidizing farmers or homeowners or whomever, they should not be subsidized.

But what if, as a practical matter, taking the subsidies away from the farmers, the homeowners, and all of the others is out of the question; is there not then a case for subsidizing the poor along with everyone else? On grounds of equity the answer is obviously yes. Other considerations than equity have to be taken into account, however, and I am afraid one of these is that it is impossible to devise a welfare system that will deal generously with all of the poor and yet be tolerable from the standpoint of voters and taxpayers who are not poor.

In order to prepare the way for this argument I shall list four sorts of undesirable side effects—social costs—that result from steps that people take either to qualify for benefits under the present welfare system or in consequence of having qualified for them. Except as these side effects can be eliminated (without in the process introducing other kinds that are as bad or worse!) one must, it seems to me, fear that extending and liberalizing the system will do more harm than good.

Moynihan in Reverse

1. The welfare system causes the breakup of a great many families. The Moynihan Report of a few years ago theorized that male Negro unemployment caused the breakup of the Negro family and that this in turn caused dependency rates to soar. I suggest that this theory would work better in reverse: it is high AFDC rates that are causing the breakup of the poor—and hence the Negro—family. Moynihan presented a chart showing a remarkable correlation between male Negro unemployment and AFDC cases opened, but the correlation ceased after 1962. What happened after that year— the continued rise of the AFDC caseload in the face of a decline in male Negro unemployment—as well as what happened before it, can be explained by putting his theory in reverse.

The fact is that the AFDC program offers low-income parents strong financial incentive to separate. The family may be able to get on welfare only if the father leaves or pretends to leave ("fiscal abandonment"). The kind of welfare that is easiest for them to get is AFDC, whose funds come almost entirely from the federal government; and in most states, this is more readily given than General Assistance, three quarters of which comes from the locality and the state. A federal AFDC program does exist under which an intact family may receive support for a short time if both parents are unemployed, but in May 1968 only 68,000 families were receiving benefits under it. Usually, federal money is available only to fatherless families. If the arrangement encourages fathers to desert their families, it also encourages mothers to kick out fathers or to make life so miserable for them that they will leave. By the same token it removes any material incentive for a pregnant girl to marry the man who made her so.

Two rather striking facts support the hypothesis that the welfare system causes the breakup of families rather than the other way around. One is that in a sample of welfare mothers in New York City, nearly 60 percent of those who were separated or divorced were separated or divorced *after* they went on welfare. The other is that the number of female-headed families in the cities increased by 660,000 from 1960 to 1968. The rate of increase was greatest among those most eligible for welfare—low-income Negroes. Nearly two thirds of all children in urban Negro families having incomes of less than $4,000 are now without fathers. I have no doubt that welfare is responsible for a great deal of this.

The breakup of families is, in and of itself, another contributing cause of the increase in caseload. An intact family normally receives welfare only during periods of unemployment, which is to say only now and then, but a broken one is likely to receive it continuously until the youngest child has grown up. The main damage, however, is not to the purse of the taxpayer but to the happiness and well-being of children who are left fatherless. Although the absence of the father is apparently nowhere near as injurious to the psychological health of children as the Moynihan Re-

port claimed, and there is little doubt that a child may be better off without a father than with one who is abusive, the breakup of families must certainly be counted as a heavy cost against the welfare system.

The Cop-outs

2. The system enables a great many people who should work to escape work. I am not referring to mothers with dependent children—in my opinion most of them ought not to work. I am referring to the men who should be supporting those women and children but who are not because welfare relieves them of the necessity. There must be hundreds of thousands of these men. Some probably work about as much as they would if their families did not receive welfare; the difference is that they spend their earnings on themselves alone. (I conjecture that a considerable part of this spending is for illicit goods and services and therefore constitutes an inducement to others to engage in criminal activities.) Most, however, probably work less, only enough to live according to the standards of a street-corner society. If I am right about this, their partial withdrawal from the labor force represents a real cost to society, not merely a transfer of wealth from one group to another. It is obviously unjust to tax those who work for the support of those who won't. Moreover, I believe that voluntary unemployment is often just as demoralizing as involuntary.

I am not speaking here of people who have learned the uses of leisure (such people are few, even among the rich); for most people, especially those who live in the present, work is the only available relief from boredom and the only source of discipline.

Keeping Them Down in the City

3. The welfare system deters people from moving to places where their opportunities will be better and where the costs of supporting them will be less. The idea seems to be gaining currency that no one should ever be expected to go somewhere in search of a job, no matter how little need there may be for his services where he is or how much need there may be for them elsewhere; instead, a job should be provided where the individual is, whatever the locational disadvantages may be, or else he and his family should be supported on welfare there indefinitely. In the case of the unemployable poor, it is taken for granted that they should be supported in whatever place they choose, no matter what the disadvantages of this to others may be. The tendency of welfare is therefore to maintain a concentration of the poor in the centers of the largest cities. The existence of huge ethnic or racial enclaves of the poor in the inner city at a time when economic growth is mostly in the suburban fringe is manifestly undesirable. When you stop to think about it, could anything be more absurd than to keep the unemployed and unemployable in those places where their long-run opportunities are poorest, and space is in greatest demand, shortest supply, and therefore highest in price?

Cheating

4. The welfare system offers an incentive to wholesale lying and cheating. No one really has any idea how many "fiscal abandonments" there are, and it is difficult to see how anyone could ever find out even by a major research project. If a mother wishes to claim more dependent children than she actually has, it is all but impossible to detect the fraud without the kind of prying that social workers are no longer supposed to do.

The example of the income tax is often cited as justification for a "declaration" procedure under which an applicant's statements are checked only if "circumstances in the particular case would indicate to a prudent person that further inquiry should be made." (The quotation is from the Wisconsin welfare statute.) After all, if we assume that income tax payers generally tell the truth, why should we not also assume that applicants for welfare do too? The answer is, first, that statistically speaking the poor are much more likely than the nonpoor to have what has been called a preconventional morality —one that says in effect that any action is "right" that serves your purpose and that you can get away with, and, second, the poor have little or nothing to lose if they are caught violating the law—parents who arrange a "fiscal" separation know perfectly well that the welfare department is not going to have them sent to jail if it finds out about it. What exactly can it do? It cannot even deprive them of support; people cannot be allowed to starve no matter what they do.

What of it if the poor do cheat on their "declarations"? Payment levels are too low anyway, it will be said, and so the cheating only results in their "taking" what they should get as a matter of right. I do not find this argument persuasive. For one thing, payment levels in the heavy caseload states are not so terribly low. But the main objection to a system that encourages cheating is that it tends to destroy honesty and fair dealing in all relations of life and thus also to reinforce the already pervasive cynicism of the "underclass" toward the institutions of government and toward authority of any kind. . . .

A SCANDAL CALLED WELFARE *
MORRIS K. UDALL

The present welfare system has few defenders, because it is expensive; administrative costs are very high; it tends to break up family groups; many of the poor are untouched; and besides there is little incentive for the poor to break out of the system.

How has the present system encouraged the migration of southern Negroes to northern big-city ghettos? Why are welfare rolls rising? What advantages does the Family Assistance Plan have over the existing system? Why does Udall believe that liberals should support it? How can a fully employed worker in the United States fall below the poverty level? What government should finance our welfare system? Why does Udall favor direct federal responsibility for welfare rather than revenue sharing?

President Nixon calls it a "monstrous, consuming outrage"; Governor Ronald Reagan, "a cancer

* Reprinted from Morris K. Udall, "A Scandal Called Welfare," The Progressive, May, 1971, by permission.

eating at our vitals"; *Time* magazine, "a living nightmare." It is a monster which affects the lives of 13.5 million Americans, costs more than $14 billion a year, and gets bigger and costlier every day.

I am referring, of course, to the national scandal called welfare, and I am disturbed by the fact that one of the main roadblocks to reform of our antiquated, cruel welfare system is a segment of the liberal community that may be putting partisanship ahead of the needs of the poor.

There are not many readers of *The Progressive* who are on welfare. And it is pretty easy for liberals to point to the bogeyman of Ronald Reagan and Richard Nixon to justify just about any position they want to take. But I think it is time that we at least start listening to some conservative voices, even if we think they are wrong, and in listening, perhaps help put poverty and welfare above partisanship.

Here is one of those voices, with a message I like:

I believe that the American people feel that with the high production of which we are now capable, there is enough left over to prevent extreme hardship and maintain a minimum standard floor under subsistence, education, medical care, and housing, to give to all a minimum standard of decent living and to all children a fair opportunity to get a start in life.

That was Senator Robert A. Taft —in 1949.

It is a sad commentary on the snail's pace of progress, and the divisions in the liberal world, that the conservative "Mr. Republican" could say that two decades ago and be regarded as marching in the ranks of liberal thinking today. It is a sad commentary on the divisions in the liberal community that a man with Richard Nixon's checkered past could be offered up as the author of welfare reform in the 1970's.

Yet in the Family Assistance Plan his Administration has offered more in the way of fundamental change for the good in the country's well-intentioned, but basically bad, welfare system than we were able to achieve in a decade of New Frontiers and Great Societies.

In 1970, I worked and voted for the House-passed version of President Nixon's Family Assistance Plan to reform that creaking, crumbling welfare machine that we built with a third of a century of disjointed social legislation. That did not rest well with some of my liberal colleagues in the House and Senate, but I think I was right.

That is not to say that the liberal opponents of the President's plan were and are wrong in their beliefs that FAP does not go far enough, and that it will not provide the poor with gate passes to the promised land as the President implies. It does not on either count.

But the fact of political life is that FAP is the only immediate move we can take, and the only alternative to taking that step this year or next is a continuation of our existing system, marked by three decades of failure.

Deep within me I have a hidden fear that perhaps some of the liberal opponents of the President's plan are spurred in part because it was Richard Nixon who proposed it. If that is true, it is a terrible price they are asking the poor to pay so that we may continue to play politics as usual.

I think I was right in working for House passage of the FAP; I am going to work in the same general direction this year, and hope that all liberals will, as a first step toward a total reform of the welfare system of the United States.

Liberals ought to take a close look at the welfare system and the chaos it has bred—and at the FAP as well, before they dismiss it out of hand. Here is what they would find:

First, all of our big cities are overcrowded, near bankruptcy; jobs for the unskilled are scarce. Yet the welfare system, like a huge magnet, draws millions of poorly trained, poorly educated people off the farms and out of the rural areas of our country and into the already crowded cities. There many of them, whether they want to or not, end up on welfare. Compounding the disaster, we have not one welfare system, but fifty—a different set of rules for each state. Thus, a deserted mother of three living in Mississippi, where farm jobs have been mechanized, will receive $840 a year if she tries to keep her family together at home among her relatives and friends. But if she can get to Tucson, Arizona, with her children, she will receive $2,004. And if she had gone to Newark, New Jersey, she would have received $4,164.

Second, as welfare developed it incorporated a basic evil principle —the proviso that denies relief to a family with "a man in the house." This often forces an unemployed, or under-employed, father to abandon his family so that his children may eat. And that includes millions of men who willingly work, but do not earn enough to feed their families. How can anyone defend a system designed to drive families apart?

Third, welfare's stated goal has always been to provide temporary help until a family could get back on its feet. But in practice welfare rules usually penalize those who try to work themselves off welfare. Suppose the Mississippi mother goes to Newark and gets $4,160 a year in welfare. But she hates welfare and wants to get off. Suppose she finds a $4,800-a-year job as a waitress. Here comes the rub: transportation, uniforms, and day care for her children come to $1,200 a year. Thus, if she takes the job she may become ineligible for any welfare, though she is *worse off by $500*. The senseless result: she may become a permanent rider of the welfare rolls. Common sense would suggest that we encourage her to take her $4,800 job and let her keep perhaps $1,500 of the welfare check. The taxpayers are ahead by $2,600, she is ahead, and eventually she may get off the rolls entirely. But common sense is not so common in the welfare jungle.

The main roadblocks to passage of FAP are these:

There are some liberals who agree that the present system is a mess, but say that FAP does not go far enough, and that its support levels are ridiculously low. They are linked in a strange alliance with some conservatives who think that FAP is "something for nothing" and amounts to a guaranteed annual income for people who do not deserve it.

There is a big push by the country's mayors and governors for a massive revenue sharing plan. But along with many others, I am beginning to wonder whether the best way to get more Federal dollars for cities and states might not be for Uncle Sam to pick up the whole welfare check for all levels of government, including the $7.5 billion paid this year at local levels. This would quickly relieve states of a huge and growing drain on their budgets and free a lot of local tax dollars for education, health, crime control, and all the urgent needs. These two possibilities have become entangled and we will have to resolve them together.

A good first step would be to enact FAP, followed by a federalization of the entire welfare system. That would save state and local governments $9.7 billion next year alone.

Here are just a few exhibits from today's chamber of welfare horrors:

¶ Thirteen million Americans now receive some kind of public assistance. This is up from 7.7 million just five years ago. In that time the cost has skyrocketed from $5.3 billion to $14 billion. Today the United States has the largest number of people drawing public aid since the 1930's. Ironically, the explosive growth of welfare rolls came during the late 1960's in a period of full employment and peak prosperity.

¶ If present trends continue to 1975, more than sixteen million Americans will be on welfare, collecting something like $25 billion each year. New York City's welfare population—1.1 million people. That city's welfare bill will total $1.7 billion this year, a jump of 600 percent in just one decade.

¶ California and New York together have a total welfare load of three million people. They distribute almost thirty-seven percent of the nation's welfare money. In Los Angeles, one of eight residents draws a welfare check, and in the face of a faltering economy and heavy layoffs in the aerospace industry, welfare rolls climb by as much as 15,000 new cases every month. As a small state faced with many of those same strains, Arizona's welfare budget has soared from $10.8 million to about $26.1 million a year in the last decade. The frightening rise in welfare budgets is forcing many states to cut back on schools and other desperately needed services.

¶ Part of welfare's staggering costs arise from a fantastic administrative apparatus, with an enormous army of caseworkers required to visit homes and pry into people's lives. The whole monster is controlled by a jungle of laws and regulations which could and does baffle Philadelphia lawyers.

Trapped in this welfare maze, we have lost our way. But one thing is clear: unless something drastic, fundamental, and far-reaching is done we can be sure that next year, and every year, costs and taxes will go up and up in a deadly drain of the nation's resources. I think it vital that we come up with a new approach to welfare.

The Family Assistance Plan represents that new approach to helping poor families. It is not just an enlarged welfare system; it is founded on some principles fundamentally different from "welfare" as we now know it. As our present system grew, a basic principle was fostered forbidding help to an able-bodied adult, or to children dependent on him. In recent years this concept has begun to change, and it will be altered even more under FAP.

It is important to understand why that change is necessary. Two basic American beliefs are that work is good for an individual, and that people physically able to work should do so. Coupled to those beliefs is the attitude that an able-bodied person willing to work can find work and therefore needs no public aid or charity. This set of attitudes has formed the bedrock of our welfare system since the 1930's.

Thus from the start the system offered aid only to certain categories of needy adults—the blind, the aged, the crippled, those physically unable to work. Our welfare system continues to care for these people today.

No one expects those three million people—mainly hard core unemployables—to work. And the FAP will protect the rights and needs of the overwhelming majority of those now receiving public assistance—the ninety-five percent who, according to Department of Health, Education and Welfare statistics, cannot work because of handicaps, or because they are mothers who have nowhere to leave their children in order to take a job—if one exists.

In our concern for hungry or neglected children, we added a further category, aid to families with dependent children (AFDC), which now supports 9.5 million people. At the heart of today's problem is this AFDC program, for until recently we carried forward into AFDC that basic notion of refusing help, in theory at least, to all able-bodied men and their dependents. Thus in many states, AFDC will not help a family with children if there is an able-bodied working man in the house capable of contributing to his family's support. This attitude may have made some sense in a rural society or in simpler times, but the FAP challenges the idea that it makes good sense in the 1970's.

The Army treats its seriously hurt, but it also cares for the "walking wounded." And, economically speaking, there are 10.5 million Americans today who are "walking wounded." These are people who want to work, and who work hard, but who remain desperately poor and so their children suffer.

Consider these statistics:

If the head of a family of four worked forty hours a week for fifty-two weeks a year at the Federal minimum wage of $1.60 an hour, he would earn $3,328—the current Federal poverty level for a city family is $3,967. Unfortunately, there are more than ten million jobs in this country, including many offered by state and local governments, which do not pay even that Federal minimum wage.

The median earnings of domestic workers in 1969 was $1,061; for laundry workers, $2,729; restaurant employees, $2,147; health service workers, $3,156. America badly needs people who will work in these jobs, yet our present welfare system says two crazy things: "We'll help the children of men who desert them, and who don't work at all . . . but rather than give 'something for nothing' we won't help the children of men who don't earn a living wage."

The heart of the FAP proposal is that all of this will be changed. We will help both kinds of poor families, and there will be job training and incentives for people to work their way out of welfare.

Briefly put, the FAP will combine and streamline assistance programs for the blind, aged, and disabled. In addition, it will junk the existing Aid to Families with Dependent Children program as a means of helping children of the poor. In its place we will have a new agency to administer a new FAP. It will be a system designed, as President Nixon said, to "place a floor under the income of every family with children in America—and without those demeaning, soul-stifling affronts to human dignity that so blight the lives of welfare children today." Every poor family of four will be guaranteed a money income of at least $1,600. Food stamps will push its purchasing power up to $2,400. These benefits will be provided regardless of the health or presence of a father. This plan will reduce snooping; it will be administered by fewer people; and it will eliminate many other evils of the present system.

No one is going to argue that the $2,400 is adequate as a living level. It isn't. But it is a place to start. On top of that, under a sliding scale, would be wages the poor would be allowed to keep from jobs encouraged under the FAP. This would particularly help our working poor, totally unaided now. And on top of that would be continuing state contributions, meaning that in high benefit states most recipients would continue to receive at least as much as they are granted now. The change in many states, particularly in the South, would be dramatic. The lesson we have to remember is that, in the history of Congress, once a Federal social program of this sort is started, benefits do rise if pressure continues to be applied. I have no doubts that we could get the benefit level up to a basic $4,000 or so within a couple of years—if we can get the program started *now*.

Beneficiaries of the FAP would be expected to meet one requirement—to register and be available for work. Mothers with pre-school children would be exempt from that requirement, naturally. A parent, if covered by the registration requirement, would lose his or her $500 in benefits upon refusal to register, but the children would not be penalized (as now), and payments for them would continue. This work requirement might well be coupled with a program of Federally subsidized public service employment. Instead of hopeless, idle people on the dole, we can provide desperately needed helpers in public service: teacher's aides, day care workers for parents who want to take jobs, hospital aides, people to beautify our parks, and other services badly needed today. This could be a tremendous boost for bills such as Senator Gaylord Nelson's public employment manpower proposal to provide jobs in that sector for 300,000 needy Americans.

Each year a parade of officials and individuals comes through my office seeking "Federal grants"—to cities for building sewers, grants to students to pursue an education, grants to farmers to stabilize production and improve the land. These are all subsidies given for the "welfare" of particular people.

In each of these cases, we grant Federal money because society supposedly gets something valuable in return: agricultural stability, an educated nation, clear water. Maybe we will have to come to look on welfare as a "people subsidy" given in return for family stability, healthy children, and for services and facilities the public needs.

This "people subsidy" can become a reality if liberals back FAP. But we cannot be content with simply accepting what President Nixon has proposed; it stops short of our real social needs.

It seems certain that "revenue sharing" is not going to pass this year or next—and I do not think it should. But we do have a chance to provide a true alternative that will accept the best parts of the FAP and provide local relief from spiraling tax pressures as well.

The best way to help states and localities, as well as the poor, is to act now on the President's Family Assistance Plan, put it into operation immediately, and then federalize the system so that all of the costs are paid on the national level. This program could save a total of $7.5 billion at the state and local levels this year alone, $27 million of it in a fairly small state such as Arizona. As a direct result, those funds could be put to local uses.

There is some real justice in federalizing welfare. The broad trends which have drawn some twenty million people off farms and out of the small towns into the big cities are a direct product of a national, highly centralized, mechanized, computerized society. Chicago and New York did not produce these trends, yet they are being asked to pay the welfare bills that come due at the local level.

A direct result of a federalization of the welfare system would be a national set of welfare standards that would end the inequities which are the hallmark of the patchwork system we have built. A poor child in Arkansas deserves the same level of nutrition and clothing as one in Arizona or Ohio. If we federalize the system we can compel a complete overhaul. We could take one of our most pressing social problems and devote concentrated attention to it with the urgency of a "space race," a race aimed at providing a decent life for the poor.

Much has been written about the polarization of our society—and the growth of the divisions splitting us. We have to face facts and admit that our welfare system has continually contributed to that process, no matter what our intentions when we started it. We have a chance to make some fundamental changes. I would hate to think that liberals were standing in the way.

THE IMPOSSIBILITY OF WELFARE REFORM *

EDWARD C. BANFIELD

Professor Banfield insists that we are considering a fundamental reordering of our society under the guise of welfare reform. The original welfare system was created to help people who had temporary economic problems. Present reform plans are keyed to a redistribution of income and the elimination of poverty. If our goal is a reshuffling of income, we should face up to this fact squarely, rather than saying we are tinkering with bits and pieces of the welfare system.

Why does Banfield believe that proposed welfare reforms will not keep families intact, provide work incentives, get the poor out of the inner city, or minimize cheating? Why does he believe that a more generous welfare system would be swamped and break down? Will taxpayers ever support an "adequate" welfare system? Why can no welfare system be satisfactory?

. . .

* Reprinted from Edward C. Banfield, "Welfare: A Crisis Without Solutions," The Public Interest, Summer, 1969, pp. 97–101. Copyright © National Affairs, Inc., 1969. Reprinted by permission of the author.

The Impasse

What sort of a welfare system would eliminate . . . undesirable side effects, or reduce them to tolerable limits, and yet afford generous support to all who are by some reasonable definition poor? I believe the answer is: none—not even the much talked about negative income tax.

It would be a simple matter to extend the AFDC program to intact families, including those in which both parents are employed. This would eliminate the incentive to "fiscal abandonment" to be sure. But the husband could still desert his family secure in the knowledge that it would be well provided for, and the wife could still kick him out secure in the same knowledge. No doubt many middle class husbands would leave or be kicked out if this would not create a financial problem for the family; in the lower class the pattern of husband-wife relations makes this even more likely. In the Negro lower class, Rainwater says, if the wife works she and her husband treat their earnings not as "family" income but as "yours" and "mine." Presumably when a family is on welfare the husband's earnings are "his" and he accordingly leaves the support of the family largely or entirely to welfare. If this is indeed what he does, his wife has no material incentive to let him remain. (When a husband fails to provide, Rainwater says, "the wife increasingly refuses to perform her usual duties for him." Kicking him out is the eventual outcome that is logically implied by this.) In the white lower class the pattern is probably much the same.

A welfare system can be designed to make those on welfare who work benefit more than those who do not. The incentives that such a system would offer, when piled on top of a decent minimum, might make the system enormously expensive. But let's ignore the cost. The fact remains that, even with incentives, anyone who prefers a minimum income without work to a higher one with work can still escape work, and unless the minimum is set very low—below what most of us would consider a decent level—it is likely that many would choose not to work. Moreover, the number who will choose not to work is likely to be vastly greater in the next generation than in this one, for it must be remembered that new tastes and habits will over the long run be formed in response to the incentives and opportunities that the new situation provides. The more ample and dependable the provision that society makes for the individual's future, the more encouragement it gives him to live only for the present.

Establishing equal standards in all states—and the standards would presumably be closer to New York's than to Mississippi's—would, to be sure, eliminate any incentive to go from Mississippi to New York for the purpose of getting on welfare. It would not, however, cause any movement out of the cities or from places of relatively poor to relatively good opportunity. In order to induce people to leave the city it would be necessary to reestablish inequality of payment levels with higher payments going to persons who did *not* live in big cities. It is of course hard to imagine this as a practical possibility: so long as most of the money comes from the federal government, New York will not stand for its poor receiving less than the poor of some other place, and Los Angeles and every other city will have the same attitude.

Cheating could be made difficult by returning to old fashioned methods involving frequent inquiry by case workers. But this would make the process of getting welfare so embarrassing, time-consuming, and uncertain that many who genuinely need help would be deterred from applying for it.

I am not claiming that any step in the direction of liberalizing our welfare system will entail significant amounts of these social costs. I doubt, for example, if tripling the average AFDC payment in Mississippi would cause the breakup of many families. Even if it would, I would favor the increase because it seems obvious to me that intended benefits in terms of the relief of suffering would more than offset such unintended costs. The practical question is, however, how far can we go in raising benefit levels before the unintended costs become unacceptably high? I am afraid, the answer is not as far as one might think and certainly not as far as most of us would wish. The costs that I have been discuss-

ing tend to rise at an increasing rate as a welfare system is liberalized, whereas the additional benefits tend to decrease. Imagine the effect of tripling the average AFDC payment not in Mississippi but in New York. An increase like that would not greatly reduce suffering because the payment level in New York is already high enough to prevent extreme suffering. On the other hand, hundreds of thousands of people would probably take some of the socially undesirable steps that I have listed if an average family on welfare were assured a monthly income of $1,000 rather than $300.

Swamping the System

These considerations are sufficient to justify the conclusion that benefit levels ought not to be allowed to rise as high as generosity, or guilt, might prompt. Another consideration tends almost as strongly in the same direction. A high benefit level will tend to swamp the system by increasing the demand for welfare. Those who decide about the funding of a system naturally base their decisions on estimates of the number of persons who will be eligible and will apply for benefits under its terms. Characteristically they underestimate these numbers seriously. They fail to realize that the substantial increase of benefits may induce many people to take steps —often simple ones that do not constitute "chiseling" by any stretch of the imagination (e.g., ceasing to work overtime)—to reduce their incomes enough to make themselves eligible. They tend to assume that the percentage of eligibles actually applying will be no greater in the future than in the past. As a result of these errors, the demand for welfare frequently exceeds the amount of funds available to meet it and a "crisis" exists. Obviously the "crisis" could eventually be met by increasing appropriations *if* benefit levels were not allowed to rise further. In practice, however, they are allowed to rise, perhaps at an even faster rate than appropriations, and so the "crisis" grows. Eventually, of course, the taxpayer will put his foot down, for there must be some limit to the number of persons he is willing to support, or that he *can* support. When he does put it down, the number of persons eligible and applying for benefits will still exceed the available funds but it will no longer be possible to increase appropriations (the taxpayer having finally concluded that generosity to the poor only increases their numbers) and a real crisis—the swamping of the system—will have occurred.

I conclude that *no* welfare system can be satisfactory. A system that provides a high level of support for all who are by some reasonable definition poor will *ipso facto* offer powerful incentives that will induce a great many people to become (or pretend to become) poor in order to qualify for benefits and will in the process give rise to intolerable side effects of the kinds that I have mentioned. On the other hand, a system that does *not* offer incentives powerful enough to produce these effects will *ipso facto* not provide generously, or even adequately, for the poor. There is no way out of this bind. One must make a choice among evils.

Two Lesser Evils

Two possibilities, each with some claim to being the least among evils, recommend themselves. One is to replace all assistance programs with a negative income tax. The other is to make *everyone*, whether employed or not, whose income is below standard, eligible for the equivalent of AFDC. Either arrangement would much reduce the incentive now being given to break up families, and either would give the welfare recipient some incentives to increase his income by working.

Perhaps the greatest advantage of the NIT is that it would not require a horde of social workers to operate it. This would not be all net gain, however, for the Internal Revenue Bureau would probably have to employ a great many social workers under another name in order to keep cheating within tolerable limits. Moreover, on certain assumptions a welfare bureaucracy may be a good thing. In bringing knowledge about the special circumstances of particular cases to bear upon decisions as to which of the poor are to receive assistance, it could perform an invaluable function. By distinguishing the technically poor—that is, those eligible only because they have taken steps to become so—from the really poor such a bureaucracy could check the production of side effects of the sorts that I listed above. And, by keeping the effective demand for benefits within manageable bounds, it could also make feasible higher payment levels than could otherwise be allowed without swamping the system. By contrast, the NIT being almost automatic in its operation, could not distinguish between the technically poor and the really poor and would therefore, if grave injury to the society were to be avoided, have to have rates so low as to be deemed seriously inadequate by many well-meaning people who have not fully considered the costs and benefits involved.

There would be no "welfare crisis" if welfare were regarded as still being for the purpose for which it was originally intended—helping those poor people who, because of unemployment or other causes beyond their control, are *temporarily* in need. Instead, welfare has gradually come to be regarded as a means of bringing about a more nearly equal distribution of income. The question has to be faced whether it is a fit instrument for its purpose. There are, of course, numerous other ways of redistributing income, and a rational policy would use them in combination. The experience of recent years demonstrates welfare cannot *in and of itself* constitute a satisfactory answer to the problem of income redistribution. . . .

11. The Educational Dilemma: Empty Tills, Community Control and Quality Education

Education is frequently put forward as a panacea for all of America's social ills. In the past, much of this faith has been justified. A public school diploma was supposed to be the great leveller, that equalized economic opportunity and provided a common cultural base. Despite the billions of dollars spent on public education today, evidence mounts that slum children are not being educated in their schools to enter the mainstream of American life. In fact, ghetto schools are a mirror that reflects slum crowding and decay.

The Ghetto School

Ghetto schools are overcrowded and old. For the most part, the teaching faculty is made up of inexperienced and marginal teachers who try to escape at the first opportunity. This teacher turnover is matched by student turnover. All of the ghetto culture seeps into corridors of the slum school—violence, family instability, emotional disturbances, vice, and the general disorganization, clutter and turmoil.

Centralization vs. Decentralization

Until very recently the whole trend in public education was toward centralization. School funding steadily shifted from local tax units to the city or state. A similar pattern of decision-making emerged, with most policies being fixed by regional or state boards, rather than by local districts. The neighborhood school had largely lost its identification with its community.

Recent years have witnessed a demand for restoration of the neighborhood school. Dissident ghetto residents, teachers and social workers declare that the prevailing middle-class curriculum has little relevance for the ghetto child. The all-white, tidy neighborhood of the Dick and Jane series, according to the critics, is far removed from the world of the slum child. The Bedford-Stuyvesant first-grader brings to school a far different cultural background and skills than does the child from upper-middle-class Scarsdale. Quite possibly, if he comes from Spanish Harlem, his English is only a second language. A standardized curriculum in the midst of this diversity is ridiculous, say the critics.

If something approaching local automony is granted to neighborhood schools, however, other problems arise. Slum neighborhoods have a low tax base. If the city or state becomes a minor voice in local school matters, why should it finance the operation? If the curriculum is hand tailored for the chicano section of San Antonio, have we not locked another generation into the ghetto subculture?

Improving Ghetto Education

Ghetto education today is a failure when measured by any objective standards. An alarming number of students become dropouts, joining the ranks of the untrained. Those that graduate are several grades behind their suburban counterparts in terms of achievement. Segregation in the northern ghetto schools is far more rigid than in the Old South. Although most educators insist that smaller classes, more money and better classroom equipment will close the educational gap between slum and suburb, the skeptics are doubtful. It is true that many of our middle-class schools are working well. With their adequate tax base, a great deal of innovation and experimentation is going forward. But in our difficult schools, where major problems exist, a minimum amount of educational research is funded. We actually know very little about the learning process and only a budget approaching the percentage that industry spends on research will give us the necessary insight.

The recent Coleman Report suggests that school and teacher quality have their greatest impact on minority groups. If we infer that the slum family is something of an educational handicap, perhaps we should convert the ghetto school into a round-the-clock substitute for the family, that offers the services of a cafeteria, gymnasium, and classroom, while providing artistic, dramatic, and health facilities.

We may also want to make the school more accountable for its performance in teaching reading, math, and science. One radical suggestion would encourage business to teach basic skills in the schools, thereby introducing a competitive note into what has become a monopoly enterprise. Perhaps we should engage in school busing on a massive scale to break down racial barriers. (A list of possible educational experiments would run on for pages.)

We do know that in the past our public schools have been an important instrument in providing social and economic upward mobility. Today that instrument seems blunted. Yet, new ideas are needed if ghetto America is not to become a separate society.

PUBLIC SCHOOL 60:
SOUTH BRONX, U.S.A. *
DONALD MOFFITT
AND ART SEARS, JR.

Slum children have a far different experience in the public schools than do middle-class children. Ghetto schools are physically run down; they are overcrowded; they have inferior teachers; in the hallways profanity and obscenity and vandalism are commonplace. The children themselves often come from fatherless welfare homes that have little concern for the educational process. The communities have far more than their share of prostitutes, winos and drug addicts. Under these adverse conditions do the schools have any successes? What factors seem to promote education? Would more black male teachers improve the schools? Would more money change things noticeably? What happens to P.S. 60 graduates?

Public School 60 in the South Bronx is a slum school and it looks it.

---

* Reprinted from Donald Moffitt and Art Sears, Jr., "Kelly Street Blues," Wall Street Journal, January 16, 1969, by permission.

The windows of the big, dingy red-brick building are covered with heavy steel mesh to ward off stones and bricks and to discourage burglars, and the school is surrounded by a five-foot-high grillwork fence of black wrought iron. The concrete playground is littered with broken glass. A section of 12-foot-high chain link fence has been torn down and dragged onto the playground, where it provides an obstacle course for youngsters. Occasionally teachers find burned, gutted autos abandoned on the playground. On school days, the street in front of P.S. 60 is jammed with double-parked cars that belong to the teachers. They are afraid to park on side streets lest thieves strip their cars.

Grim as it is on the outside, however, P.S. 60's worst problems are in its classrooms. The school is overcrowded and lacking in teachers trained to meet the needs of slum children. "We don't have any 'special' problems," says Henry Schechtman, principal of P.S. 60. "We seem to have all the problems."

P.S. 60 is one of two elementary schools attended by the children who live in the 800 block of Kelly Street, which is part of a black ghetto that, in turn, lies inside a Puerto Rican ghetto. The student bodies of the two schools are almost entirely Negro or Puerto Rican, with a handful who are of Chinese ancestry. Whether a Kelly Street child attends P.S. 60 or P.S. 39, both a short walk from the 800 block, is determined by which side of the street he lives on. Either way, his educational experience is quite different from that of a typical white, middle-class child in the suburbs or even elsewhere in New York City.

The most obvious of the schools' problems is the ghetto culture in which they exist. The impoverished and often chaotic home lives of most Kelly Street children do little to prepare them for school or to sustain them once they are there.

Most Kelly Street families are on welfare. Many of the children were born out of wedlock, and many others have been deserted by their fathers. Few parents are willing or able to help their children with school work and only a handful exhibit any interest in the operation of the schools. School officials say the children tend to lack self-discipline, and often they suffer from deep emotional problems.

Community life scarcely compensates for the deficiencies in family relationships. Merely walking to school in the morning can be a jarring experience on Kelly Street. The children step out of their drab tenements and often must immediately pick their way around grizzled winos sleeping on the stoops of the buildings. Along the sidewalks, they wind through a maze of broken, discarded furniture stacked against overflowing garbage cans. They pass a few neighbors going to work, and they also pass narcotic addicts and prostitutes headed home after a long night.

High Turnover Rates

In strictly academic terms, a major problem is the lack of continuity in the educations of ghetto children. Families like those on Kelly Street tend to move frequently, seeking roomier quarters and lower rents or fleeing debts and other troubles. P.S. 39 has a student turnover rate of almost 30% a year, and at P.S. 60 it's closer to 50%.

"It's tragic," says Mr. Schechtman of P.S. 60. "You begin working with children, and before you can achieve anything they're gone. They're in school one day, the next day they're gone."

Isidore Greenberg, principal of P.S. 39, says it isn't uncommon for a fifth or sixth grader there to have attended as many as 12 schools. The results are apparent in the findings of a study conducted recently by Seymour J. Perlin, an assistant principal at P.S. 39. He found that sixth-grade children who have been at P.S. 39 five or more years can read at a 6.4 level (sixth grade, fourth month), only two months behind the citywide average of 6.6. But those who have been in two to four different schools have an average reading level of 4.8, and those who have attended five or more schools read at a 3.6 level.

To compensate for such deficiencies, teachers at both schools devote an unusually large part of their time to reading drills, sometimes at the expense of subjects such as history or science. "Everything we do, we try to hit that reading," says P.S. 60's Mr. Schechtman. "I don't care how my teachers get through to the children—using comics or whatever. We stress trying to close the reading gap."

Thwarted By Overcrowding

Such efforts are often thwarted, however, by the overcrowding at both schools. Six years ago P.S. 60 was converted from a junior high to an elementary school. Its student body was transferred from three other schools. P.S. 39 contributed about 400 students, dropping its own enrollment to a comfortable 1,400.

But now, says Principal Greenberg, enrollment at P.S. 39 is back up to 1,600. The school's 260 first graders are on double shifts, and Mr. Greenberg figures there's a critical need for at least four additional classrooms—which, he says, aren't likely to be built.

At P.S. 60, which has 1,850 students, double shifts have been avoided by using some rooms not originally intended as classrooms. Some classes are held in rooms that are smaller than standard classroom size, including teachers' lunch rooms, and a music room and an art studio have been converted to classrooms. That leaves only one music room and no art room.

An old gymnasium at P.S. 60 has been converted into three classrooms. There is another gym in the building, but Principal Schechtman says it is situated in a wing that's so far from some classrooms that many children aren't sent to gym classes.

To help children with nonacademic problems, P.S. 60 has a part-time social worker, a part-time psychologist and guidance counselors. P.S. 39 also has a small stable of counseling experts.

But the numbers of emotionally disturbed children overwhelm the schools' staffs, particularly at P.S. 60. It has 90 pupils, or 5% of the student body, who are classified as mentally disturbed or maladjusted and "don't fit into our regular classes," says Mr. Schechtman. Nonetheless, he adds, most of them are in the regular classes because no other facilities are available.

One such problem child is a 12-year-old boy who has been designated by the board of education for admission to a school for aphasics —persons whose ability to speak has been impaired by brain lesions. But the boy is still at P.S. 60 because the special school is overcrowded. "We simply aren't geared to help children like this," says Mr. Schechtman.

One nine-year-old boy from Kelly Street, attending P.S. 60, habitually exposes his genitals in the classroom and pulls up the dresses of girls. He also has slapped a teacher. A reporter visiting the school watches as the boy, crying loudly, pulls away from an assistant principal who is trying to lead him down a hall. The boy runs down the hall and then, reaching a set of doors, turns and screams: "Bastard! Bastard! Bastard!"

Normal Hallway Din

"We have several disturbed children who don't do any schoolwork," says Mr. Schechtman. "One boy sits in classes and works on puzzles or plays with educational games."

Profanity and obscenity are part of the normal hallway din at P.S. 39 and P.S. 60. Even the youngest children are often proficient at swearing. A school aide at P.S. 60, one of several neighborhood women employed at the schools to help teachers and assist in keeping order, says of her charges: "Sometimes I have to remind myself the kids are not mine so I don't smack them. They curse and swear. One kid in kindergarten is a bully, always holding other kids down. When I make him get off, he calls me all kinds of dirty names."

Only a handful of the regular teachers at P.S. 39 and P.S. 60 live in the neighborhood they serve. They commute from suburban Westchester or Rockland Counties or from other areas of New York City. Most are white; of the 170 teachers at the two schools, only 14 are Negro and only five are Puerto Rican. Neither school has any black or Puerto Rican administrators.

More Male Teachers

Many of the teachers are young and relatively inexperienced, including a large complement of young men who have joined the staffs in recent years—many of them, according to some faculty members, because teachers are draft-exempt. An older woman teacher at P.S. 60 notes that prior to the Vietnam war the school only had four male teachers and now it has 30. "Some day they'll be moving to something else as soon as the war ends," she says.

Both P.S. 60 and P.S. 39 provide hot lunches for students. For children whose families are on welfare —which includes all but a few of the schools' pupils—the lunches are free; sometimes they are the only balanced meals the children receive. "We used to find kids slipping in for lunch from as far away as Harlem," says Mr. Schechtman of P.S. 60, "so we began issuing lunch tickets to our children."

Both schools suffered losses to thieves and vandals during the nearly six weeks last fall when New York City schools were disrupted by a strike of teachers. At P.S. 60, for example, thieves stole thousands of dollars worth of television sets, phonographs, tape recorders and other equipment. Hundreds of windows were broken by vandals despite the heavy mesh screens, and many are still boarded up.

Little Parental Interest

Mr. Schechtman and Mr. Greenberg say they have little contact with parents in the area, though some community groups such as the Kelly Street Block Association take an active interest in school affairs. One indication of the lack of parental interest: During the teachers' strike, the block association had to pay parents to persuade them to help keep the school open and at least partly in operation.

There are, however, a few parents who are fiercely determined that their children will receive adequate educations. "Even when you're on welfare," says Mrs. Betty Alston, a mother of three, "there isn't any reason in the world not to get your children educated. It doesn't cost you a penny." Her own children are industrious students, and when they come home they often play chess or peruse the stacks of paperback books Mrs. Alston has collected.

Another Kelly Street mother became so incensed at the teachers' strike last fall that she called the Board of Education and demanded that a tutor be sent to teach her daughter. She got her wish: Her daughter and neighbor boy met daily with a teacher to do their lessons at a public library.

After they complete elementary school, the children of Kelly Street attend one of two junior high schools that serve the area. There are no high schools in the immediate neighborhood; depending on their interests and abilities, students attend vocational or academically oriented high schools scattered throughout the city.

Many Become Dropouts

Though no statistics are available, it's apparent from conversations with Kelly Street residents that only a minority of their children ever complete high school. "Children on a block like this learn at a very early age by their environment that they're not going to get very far in life, so they don't try hard," contends Peter J. Akam, an African-born Negro who holds a master's degree in economics and has lived on Kelly Street for seven years.

Few of the dropouts wind up in job-training or other compensatory programs, though such opportunities are available on Kelly Street through the welfare department or the block association.

A few adults on Kelly Street, most of them dropouts themselves, are now trying to further their own educations. One mother of nine, who receives welfare, has nearly completed studies to receive her high school equivalency diploma. Another welfare mother is taking a secretarial course she hopes will enable her to get a job.

THE CASE FOR
LOCAL CONTROL *
KENNETH W. HASKINS

Opponents of community control of schools express concern over the probability that standards will decline, segregation will be encouraged, and local leaders will lack an understanding of modern educational goals. On the other hand, Mr. Haskins contends that this proposal has great promise. Why does he believe that school conditions will be improved? How will a community school reduce social problems? Is the possibility of radical control a real danger? Has traditional school organization failed in the ghetto?

Community control means only one thing: the public institutions that serve a particular community should be controlled by it. In education this movement has grown out of the failure of existing institutions to meet the needs of the children of the black community.

* *Reprinted from Kenneth W. Haskins, "The Case for Local Control," Saturday Review, January 11, 1969 by permission of The Saturday Review, Inc. and the author. Copyright © 1969 by The Saturday Review, Inc. A special issue produced in cooperation with The Committee For Economic Development.*

The term "racism" is often used in discussions of community control, and people recoil from it. But racism doesn't always mean racism of, say, the George Wallace type. It means, for example, that a public school system that fails poor black children can be tolerated, while a public school system that fails white middle-class children cannot. The black community, therefore, has decided that it has to make the decisions about what can and cannot be tolerated for its children because society as a whole has largely failed the black community in this respect.

I am the principal of the Morgan Community School in Washington, D.C., a school that is now community controlled. Four years ago, before I came, the school had four classes in the auditorium. It is a very old building, and the auditorium was the only extra facility. Parents could no longer register their children in kindergarten because it was overcrowded, and the first, second, and third grades were on half-day sessions. Textbooks were poor and in bad condition, and the school had very little equipment. It wasn't until the parents really got concerned and organized that things began to change.

If a community school is to have any meaning, it must take its character from the nature of the people living in the community and from the children utilizing the school—rather than rigidly defining itself as an institution that accepts only those people who fit into a preconceived definition. This would mean that there would be a minimum of social problems in the school because what is socially acceptable in the community would be worked with and tolerated within the school setting. Such terms as "uneducable" or "unteachable" must be separated from forms of social behavior.

For example: I live in a community where children fight in the street. It doesn't bother me particularly; that is the way they get their reputations. I grew up in the same kind of neighborhood, and I don't believe that children who fight at the age of five, six, or seven necessarily grow up to be criminals. But because there are a few middle-class children in my school whose parents don't want their children exposed to fighting, should I call every child who fights a criminal and force him into a pattern of conformity that is alien to him? If the child is not a problem at home or in the community, but he fights in school, should I consider the fighting in itself a problem? If so, I become obligated to solve it, and that usually means calling in a psychologist and giving the child labels such as "emotionally disturbed" or "aggressive." This gives the school ammunition to push the child further away.

I have found that once you stop fighting with children about fighting, the incidence of fighting diminishes because you no longer have teachers and students acting like prison guards and inmates. You don't condone fighting, but you don't stop it simply because some-one labels it a problem; you stop it because young people should be taught that there are better ways of handling social relationships.

In a sense, schools should relate to the people who use them in much the same way that any other producer relates to a consumer. I would like to see schools in Spanish-speaking neighborhoods be forced, because of their relationship to the community, to put up signs saying SE HABLA ESPAÑOL as quickly as every store in the community had to put up one in order to stay in business. I have seen stores do this in one or two days, but schools spend fifteen years in a Spanish-speaking neighborhood without one Spanish-speaking teacher in the school. The teachers merely speak English louder, and the louder they talk the less the pupils understand them—so the more ignorant the pupils are.

When you talk about community control, questions are always raised about who is asking for control—about making certain that the militants don't take over. The people of the black community can take care of their own militants. They really don't need anybody else to define for them who are militants, particularly not those who three or four years ago were calling Roy Wilkins a militant. People learn by their mistakes. The right to vote means that you can vote again in two or three years; if someone doesn't represent you, you can get rid of him. You don't need people from outside to make definitions and selections for you, unless, of course, you really feel you are not capable of making decisions for yourself.

A lawyer recently told me that we were extralegal. Now he might be right. But I am talking about black people in this country. And in the 1800's if someone had been teaching me how to read and write, that would have been extralegal. Extralegal means one thing for people who are afraid of breaking the law because they have something to lose, and another for those who don't. What does it mean if I am extralegal? Are they going to put me in jail? What sort of crime is it when people are trying to educate their children in a way that somehow doesn't fit with the organic law of 1906?

The community-control movement is irreversible, and I think it is time for people to recognize this. I say this not as a threat but because I am part of the movement and I wouldn't know how to stop it if I wanted to. So if industry has something to offer the movement, it should offer it to the parents. And if the educators have something to sell, they should learn how to talk to the people who are buying. It makes very little sense for school superintendents to talk among themselves about "cognition" and things they can't even define in their own circles when they should be talking to the parents.

Despite the fact that community control is moving with such force, no community has yet achieved the degree of control that it needs to make the movement succeed. Yet the success—and failure—of community control is already being discussed. Community control has emerged not because of the great promise that it holds for the education of black children, but because of the failure of what has taken place so far.

INEQUITIES OF SCHOOL FINANCE *

ALAN K. CAMPBELL

Very little relationship exists between educational needs and the tax base. Inner cities depend largely on property values that are stationary or declining. Although it costs more to educate a slum child properly, the funds for his education are less. National and state aid is allocated in a manner that discriminates against central city schools.

* *Reprinted from Alan K. Campbell, "Inequities of School Finance," Saturday Review, January 11, 1969, by permission of The Saturday Review, Inc. and the author. A special issue produced in cooperation with the Committee for Economic Development. Copyright © 1969 by The Saturday Review, Inc.*

What relationship exists between population shifts and the tax base? Where is industrial and personal wealth increasingly apt to be found? In relationship to their tax resources, which government spends most on education? Which local governments get the least federal aid? Is it politically possible to favor inner city children by giving their schools the highest per capita allocation of state and federal funds?

Throughout its history this nation has stressed education as the primary means of guaranteeing every citizen an equal chance at obtaining the rewards of an open society. If educational opportunities are unequal, then the American experiment in equality of opportunity must fail. The evidence indicates that we are indeed failing. Nor is there any strong indication that we are about to correct this failure.

It is possible, of course, to read the evidence differently. The proportion of national income devoted to education is increasing, as is the proportion of total public expenditure for education. But these favorable trends do not overcome one of the fundamental weaknesses of our educational system—the basic mismatch between inadequate educational resources and great educational needs. This inequality is the result of an allocation system which provides more resources for educating the suburban child than

the city child. Such differences would make sense, if it were easier to educate the city child than the suburban child. Just the opposite, of course, is the case.

The problem of matching resources to needs in education was created by a redistribution of population in the United States. The result has been that poor, less educated, non-white Americans are staying in the central cities, while higher-income, white families, and a substantial part of the industrial sector are moving to the suburbs and taking their tax base with them. This phenomenon varies with the size of the metropolitan area and the region of the country, but it applies with force to most large metropolitan areas.

While this shift in population was occurring, research studies were demonstrating that the single best indicator of educational achievement is the family background of the pupil. Thus, it was made clear that a lower-income city student was at a significant educational disadvantage when compared to a more affluent student in a suburban community. Further, it became apparent that educational programs were essentially designed by middle-income people for middle-income students. Educational materials are full of examples and illustrations drawn from the life of the suburban middle class. Teachers are recruited largely from the middle-income stratum and are trained in schools of education and liberal arts colleges by faculty members who come from this same background.

All of this demonstrates that present personnel and educational practices are not equal to the needs of the city child. Curricula must be revised, teacher-training changed, and teaching methods adjusted to his needs. To do all these things will require new and massive resources. Small incremental differences will not do the job.

Despite the obvious need for more resources in city schools, we are spending less—any way you measure it—in the cities than in the suburbs. For the thirty-seven largest U.S. metropolitan areas, the average per capita expenditure for education in the central cities is $82; the same expenditure in the suburbs is $113. On a per student basis, the comparable figures are $449 for the cities and $573 for the suburbs. These figures would not be so startling if the gap between city and suburb appeared to be closing. It is widening, however. To compete with the suburbs, central cities must have a resource advantage. Yet, the present system of resource allocation clearly discriminates against the city. Why?

Because of educational difficulties in many central-city schools, experienced teachers seek assignments in the so-called "better" schools within the city system; many abandon the central city entirely for more attractive suburban districts. Schools are older, and site costs for new buildings are higher in the city than in the suburbs.

Moreover, the pressure for other public services—police protection, welfare, and the like—is greater in the city.

To a large extent, it is the available income which influences the ability of a governmental unit to meet the service requirements of its population. Central cities are losing ground in this respect, while their functional needs are increasing simultaneously. As part of the metropolitan pattern, economic activities are becoming decentralized, moving from the core city to the surrounding areas and weakening the central-city tax base in the process. An examination of the central cities of twelve large metropolitan areas demonstrates that the proportion of manufacturing compared to that of suburban areas has clearly declined over the past three decades, especially in the post-World War II period. In 1929, these twelve cities accounted, on the average, for 66 percent of manufacturing employment. This percentage decreased to 61 percent by 1947, dropped to 49 percent by 1958, and has since declined even further.

As industries continue to move outward, taxable assessed valuation —the source of local property taxes —has barely held its own in many localities and has actually declined in several large cities. For example, in a recent five-year period, the percentage changes in taxable assessed valuation for seven cities were: Baltimore, —11 percent; Boston, —1 percent; Buffalo, —1 percent;

Detroit, −2 percent; St. Louis, +1 percent; Philadelphia, +3 percent; and Cleveland, −3 percent.

Translated into educational terms, the tax base in large cities has not kept pace with the recent growth and changing nature of the school population in these cities. Indeed, an examination of the per pupil taxable assessed valuation over a five-year period shows that ten large cities out of fourteen experienced a decrease in this source of revenue. Since local property taxes are the major source of local educational revenues, large city schools can barely meet ordinary education needs, let alone resolve problems resulting from shifting population patterns. Complicating the picture is the burden which non-educational services place on the tax bases of central cities. Non-educational expenditures constitute 68 percent of total public expenditures in the central cities of the thirty-seven largest metropolitan areas. The comparable percentage for the suburbs is only 47 percent. Accordingly, the distribution of needs and resources creates heavier total local tax burdens in cities than in suburbs. Measured against personal income, local taxes constitute 8 percent of that income in cities and only 6 percent in suburbs, or a one-third greater burden on city taxpayers.

One of the means by which the American fiscal system can overcome such disparities is intergovernmental aid. By this device, aid should flow from areas of greater than average resources to areas of greater than average need. Until recently, state and federal aid systems for education worked just that way. It took resources from centers of wealth, the cities, and provided it to the less affluent rural areas. But today, the aid system does not allocate resources relative to need, whether measured as total need or for education alone. Most revealing about the present fiscal system is the failure of aid, either state or federal, to fill the gap left by the unequal distribution of local resources available. For example, state and federal aid supports 27 percent of public expenditures in central cities, while supporting 29 percent of those in suburban areas, and 37 percent of all local expenditures in the rest of the nation. Considered as a proportion of local tax effort, federal and state aid represents only 44 percent of central-city taxes; the comparable figure for suburbia is 53 percent, and for the rest of the nation, 74 percent.

It may be that the single greatest failure of the aid system is in the field of education. State education formulas provide substantially greater aid to suburban districts than to city districts. Completely current data is impossible to obtain, but in 1962, per capita education aid in the central cities was $20.73, while in the suburban areas it was $37.66. On a per student basis the gap is equally dramatic, as shown by data for New York State. In New York State's six metropolitan areas during the school year 1966–67, the average difference between educational aid to the central cities and that to the school districts in the rest of the counties in which the central cities were located was more than $100 per pupil. Recently enacted federal education aid programs may help to close the gap between city and suburb, but thus far the funds involved are painfully insufficient. Is there any evidence that this allocation pattern will be corrected?

The disparities certainly cannot be overcome by increased local tax effort; the fiscal bind in which most cities find themselves is well known. And the behavior of city school boards does not indicate any sweeping changes in the allocation of resources. Nor is there much evidence that states are likely to provide greater assistance for their cities. The states have the power to assume functions which are performed locally. They could adapt their aid systems to current metropolitan patterns, and they could adjust the boundaries of local government accordingly. However, these powers and responsibilities have been exercised sparingly, if at all. The former bias of state legislatures in favor of rural areas seems to have been translated by reapportionment into a bias in favor of suburban areas.

There has been much controversy and uncertainty about how educational disadvantage can be overcome. But one thing is clear, it cannot be done cheaply. Whether the answer is integration, compensatory education, community control, more private schools, or some combination of these and other approaches, the cost will be high. To substitute educational experimentation and innovation for increased resources is to sentence those experiments to failure.

Further, the educational problems now found in cities are becoming increasingly apparent in some suburban areas. As more and more people move to suburbia, communities are being created with many central-city characteristics. Tax burdens are high, educational disadvantage is growing, and political resistance to applying increased local resources to education is on the rise. Unless major breakthroughs in central city education are made soon, the same problems will spread throughout metropolitan areas.

The present allocation of resources may match the distribution of political power in American society; but it does not match the distribution of need. If we are to make breakthroughs, it must.

THE REJUVENATION OF URBAN EDUCATION *

JAMES E. ALLEN, JR.

Dr. James E. Allen, Jr. served as U.S. Commissioner of Education during the early Nixon years. His appointment was widely hailed as a promise of new leadership at the national level.

In the interview that follows he touches on nearly every aspect of contemporary urban education. How does he evaluate the quality of current education? What does he propose regarding school finance? Why is urban education an especially difficult area? What role should parents have? Is desegregation a valid goal? What is the real value of busing?

Q Dr. Allen, what kind of job are American schools doing today— good or bad?

A I think the American schools, by and large, are doing a very good job. When you compare school achievement statistically, you find:

A generation ago, the average length of time that a person went

* Reprinted from *James E. Allen, Jr.,* *"Crisis In City Schools,"* U. S. News & World Report, *June 30, 1969,* *Copyright © 1969 by U. S. News & World Report, Inc.*

to school was only eight years, and now it is 12 years. The number of Americans who go on to college has more than tripled since 1946. Only about 1 in 5 persons of college age was in college in 1946; today it's 1 in 2. A generation ago, only about 50 percent of our teachers had bachelor's degrees; today, virtually all of them do—about 96 percent, I believe.

Also, looking at the intellectual and social interests and activities of our young people, the questions they are raising and so on—these, in my judgment, are indications that the schools are doing a good job.

Now, obviously, the expectations of society for education are far greater today than they were a generation ago. We are now trying to educate everybody, to reject no one. And we're finding that for many young people, the traditional educational system does not do a good job.

To this degree, there would appear to be some substantial failures. But I look upon this not so much as a failure of the educational system as a failure of our society to provide adequate educational opportunities for large numbers who have been neglected or have suffered deprivations or discrimination of various kinds.

In terms of the dimensions of the task that we have to do, I would say that the American schools are doing a good job.

Q Better than in the past, do you think?

A It's difficult to compare it with

past years, because we have a different society today. I recall a few years ago in New York State we gave that year's graduating class the Regent's examinations that had been given 50 years ago—and the students of that year did much better on those same examinations than the students of 50 years back.

In other words, schools today are doing better at teaching the kind of knowledge that was expected 50 years ago.

But, again, if you make your comparison in terms of what the people expect of the schools today, we have a long way to go to do as good a job as needs to be done.

Q What, most of all, needs to be done to improve schools?

A I think that many things need to be done:

One is that we need to develop a kind of nationwide strategy for the improvement of education. We need more money for research to find out how to teach children better. In business, you set aside 10 percent or more for research and development. I'm told that less than one half of 1 percent of the 60 billion dollars we spend annually for education in this country goes for research and development. And education is big business.

We need to bring together in a better way than we do now the information we already have about better ways of education, and to disseminate that information more widely through our educational system. Furthering research in education and disseminating information are things in which I think the U. S.

Office of Education could be very helpful.

Also, I think we need to enlist more outside help in education—business help, for example. I don't think we've begun to tap the potential of business enterprise for help in making our educational system more effective.

We need to do a better job of training and retraining teachers—particularly retraining. A large proportion of our teachers were prepared for a kind of school system that is quite different from that in which they now find themselves. This is especially true with respect to dealing with new approaches and concepts related to the needs of the disadvantaged.

We also need to make better use of the technology that is available today—technology that can enable us to learn much more about a student through computers and other measurement systems and to apply the school programs more effectively to meet the needs of each individual.

What we really need to do, to sum it all up, is to make our advanced methods more available to all our schools.

Q Is this going to require the setting of federal standards for education.

A No, I don't think it is at all. If you mean uniform standards laid down at the federal level, I would not like to see that.

I do believe, however, that the Federal Government has the obligation to insist upon high standards, and to encourage and help every State and locality to maintain them. The setting of standards and their enforcement, however, is a State and local responsibility, and it is up to the people to hold their school officials accountable for achieving high standards.

Q One hears a lot of criticism about big-city schools. Are they really worse than rural schools?

A Some of the best schools we have are in the cities. New York City, for example, has some outstanding schools—though New York schools vary.

But the problem is not solely the quality of the school. It's the students they have to educate. If students come to school from home well prepared, it's much easier for the school to teach them. But if they come from families—or from lack of families—where they do not have the advantages of home preparation for schools, then the problem of teaching them is more difficult.

Many of our children who are behind in reading come from homes where education was not regarded as important, or at least where the parents were not able to provide the kind of help and atmosphere that you find in the middle-class or upper-middle-class homes. They arrive at school with great disadvantages. And in school they are faced with a whole new world. Some of them have never had books before. The teachers speak a language they've never heard before —or a different type of language, at any rate. These are some of the things that such children have to

overcome in order to take advantage of what the school has to offer.

So it isn't entirely a question of the schools failing in the cities. I think it's society failing to provide the educational opportunities for those children who have not had the kinds of opportunities that children in other schools have had.

Q Is more money the answer for these city schools?

A More money is only part of the answer. I think that we are going to have to help these school systems renew themselves—give them the kind of expertise, technical assistance and encouragement to make the changes that are needed.

I am not at all sure that the school as we have thought of it in the past—a four-walled building with a lot of egg-crate-like classrooms—is any longer the proper educational instrument for the inner cities.

It may be that a different kind of school—a sort of educational center—is needed, where some students may remain in school for longer than the traditional hours, where they are given all kinds of help—nutrition, health services and so on—and parents are brought in to work with them.

Other youngsters may achieve more by studying on their own, out of school—working in libraries, art centers, with businesses or in other situations better suited to their needs and abilities.

Q Would you do this in the earlier grades of school?

A No. I would begin it later on. But even in the early grades, I think there can be a great deal more diversity and flexibility.

Q How many hours a day would you have the school take over a youngster who is hard to educate?

A This is a question that would have to be worked out with the parents and the school people. Right now, more and more schools are staying open afternoons for special remedial programs. Some are opening schools in the evening, so that students who want to can go back.

Q Would these longer hours be optional, or would you tell some children that they have to go to school longer than other children?

A I don't think you would want to order anybody. This would be a question to be worked out among teachers, pupils and parents.

In other words, the school should find out what each child needs, and then shape an educational program especially suited to him. And, wherever possible, his parents should be involved, so they can understand what is taking place and why.

Q Wouldn't such a system be much more expensive?

A Yes, it would probably be more expensive—but not in terms of the results that could be obtained. What we're after is the best possible education of each individual. You can't think just in terms of a group, which is what we've been doing to too large an extent.

Q What other changes would you suggest in schools?

A We need changes to make our schooling more relevant—to use a word that is too much used these days.

A great part of our educational system—and this is true especially at the college level, as the students are reminding us—seems to give both young people and society a feeling that the schools are really preparing students for the world of the past more than for the world of the future.

So I think we need changes in programs, as well as in techniques in many school systems. But you have to leave this to the local community, by and large, and then make the resources available to them so that they can make changes. I believe very strongly that you get better schools by a diversified approach. It is important for all communities to experiment, to evaluate their schools in terms of the quality and the relevance of their efforts.

Q In many cities we find a growing demand for what is called decentralization of schools—breaking up the citywide system into smaller districts under "local" or neighborhood school boards. Is this a part of the change that you are suggesting?

A In some cases, it may be. I have been active, as you know, in seeking decentralization in New York City. I believe that this is a proper approach to problems there. I am not ready to say that this should be the pattern for every other city—not developed in the same way, at any rate.

But I am convinced that the best schools are those where parents and other local people can have and take a real interest in what is being taught, and how.

In a school system as large as New York City's, with more than a million pupils, this lack of a say by parents is one of the things that have brought about so much unrest. Parents see their children coming home unable to read, but they find it very difficult to make any change in the system in order to correct such a deficiency, because they have to go through a large, bureaucratic organization where everything is handled at the center.

Q Aren't those parents who send their children to school unprepared for education the same parents who would be given control over the neighborhood schools by a system of decentralization?

A I am not speaking of control in the sense of turning the whole system over to them. They shouldn't have power to assume professional duties. And I think protection has to be provided to insure that the teachers who are employed are the best available for the children to be taught.

But city parents should have authority to make some decisions— as people do in suburban communities—about what things the school should teach and how they should be operated and managed.

When I say that some parents don't prepare their children for school, I don't mean that it's a case of the parents not wanting to do so. In many cases the parents simply cannot, because of circum- stances. I believe that inner-city parents who have not had the kind of advantages that suburban parents have had would nonetheless accept responsibility for helping to direct their schools if given the chance. They want good schools. They want their children to learn.

Q Is there a problem in finding the right kinds of teachers for schools in "ghetto" areas?

A There is that problem. Some teachers in "ghetto" schools are really not prepared to teach the kind of student who attends those schools. Most teachers have middle-class backgrounds. They often don't understand the culture of the community. Some do not really believe that poor children or black children can learn. Of course, the child quickly becomes aware of this, as do the parents, and the child loses his motivation. We all know that when the teacher has faith in the child's ability to learn, and lets the child know this, the child is far more likely to learn.

Q How effective are programs of compensatory education for disadvantaged children?

A In general, I think they are necessary and helpful. Despite some well-founded criticism, Head Start, for example—the preschool training of small children—is an excellent program. Other good compensatory programs include the "More Effective Schools" in several of our cities. Ineffectiveness in such programs is usually due to poor planning and lack of adequately prepared teachers.

I think these compensatory programs should be enlarged. But, more importantly, I think the need to improve the quality of education from the very beginning—from early childhood—and then continue that improvement all the way through the educational system so that it will become unnecessary to have these large programs of remedial action.

Q When you say from early childhood, do you mean as early as age 2 or 3?

A That's right. This is being done in some communities now. And we know that young people at a very early age can learn a lot more than we once thought they could.

. . .

Q Do you favor cross-busing for . . . integration?

A Busing is a means to an end, and the end is a better education for all children. The only real justification for busing is to get a child safely to a better education than the one he otherwise might have. I happen to believe that an integrated situation is part of a good education. So I would say that if busing were the only way to bring about a good, integrated situation, then I would bus.

Q What is the educational advantage of having a mixture of black and white children in a school?

A It seems to me to be very important that children learn how to live together, respect each other, and not feel that they are in a particular school simply because they happen to be black or white.

Q If you cross-bus, aren't you sending a black child to a certain school because he is black, and a white child to another school because he is white? Isn't this actually assignment of pupils on a racial basis?

A Only as an incident of a larger purpose. Basically, you are making the assignment to overcome educational deficiencies that result from racial discrimination.

If a child is in a "ghetto" school where the neighborhood is all black and run-down, and the child knows that his chances in life are limited because of that situation, his motivation in school is going to be greatly impaired. If he gets into a school where he feels on a par with all other children, then I think his motivation for learning is going to be much greater.

Q What about the so-called neighborhood school, where children attend the school nearby—in their own neighborhood? Is this kind of school on the way out?

A I'm for the neighborhood school, believe me. But if the neighborhood school can't produce good education, if it is considered as exclusive for one race or creed, then I think that particular neighborhood-school area ought to be enlarged or changed to correct that situation.

Q When you were commissioner of education in the State of New York, didn't you suggest enlarging

city districts to include the predominantly white suburbs in order to get more integration?

A I think the people in the suburbs—many of whom left the cities and have helped to create the problems in the cities—have an obligation to help the cities find answers to their problems.

Q How could suburbs be compelled to do this?

A I would hope it could be done through a change in attitude, through more understanding. But if some people are not willing to face up to this kind of educational problem, then somebody must seek to protect the educational well-being of the children. And it seems to me it has to be the State.

The constitution of the State of New York, for example, says that the State shall provide equal educational opportunities for every boy and girl. And if it is true, as the courts and educators have said, that equal educational opportunity cannot be provided in separate setups, then the State has an obligation to try to correct this situation.

DEAD END IN
AMERICAN EDUCATION *
ROGER A. FREEMAN

In this article Mr. Freeman summarizes many of the reservations offered by critics of recent experimental educational programs. At what rate have educational expenditures increased in the past decade? What success have "compensatory programs" had? Do specially trained teachers and smaller classes make a difference? Does Head Start make a lasting impact? What success has New York City had with community schools? What conclusions regarding schools did the Coleman Report reach? What relationship exists between the parent's socio-economic level and pupil achievement? Why does Freeman advocate "Track" schools?

Certain basic assumptions that have long dominated the thinking of American educationists are now being increasingly called into question. Almost no one used to doubt that children learned more in direct proportion to additional inundations of a) money, b) teach-

* Reprinted from Roger A. Freeman, "Dead End In American Education," National Review, *January 14, 1969, by permission.*

ers, c) classrooms and d) integration: all appropriately nursed and coerced by the Federal Government since the states, naturally, could not be expected to be other than slightly Neanderthal. It now transpires, however, that since the passage of the "landmark" 1965 School Aid bill that was supposed to have favored disadvantaged children, not a shred of evidence has surfaced to support the contention that such children are helped by a, b, c, or d. Quite the contrary.

One must begin by comprehending the gigantic proportions of America's recent educational efforts. While the country's business and other private investment tripled over the past twenty years, investment in education increased eightfold, reaching about $52 billion in the school year 1967–68. Public school revenues account for more than half of that, having increased by more than 150 percent in the last decade. (Only a tenth of the increased funds came from the Federal Government.) Congress has passed forty major education laws in the last four years. It spent over $4 billion on education this year alone.

Under Title I of the 1965 bill, "compensatory" programs were set up across the country to help children who grew up in poor families, an attempt that was, I felt at the time, probably doomed to failure ("How to Railroad a School Bill," NR, May 18, 1965).

Three years have passed since that bill, time enough for signs of success or failure to have appeared: the signs have indicated, alas for the children involved, failure. The Associated Press conducted a nationwide survey of the program's results in May and found that both critics and supporters now agree that it is not working. "It is a monumental flop, and the outbreak of recent riots speaks louder than anything I can say about the total collapse of the program," said Rep. Roman Pucinski (D., Ill.), chairman of the House general subcommittee on education, and one of the bill's original sponsors. Said Assistant U.S. Commissioner of Education Joseph Fromkin: "We still have little evidence that the problem is being licked; in fact, we may even be falling behind." And Alice M. Rivlin, assistant secretary for program analysis at HEW: "I think we have found the task is much tougher than we thought at the start. . . .When it began, we really didn't know how to go about it. We still don't. . . ."

Professor Edmund Gordon, writing in the Winter 1966/67 issue of *College Board Review*, came to the astounding conclusion that "for all their variety the programs have generally suffered from one fundamental difficulty: they are based on sentiment rather than on facts." Actually, the programs were designed and authorized in the face of overwhelming evidence that they could not produce what their sponsors promised, and such evidence continues to pour in.

The U.S. Office of Education, in

its first reports on Title I in 1967, published a statistical table revealing that in nineteen tests ranging from reading comprehension to arithmetic the educational lag of participating children had been slightly reduced on ten tests but had actually increased on the other nine. Over all, the measurable advance was negligible, which was highly significant since three out of every four school districts in the United States were participating in Title I. The second-year report disclosed that the average disadvantaged child was farther behind national norms in reading and arithmetic *after* going through Title I programs than he had been before.

This did not come as a surprise to students of earlier compensatory programs. In 1959, New York City had initiated a Higher Horizons (HH) project involving 100,000 children in 76 grade and high schools, the most extensive undertaking of its type up to that time. HH was hailed as the solution to the problem of bringing underprivileged children up to the norm, was copied by dozens of school systems across the country, and served as a model for Title I. In 1965, however, the New York City Board of Education reluctantly made public the results of a report on the program, which concluded that HH had virtually no effect in improving education. Investigators had found "no significant differences between students in schools with the HH program and similarly situated students in schools without the program." HH was closed down.

New York subsequently initiated an even more generously endowed project called More Effective Schools (MES): in 21 grade schools class sizes were cut to between twelve and twenty pupils and annual per-pupil costs boosted to $1,263, about twice the regular amount. Senator Joseph Tydings declared that the program was a "remarkable example of what can be done in slum schools with small classes, special instruction services and striking teaching techniques; what can be done, in short, if the educational expenditures for ghetto schools are geared to the disproportionate needs of disadvantaged children." But a report on MES prepared by the Center for Urban Education at the request of the city Board of Education provided another big shock. The report (September 1967) noted an atmosphere of enthusiasm and hope and "a belief among all levels of staff that they were in a setting in which they could function." But it went on:

Equally clear are the data which indicate that the MES program has made no significant difference in the functioning of children, whether this was measured by observers rating what the children did in class, and how they do it, or whether it was measured by the children's ability in mathematics or reading on standardized tests. The data of this evaluation show that children in classes in MES schools were not behaving differently from children in classes in the officially designated control schools or in classes in other special service schools. *The achievement test data showed that the profiles of MES schools were no different from the profiles of these same schools before the program was instituted.* Moreover, the academic year gains which previous evaluations had noted were not maintained over the calendar year so that over all, in most grades after three years of MES, the retardation below the urban norms used for reading was no better, and in some cases, worse. [Italics added]

Similar endeavors in Syracuse, St. Louis, Berkeley, Seattle, Philadelphia and dozens of other cities proved equally ineffective. Large numbers of specially trained teachers, sharp reductions in class size, and large infusions of money had not helped. Even extending school hours didn't pay off: New York City's All-Day Neighborhood School program, for example, revealed no significant difference in achievement levels among the 7,000 economically deprived children participating.

Temporary Gains

If compensatory programs could raise lagging children to significant new levels of attainment and enable them to succeed in better-paid occupations, several billions of dollars annually would be a cheap price. Perhaps it is because of this feeling that the facts are so often ignored. In November 1967, the Urban Coalition recommended "concentrated compensatory pro-grams to equalize opportunities for achievement." The ten-year cost of such a program on an "adequate" national scale was estimated at $100 to $150 billion. This is roughly the equivalent of a national extension of New York's MES program. But what reason is there to believe that MES will prove more effective nationally than it did in New York?

Or consider Project Head Start, which aims at helping children from poor families to enter school on a par with children of more affluent parents. This was the most enthusiastically received of all the war on poverty programs: it had an almost irresistible emotional appeal, and was noncontroversial until recently. More than 600,000 children have participated each year for the past four years at a cost of more than $300 million annually. But while initial results showed an average gain of eight to ten points on I.Q. verbal tests, it soon became apparent that the gain was only temporary: it disappeared entirely within a few months. Studies by Dr. Gerald Alpern, director of the Research Child Psychiatry Services at Indiana University Medical School, Dr. Max Wolff of the New York Center for Urban Education, and others, found no lasting progress when Head Start children were compared with other control groups.

A recent report by the U.S. Commission on Civil Rights found that none of the many compensatory education programs "appear to have raised significantly the achievement of participating pupils" and noted that the programs tended to strengthen growing *de facto* racial segregation in the schools. The report stated that integration was an important factor in helping disadvantaged children, yet there is no evidence that racial mixing *per se* advances the measurable achievements of lagging children, *vide* the experience of PS 7 and PS 8 in Brooklyn, one black and one white. With the enthusiastic support of parents the schools were paired, whereupon the over-all educational level dropped, parental enthusiasm turned to panic, and within one year both schools were black.

Black children tend to be, on the average, several months behind whites when they enter school, and the discrepancy widens as they are promoted each year until at the beginning of the twelfth grade the average black child lags from three to six years behind national norms, no matter what sort of school he has been attending.

Nevertheless, in order to prove that such differences are largely the result of inferior schools, the U.S. Office of Education in 1965 sponsored the most extensive study of the subject ever undertaken. Headed by James S. Coleman of Johns Hopkins University, it covered 4,000 schools with 600,000 children in grades one through twelve. To almost everyone's surprise, the Coleman report showed that the differences in the physical and economic resources of schools attended by Negro children and by

white children are not significant: "The evidence revealed that within broad geographic regions, and for each racial and ethnic group, the physical and economic resources going into a school had very little relationship to the achievements coming out of it. . . . If it were otherwise, we could give simple prescriptions: increase teachers' salaries, lower classroom size, enlarge libraries, and so on. But the evidence does not allow such simple answers." Among the specific findings of the report was the startling datum that pupil-teacher ratios "showed a consistent lack of relation to achievements among all groups under all conditions." (Again, this should really have come as no shock. The *Encyclopedia of Educational Research* of 1950 summarized more than 200 studies of class size, concluding: "On the whole the statistical findings definitely favor large classes at every level of instruction except the kindergarten . . . the general trend of evidence places the burden of proof squarely upon the proponents of small classes.")

School's Fault?

The burden of the Coleman report was a repudiation of the entire mode of thinking that holds environment entirely responsible for whatever shortcomings are apparent in individual pupils. Yet spokesmen for this position have failed to demonstrate why achievement differences are far wider among the children in a given school than between the test-score average of the various schools. If it were all the schools' fault, the impact of each school on its pupils ought to be more uniform than this.

Parents whose children attend schools with low average scores increasingly tend to blame school boards, administrators, teachers, curricula, a trend that is resulting in demands that school control in urban poverty areas be transferred to local communities on the theory that parents, with their children's interests at heart, will see to it that the schools provide a good education. In order to test this concept, the New York City Board of Education built a "dream school"—IS 201 in Harlem which opened in 1966. It cost $5 million, much of the decision-making was left to parents, the teacher-pupil ratio was 1:13.8. On February 1, 1968, this school was described as a "bedlam" by the New York Times and later as a "model mess" by the Associated Press. By December 1968 IS 201 was in a state of revolt while reports on tangible accomplishments were conspicuous by their absence. Even worse was the experience with the Ocean Hill-Brownsville district in Brooklyn, whose schools were controlled by the local board. Shortly after they were described as "a failure by any known measurement" in the New York Times Magazine, growing conflicts between the teachers and the parents paralyzed not only the schools in the demonstration project but led to a closing of the entire New York City school system for most of the fall of 1968. While the idea of school control by local communities has some merits, its translation into practice in three New York "disadvantaged" areas has not only resulted in no improvement in the children's education but created chaos and caused the skill and knowledge of New York's school children to fall farther behind.

Christopher Jencks, writing in the New Republic, concluded that the Coleman report "makes a convincing though not a definite case for the view that student achievement depends largely on forces over which today's schools exercise little control." What about those forces? What determines student ability?

Harry Levin of the Brookings Institution observed, in the Saturday Review, that since children possess a wide range of inherited abilities and are products of different family and community influences, it is hardly surprising to learn that most variation in performance is not attributable to the schools: "The literature on testing suggests that from 60 percent to 90 percent of the variance in standardized ability tests is attributable to genetic differences among individuals."

At this point, the debate usually tends to become irrational, and Coleman was concerned lest some of his findings be misinterpreted as permitting racist implications. He was careful to emphasize that "racial composition *per se* of the school was not related to achievement when the social class composition was controlled." In other words, individual attainment is unrelated to racial background although it is indeed related to personal background.

The most significant statistical correlation was found to exist between the pupil's achievement test scores and the socio-economic level of his parents. However, until continued research has resolved the existing heredity-environment uncertainty, explanations of the close relation between parental income and children's educational attainment scores will remain hypothetical.

What, then, to do? The answer is simply that nobody knows. Coleman submitted no recommendations: "Indeed, if recommendations had been requested, they could hardly have been given, for the facts themselves point to no obvious solution." Participants in the Civil Rights Commission's national education conference in November of 1967 "reflects a general feeling of frustration," according to the *New York Times,* and while everyone thought more money should be spent, the conference made no recommendation on *how* it should be spent. All this does not mean that we should give up attempts to offer all children an opportunity to acquire an education to the limits of their abilities. But unless certain facts of life are recognized, we will only continue the frustrating experience of the past few years.

'Track' Schools

Children differ widely in their aptitudes, and no power on earth can make *all* of them perform at or near the norms for their ages. Differences between the more and less gifted widen with age. This is why virtually all countries operate two or more parallel secondary school systems, and why some of our own schools run several "tracks." But in the great majority of American public schools, heterogeneous grouping and automatic annual promotion are now common practice, confronting the teacher with the almost impossible task of simultaneously educating in one classroom three or more grade levels of children. It is just as wrong and destructive not to segregate children for educational purposes according to their measurable innate capacity as it is to segregate them deliberately by color of skin. Most European countries run schools which for low-ability children combine teaching of basic essentials with training in marketable skills. From a certain age, schools provide part-time classroom instruction tied in with apprenticeship training by potential employers. The prejudice against vocational education in this country must be overcome and the myth destroyed that chronological age is the only criterion by which children should be assigned to schools, classes, grades, and curricula.

Beyond this, time alone will provide the development in our general and scientific understanding that will permit us to find solutions. In the meantime, educationists must at least be honest with themselves in examining their failures, and must not be afraid to retrace their steps before beginning afresh.

12. The Good Life: An Impossible Dream?

Mankind has always dreamed of a society in which the unending struggle for food, clothing and shelter was solved. Then, and only then, said the philosophers, would men truly become men in the fullest sense. Freed from their constant preoccupation with dull, routine work, they would walk erect and enjoy the amenities of life.

Americans As a Leisure Class

Within the memory of living Americans this age-old dream has come true. The work week has fallen steadily from six days (72 hours) to five days (40 hours) with a new target of four and one-half days (36 hours). But this is far from the full story. On the job, half-hour coffee breaks are common. A three-week vacation is standard. A new national law has juggled traditional holidays to create mini-vacations (from Thursday till Tuesday). Sabbaticals have spread from college professors to business executives and steel workers. With few exceptions all Americans are now part of the leisure class. Even those unemployed Americans who live below the poverty level are part of this leisure society, although they are obviously excluded from the wealth that is normally associated with leisure.

Gaps in the Good Life

This new leisure has not brought Americans to the threshold of

Utopia. As a nation we are deeply committed to a work ethic. Faced with a shorter work week, many Americans seek a second job (moonlighting). Others wander about aimlessly, staring for hours at their TV, lounging in bars, or getting underfoot at home. Many a housewife dreads the day that her husband retires.

In fact, the aged in our society are a subculture, cut off from the mainstream of American life. Thus far we have provided no gradual transition from full time employment, dominated by the work ethic, to full time leisure, that ranks as an aimless, degrading and parasitic existence. The aged share with all of the unemployed an "unAmerican" stigma, that is even more pronounced because their condition is permanent. Most men (and many women) are fully employed, functioning citizens at age 64. At 65 they are abruptly "retired" to the discard pile where they live out their remaining years as second-class citizens.

This waste of human resources need not continue. Many retired persons are capable of providing the social services that government cannot afford. These services might include the operation of day-care centers and nurseries (grandmothers have a hard-earned expertise with children). Many older men could bring a lifetime of experience to the young and middle-aged; seminars on small business operation by former top executives; legal aid and advice given to ghetto residents by retired lawyers. Overseas, these people might greatly expand the work of the Peace Corps. At home they could apply their knowledge to the complicated ills of American urban society. The catalogue of socially-useful, part-time jobs that the aged could fill has yet to be written.

In exchange our society can surely provide something beyond the shabby arrangements that presently exist for the elderly. Conditions in many nursing and rest homes at the moment are not far removed from slum conditions. Although we have made a beginning at providing health services for the aged, much more needs to be done.

In truth, the health services available to many other Americans represents a serious gap in the good life. Although the professional competence of our physicians is recognized worldwide, the availability of health care is insufficient and badly distributed. Rural areas are especially short-changed. The price tag on medical care all too frequently makes it a luxury item fully available only to high income groups. Our present voluntary plans leave major gaps (prolonged illness, specialized surgery). Above all else our medical profession is so understaffed that other nations have assumed the leadership in providing medical care for all of their citizens.

Another gap involves the humanistic aspects of our national life. Consider education: the school has always been regarded as an apprentice system for the world of work. Students are molded into employees in the classroom. Such "frills" as music, art and physical education are tolerated in good times, but are the first to get the economy axe in hard times. In today's world we might argue that these priorities should be reversed. If future Americans are to spend twice as many of their working hours at leisure as they do at work, Leisure 101 should become a required course, with Remedial Leisure 001 for those who have absorbed too much of our present culture. In fact, education may become a life-long activity, dedicated to the development of the whole person. The fine arts and performing arts have heretofore been restricted to highly skilled professionals. Hopefully they will now be recast into a form that makes them part of everyone's life. There is no logical reason why the steelworker should not paint on weekends; the secretary take ballet; the mechanic play the flute in a little symphony; the lawyer carve wood sculptures.

The arts will not attract everyone. Recreation has a widespread appeal and is necessary for good mental and physical health. A look at any city swimming pool, golf course or tennis court on a summer day will dramatize our lack of facilities. Any visit to a national or state park will show how demand has outrun supply. With a much larger population and more leisure time in the offing the need for city, state and national action is clear.

The American Dream

Our 200-year-old Declaration of Independence refers to the "pursuit of happiness." Today our search for the good life has proved to be elusive. We know that we will not automatically stumble onto it—that more than money and leisure are needed. In an individualistic society, each man must find his own version of those activities that raise him to his highest potential as a human being. Government cannot prescribe: it can only provide the atmosphere and the opportunities for the good life.

Do contemporary Americans actually have a vision—a dream of the good society? Available evidence is conflicting. At an earlier date American goals were widely agreed upon, no matter how much they might be violated in practice. Such terms as human brotherhood, equality of opportunity, individual freedom, liberty and justice (however ill defined) were common rallying points for the average American. There was no claim that America was perfect, but we were committed to the building of a society greater than any the world had ever known.

That spirit is captured in the lyrics of "America The Beautiful," to be found in this chapter. A modern version might be the "Dream" speech of Martin Luther King, Jr.

But in some quarters doubt, uncertainty and pessimism seem to have replaced this earlier American spirit. A British commentator has described modern America as a nation that has "lost its nerve" and no longer believes in its destiny. Somewhere between these extremes Americans as individuals and as a nation pursue their quest for the good life.

FROM INDUSTRIAL SOCIETY TO HUMAN CIVILIZATION *

RENE DUBOS

Americans are increasingly concerned with an apparent deterioration in the quality of American life. Fixing their eyes on the year 2000 the pessimists see some new version of the Dark Ages emerging, in which men will be surfeited in a sea of material goods while their spirits atrophy. The optimists see a reordering of priorities that will redirect technology to serve the humanistic concern for the good life.

If we truly set out in search of the good life, will we recognize the object of our search? What role should the general public have in determining the good life? What role should be reserved for the expert? Do technological societies have their own built-in patterns of evolution? Or can men determine the direction of social development? Who is in the saddle—men or machines?

It is traditional to make fun of commencement speeches. Students regard them as the high mark of the academic year for pompous platitudes. So if you'll allow me, I shall limit myself to very prosaic language.

An anthology of commencement speeches would certainly make for dreary reading. Yet it would constitute, I believe, a valuable social document because it would reflect the beliefs, hopes, fears, and especially illusions, of each historical period. What an entertaining exercise it would be to compare the pronouncements made at different times in history by learned, and supposedly wise, adults, as they try to convey to the younger generations their own sense of value and their advice as to the proper way to carry on the torch of life. I shall play this game with you, and to this end I shall evoke the changes of mood concerning the future that I have experienced and witnessed since graduating from a French technical school exactly half a century ago today.

As a member of the scientific community, I was, of course, indoctrinated into the belief that science and technology would soon solve all the important problems of mankind. Now what an extraordinary piece of academic wisdom! I wonder whether any commencement speaker would dare, in our times, to offer science as the savior of mankind. He would, I believe, defend the view, as I shall, that scientific knowledge does contribute or can contribute to health and happiness, but he would hastily introduce many conditioning ifs and buts.

* Reprinted from the commencement address at Williams College, June 6, 1971 from Williams Alumni Review, Summer, 1971, by permission.

Commencement speakers are now much more likely to emphasize the folly of identifying progress with our current practice to produce on an increasing scale, faster and faster, everything and anything that science and technology enables us to produce. As its etymology indicates, the word "progress" just means moving forward, in a certain direction, even when this direction takes us on a dangerous road. And there are, as we well know, many indications that we are now moving on a road leading to despair and disasters.

I believe the atmosphere in which we considered progress as just moving forward was expressed at its best, in some of the worst verses written in the English language, namely, in Stephen Vincent Benét's poem, "The Western Star." You probably recall those extraordinary verses, "We don't know where we are going, but we are on our way!" Being of French origin, I take pride in the fact that a much wiser statement of progress was made by one of the French wits who was my contemporary, namely, Jean Cocteau. A few years before his death, he remarked facetiously, as he was prone to do, that progress might be nothing else than a logical development from false premises. . . . And indeed we do know that growth, prosperity, and abundance of goods become meaningless beyond a certain point and that great economic affluence constitutes in fact an ethical absurdity when it coexists with abject poverty.

But to be really up-to-date, [we] . . . should, I believe, emphasize that inescapable limitations which are built into the laws of nature will soon compel us, whether we want it or not, to change the course of industrial societies.

Our technological enterprise presently operates on the assumption that the production of goods and especially the use of power, of electric power, will continue to increase at the rate of approximately seven percent a year. It does not take much knowledge of mathematics to realize that seven percent a year means doubling every 10 years, which would mean a level 6 to 10 times the present one by the year 2000. And I only ask you to imagine what the world would be like, what our world would be like, with 10 times as many power plants and transmission lines, 10 times as much junk in our air, streams and lakes, ten times as much garbage in our cities! And yet this is what would happen by the year 2000 if we do not change our ways.

You will now perceive that the theme . . . is to convey to you my belief that before the year 2000, in other words, during your adult days, natural forces will slow down the rate of technological growth which has prevailed in the industrial world throughout the 19th and 20th centuries. Whether we want it or not, we shall soon enter a phase that one might call one of steady state, hopefully, permanent steady state.

And my larger theme is that we have the opportunity to take advantage of this situation to become more directly concerned with improving the quality of life. The change from quantitative growth to improvement in the quality of life, will certainly be painful. We shall find it difficult to refrain from continuing to exploit nature in a wasteful way, the way we have been doing during the past two centuries because we have been brainwashed into the belief that progress depends on quantitative growth, and that a steady state means stagnation to be followed by decadence. But, in fact, I believe that history shows that qualitative changes do not depend on quantitative growth.

And if I have time, I would like to illustrate before you, how the Minoan civilization on the very small island of Crete continued to evolve for 6,000 years, becoming more and more sophisticated, more and more pleasant, without growing in size. Now, during the past 10 years, some prophets have asserted that the year 2000 will see the beginning of a technologic utopia. But other prophets believe, on the other hand, that the progressive degradation of life and the environment we are now experiencing is the forerunner of a gloomy sunset for the human race. My own view is that the future will be nothing of the sort. Human beings, and that means especially you, your generation, will not accept present trends as their destiny. They will not want either to become robots, or to return to the Stone Age cave. In fact, I believe that we are witnessing,

right now, the beginning of a new phase in the human adventure. Instead of continuing to struggle in a suicidal way for quantitative growth, we are beginning, I believe, to become concerned with improving the quality of life.

One begins to sense this preoccupation even in the political world, certainly the last place where one would expect to find it. The present concern of legislators and government bodies for "technological assessment" is evidence that social goals have finally come to be recognized as more important than technological means for the future of industrial civilization.

Finally, one has come to recognize that present trends, if continued much longer, would result in a new version of the Dark Ages, an intellectual and social paralysis caused by the overdevelopment to the point of absurdity of our misdirected technological skills. In contrast, a change of direction will generate, I believe, a social and scientific renaissance. For example, we all know that we need better political and economic systems for a more adequate distribution of wealth and for greater social justice. We need better planning of our environments, to enlarge and enrich the human encounter. We need better engineering for more efficient use of available energy. And we need much better chemical and biological methods to improve industrial technology by an intelligent policy of recycling that would make it possible for us to imitate the wonderful economy of nature, an economy in which there are no wastes, there is no pollution.

The most notable aspects of the forthcoming decades, in my opinion, will be that social, natural sciences will be redirected so as to make them really serve the ancient humanistic concern for the good life. Emphasis will increasingly shift from technologic and economic feasibility to value judgments as to what *ought* to be done among all the things that *can* be done.

And when social and technologic problems are considered from this humanistic point of view, no specialist can claim exclusive rights as an expert. Specialized knowledge and skills are needed, of course, for the planning and execution of social programs, as well as for the prediction of their likely consequences. But each one of us, that is, the general public, has a role just as important as that of the experts in decision-making, because goals are just as important as means in the formulation of all social enterprises. A society which accepts the tyranny of the expert is a sick society. And our form of technological civilization will die if it continues to accept to be governed by experts or at least if it continues to regard efficiency in the pursuit of life as a substitute for the quality of life. One of the hopeful aspects of our time is the increasing awareness that, if *things* are in the saddle, it is because *we* have put them there. The demonic force in our life is not technology *per se*, or the social structure, but our propensity to consider means as ends in themselves.

In our search for the good life, we shall often move in the wrong direction, and even initiate destructive trends. But this is no reason for despair. Men are not robots and they are able to retrace their steps when they recognize they have taken the wrong road. Wherever free human beings are involved, trend is not destiny.

Many of you may see the future as dark, but I would like to end with a statement of faith in man, which is one that I have not formulated for the occasion, one which I believe has sustained human life for the past 10,000 years. In my judgment, you will not live in a technologic utopia, but neither will you have to watch gloomily the sunset of the human race. Instead you will have the exciting experience of redirecting technological civilization into a truly organic, humane way of life.

ACHIEVING PARITY
FOR THE ARTS *
ROGER L. STEVENS

Mr. Stevens is chairman of the John F. Kennedy Center for the Performing Arts in Washington, D. C. In this capacity he has had ample opportunity to reflect on traditional American reluctance to use public funds to underwrite the arts. What follows is his prescription for a revitalization of the arts in America. Is it true that socialist-communist countries have had greater success then we have in stimulating artistic endeavor? Are the arts really a component of the good life? Or are they a "fringe" operation that should be supported by wealthy patrons? What sum represents minimum financial support for the arts, according to Mr. Stevens? How should this cost be apportioned? Can the arts be expected to "break even" financially from admission charges? Are the arts that stress achievement and excellence compatible with democracy?

With the thousands of words that have gushed forth from all direc-

* *Reprinted from Roger L. Stevens, "America's Stake In the Arts,"* Saturday Review, *February 28, 1970, by permission of the author and The Saturday Review, Inc. Copyright © 1970 The Saturday Review, Inc.*

tions about the sad condition of the arts, the importance of the arts, and the financial problems of the arts, I think it is time that we ask some fundamental questions. What stake does this country have in the arts? Why should we all be concerned? Actually, there is great need for concern, if for no other reason than that the world's most prosperous civilization is suffering from a malaise that seems to defy explanation.

Ironically, socialist and communist countries that are trying desperately to raise their living standards and create an economic system that will excel U.S. achievements do not seem plagued with the problems besetting our country. Their struggle to overtake us seems to provide a motivation and *esprit de corps* that we no longer have. In spite of our affluence there is general discontent—youths are disillusioned; the poor are dissatisfied; the wealthy are bored; the blacks are angry; the middle class is frustrated and bewildered by rapidly changing values and mores; and ever increasing violence occurs. It seems obvious that we must develop a new approach to life through which we can utilize our new affluence in a more meaningful way. It is at this point that we should consider what role the arts can play in enriching our lives and curing the malaise that permeates our society.

If only for a purely selfish reason, each individual should become personally involved in the arts. There always are new pleasures and excitement to be derived from day-to-day living if one expands his interest in every field of the arts. And if one is willing to devote the time and effort necessary to specialize in one area, the rewards will be even greater.

Whether one is an artist developing his talent or an individual developing an appreciation of the arts, one must expend discipline, training, and effort. Unfortunately, many people tend to expect instant satisfaction when they dabble with the arts, failing to realize that reaping true benefits requires as much preparation and hard work as any other field of endeavor, if not more. The simple fact is that there is so much music to hear, so much literature to read, and so much visual art to see that if one spent all his life attempting to absorb the arts he would merely scratch the surface. If one stops to contemplate the personal rewards received from exploring these areas, it is difficult to understand why most of us do not realize the opportunities. Were we more successful in utilizing these vast resources and incorporating the arts into our daily lives, we would undoubtedly be closer to the utopia promised us by religions and political systems for centuries.

With today's shortened work week and lengthened life span, the average American is left with a tremendous increase in leisure time. Many people faced with retirement seem to wither away because they failed to acquire outside interests during their more active years. When they no longer have jobs, boredom and depression set in. Had they developed the necessary mental resources and habits of concentration, they could enjoy their free time.

The disaffected youths of today seem more and more attracted to the arts, even to the point of making their careers in this field. Many see weaknesses and faults in business and feel that the arts are more compatible with their views of life. Unfortunately, our educational system has performed miserably in the arts. The presentations made by most art teachers are so dull and unimaginative that they deaden student interest. As a result we lose many potential audiences and much potential talent.

The failure to teach students to appreciate design and beauty at an early age has appreciable impact on the appearance of our cities and roadsides. The squalor in most American cities is beyond belief; what the automobiles, parking lots, highways, and utilitarian buildings have done to our cities is criminal. Were Americans taught to become more concerned with shaping their environment, they would not allow their cities to be desecrated with the usual hot dog stands, gaudy gasoline stations, garish store fronts, and generally bad designs. If esthetic principles instead of purely utilitarian ones carried the day and the ugliness of our cities were not so pronounced, one could enjoy the exhilaration that comes from beautiful surroundings.

Our image abroad is deteriorating continually in spite of the billions spent to foster good will. If we would stop feeling that our greatest threat is atomic war and waken to the fact that the real battle is for the minds of men, we would realize the importance of the arts in securing the good will of intellectuals and artists who are world opinion-makers.

There is, however, an ever-present problem of financing. To deal with that, we must get rid of the general notion that art should pay for itself like a manufactured product. It is time, too, to stop asking the artist to subsidize the arts indirectly by accepting inadequate compensation for his work. It has always seemed strange to me that this nation, which was the first to recognize the importance of making free education available to everyone, has failed to understand the importance of making the arts available for all.

It took *Sputnik* to awaken this country to the necessity of vastly increasing its budget for scientific research and development. We who have been trying to promote support for the arts have always said that what we needed was our version of *Sputnik*. It may be that the revolt of today's disillusioned youth will provide the impetus we have needed. Government, foundations, and business might then decide to allot the kind of resources necessary for real development in the arts—the long-term benefits of which could possibly be even more exciting than a moon landing.

We should spend at least $5-billion a year on the arts—which is less than 10 percent of the total spent on education. This would finance building of museums, performing arts centers, and other necessary facilities throughout the country, and provide sufficient subsidy to enable everyone who wishes to participate in some artistic endeavor to do so. The ideal situation would be to secure combined support from government, foundations, business, and individuals, so that no one group would dominate.

Actually, there is much more government money available for the arts than might appear at first glance—if we include funds available through individual and corporate tax deductions, as well as indirect educational aid. But it is not nearly enough to do an adequate job of attaining the artistic development that the American people deserve. Government budgets for the arts—federal, state, and municipal —must be increased substantially. Government is the appropriate source of assistance to organizations such as performing arts groups that are in desperate financial straits, since the political overtones would be considerably less than in more controversial individual grants. The latter could be handled by foundations and private individuals.

Among the principal villains responsible for the arts' financial problems are the foundations, which, according to statistics, give less than 4 percent of their total income to arts programs. With the government increasing yearly the money available for education and health, the arts would seem to be the logical alternate place for foundations to put their money. The foundations should function halfway between government and individuals. If properly operated, they could be the ideal source of funds. There is always the danger of too much control when government supplies most of the money, and individuals can be just as dominating as government, as evidenced by the experiences of painters, sculptors, composers, and writers who were financed by individual patrons.

Unfortunately, however, foundations often suffer the same disease that can afflict federal agencies— the tendency to "play it safe." In the arts this can be fatal. One reason for the weaknesses in the operation of foundations is that many were formed by those who wished to avoid taxes rather than undertake good works. As time goes on, however, and the foundations mature—and laws make them live up to their credos—it is hoped they will all operate in the manner in which the Ford, Rockefeller, and Mellon Foundations do.

Corporations are another source of funds that have hardly been tapped, and they must be brought into this alliance. The time is long overdue for big business to face its responsibility of improving the society that has allowed it to become so successful. One very encouraging development has been formation of the Business Committee for the Arts. If, as hoped, committee members are able to convince the business community to increase its appropriations to the arts twentyfold, as was done for education by the Council for Financial Aid to Education, it could mean an increase of hundreds of millions of dollars for the arts.

Assuming we are fortunate enough to obtain the funds necessary for the arts to fill their proper role in our civilization, it must then be decided how to disburse the money in a manner that will insure the maximum benefits. In the space available here it would be hard to detail the specific uses of the $5-billion mentioned earlier, but I can briefly mention some categories that must receive attention.

ART EDUCATION

A first order of business should be completely to overhaul our system of art education at all levels. The quality of teachers must be improved by better training and more attractive rewards. One way to insure good instruction might be to require artists receiving government aid during their developing years to devote a certain amount of their time to teaching. Outstanding art teachers should be recognized, and suitable awards of money and prestige should be made.

More imaginative programming must be introduced. Methods and techniques must be updated. Some strongly advocate use of audiovisual materials. Development of cassettes for TV sets could drastically change present teaching methods. The Kodály system, developed in Hungary, goes to the other extreme: It teaches music using only voice. Instruction begins at the age of five and continues through high school. It will take time to measure the benefits of these relatively new methods, with many controlled experiments.

If properly mobilized, local museums and performing arts groups can be used effectively to help educate the community by working with schools and local groups. Although there has been some cooperation in this area recently, it can be greatly increased.

Traditionally, professional artists go through basic training at specialized schools and then undertake advanced individual tutorial study. But conservatories and private art schools are suffering serious financial problems, and their costs are rising rapidly. Federal programs, for the most part, have been oriented toward the sciences. The young scientist is usually attached to an institution that is well equipped, and he is taught by teachers who have research opportunities and above-normal salaries because of federal programs and other aid. On the other hand, the young artist usually finds himself with a school that has an obsolete physical plant, poor equipment, and underpaid teachers. Private gifts to such institutions are rare, and alumni usually can barely provide for their own needs, much less help their alma mater. We must institute a program of substantial aid immediately or expect to see a considerable decrease in the amount and quality of pro-

fessional training available to young artists.

SUPPORT AND ENCOURAGEMENT OF THE INDIVIDUAL ARTIST

Recently I attended a meeting of arts deans, who unanimously agreed that one of the most serious problems facing the arts is the large percentage of individuals with talent who do not pursue arts careers because of economic considerations. Young people with talent first must be persuaded to enter the field, and then they must receive financial support during the difficult time of adjustment between their university training and the development of sufficient ability to support themselves. Socialist and communist countries, whose repressive controls hardly provide ideal climates for the artist, at least always have recognized the importance of his influence on society and offered him financial security. The artist in these countries enjoys great community respect, as well as a high standard of living. Hopefully, the day will come in this country when our artists will enjoy the same admiration and prestige that we offer athletes.

For an example of what financial assistance to individual artists can accomplish, we need only look at the WPA and PWA programs, which offered assistance to all needy visual artists during the Thirties. Although no accurate study has been made, it is generally acknowledged that about 80 percent of the painters and sculptors who gained world recognition in the Forties and Fifties were supported during the Depression by government funds—not to develop art, but for sociological reasons. Obviously, a percentage of the artists would have continued their work even if these funds had not been available, but a great many would have had to turn to other endeavors to survive. As a result of this subsidy, so many great artists were developed that New York is now generally acknowledged to be the center of the visual art world, which previously had been Paris. An interesting question is, "What panel of experts in the Thirties would have picked people like David Smith, Mark Rothko, or Jackson Pollock as the most promising artists of the future?" In other words, this shotgun approach gave all outstanding talent a chance to develop and brought our country to its present eminent position in visual art. Ironically enough, the financial gain from increased taxes and values has far exceeded the government cash outlay.

DEVELOPMENT OF MANAGERIAL TALENTS

There is an acute shortage of administrators for museums and the performing arts. In fact, the lack of qualified people has resulted in much justified criticism from potential contributors, and in many cases has meant the loss of a great deal of money. It is difficult for a non-artist to do a good job in this field even though he may be a capable administrator. What is really needed are individuals with artistic

bent, although not necessarily with great talent. However, it is frequently difficult to get an artist to admit his lack of progress and persuade him to undertake the immensely important job of administration, which can be so important to all concerned and often can improve his own position in life. But again, if we are to receive additional funds, we must make this field more attractive to qualified people.

PLANT AND EQUIPMENT

There is a great need for additional facilities and equipment, the provision of which is taken for granted in such fields as education and manufacturing. Though financial assistance to many new arts centers is constantly questioned and criticized, I think one would be hard put to deny that uncomfortable, unpleasant surroundings cannot produce the best art—from the point of view of either creator or audience. We must continue to provide more theaters, opera houses, studios, and museums to communities throughout the country.

IMPROVEMENT OF ARTISTIC STANDARDS IN URBAN DEVELOPMENT

Good architects and designers should be given many more opportunities to protect our cities and roadsides from being continually despoiled. A massive program should be instituted that would take advantage of the natural beauty of our rivers and harbors, which, if properly developed, could add immeasurably to the appearance of our cities. Insurance companies and banks, which, along with government, finance most of the building in this country, could easily insist that certain esthetic standards be met. There will be those who say that this will mean too much control, but, on the other hand, what right do some individuals or business concerns have to inflict ugliness upon the rest of the community and desecrate its environment?

An interesting example of how a city can improve its architectural environment exists in the little town of Columbus, Indiana, where the progressive Cummins Engine Company donated the architect fees for new public structures, provided they were designed by one of five or six of the leading architects in the country. Consequently, this little city has more beautiful schools, churches, and other public buildings than many other cities twenty times its size. This kind of a program should be adopted in more cities.

DEVELOP MORE DISCERNING AUDIENCES

Developing more intelligent audiences for all art forms is a gigantic task but one that must receive top priority, not only because it will provide the artist with a greater opportunity to become self-supporting but also because it will guarantee a much happier public. People who do not necessarily have creative talents, but who are interested in painting, theater, music, and the dance, should be encouraged to become "Sunday painters" or to become involved in amateur musicals, theatricals, and concerts. Facilities and equipment should be made available so they may sense the excitement of personal involvement and better understand the work that goes into these productions.

Television offers an excellent vehicle for introducing good art to the public, as well as offering a showcase for artists. If one considers that the average child watches TV twenty hours a week, one realizes the marvelous educational opportunities that could be exploited. Unfortunately, to date, very little quality art is being produced for TV. We must make every effort to see that this is changed. Since many sections of this country rarely, if ever, are exposed to quality performing arts groups, touring companies should be subsidized. Touring dance programs sponsored by the National Council on the Arts have been extremely well received throughout the country.

EXCHANGE OF ARTISTS FROM ALL NATIONS

A proper exchange of leading artists the world over should be adopted as a major part of our foreign policy, so the best ideas can be exchanged and evaluated. If this exchange were increased as much as it should be, the cost would be heavy; however, we could take some of the funds from the national defense budget and use them for this purpose. The benefits in increased knowledge, influence, and understanding might provide a higher return for money spent than the very expensive military equipment we have been supplying to date to other nations.

ASSISTANCE TO ART INSTITUTIONS

Finally, we must face the fact that if our leading art institutions are to survive we must be prepared to subsidize them. With the profit-minded mentality in this country it is often considered disgraceful for institutions to operate with deficits. But it is virtually impossible for most orchestras, opera companies, dance groups, and theater groups to operate without deficits, even when playing to capacity audiences. In a machine age, it is impossible for the arts to mechanize, and therefore they feel rising costs more than most businesses.

There are frequent complaints about the price of theater tickets. While doing some research on ticket prices, I found that the Globe Theater, which was built on Broadway in 1908, originally charged $3 for an orchestra seat. Considering the depreciation of the dollar, it would be necessary to receive ten times that amount today—which is seldom the case. So unless admission prices are raised considerably —which, whether one likes it or not, would eliminate most of our audiences—our performing arts groups will never be solvent. The use of the word "deficit" actually is unfair and should be applied to operations in the performing arts only when the receipts, gifts, and any government aid are less than planned expenditures.

Generally speaking, we should charge admission for the performing arts, except in the case of school children. In addition to the economic considerations, people tend to appreciate something more if they are required to pay a slight fee. I even advocate charging admission to museums that are now free. In Europe, which has had a long tradition of subsidizing the arts, there has always been a charge for attending museums and the performing arts, even though the amount may be small. However, if prices are to be kept reasonable, some form of subsidy always will be necessary to make up the difference between receipts and costs.

We Americans, who are renowned for our ability to achieve almost anything, once more need to regain our feeling of purpose as well as our sense of the marvelous in life. There are still discoveries to be made, unknown frontiers to be crossed, great things to be accomplished. Not least, we are challenged by that long line of social philosophers and critics who delight in pointing out the fact that no great democracy has ever lasted long enough to produce a high culture. We are today the oldest democracy in the world, and we are now faced with having to prove those critics wrong.

I believe the arts and our democracy are compatible, and that we have every reason to aspire to that high culture. I believe that we can achieve that high culture, especially when we as a people learn that the arts are not the province of the few, but the staple of the many. Bernard Berenson, just before his death, had a vision of what we might become through the genius of the arts. "All the arts," he wrote, "poetry, music, ritual, the visible arts, and the theater, must singly and together create the most comprehensive art of all, a humanized society, and its masterpiece, free man."

OUR SICK MEDICAL
SYSTEM *
THOMAS J. WATSON, JR.

For a quarter century Americans have agreed on the goals of medical service, while they have violently disagreed over the means. The American Medical Association has urged a voluntary, private insurance program for hospital-medical care. Labor leaders have advocated a national health

---

* Reprinted from Thomas J. Watson, Jr., "Health Service," Vital Speeches, February 1, 1971 by permission of Vital Speeches of the Day, and the author.

insurance plan operated by government. The issue has been clouded by emotional cries of "socialism" and "free enterprise." Meanwhile, we have been outdistanced by other nations which have done a better job of putting health care within the reach of everyone.

Where do we now rank in infant mortality? Female life expectancy? Male life expectancy? How does the percentage of gross national product that we spend on health care compare with other nations? If more money were made available, how should we spend it? Under our present system, who suffers the most? Can our goals be met by repairing the present system? Why will it be politically difficult to create a national health insurance system?

. . . How would you like to live in a country which—according to the figures available in the United Nations—during the past two decades has dropped from seventh in the world to sixteenth in the prevention of infant mortality;

—Has dropped in female life expectancy from sixth to eighth;

—Has dropped in male life expectancy from tenth to twenty-fourth,

—And which has bought itself this uneviable trend by spending more of its gross national product for medical care—$1 out of every $14—than any other country on the face of the earth?

You know the country I am talking about: Our own U.S.A., the home of the free, the home of the brave, and the home of a decrepit, inefficient, high-priced system of medical care.

Just look for a moment at what some of the figures mean. They mean that in infant mortality we have been overtaken by France, the U.K., and Japan; that in male life expectancy we have been overtaken by France, Japan, West Germany and Italy.

I know experts can disagree over our precise international standing. And I realize that medical problems in the United States, Europe and Japan are not identical.

But the evidence overwhelmingly indicates that we are falling down on the job, heading in the wrong direction, and becoming as a nation a massive medical disgrace. . . .

We have an outstanding record of individual achievement across the whole medical spectrum.

But despite all that, when I look up at the international scoreboard, I can come to only one conclusion: We are failing to fulfill adequately for all our people the first right set down in the Declaration of Independence—the right to life.

What do we have to do to restore that right to every man, every woman, every child in America?

First, as the Carnegie Commission said last month, I believe we have to beef up our arsenal: Train more doctors, more nurses, more paramedics;

Bail our medical and dental schools out of their present deep financial troubles;

Break ground for new hospitals and clinics;

In a word, spend more money.

We Americans are great on that.

Show us a shortage—of airplanes or tanks or trucks or scientists or engineers or satellites—and we'll fix it.

And I believe we can do that kind of job just fine in medicine.

Second, we must build into the system better management, better organization, more incentives to increase productivity and cut inefficiency.

I find it shocking, for example, that comprehensive pre-paid group practice, which has repeatedly delivered better care at lower costs, encounters legal roadblocks in more than half our states.

I find it shocking to read of Americans living in backwoods towns and city slums without a doctor or a dentist or a clinic.

I find it shocking that as 30,000 highly trained medical corpsmen return to civilian life every year— many from the field of battle—they too often discover, if they want to enter medicine as a career, that they have just one job open to them —hospital orderly.

We cannot continue to live with facts like these. We have to overhaul the system.

But as we do so, we should begin simultaneously to do the third part of the job: put health care within reach of everyone in America.

And that means putting it within the reach of the poor.

I do not really believe, of course, that you can ever make the poor rich and the rich poor. But I do think we should have a floor for each American below which he cannot fall, and I believe this applies not only to his economic status, but also to his medical status.

For the plain fact is that under our present medical system, the poor suffer by far the most.

Moreover, if a person happens not to be white, the picture is even bleaker.

A non-white infant can expect to live six years less than a white infant.

The non-white infant mortality rate is the white rate multiplied by *two*.

The non-white maternal death rate is the white rate multiplied by *four*.

To me, all this adds up to a completely unacceptable situation, which I think is un-American, undemocratic and unfair.

How do we correct it, and extend coverage for medical bills to everyone?

Not just through tinkering with our present system of paying for health care.

Not just through trying to stretch the umbrella of private health insurance, which, despite its costliness, still doesn't come close to covering Americans today.

No, we need a far more thorough-going reform.

And that brings us up against that old taboo—"Socialized Medicine."

I completely believe in the American free enterprise system. But when the system clearly fails

to produce a much needed good, I think we should not flinch from looking to some sort of government intervention to get the job done.

Frequently in the past, we have faced up to such a requirement with new legislation: on workmen's compensation, child labor, the reduction of the work week, unemployment insurance, and social security.

I believe we face today the same kind of moment of truth in medicine.

And I believe we have only one choice before us that will work: some very new form of national health insurance.

Twenty-one years ago, we looked at national health insurance when President Truman urged it, and we rejected it.

And in 1949 we rejected it in part because of arguments like this which appeared that year in the June issue of the magazine of the American Medical Association under the title: "Wake up, America!"

"The private profession of medicine is taking rapid strides toward the solution of this problem (of medical aid for the poor). Voluntary, pre-paid hospitalization and professional insurance plans now protect 56 million Americans . . . The American people enjoy a state of good health unequaled in the world today."

As a dyed-in-the-wool free trader, free enterprise, and hater of bureaucracy, I accepted that argument in 1949, and I bet nearly everyone else in this room did, too.

But on the evidence—particularly the international evidence—I cannot accept it in 1970.

We need a dedicated and total effort to find a way to build a floor under each citizen of this country that assures much better quality and equality of medical services for all.

A variety of plans have been advanced to this end in the Congress, by representatives of government, labor, business and the medical profession, but none of these plans are moving very fast, and our problem is compounding.

We do not need national health insurance as a political football.

We need a new national health insurance law, and we need it now —in the next session of the Congress. Indeed, I hope the Administration will put this at the top of its priority list.

To get that legislation, the partisans of varying plans—in the Congress, the American Medical Association, the AFL-CIO—must get together and compromise their differences.

And to speed such compromise, I believe all of us as citizens—and I dare to include doctors—should start now to build a bonfire of persuasion—to speak out, to demand change, and not stop pushing for action until we get the legislation we need.

We can take pride in our system of universal public education, social security, and work laws.

The time has now arrived for us to have a system of universal public medicine in which we can also take pride.

A national program, of course, is not a panacea in itself. But as we look toward some sort of governmental approach to this problem, let us remember that the plans in Britain and the Scandinavian countries have proved very successful in keeping those countries in the front rank internationally. And certainly they have provided better medical service for all of the people than the systems they supplanted. To me, this is a tremendously compelling argument for keeping an open mind as we look for a solution.

Not long ago, on a visit to the California Institute of Technology, I read these words on a student poster: "Our age is characterized by the perfection of means and confusion of goals."

The goal before us in medicine is clear.

But we shall reach it only by doing what we have always done with our magnificent American system: fearlessly facing its faults, cutting them away, replacing them with something better, and moving on.

.   .   .

We must begin it now.

As the wealthiest, most powerful, best educated nation in the world— a people with a heroic history of pioneering and justice and compassion—I believe we can do no less.

THE OLD IN THE COUNTRY OF THE YOUNG *

TIME MAGAZINE

*In the 1970's as never before,
America has become a youth culture. Public relations men have
dutifully coined the phrase "golden
years" to describe old age, but
most Americans either consciously
or unconsciously identify youth
with the "golden years." Old age
and death are unpleasant realities
that are brushed aside and never
discussed in polite company. In
the face of this discreet discrimination, the proportion of Americans
over 65 has reached 10 percent
and is rising.*

*How can the problems of the
aged be likened to those of youth?
Why are the aged isolated in
modern western culture? What
discrimination do they encounter?
Where do they live? Why do so
many fall below the poverty line?
Can the aged contribute anything
to society? What reordering of
American values would be necessary to provide a good life for
Americans from cradle to grave?*

Edward Albee once wrote a play
about a middle-aged couple who,

* *Reprinted from* Time *Magazine, August
3, 1970, by permission from* Time, *the
Weekly News Magazine; Copyright Time,
Inc., 1970.*

before putting Grandma permanently in the sandbox with a toy
shovel, gave her a nice place to live
under the stove, with an Army
blanket and her very own dish. The
play contains more truth than alle-
gory. One of the poignant trends
of U.S. life is the gradual devalua-
tion of older people, along with
their spectacular growth in numbers. Twenty million Americans are
65 or over. They have also increased proportionately, from 2.5%
of the nation's population in 1850
to 10% today.

While the subculture of youth
has been examined, psychoana-
lyzed, photographed, deplored and
envied, few have wanted even to
admit the existence of a subculture
of the aged, with its implications
of segregation and alienation.
Strangely enough, the aged have a
lot in common with youth: they are
largely unemployed, introspective
and often depressed; their bodies
and psyches are in the process of
change, and they are heavy users
of drugs. If they want to marry,
their families tend to disapprove.
Both groups are obsessed with
time. Youth, though, figures its passage from birth; the aged calculate
backward from their death day.
They sometimes shorten the wait:
the suicide rate among elderly men
is far higher than that of any other
age group.

The two subcultures seldom in-
tersect, for the young largely ignore
the old or treat them with what
Novelist Saul Bellow calls "a kind
of totalitarian cruelty, like Hitler's
attitude toward Jews." It is as

though the aged were an alien race to which the young will never belong. Indeed, there is a distinct discrimination against the old that has been called age-ism. In its simplest form, says Psychiatrist Robert Butler of Washington, D.C., age-ism is just "not wanting to have all these ugly old people around." Butler believes that in 25 or 30 years, age-ism will be a problem equal to racism.

We have time to grow old—the air
   is full of our cries.
          —Samuel Beckett

It is not just cruelty and indifference that cause age-ism and underscore the obsolescence of the old. It is also the nature of modern Western culture. In some societies, explains Anthropologist Margaret Mead, "the past of the adults is the future of each new generation," and therefore is taught and respected. Thus, primitive families stay together and cherish their elders. But in the modern U.S., family units are small, the generations live apart, and social changes are so rapid that to learn about the past is considered irrelevant. In this situation, new in history, says Miss Mead, the aged are "a strangely isolated generation," the carriers of a dying culture. Ironically, millions of these shunted-aside old people are remarkably able: medicine has kept them young at the same time that technology has made them obsolete.

Many are glad to end their working days. For people with money, good health, careful plans and lively interests, retirement can be a welcome time to do the things they always dreamed of doing. But for too many others, the harvest of "the golden years" is neglect, isolation, anomie and despair. One of every four Americans 65 or over lives at or below "the poverty line." Some of these 5,000,000 old people were poor to begin with, but most are bewildered and bitter *nouveaux pauvres,* their savings and fixed incomes devoured by spiraling property taxes and other forms of inflation. More than 2,000,000 of them subsist on Social Security alone.

Job discrimination against the aged, and increasingly against the middle-aged, is already a fact of U.S. life. While nearly 40% of the long-term unemployed are over 45, only 10% of federal retraining programs are devoted to men of that age. It is often difficult for older people to get bank loans, home mortgages or automobile insurance. When the car of a 68-year-old Brooklyn grocer was stolen last winter, he was unable to rent a substitute. Though his driving record was faultless and he needed a car for work, he was told falsely by two companies that to rent him one was "against the law."

Youth is everywhere in place
Age, like woman, requires fit surroundings.
          —Ralph Waldo Emerson

Treated like outsiders, the aged have increasingly clustered together for mutual support or simply to enjoy themselves. A now familiar but still amazing phenomenon has sprung up in the past decade: dozens of good-sized new towns that exclude people under 65. Built on cheap, outlying land, such communities offer two-bedroom houses starting at $18,000, plus a refuge from urban violence, the black problem (and in fact blacks), as well as generational pressures. "I'm glad to see my children come and I'm glad to see the back of their heads," is a commonly expressed sentiment. Says Dr. James Birren of the University of·Southern California: "The older you get the more you want to live with people like yourself. You want, to put it bluntly, to die with your own."

Most important, friendships are easy to make. One relative newcomer to Laguna Hills Leisure World, Calif., received more than 200 get-well cards from her new neighbors when she went to a hospital in Los Angeles. There is an emphasis on good times: dancing, shuffleboard, outings on oversized tricycles and bowling (the Keen Agers *v.* the Hits and Mrs.). Clubs abound, including Bell Ringing, Stitch and Knit, Lapidary and "tepees" of the International Order of Old Bastards. The I.O.O.B. motto: "Anything for fun." There is, in a sense, a chance for a new start. "It doesn't matter what you used to be; all that counts is what you do here," said a resident of Sun City, Ariz.

To some residents the communities seem too homogeneous and confining. A 74-year-old Cali-fornian found that life was flavorless at his retirement village; he was just waiting for "the little black wagon." Having begun to paint seascapes and landscapes at 68, he moved near an artists' colony, where he now sells his landscapes and lives happily with a lady friend of 77.

In silent synods, they play chess or
   cribbage . . .
                          —W.H. Auden

In fact, less than 1% of the elderly leave their own states. The highest proportion of the aged outside Florida is in Arkansas, Iowa, Maine, Missouri, Nebraska and South Dakota—on farms and in communities from which youth has fled. In small towns, the able elderly turn abandoned buildings into "senior centers" for cards, pool, slide shows, lectures and pie socials. In Hebron, N. Dak. (pop. 1,137), grandmothers use the balcony of the former J.C. Penney store for their quilting. But there is little socializing among the rural aged, who often subsist on pittances of $60 a month, and become even more isolated as public buses disappear from the highways, cutting off their lifelines to clinics, stores and friends.

A third of the nation's aged live in the deteriorating cores of the big cities. On Manhattan's Upper West Side, thousands of penniless widows in dingy single-room-occupancy hotels bar their doors against the alcoholics and dope addicts with whom they share the bathroom, the padlocked refrigerator and the telephone down the hall. "Nine out of ten around here, there's something wrong with them," says a 72-year-old exhousekeeper living on welfare in a hotel on West 94th Street. "I get disgusted and just sleep every afternoon. Everybody dying around you makes you kind of nervous." Terrified of muggings and speeding cars, the disabled and disoriented do not leave their blocks for years on end, tipping anyone they can find to get groceries for them when their welfare checks arrive.

Close to a million old people live in nursing homes or convalescent facilities provided by Medicare. A new growth industry, nursing homes now provide more beds than hospitals. They are badly needed. But in many of the "homes," the food and care are atrocious. Patients have even been confined to their beds merely because bed care entitles the owners to $2 or $3 more a day. Mrs. Ruby Elliott, 74, recalls her year in a California nursing home with fear and bitterness: "It's pitiful, but people are just out for the money. That whole time I was among the living dead."

Fewer than half of the country's 25,000 nursing homes actually offer skilled nursing. Arkansas Congressman David Pryor recently visited twelve nursing homes near Washington, D.C. "I found two where I would be willing to put my mother," he said. "But I don't think I could afford either one on my $42,500 congressional salary." Pryor is trying to set up a congressional committee to investigate long-term care for the aged. . . .

Better to go down dignified
With boughten friendship at your side
Than none at all. Provide, provide!
—Robert Frost

The problems of the aged are not their concern alone. Since reaching the age of 70 or 80 is becoming the norm rather than the exception, more and more of the middle-aged —even when they retire—have elderly parents and other relatives to care for. For the "command generation" there are two generation gaps, and the decisions to be made about their parents are often more difficult than those concerning their children. Various community agencies sometimes help, and in Manhattan a private referral service is kept busy helping distraught people find the right place for parents who can no longer live at home. One 81-year-old woman was persuaded to go to a nursing home when her daughter, with whom she had always lived, married late in life. To her own surprise, she is happier than she was before, taking great pride in reading to and helping her older roommate. A difficult decision of the middle-aged is how to allot their resources between children and parents and still provide for their own years of retirement, which may well extend for two decades.

The next generation of the aged may be healthier, certainly better educated and perhaps more politically aware. Those over 65 are now a rather silent minority, but in number they are almost exactly equal to the nation's blacks. Since none are below voting age, the aged control a high percentage of the vote—15%. More and more are banding together. The American Association of Retired Persons, for example, helps its nearly 2,000,000 members get automobile insurance, cheaper drugs and cut-rate travel. A more politically oriented group, the 2,500,000-member National Council of Senior Citizens, played a major role in pushing through Medicare. Now the group is lobbying to improve Medicare, which helps the sick but does not provide checkups, by including some sort of Preventicare.

Aside from health, money is the most pervasive worry of the aged; income maintenance is a major need. Private pension plans need attention too. According to one informed estimate, only 10% of the people who work under pension plans actually receive any benefits, usually because they do not stay long enough to qualify. As presently arranged, pensions also tend to lock older workers into their jobs and, if they become unemployed, to lock them out. They are then denied jobs because it is too expensive to let them join a pension plan.

Come, my friends,
'Tis not too late to seek a newer
    world.
                    —Tennyson

Will able 70-year-olds have more opportunities to work in the future? Probably not. Instead of raising the age of mandatory retirement, business and labor may lower it, perhaps to 50 or below—making workers eligible even earlier for social insecurity. Aside from those fortunate few in the professions—law, medicine, dentistry, architecture— most of the people over 65 who are still at work today are farmers, craftsmen and self-employed tradesmen, all categories whose numbers are shrinking. Of course, people cannot work hard forever. Each man ages according to his own clock, but at long last he is likely to lose much of his strength, his drive and adaptability. Witness the gerontocracy that slows down Congress and the businesses that have failed because of rigid leadership. But there are still many areas where the aged can serve and should, for aside from humane consideration, they can provide skill and wisdom that otherwise would be wasted.

New plans to recruit, train and deploy older workers to provide much needed help in hospitals, special schools and elsewhere will be discussed at the White House Conference on Aging scheduled for November 1971. Meanwhile, a few small-scale programs point the way. One is Operation Green Thumb, which hires retired farmers for landscaping and gardening. Another is the International Executive Service Corps, which arranges for retired executives to lend their management skills to developing countries. Hastings College of Law in San Francisco is staffed by law professors who have retired from other schools. A federally financed program called Foster Grandparents pays 4,000 low-income "grandparents" to care for 8,000 underprivileged youngsters. Although they have numbered only in the hundreds, most elderly volunteers in Vista and the Peace Corps have been great assets. "We know about outhouses and can remember when there weren't any refrigerators," says Nora Hodges, 71, who spent two years in Tunisia and is now associate Peace Corps director in the Ivory Coast. "People in underdeveloped countries rate age very highly. When we meet with this appreciative attitude, we outdo ourselves."

Begin the preparation for your
    death
And from the fortieth winter by that
    thought
Test every work of intellect or faith.
                            —W.B. Yeats

Life would be richer, students of aging agree, if a wider repertory of activities were encouraged throughout life. Almost everyone now marches together in a sort of lockstep. They spend years in school, years at work and years in retirement. Youth might well work more, the middle-aged play more, and the older person go back to school. Former HEW Secretary John Gardner wants to see "mid-career

clinics to which men and women can go to re-examine the goals of their working lives and consider changes of direction. I would like to see people visit such clinics with as little self-consciousness as they visit their dentist." As Psychiatrist Robert Butler puts it: "Perhaps the greatest danger in life is being frozen into a role that limits one's self-expression and development. We need Middle Starts and Late Starts as well as Head Starts."

To get a late start does not necessarily require a federal program. Many an enterprising individual has done it on his own. Mrs. Florida Scott-Maxwell, who at the age of 50 began training to become a psychotherapist, recently wrote down her reflections about aging in *The Measure of My Days*. "My seventies were interesting and fairly serene," she noted, "but my eighties are passionate. I am so disturbed by the outer world, and by human quality in general, that I want to put things right as though I still owed a debt to life. I must calm down."

Old age should burn and rave at
    close of day.
                            —Dylan Thomas

How socially involved older people should be is a question in hot dispute among students of aging. Some believe in the "theory of disengagement," which holds that aging is accompanied by an inner process that makes the loosening of social ties a natural process, and a desirable one. Others disagree. Says Harvard Sociologist Chad Gordon: "Disengagement theory is a rationale for the fact that old people haven't a damn thing to do and nothing to do it with."

After analyzing lengthy interviews with 600 aged San Franciscans, Anthropologist Margaret Clark found that engagement with life, rather than disengagement, contributed most to their psychological well-being. But not when that engagement included acquisitiveness, aggressiveness or a drive to achievement, super-competence and control. To cling to these stereotypical traits of the successful American seems to invite trouble, even geriatric psychiatry. The healthiest and happiest of the aged people in the survey were interested in conserving and enjoying rather than acquiring and exploiting, in concern for others rather than control of others, in "just being" rather than doing. They embraced, Dr. Clark points out, many of the values of today's saner hippies. Similarly, religion often teaches the aged, in spite of their physical diminishment, to accept each day as a gift.

The ranker injustices of age-ism can be alleviated by government action and familial concern, but the basic problem can be solved only by a fundamental and unlikely reordering of the values of society. Social obsolescence will probably be the chronic condition of the aged, like the other deficits and disabilities they learn to live with. But even in a society that has no role for them, aging individuals can try to carve out their own various niches. The noblest role, of course, is an affirmative one—quite simply to demonstrate how to live and how to die. If the aged have any responsibility, it is to show the next generation how to face the ultimate concerns. As Octogenarian Scott-Maxwell puts it: "Age is an intense and varied experience, almost beyond our capacity at times, but something to be carried high. If it is a long defeat, it is also a victory, meaningful for the initiates of time, if not for those who have come less far."

AMERICA THE BEAUTIFUL *

KATHERINE LEE BATES (1893)

Nearly a century ago the American dream was set forth in verse and song that captured the imagination of generations. A modern cynic may rate the aspirations described here as naive relics of our rural heritage.

Are we moving toward or away from the goals described here? How does our contemporary pollution record detract from the first stanza? Do we still have a thoroughfare for freedom? How does the philosophy of the New Left, campus unrest, and urban riots conflict with "self control," "liberty" and "law"? Has the Vietnam war destroyed the kind of patriotism that "more than self their country loved"? Are the references to divine intervention archaic in a society where "God is Dead"? Is there a fighting chance that we will see either brotherhood or alabaster cities?

O beautiful for spacious skies
For amber waves of grain
For purple mountain majesties
Above the fruited plain
America! America!
God shed his grace on thee
And crown thy good with brotherhood
From sea to shining sea

O beautiful for pilgrim feet
Whose stern, impassioned stress
A thoroughfare for freedom beat
Across the wilderness
America! America!
God mend thine every flaw
Confirm thy soul in self-control
Thy liberty in law

O beautiful for heroes proved
In liberating strife
Who more than self their country loved
And mercy more than life
America! America!
May God thy gold refine
Till all success be nobleness
And every gain divine

O beautiful for patriot dream
That sees, beyond the years
Thine alabaster cities gleam
Undimmed by human tears
America! America!
God shed his grace on thee
And crown thy good with brotherhood
From sea to shining sea

AMERICA *

PAUL SIMON

Many young Americans today re-gard Paul Simon as a spokesman who has eloquently set forth their mood, aspirations, and feelings. Superficially, at least, what Simon has been recording is a general feeling of disillusionment, ennui, and malaise. In this version, the American dream seems dead. Modern American youth can recite, with Swineburne's Roman pagan:

From too much love of living
From hope and fear set free . . .

If these poets have accurately gauged the mood of contemporary youth, several questions remain unanswered. Why has American youth become so disenchanted? Does Simon speak for all youth, or is the malaise he reports restricted to an affluent middle-upper class? Is America something that one looks for as an observer, or is that attitude a cop out? In the depths of our bloody civil war Julia Ward Howe wrote "Mine eyes have seen the glory of the coming of the Lord." Katherine Lee Bates (see preceding poem) at the turn of the century had a dream of a future, glorious America. Is that dream now dead? Can any nation survive for long if its young people do not dream? What is the stuff that dreams are made of?

"Let us be lovers,
We'll marry our fortunes together.
I've got some real estate
Here is my bag."
So we bought a pack of cigarettes
And Mrs. Wagner's pies,
And walked off
To look for America.

"Kathy," I said,
As we boarded a Greyhound in Pittsburgh,
"Michigan seems like a dream to me now.
It took me four days
To hitchhike from Saginaw.
I've come to look for America."

Laughing on the bus,
Playing games with the faces,

She said the man in the
    gabardine suit was a spy.
I said, "Be careful,
His bow tie is really a camera."

"Toss me a cigarette,
I think there's one in my raincoat"
"We smoked the last one
An hour ago."
So I looked at the scenery
She read her magazine.
And the moon rose over an open field.

"Kathy, I'm lost," I said
Though I knew she was sleeping
"I'm empty and aching and
I don't know why."
Counting the cars
On the New Jersey Turnpike.
They've all come to look for America,
All come to look for America.
All come to look for America.

I HAVE A DREAM *

MARTIN LUTHER KING, JR.

In contemporary America there are still people who dream. Early in the 1960's one such dream was eloquently set forth by the black leader, Martin Luther King, Jr., addressing a massive rally in Washington. The speech, that immediately captured national attention, has in it the ring and majesty of ancient Hebrew prophecy. Looking far beyond racial strife of the moment, he saw an America free at last from the corrosion of prejudice.

* Reprinted from Martin Luther King, Jr., "Though We Face Difficulties, I Have A Dream," The National Observer, September 2, 1963 by permission.

. . .

Five score years ago, a great American, in whose symbolic shadow we stand today, signed the Emancipation Proclamation. This momentous decree came as the great beacon light of hope for millions of Negro slaves who had been seared in the flames of withering injustice. It came as the joyous daybreak to end the long night of their captivity.

But one hundred years later the Negro still is not free. One hundred years later, the life of the

Negro is still badly crippled by the manacles of segregation and the chains of discrimination. One hundred years later, the Negro lives on a lonely island of poverty in the midst of a vast ocean of material prosperity. One hundred years later, the Negro is still languished in the corners of American society and finds himself an exile in his own land. So we have come here today to dramatize this shameful condition.

In a sense we've come to our Nation's Capital to cash a check. When the architects of our republic wrote the magnificent words of the Constitution and the Declaration of Independence, they were signing a promissory note to which every American was to fall heir. This note was a promise that all men, yes, black men as well as white men, should be guaranteed the unalienable rights of life, liberty and the pursuit of happiness.

It is obvious today that America has defaulted on this promissory note insofar as her citizens of color are concerned. Instead of honoring this sacred obligation, America has given the Negro people a bad check, a check which has come back marked "Insufficient Funds." But we refuse to believe the bank of justice is bankrupt. We refuse to believe that there are insufficient funds in the great vaults of opportunity of this nation. So we have come to cash this check, a check that will give us upon demand, the riches of freedom and the security of justice. We have also come to

this hallowed spot to remind America of the fierce urgency of now.

This is no time to engage in the luxury of cooling off or to take the tranquilizing drug of gradualism. Now is the time to make real the promises of democracy. Now is the time to rise from the dark and desolate valley of segregation to the sunlit path of racial justice. Now is the time to lift our nation from the quicksands of racial injustice to the solid rock of brotherhood. Now is the time to make justice a reality for all of God's children.

It would be fatal for the nation to overlook the urgency of the moment. This sweltering summer of the Negro's legitimate discontent will not pass until there is an invigorating autumn of freedom and equality. Nineteen sixty-three is not an end but a beginning. Those who hoped that the Negro needed to blow off steam and will now be content will have a rude awakening if the nation returns to business as usual. There will be neither rest nor tranquility in America until the Negro is guaranteed his citizenship rights. The whirlwinds of revolt will continue to shake the foundations of our nation until the bright day of justice emerges.

But there is something I must say to my people who stand on the warm threshold which leads them to the palace of justice. In the process of gaining our rightful place we must not be guilty of wrongful deeds. Let us not seek to satisfy our thirst for freedom by drinking from the cup of bitterness and hatred. We must forever conduct our struggle on the high plane of dignity and discipline. We must not allow our creative protest to degenerate into physical violence. Again and again we must rise to the majestic heights of meeting physical force with soul force.

The marvelous new militancy which has engulfed the Negro community must not lead us to a distrust of all white people, for many of our white brothers, as evidenced by their presence here today, have come to realize that their destiny is tied up with our destiny. They have come to realize that their freedom is inextricably bound to our freedom. We cannot walk alone.

And as we walk we must make the pledge that we shall always march ahead. We cannot turn back. There are those who are asking the devotees of civil rights: "When will you be satisfied?" We can never be satisfied as long as our bodies, heavy with the fatigue of travel, cannot gain lodging in the motels of the highways and the hotels of the cities. We cannot be satisfied as long as the Negro's basic mobility is from a smaller ghetto to a larger one. We can never be satisfied as long as our children are stripped of their self-hood and robbed of their dignity by signs stating: "For Whites Only." We cannot be satisfied as long as the Negro in Mississippi cannot vote and the Negro in New York believes he has nothing for which to vote. No, no, we are not satisfied and we will not be satisfied until

justice rolls down like the waters and righteousness like a mighty stream.

I am not unmindful that some of you have come here out of great trials and tribulations, some of you have come fresh from narrow jail cells, some of you have come from areas where your quest for freedom left you battered by the storms of persecution and staggered by the winds of police brutality. You have been the veterans of creative suffering. Continue to work with the faith that unearned suffering is redemptive.

Go back to Mississippi, go back to Alabama, go back to South Carolina, go back to Georgia, go back to Louisiana, go back to the slums and ghettos of our northern cities, knowing that somehow this situation can and will be changed. Let us not wallow in the valley of despair.

I say to you today, my friends, even though we face the difficulties of today and tomorrow, I still have a dream. It is a dream deeply rooted in the American dream. I have a dream that one day this nation will rise up and live out the true meaning of its creed: "We hold these truths to be self-evident that all men are created equal."

I have a dream that one day on the red hills of Georgia the sons of former slaves and the sons of former slaveowners will be able to sit down together at the table of brotherhood.

I have a dream that one day even the State of Mississippi, a state sweltering with the heat of injustice, sweltering with the heat of oppression, will be transformed into an oasis of freedom and justice. I have a dream that my four little children will one day live in a nation where they will not be judged by the color of their skin but by the content of their character. I have a dream today.

I have a dream that one day down in Alabama with its vicious racists, with its Governor having his lips dripping with the words of interposition and nullification—one day right there in Alabama, little black boys and black girls will be able to join hands with little white boys and white girls as sisters and brothers.

I have a dream today.

I have a dream that one day every valley shall be exalted, every hill and mountain shall be made low, the rough places will be made plain and the crooked places will be made straight, and the glory of the Lord shall be revealed, and all flesh shall see it together.

This is our hope. This is the faith that I go back to the South with. With this faith we will be able to hew out of the mountain of despair a stone of hope. With this faith we will be able to transform the jangling discords of our nation into a beautiful symphony of brotherhood. With this faith we will be able to work together, to pray together, to struggle together, to go to jail together, to stand up for freedom together, knowing that we will be free one day.

This will be the day when all of God's children will be able to sing with new meaning:

My country 'tis of thee,
Sweet land of liberty,
Of thee I sing:
Land where my fathers died,
Land of the pilgrims' pride,
From every mountain-side
Let Freedom ring.

And if America is to be a great nation, this must become true. So, let freedom ring from the prodigious hill tops of New Hampshire. Let freedom ring from the mighty mountains of New York. Let freedom ring from the heightening Alleghenies of Pennsylvania. Let freedom ring from the snowcapped Rockies of Colorado. Let freedom ring from the curvaceous slopes of California. But not only that, let freedom ring from Stone Mountain of Georgia.

Let freedom ring from Lookout Mountain of Tennessee.

Let freedom ring from every hill and molehill of Mississippi. From every mountainside, let freedom ring. And when we allow freedom to ring, when we let it ring from every village, from every hamlet, from every state and every city, we will be able to speed up that day when all of God's children, black men and white men, Jews and Gentiles, Protestants and Catholics, will be able to join hands and sing in the words of the old Negro spiritual: "Free at last! free at last! thank God almighty, we are free at last!"

13. Superpower USA: The High Price Of World Leadership

By any yardstick the United States today looms as a superpower in world affairs. We share with the Soviet Union a special preeminence based on our military strength, our diplomatic commitments and our economic power. Because something approaching anarchy prevails in international relations, we have armed ourselves against all potential enemies, fought a series of limited, brush-fire wars, and played the role of world policemen. But this preeminence has been purchased only at a very high cost in money and lives. For a generation, foreign policy and national defense have held a top priority over domestic demands. Pentagon planners have steadily escalated their requests for funds. The Defense Department spends half of the national budget. Our State Department has extended economic aid to over a hundred nations.

Now we have reached something of a crossroads. At the same moment that defense officials are requesting larger budgets for more sophisticated, more expensive weapons systems (MIRV, ABM) our neglected domestic problems cry out for attention. Public support for our role as world policeman is fading. This new assessment is fueled by an increasingly unpopular war in Vietnam, and a growing belief that the Pentagon bureaucracy plays a self-serving role. Basing their challenge on the warning of President Eisenhower, critics talk of an ever-rising military-industrial complex. They charge that the generals have shoved aside the diplomats in charting foreign policy. Having ridden high for a quarter century, we are now buffeted at every turn. The college students concentrate their attack on the military draft and ROTC. The Vietnam war produces such horror tales as My Lai; corruption is unmasked in the PX system; drug addiction spreads like wildfire through the ranks; military morale sinks lower month by month. This "time of troubles" is topped off by publication of the "Pentagon Papers" that reveal a condescending, callous contempt for public opinion on the part of governmental policy-makers.

In the face of this disillusionment, the execution of foreign policy becomes increasingly difficult. President Nixon has termed the growing attitude a "neo-isolationism" that would force us to retreat completely from world leadership. Although his concern appears exaggerated, there is little question that foreign policy needs will be subjected to increasingly critical examination. Congress in its present mood is not apt to give future Presidents a free hand in foreign affairs. In this new environment, Congress has become the spokesman for domestic priorities while demanding a greater voice in international affairs.

Defusing the Atom

If neither the "isolationist" nor the "world policeman" concept is workable, we need a new set of guidelines for foreign policy. We cannot withdraw completely from the world; nor can we control it. The first priority must be a redefinition of our vital interests. Is the election of a Communist president in Chile a threat to our national security? Would the defeat of Israel by her Russian-backed Arab neighbors be worth an all-out war? Can we tolerate the confiscation of American property in Iran? Were our vital interests ever involved in Vietnam? Human history suggests that total appeasement only delays the hard answers. On the other hand, total involvement will drain our human-economic resources. In an effort to recast foreign policy thinking, President Nixon proclaimed in the "Nixon Doctrine" that "Our interests must shape our commitments, rather than the other way around." As a generalized policy, few Americans would quarrel with this concept. The difficulty arises in its application. Who is to define the "national interest" in foreign policy? The President? Military leaders? The Congress? Public opinion? There is no textbook answer to these questions, but national policy requires a blending of many opinions.

Foreign Policy For the Seventies

Our relationships with the Soviet Union and Communist China fall in a special category because of their actual or potential nuclear capability.

The possibility of world destruction has existed since 1945. With the weapons technology of the 1970's it is possible for an enemy to wipe out dozens of great cities without invasion. The resulting fear and distrust has poisoned all international relations and diverted billions of dollars, rubles and yuan to a vain search for security. If the other nation has a 500 megaton bomb, can you gain security by stockpiling a 1000 megaton bomb? If they stockpile 3000 bombs, can we build a defense based on 5000? If they have intercontinental missiles, can we put together a defense based on anti-missile missiles. If they built an anti-missile, can we win with a MIRV? If they have a very great "first strike" capability, does our defense lie in "doomsday machines" and powerful "second strikes"? Is this for real? This literature of projected warfare makes *Alice in Wonderland* seem like a course in logic.

Is there any alternative? Can political leaders find a way to defuse the atom? Some slight evidence exists that all sides realize the futility of the present mad caper. Serious talks over deescalation (SALT) have occurred between the U.S. and the U.S.S.R. The futile arms race plus the challenge of unresolved domestic problems may provide the impetus for future consultation between Washington, Moscow, and Peking.

THE DISTORTION OF NATIONAL PRIORITIES *

JOHN KENNETH GALBRAITH

*Before World War II the topmost
American priorities were assigned
without question to peace time
pursuits. Wars brought brief national mobilization, but not until
the cold war did military priorities
dominate the national budget
year after year. In the late 1960's
it became evident that the national
government could not finance both
guns and butter—either Americans
would have to forego some domestic programs or they would have
to curb military spending.*

*In the article that follows Mr.
Galbraith makes the case for
domestic priorities. Why would
he argue that his point of view is
not anti-military? How has the
Pentagon bureaucracy used fear
to promote its power? Why does
he reject the idea of a unified
Communist threat? What is the
greatest U.S. crisis today? What
political body must redefine our
national priorities?*

We shall have accomplished little
if we get out of Vietnam and leave

* *Reprinted from John Kenneth Galbraith,
"The Distortion of National Priorities,"*
The Progressive, *June, 1969, by permis-
sion of The Progressive.*

uncontrolled the influences that
were responsible for this disaster,
for the Bay of Pigs, and for the
Dominican Republic.

We are not concerned in these
discussions, I would suggest, with
making the Pentagon more efficient.
Bob McNamara made as good an
effort on that as could be made. We
are not, I think, concerned with
making the Pentagon and its suppliers more honest, or with eliminating graft. These things can, indeed, be diversions from the basic
problem, and can leave the basic
problem unsolved.

I would suggest, too, that we
can't have a crusade against military men as such. Indeed, our purpose is to restore the military profession to its historic and honored
role. The armed services were
meant to be the servants and not
the makers of national policy. They
were never intended to be commercial subsidiaries of General Dy-
namics.

Our problem is essentially one of
bureaucratic power, of uncontrolled
bureaucratic power which, in the
manner of all bureaucracies, including those which many of us
here at this table have been associated with, governs in its own interest and in accordance with its
own parochial view of the world.

It is the problem of a vast bureaucracy going considerably beyond the Pentagon, embracing the
intimately associated industries
where increasingly the line between
what is public and what is private
can't be distinguished; and to all
its outsiders and intellectual allies

in the Department of State and the intelligence agencies, including members of the Congressional armed services committees.

The principal instrument of power of this bureaucracy is fear. It is fear that gave it this enormous power and autonomy in the 1950's and early 1960's. This fear caused us to consolidate and delegate power—in effect to say, "Here, we will give you all the money you can use, all the authority you need, and you deal with the danger of the Soviet Union and the Communist world."

It is interesting proof of the role of fear that the Secretary of Defense, when he was up here talking about the ABM, when he was seeking approval of the so-called "Safeguard" system, immediately resorted to the tactic of trying to scare the hell out of everybody. I think one can say of the Secretary of Defense that he is a man who fully learns his business.

Since this power was born in an age of fear, it will be curbed only as we resist fear; only as we resist the temptation to scurry for cover when anybody talks about Communism; only as we look upon the world, Communist and non-Communist, with a certain calm intelligence.

I think we should also bear in mind this is a power which traces to a period in our history not distant in time, but quite different in character. This delegation of our power of the late 1940's and through the 1950's was in a period when it was possible to believe

Secretary Rusk's haunting dream of a Communist imperium, completely united and probing out at any soft point on its perimeter and without —and with no objective short of the ultimate destruction of its opposition.

We must remind ourselves how distant that world is from the world that we now see—a world of bickering Communist states coming to the edge of actual conflict on some obscure island in Asia, a world where the Soviets have to move troops into Czechoslovakia "to have comradely talks." The most pregnant fear in the world today is the fear some Communist states have of other Communist states. There has been in the past twelve months no depth of alarm in the West comparable to that felt in Yugoslavia and Czechoslovakia about the intentions of the Soviet Union.

There was another aspect of the 1940's and 1950's that we must also bear in mind. This was a period when the memory of the Great Depression was strong in all of our minds. In some measure we were spending money because we did not have an easy alternative to sustain employment. Liberals, those of us around the table who went through that period, never liked to say that was one justification of the military budget, but it is in some measure the truth. In 1964 we were forced to reduce taxes essentially because we could not find civilian objects of expenditure that were acceptable to Congress.

We have now moved, in less than

a decade, into a drastically different society in which the balance which all societies must sustain between their public and private outlays has been deeply disturbed. This is a practical matter. We must have a balance between what kids see on television and the quality of the schools they attend. We must have a balance between the concentration of urban work forces and what we do to make our cities livable. We must have a balance between the living standard that we have and the enormous amount of refuse in which that living standard comes packaged and which has to be disposed of.

It is a pervasive thing. For nearly twenty years we have allowed this enormous military budget to preempt a large part of the public expenditures which maintain this balance. We have expansive private consumption and tight public expenditure designed to balance off this growth.

There is much psychological speculation involving race, the nature of poverty, and the like, to explain the agony of our cities. I am forced to confess to the somewhat old-fashioned view that damn few of these problems would not be substantially solved by a considerable increase in the budget.

Twenty years ago, we were alarmed about the vision of the Communist imperium, but everybody around this table today is far more alarmed about the crisis of our cities. Therefore, the ultimate task which confronts us is to bring the sense of priority that we have of

our national responsibility abreast of the anxiety we all manifest.

I see this in no radical terms. I see only one possibility of doing this: through the Congress. Congress is the instrument which must do this. I don't think it will require great political sacrifice, because I think the public has come to share this concern.

THE MILITARY ROLE
IN FOREIGN POLICY *
RICHARD M. NIXON

Although extremists may argue that all military force leads inevitably to war, a better case can probably be made for an adequate military force that keeps the peace. As one of the major military powers of the world, the United States is faced with the problems of balancing her military might between weakness and overkill. New weapons that are constantly being introduced result in an ever-changing equation. In the following

* Extracts from the Nixon "State of the Union" message, January 22, 1971 and his "State of the World" message, February 25, 1971.

article President Nixon tries to define the proper level of U.S. military strength.

Do strategic arms limitations fit into the total military pattern? What role should our allies play in our total military planning? Why does the President recommend an increased military budget?

. . . This Nation's strategy for peace will—as it must—be based upon a position of military strength. The purpose of this strength is to prevent war; and, to this end, we will negotiate with those whose vital interests and policies conflict with our own.

We are pursuing negotiations on strategic arms limitations, on Vietnam, on Berlin, and on the Middle East. These negotiations are difficult and often slow, but we have the stamina and commitment necessary to proceed with patience and purpose.

As we carry on negotiations, we couple them with other efforts to achieve the same goal. The Vietnamization program is an example, and we are making good progress. By this spring, our authorized troop strength will have been cut approximately in half since the time I took office, and we will continue to bring American troops home.

Supporting these efforts, the military forces of this Nation and its allies will provide the armed might necessary to deter aggression or to deal with it effectively where necessary. We expect our allies to do more in their own behalf, and, in

the spirit of the Nixon doctrine, many are taking steps in that direction. But we must also do our share. The kind of partnership we seek to forge works both ways. We have a vital interest in peace and stability abroad and we plan to maintain the capabilities necessary to protect that interest.

Our withdrawals from Vietnam and the change in our general purpose force planning and strategy permit a smaller force structure than in the past. At the same time, the preoccupation with Vietnam has limited our ability to meet some of our military needs elsewhere, particularly in NATO. We must be certain that our military forces are combat-ready and properly equipped to fulfill their role in our strategy for peace. In addition, we face formidable Soviet nuclear and conventional forces, including increased naval forces, and a further rise in the costs of our military equipment and personnel.

For these reasons, I am recommending an increase of $6 billion in budget authority for military and military assistance programs. This Nation has the will and the resources to meet its vital national security needs. At a time when we are urging our allies to do more and when our potential adversaries may seek military advantage, I cannot in good conscience recommend less.

We often think of military strength primarily in terms of equipment and massive organizations. While these are important, attracting and holding able citizens in the Armed Forces is the key to an effective and efficient military force. The service of Americans in uniform is worthy of respect, and I am dedicated to the goal of making all such service voluntary. This budget, and subsequent legislation which I will recommend to the Congress, will make significant progress toward ending reliance on the draft.

. . .

Strategic Policy and Forces

Strategic forces, both offensive and defensive, are the backbone of our security.

—They are the primary deterrent to strategic attacks against us or our allies.
—They face an aggressor contemplating less than all-out attacks with an unacceptable risk of escalation.
—They are essential to the maintenance of a stable political environment within which the threat of aggression or coercion against the U.S. and its allies is minimized.

Our strategic forces must be numerous enough, efficient enough, and deployed in such a way that an aggressor will always know that the sure result of a nuclear attack against us is unacceptable damage from our retaliation. That makes it imperative that our strategic power not be inferior to that of any other state. Thus I am committed to my pledge to keep our strategic forces strong. I am equally committed to seeking a stable strategic relation-

ship with the Soviet Union through negotiations. There is no inconsistency between those goals; they are in fact complementary.

. . .

THE STRATEGIC BALANCE

Last year I reported on a new strategic policy for the 1970's. In assessing the changed strategic relationship, we faced the following realities:

—Until the late 1960's, we possessed strategic forces that provided a clear margin of superiority.
—In the late 1960's, however, the balance of strategic forces changed. While our forces were held at existing levels, the Soviet Union moved forward vigorously to develop powerful and sophisticated strategic forces which approached, and in some categories exceeded, ours in numbers and capability.

By any standard, we believe the number of Soviet strategic forces now exceeds the level needed for deterrence. Even more important than the growth in numbers has been the change in the nature of the forces the USSR chose to develop and deploy. These forces include systems—particularly the SS-9 ICBM with large multiple warheads—which, if further improved and deployed in sufficient numbers, could be uniquely suitable for a first strike against our land-based deterrent forces. The design and growth of these forces leads inescapably to profound questions concerning the threats we will face in the future, and the adequacy of our current strategic forces to meet the requirements of our security. Specifically:

—Does the Soviet Union simply seek a retaliatory capability, thus permitting the pursuit of meaningful limitations on strategic arms?
—Or does the Soviet Union seek forces which could attack and destroy vital elements of our retaliatory capability, thus requiring us to respond with additional programs of our own, involving another round of arms competition?

The past year has not provided definitive answers. Clearly, however, the USSR, over the past year, has continued to add significantly to its capabilities.

OPERATIONAL UNITED STATES AND SOVIET MISSILES

	1965	End 1969	End 1970
Intercontinental Ballistic Missiles:			
United States	934	1054	1054
USSR	224	1109	1440
Submarine-Launched Ballistic Missiles:			
United States	464	656	656
USSR	107	240	350

By the mid-1970's we expect the Soviets to have a force of ballistic missile submarines equal in size to our own. Furthermore, the Soviet Union has continued to make significant qualitative improvements in its strategic forces. These include new and improved versions of their Minuteman-size SS-11 missile, continued testing of multiple warheads, research and testing of ABM components, and improved air defense systems.

An additional source of uncertainty is China's possession of nuclear weapons. China continues to work on strategic ballistic missiles and, by the late 1970's, can be expected to have operational ICBM's, capable of reaching the U.S.

On the other hand, the Soviet Union in the past few months appears to have slowed the deployment of land-based strategic missile launchers. The significance of this development is not clear. The USSR could be exercising self-restraint. Its leaders may have concluded, as we have, that the number of ICBM's now deployed is sufficient for their needs. Or, the slowdown could be temporary and could be followed, in due course, by a resumption of new missile deployments. The delay could mean that the Soviet Union is preparing to introduce major qualitative improvements, such as a new warhead or guidance system. Finally, the slowdown could presage the deployment of an altogether new missile system.

.   .   .

Conclusion

It is essential that the United States maintain a military force sufficient to protect our interests and meet our commitments. Were we to do less, there would be no chance of creating a stable world structure.

We will continue to watch Soviet deployments carefully. If the USSR is in fact exercising restraint, we welcome this action and will take it into account in our planning. If it turns out to be preparatory to a new intensification of the strategic arms race, it will be necessary for us to react appropriately.

THE DOCTRINE OF STRATEGIC SUFFICIENCY

Our policy remains, as I explained last year, to maintain strategic sufficiency. The concept of sufficiency is not based solely on debatable calculations and assumptions regarding possible scenarios of how a war might occur and be conducted. It is in part a political concept, and it involves judgments whether the existing and foreseeable military environment endangers our legitimate interests and aspirations.

Specifically, sufficiency has two meanings. In its narrow military sense, it means enough force to inflict a level of damages on a potential aggressor sufficient to deter him from attacking. Sole reliance on a "launch-on-warning" strategy, sometimes suggested by those who would give less weight to the protection of our forces, would force us to live at the edge of a precipice and deny us the flexibility we wish to preserve.

In its broader political sense, sufficiency means the maintenance of forces adequate to prevent us and our allies from being coerced.

Thus the relationship between our strategic forces and those of the Soviet Union must be such that our ability and resolve to protect our vital security interests will not be underestimated. . . .

. . .

But it is an illusion to think that the ideal guarantee of security— for ourselves or for the world— rests on our efforts alone. While maintaining our strength, therefore, we are also making a sustained effort to achieve with the Soviet Union agreement on arms limitations. Only a designed balance of armaments can insure security that is shared and equitable, and therefore durable.

It is for that reason that we have defined our security requirements in terms that facilitate arms control agreements. The doctrine of strategic sufficiency is fully compatible with arms limitations. So too are the role of our conventional forces and the purpose of our security assistance.

Our goal is security—and if others share that goal, it can be assured through mutual design, rather than mutual exertion. It will, in any event, be maintained.

THE GOVERNANCE OF
THE PENTAGON *

J. WILLIAM FULBRIGHT

For most of her history the United States has had only a skeletal military force except in wartime. This historical pattern has been shattered by the cold war with Russia since 1947. Under the cloud of instant nuclear attack we have developed a permanent military establishment. This Pentagon power is a new force in our national political life. It is an immediate or latent threat to civilian control. One of the outspoken critics of this new power has been J. William Fulbright, chairman of the Senate Foreign Relations Committee.

Why does he believe that militarism is a threat to democracy? How does he explain the ready acceptance of militarism by the American people? What evidence does he offer that our moral sensitivity is being eroded? How have the power of the Senate and the Secretary of State been lessened? In what directions has the power shifted? Why should the public relations program of the Defense Department be challenged? Why

* Reprinted from The Pentagon Propaganda Machine by J. W. Fulbright. Copyright © 1970 by Liveright Publishing Corp. Reprinted by permission of the publisher.

does he believe that young people are more apt to challenge the military power than are older people?

Although I cannot conceive of a single top-ranking officer in any of the U.S. armed services who would consider an attempt to overturn our Constitutional government—in the manner of *Seven Days in May* fiction—militarism as a philosophy poses a distinct threat to our democracy. At the minimum, it represents a dangerously constricted but highly influential point of view when focused on our foreign relations. It is a viewpoint that by its nature takes little account of political and moral complexities, even less of social and economic factors, and almost no account of human and psychological considerations.

Rarely does a general officer invoke the higher loyalty of patriotism—his own concept of it, that is—over loyalty to civilian authority, as Douglas MacArthur did in his defiance of President Truman. But if, as time goes on, our country continues to be chronically at war, continues to neglect domestic problems, and continues to have unrest in its cities and on its campuses, then militarism will surely increase. And even if the military do not take over the government directly, they could—because of increasing use in domestic crises—come to acquire power comparable to that of the German General Staff in the years before World War I. I hope this never comes to pass.

It may not seem likely now, but it is by no means so inconceivable that we need not warn against it and act to prevent it.

I have often warned those students who talk of the need to revise our system by revolution that if such a revolution were to take place, the government that would emerge for our country would not be the one they seek. Rather it would be authoritarian and controlled by the very forces who today promote military solutions to foreign policy problems.

The leadership of professional military officer corps stems from a few thousand high-ranking officers, whose unusual ability and energy come of single-mindedness. Marked as men of talents by their rise to the highest ranks through the rigorous competitiveness of the military services, they bring to bear a strength in conviction and a near unanimity of outlook that afford them an influence on public policy, in government councils and in Congress, disproportionate to their numbers. Disciplined and loyal to their respective services, with added prestige derived from heroic combat records, they operate with an efficiency not often found among civilian officials.

The danger to public policy arises from civilian authorities' adopting the narrowness of outlook of professional soldiers—an outlook restricted by training and experience to the use of force. As we have developed into a society whose most prominent business is violence, one of the leading profes-sions inevitably is soldiering. Since they are the professionals, and civilian bureaucrats refuse to challenge them, the military have become ardent and effective competitors for power in American society.

The services vie with one another for funds, for the control of weapons systems, and for the privilege of being "first to fight." Constantly improving their techniques for rapid deployment, they not only yearn to try them out but when opportunities arise they press their proposals on civilian authorities. The latter all too often are tempted by the seemingly quick "surgical" course of action proposed by the military in preference to the long and wearisome methods of diplomacy. For a variety of reasons—from believing it to be the only possible course of action in the national interest to testing equipment and techniques of counter-insurgency, or just to avoid the disgrace of being "left out"—all the military services were enthusiastic about our initial involvement in Vietnam. By now they should have had their fill, but they still push on, trying out new weapons and new strategies—such as "destroying sanctuaries" in Cambodia.

The root cause of militarism is war, and as long as we have the one we will be menaced by the other. The best defense against militarism is peace; the next best thing is the vigorous practice of democracy. The dissent against our government's action in Southeast Asia, the opposition to the ABM and MIRV, and the increased willingness of many in the Congress to do something about the hitherto sacrosanct military budget are all encouraging signs that democracy is being practiced. But there is much in American policy these days that is discouraging.

There seems to be a lack of concern among too many people about the state of the nation, and a too easy acceptance of policies and actions of a kind that a generation ago would have appalled the citizenry. The apparent broad acceptance of the "volunteer army" idea comes to mind—a concept completely at variance with our historic development. Up to now, a blessing of our system has been that those who go into the military service, whether by enlistment or through the draft, could hardly wait to get out. (Despite attractive re-enlistment bonuses, the Army's rate of retention in 1969 of men finishing their first term was 14.6 percent for volunteers and 7.4 percent for draftees.) But today, because of the exigencies of the times, there is a chance that we may turn our back on this fundamental principle. A large, standing professional army has no place in this Republic.

Along with promoting militarism as part of our society, the mindless violence of war has eaten away at our moral values and at our sensitivity. Reporters covering the domestic aspects of the My Lai massacre story in the home area of Lt. William Calley were surprised to find loud support for the accused —not sympathy, which might be expected, but support. Among these people, there seemed to be no recognition of a possible wrongdoing or criminal act in the alleged massacre.

Beyond the discouragements—and even such disturbing events as the Cambodian adventure and our activities in Thailand and Laos—one has to hope, with reason drawn from our nation's history, that the traditional workings of our system and the innate common sense of Americans will prevail. The task certainly is not going to be easy. We have been so stunned, almost desensitized—like Lieutenant Calley's supporters—by what has gone on during the recent past that it is almost possible to turn to total pessimism. History did not prepare the American people for the imperial role in which we find ourselves, and we are paying a moral price for it. From the time of the framing of our Constitution to the two world wars, our experience and values— if not our uniform practice—conditioned us not for the unilateral exercise of power but for the placing of limits upon it. Perhaps it was vanity, but we supposed that we could be an example to the rest of the world—an example of rationality and restraint.

Our practice has not lived up to that ideal, but, from the earliest days of the republic, the ideal has retained its hold upon us, and every time we have acted inconsistently with it—not just in Vietnam and Cambodia—a hue and cry of opposition has arisen. When the United States invaded Mexico, two former presidents and a future one—John

Quincy Adams, Van Buren, and Lincoln—denounced the war as violating American principles. Adams, the senior of them, is said to have even expressed the hope that General Taylor's officers would resign and his men desert. When the United States fought a war with Spain and then suppressed the patriotic resistance of the Philippines, the ranks of opposition numbered two former presidents—Harrison and Cleveland—Senators and Congressmen, including the Speaker of the House of Representatives, and such distinguished —and differing—individuals as Andrew Carnegie and Samuel Gompers.

The incongruity between our old values and the new unilateral power we wield has greatly troubled the American people. It has much to do, I suspect, with the current student rebellion. Like a human body reacting against a transplanted organ, our body politic is reacting against the alien values that, in the name of security, have been grafted upon it. We cannot, and dare not, divest ourselves of power, but we have a choice as to how we will use it. We can try to ride out the current convulsion in our society and adapt ourselves to a new role as the world's nuclear vigilante. Or we can try to adapt our power to our traditional values, never allowing it to become more than a means toward domestic societal ends, while seeking every opportunity to discipline it within an international community.

It is not going to help us to reach these ends to have a President fearful that we are going to be "humiliated," nor for him to turn to the military as a prime source of advice on foreign affairs. In the case of Cambodia, the President accepted military advice during the decision-making process, apparently in preference to that of the Department of State, thereby turning to an initial military solution rather than a diplomatic or political one. Of course, the Senate was not consulted.

At one time, the treaty power of the Senate was regarded as the only Constitutional means of making a significant foreign commitment, while Executive agreements in foreign affairs were confined to matters of routine. Today, the treaty has been reduced to only one of a number of methods of entering binding foreign engagements. In current practice the term "commitment" is used less often to refer to obligations deriving from treaties than to those deriving from Executive agreements and even simple, sometimes casual declarations.

Thailand provides an interesting illustration. Under the SEATO alliance, the United States has only two specific obligations to Thailand: to act "in accordance with its Constitutional processes" in the event that Thailand is overtly attacked, and to "consult immediately" with the other SEATO allies should Thailand be threatened by subversion. But the presence of 40,000 American troops, assigned there by the Executive branch acting entirely on its own authority, creates a de facto commitment going far beyond the SEATO agreement, and one that is largely based on military recommendations and desires. On March 6, 1962, Secretary of State Dean Rusk and Thai Foreign Minister Thanat Khoman issued a joint declaration in which Secretary Rusk expressed "the firm intention of the United States to aid Thailand, its ally and historic friend, in resisting communist aggression and subversion." Obviously, this goes far beyond the SEATO commitment and omits any reference to Constitutional processes.

An even more striking illustration of the upgrading of a limited agreement into a de facto defense obligation is provided by the series of agreements negotiated over the past sixteen years for the maintenance of U.S. military bases in Spain. Initiated under an Executive agreement in 1953, the agreements were significantly upgraded by a joint declaration issued by Secretary Rusk and Spanish Foreign Minister Castiella in 1963 asserting that a "threat to either country" would be an occasion for each to "take such action as it may consider necessary within its Constitutional processes." In strict Constitutional law, this agreement, whose phrasing closely resembles that of our multilateral security treaties, would be binding on no one excepting Private Citizen Rusk; in fact, it is what might be called the "functional equivalent" of a treaty ratified by the Senate. In 1968, acknowledging even more explicitly the extent of our de facto

commitment to Spain, Gen. Earle Wheeler, then chairman of the Joint Chiefs of Staff, acting under instructions from Secretary Rusk, provided Spanish military authorities with a secret memorandum asserting that the presence of American armed forces in Spain constituted a more significant security guarantee than would a written agreement. Again, as with the Thai commitment, strategic military considerations, arrived at by military commanders with the acquiescence of civilian authorities, undoubtedly were the overriding factors in the political decision.

The Department of State is not alone among the agencies of government awed as well as outmanned, outmaneuvered, or simply elbowed aside by Executive military decision-making. The Department of Defense has established a massive bureaucracy like that in the Department of Commerce, the Atomic Energy Commission, the Department of Health, Education and Welfare, and all the others that protect their positions and interests within the mechanism of governmental power and appropriations.

When war was abhorrent to the American people, the military was considered only as a tool to be used if needed. Today, with our chronic state of war, and with peace becoming the unusual, the military has created for itself an image of a comforting thing to have around. In reality, however, it has become a monster bureaucracy that can grind beneath its wheels the other bureaucracies, whatever their legitimate needs and their prescribed roles within the process of government.

One ominously influential arm of the Defense Department is its military public relations apparatus, which today is selling the administration's Southeast Asian policy, just as it sold the Vietnam policy of the previous administration, with increasing emphasis on patriotic militarism and activity directed against its critics. The enthusiasm and dedication of the purveyors of the hard military line are such that their present course could easily be modified in order to encourage the removal of those in the Congress who question actions of the Executive branch and the growth of military influence.

Considering the normal skepticism of the American citizen, such overt political activity by the military would seem to have small chance of success. But I raise the point, nevertheless; the apparatus exists, and we of the Congress, in another context, have been put on notice that legitimate and even constitutionally required questioning is viewed by some individuals as interference with Executive prerogatives.

It is interesting to compare the American government's only *official* propaganda organization, the U.S. Information Agency, with the Defense Department's apparatus. The USIA is so circumscribed by Congress that it cannot, with the rarest of exceptions, distribute its materials within this country. Since much USIA output is composed of a filtered view of the United States and its policies, such a prohibition is eminently sensible. But the Department of Defense, with more than twice as many people engaged in public relations as the USIA has in all of its posts abroad, operates to distribute its propaganda within this country without control other than that of the Executive branch, and it floods the domestic scene with its special, narrow view of the military establishment and its role in the world.

Of course, the military needs an information program. But it should be one designed to inform, not promote or possibly deceive. There is no need for production of self-promotional films for public consumption. There is no need to fly private citizens about the country to demonstrate to the public our military might. There is no need to send speakers at taxpayers' expense anywhere from Pensacola, Florida, to Portland, Oregon, to address luncheon clubs and veterans organizations. There is no need to set up expensive and elaborate exhibits at state and county fairs. There is no need to take VIPs on pleasant cruises to Hawaii aboard aircraft carriers. There surely is no need for military production of television shows for domestic, commercial use showing "feature" aspects of the Southeast Asian war.

What can be done about the situation?

An obvious answer comes at once to mind: legislation that would again set a ceiling on Defense Department public relations spending.

It didn't work before, but perhaps this time it might be possible to require the Defense Department to report on a regular basis to the Congress and to the public on just what it is doing in the "information" field. Such legislation might also eliminate some of the activities that are far outside the military's proper role in our society—such as the "V-Series" films from Southeast Asia and the "educational" programs of the Industrial College of the Armed Forces. It also might require the State Department to enforce strict clearance of films, speeches, and other material involving foreign policy.

The passage of such legislation would be desirable, but only as a step toward limiting the other activities in which the Pentagon is engaged far beyond the true mission assigned to it—that of physically protecting this country.

The real solution to militarism, of course, is rigorous civilian—including Congressional—control of the now largely uncontrolled military establishment. The growth of military influence began in perilous times when an implacable Stalin and world communism constituted a major threat to the noncommunist world recovering from a devastating war. But the growth of real Pentagon political power did not begin until we became increasingly involved in Vietnam seven years ago. Although the Congress these days is looking more coolly at the enormous defense budget than it has in the past, the surgical process of cutting back will be a difficult

one—and not popular with many members to whose districts the military-industrial establishment has become of great economic importance.

It may help if the public starts examining carefully attempts by the military to sell them its point of view. The press, radio, and television might look more critically on the military's attempts to influence or use them. Not that the media have been remiss in their responsibilities; in fact, frequently the press has been the only source of accurate information about what is going on in Southeast Asia and throughout the world. But there are some who allow themselves to be seduced by the military with free trips and VIP treatment, and even a few who are not much more than trained seals for the Pentagon. Also, there are editors who are not skeptical enough about the material fed to them by the military. Radio and television, as we have seen, are heavy users of the military's propaganda and public relations output. Perhaps some of their executives should devote more attention to filling their public-service time examining the grave domestic problems besetting the country instead of using "V-Series" films and the Army's *Big Picture*.

Nearly ten years ago I made a speech to the National War College and the Industrial College of the Armed Forces in Washington. I said:

The effectiveness of our armed services depends upon the maintenance of their unique prestige and integrity. These will remain intact only so long as the services adhere to their tradition of nonpolitical professionalism. No group or institution can participate in political debate without itself becoming an object of partisan attack. It is precisely because of its status as a nonpolitical institution that the military in the past has enjoyed the virtually unanimous support of the American people and has thus been beyond partisan assault. . . . It is my hope that the armed services will never yield to misguided temptations, which can only shatter the high esteem in which they are held. The preservation of that esteem is essential to the success of the armed forces in fulfilling their assigned mission and essential also therefore, to the defense of the Republic.

Since I made that speech in 1961, the military has been dragged into the political arena. President Johnson at one crisis point brought General Westmoreland from Saigon to address a joint session of the Congress, in order to counter critics in the Senate with an honored officer's explanation as a means of selling administration policy. What troubles me today is that some politicians want to make regular use of the military in such a role, and would be loath to give it up.

An indication of the fondness of some in the military for a political role is contained in the "Prize Essay 1970" printed in the March 1970 issue of U.S. *Naval Institute Proceedings,* a semiofficial learned journal on naval affairs published in Annapolis, Maryland. The prize essay, chosen presumably by a group of high-ranking naval officers, is titled "Against All Enemies," and was written by Capt. Robert J. Hanks, USN, commander of a destroyer squadron who earlier had served in the Pentagon. The theme of his essay is that the military must determine the nature and the extent of external threats to our national security, and must also determine the character of our response to them. Captain Hanks also wrote that there are many individuals in the country who want to curb the military, including a fair sampling of the Senate. He names Senators Clifford P. Case and Walter F. Mondale, who have questioned the need for more aircraft carriers, Mike Mansfield and Stuart Symington, who wonder about the size of our troop levels in Europe, Charles E. Goodell, who proposed withdrawal of our troops from Vietnam by December 1, 1970, and myself —people who would in effect, he wrote, "so weaken this nation's defenses as to place the United States in the greatest jeopardy in its history."

Captain Hanks also came to the conclusion that, "while the threat from without remains, we now face an equally potent challenge from within. . . . In concentrating on the main task of the past thirty years—the external threat—some of us may have forgotten that we solemnly swore to support and defend the Constitution of the United States against all enemies, foreign *and domestic.*" (The italics are the captain's.) And that, "If the United States is to be protected against efforts of those who would place her in peril—through apathy, ignorance, or malice—we of the military cannot stand idly, silently by and watch it done. Our oath of office will not permit it."

A real hope in the fight against military influence, I believe, rests with our young. War is abhorrent to them even though it seemingly is not to many of us who have lived with slaughter for the past thirty years and who have made an apparent accommodation to the threat of nuclear destruction. The young remain unpersuaded that man is brought upon this Earth solely to find his way to the grave. There is among them a vigorous affirmation of life, a love of life that is hopeful and adventurous, if not confident of the future. The anti-life philosophy of militarism offends their minds and hearts.

An observation so widely cited that it is almost an axiom is that no one hates war more than the professional soldier. I think Alexis de Tocqueville was closer to the mark when he wrote in his *Democracy in America* in 1835:

. . . all the ambitious minds in a democratic army ardently long for war, because war makes vacancies [for promotion] available and at last allows violations of the rule of seniority, which is the one privilege natural to a democracy. We thus arrive at the strange conclusion that of all armies those which long for war most ardently are the democratic ones, but that of all peoples those most deeply attached to peace are the democratic nations. And the most extraordinary thing about the whole matter is that it is equality which is responsible for both these contradictory results.

Beyond the ambition of which de Tocqueville wrote, there is even more danger to our democracy from the dehumanizing kind of war we are fighting in Indochina. It produces among the military an insensitivity to life hard for the civilian to comprehend. We have fought many wars before, but none since our Revolution has lasted as long as the present one. Officers and noncoms go back to Southeast Asia for second and third tours of duty, to engage in second and third rounds of killing. Such long immersion in violence of the kind peculiar to this war cannot but brutalize many of those who go through it. One example of such brutalization can be found in Seymour M. Hersh's book *Mylai 9: A Report on the Massacre and Its Aftermath:*

One brigade commander ran a contest to celebrate his units 10,000th enemy kill. The winning GI received a week's pass to stay in the colonel's personal quarters. Many battalions staged contests among their rifle companies for the highest score in enemy kills, with the winning unit getting additional time for passes.

I can recall nothing during World War II that equals in callousness a statement that Hersh attributes to one colonel, the son of a famous general: "I do like to see the arms and legs fly." Horrifying words, but no more so than "body count," "free-fire zone," and other euphemisms the military use to camouflage their deadly business.

Perhaps there is something in the theory advanced by psychologist Erich Fromm, in his book *The Heart of Man: Its Genius for Good and Evil*, that in men there are polar attitudes toward life: "biophilia" (love of life) and "necrophilia" (love of death). Fromm feels that Spinoza in his *Ethics* epitomized the spirit of the biophile: " 'A freeman thinks of death least of all things; and his wisdom is a dedication not of death but of life.' " The necrophile, on the other hand, has values precisely the reverse, for death, not life, excites and satisfies him.

Fromm goes on to say that the necrophile, by extension in modern society, might be labeled *Homo mechanicus* who

has more pride in, and is more fascinated by, devices that can kill millions of people across a distance of several thousands of miles within minutes than he is frightened and depressed by the possibility of such mass destruction. . . .

If more people became aware of the difference between love of life and love of death, if they became aware that they themselves are already far gone in the direction of indifference or of necrophilia, this shock alone could produce new and healthy reactions. . . . Many might see through the pious rationalizations of the death lovers and change their admiration for them to disgust. Beyond this, our hypothesis would suggest one thing to those concerned with peace and survival: that every effort must be made to weaken the attraction of death and to strengthen the attraction of life. Why not declare that there is only one truly dangerous subversion, the subversion of life? Why do not those who represent the traditions of religion and humanism speak up and say that there is no deadlier sin than love of death and contempt for life?

These are the kinds of questions the young are asking—not only those who demonstrate and dissent but those, too, who go unwillingly aboard the jet aircraft that fly daily from the West Coast to Saigon. A very few young people have resorted to criminal violence, but only a few. The supposition that they represent an entire generation is a hysterical invention of people like Spiro Agnew, people who seem to have lost faith in America. By and large, the young of today are life affirmers; they have new ideas and new perspectives, which warrant our respectful attention.

However, the task of strengthening the "attraction of life," the core of the American optimism that built this country, is in the hands of those no longer young. It is my generation who must halt, and then turn back the incursions the military have made in our *civilian* system. These incursions have subverted or muffled civilian voices within the Executive branch, weakened the Constitutional role and responsibility of the Congress, and laid on the public an economic and psychological burden that could be disastrous.

THE END OF THE
SUPERPOWERS *

ARTHUR SCHLESINGER, JR.

as nationalism seem at least as potent as nuclear weaponry.

How does contemporary nationalism differ from that of the 1930's? What impact has it had in the United States, Canada, and Great Britain? How has it disrupted the communist world? The Third World? Must the United States choose between its role as a superpower and isolationism? What does Schlesinger mean by a policy of discrimination? What five principles does he offer for a new American foreign policy? What limits should be put on military intervention? With what problems of the post industrial age must America cope if she is to retain intellectual world leadership?

For twenty years after World War II the world seemed to be permanently organized around two giant superpowers (the U.S. and the U.S.S.R.) and their respective satellites. The two Goliaths had overwhelming nuclear superiority: no third force existed that could defy their preeminence.

In recent years this neat power structure has deteriorated to such a degree that it no longer describes the existing world order. Although the emerging pattern is still very much in doubt, older forces such

* *Reprinted from Arthur Schlesinger, Jr., "The End of the Superpowers," Harper's Magazine, March, 1969, by permission of Harper's Magazine and the author. Copyright © 1969 by the Minneapolis Star and Tribune Co., Inc.*

What was announced on March 31, 1968 [when President Johnson withdrew from the 1968 presidential race] . . . was the collapse of the messianic conception of the American role in the world—indeed, the end of the entire age in which two Superpowers dominated the planet. To understand the reasons for this collapse we must return for a moment to the Superpowers at high noon.

There were always decisive differences between the United States and the Soviet Union on internal values and policies. But their views of the world outside had remarkable similarities. Each Superpower saw mankind as divided between forces of light and forces of darkness. Each assumed that the opposing bloc was under the organized and unified control of the other. Each insisted that every nation line up on one side or the other and condemned neutralism as anomalous if not as immoral. Each expected its own side to accept its own ideas of political propriety and economic organization. Washington supposed that what was then known as the Free World should reshape itself on the American model, while Moscow, that the Communist World should reshape itself on the Russian model.

But the world itself did not sit still; it began to change. And the most basic change of all was the rise of a new force in revolt against the reign of the Superpowers—or rather the resurgence of an older force now endowed in the years after the war with new potency and purpose. That force was nationalism; and the rise of nationalism meant growing opposition to the United States in the Western bloc, growing opposition to the Soviet Union in the Communist bloc, and growing opposition to both America and Russia in the Third World.

Nationalism means, first of all, the determination to assert national identity, national dignity, and national freedom of action. It can also mean, as the memory of prewar Germany, Italy, and Japan reminds us, the determination to assert these things at the expense of other nations; and in this sense nationalism has been and will be a source of tremendous danger to the world. But the nationalism which arose after the second world war was, in the main, not the aggressive and hysterical nationalism which had led nations before the war to try and dominate other nations. It was rather the nationalism generated by the desire to create or restore a sense of nationhood.

In the years since 1945 nationalism has redrawn lines of force around the planet. Take Europe, which Churchill described twenty years ago as "a rubble heap, a charnel house, a breeding ground for pestilence and hate." Economically shattered, politically demoralized, militarily defenseless, Western Europe in the Forties was absolutely dependent on America for social reconstruction and military protection. Then the Marshall Plan set in motion the process of economic recovery. Economic recovery led to the revival of political self-confidence, and political self-confidence to a determination to assert European autonomy. No doubt the turn given this mood in recent years by General de Gaulle is exaggerated and extravagant. But it would be a great error, I believe, to suppose that Gaullism does not spring from a profoundly real impulse in contemporary Europe: a deep pride in European traditions and capacities, a growing will to reaffirm European independence against the twin colossi. And even those who reject the narrow nationalism of de Gaulle do so in the name of the larger nationalism of Europe.

The contagion of nationalism runs everywhere. Today nationalism is seeking home rule in Scotland and Wales; it is dividing the country of Belgium; it is threatening Canada with the secession of French Quebec; in our own country it finds expression in the mystique of Black Power. And it has wrought even more spectacular changes within the empire which Stalin once ruled so calmly and implacably. The Yugoslav heresy of 1948 represented the first serious rebellion of national Communism against Russian primacy. In another decade China burst forth as an independent Communist state, increasingly determined to challenge Russia for the domination of Asia and for the leadership of the international Communist movement. With the clash between China and Russia, the unified Communist empire began to break up. Moscow long ago had to accept the Yugoslav heresy, and on Yugoslav terms. It has conceded a measure of national initiative to the once cowed and compliant satellites of Eastern Europe. Albania and Romania are going their own way. In a desperate effort to preserve the dominant Russian position, the Soviet Union had to resort to military intervention in order to discipline Communist Czechoslovakia. Even Poland, even East Germany may some day insist on national freedom. "Everyone chooses the truths he likes. In this way faith disintegrates." This was said by Pope Paul VI, but it might as well have been said by Brezhnev.

The unity of Communist discipline, the unity of Communist dogma—all are vanishing as international phenomena, crumbling away under the pressure of nationalism. In the contemporary age of polycentrism there is no longer any such thing as "world Communism." A Communist takeover no longer means the automatic extension of Russian, or even of Chinese power. Every Communist government, every Communist party, has been set free to begin to respond to its own national concerns and to pursue its own national policies. One Communist state, Cuba, has even performed the ingenious feat of being simultaneously at odds with both Moscow and Peking.

As nationalism has transformed the democratic and Communist worlds, so too it has transformed the Third World. After the war, many people—Communists and anti-Communists alike—supposed that Communism was the wave of the future and accepted the thesis of its inevitable triumph. In particular, it was anticipated that Marxism would sweep through the developing world like a prairie fire. With Asia, Africa, and Latin America shaken by the deep-running demands for economic development and social justice, new states everywhere, it was believed, would turn to Communism, if only as the most efficient technique for modernization. Some in the West became mesmerized by the notion that, when a nationalist revolution began in an underdeveloped country, Communism was bound to win out. This has not happened. There has been an abundance of nationalist revolutions in these years. But the striking fact is plainly the failure of the Communists to ride to power on nationalist upheavals.

The reasons for the failure of Communism in the developing world is the same as the reasons for the expulsion of colonialism from that world: what the new nations want more than anything else is the assurance of their national freedom of decision. And this very fact too, while it has endowed the new nations with spirit and audacity, has prevented them from forming, as some once feared they might do, a unified bloc against the West. Today they are unified only in their determination to stay out of the Cold War—and in the hope of shaking down the developed countries, Russia as well as America, for all the economic aid they can get. Beyond that, they too are deeply divided by nationalist resentments and rivalries.

Nationalism has thus changed the relations between America and the Western world and Russia and the Communist world, and it has defeated expectations of Russian and American influence as well as of a unified neutralist bloc in the Third World. It has emerged as the most powerful political emotion of our time. The Age of Superpowers is coming to an end.

A Common Frustration

Or at least this is evident to everyone—except to the Superpowers themselves. A main source of trouble in the world today is, as often before, the failure of Superpowers to recognize a new historical situation. . . .

Ordinarily it takes defeat in war to persuade a Superpower that it has been living beyond its means. Sometimes one defeat is not enough. It took two defeats, for example, to convince Germany it was not a Superpower; there are those who fear that the Germans may not have learned this lesson yet. Great Britain, on the victorious side in the second world war, persisted in the illusion until the defeat at Suez terminated her imperial dream. The American failure in Vietnam has produced a striking reassessment of the world position of the United States. Vietnam has been an expensive and horrible education; but no one can question the fact that most Americans are now determined to have no more Vietnams. Only the Soviet Union, sustained by a dogmatic faith in the infallibility of its ideology, still seems dogged in the pursuit of Superpowership, and this in spite of spectacular setbacks in Cuba and the Middle East. The world must hope that Czechoslovakia may in time have the same effect on Russia that Suez had on England and Vietnam on the United States.

A New American Policy

The last-ditch champions of the American Vietnam policy like to argue that the only alternative to universalism is isolationism. This, of course, is a self-serving definition of the issues; and the debate should not be established in these terms. A headlong dash from the world, a retreat to our own shores, even a retreat to our own hemisphere: all these are impossible options. An isolationist course would be as false to our interests as it would be false to our ideals. The United States cannot resign from the task of helping to build a rational world order.

But what form is this world order likely to take? As Franklin Roosevelt construed the universalist world a quarter of a century ago, it would be a world in which order would be enforced by the great powers. The decline of the Superpowers dooms this world. But it would appear equally to doom the sphere-of-interest world sought by Stalin. Thoughtful people still argue that spheres of influence offer the only alternative to universalism. But is it probable that, in the age after the Superpowers, the sphere-of-interest policy will be as easy to work as it was in the past? Confronted by nationalism in Czechoslovakia, Russia had to use military force to maintain its sphere of influence in Eastern Europe. Confronted by nationalism in the Dominican Republic, the United States had to use (or thought it had to use) military force to maintain its sphere of influence in the Caribbean. Both Superpowers got away with their military intervention in the short run. But both know that, where they are unwilling to use military force, they can no longer count on the automatic compliance of the countries of Eastern Europe

or Latin America. It is highly doubtful whether China will be any more successful in putting together a submissive sphere of influence in East Asia.

My guess is that the most realistic evolution in the future would be along the lines of the proposal made by Churchill in 1943—a development of regional groupings within the United Nations, thereby merging universalist and sphere-of-influence conceptions, strengthening the "middle powers" and discharging the great powers from the supposed obligation to rush about putting down every presumed threat to world peace.

This would be a policy neither of universalism nor of isolationism but of discrimination. It would imply the existence of what President Kennedy called the "world of diversity"—"a robust and vital world community, founded on nations secure in their own independence, and united by allegiance to world peace." And it would imply recognition of the limits of American power. As Kennedy put it in 1961,

We must face the fact that the United States is neither omnipotent nor omniscient—that we are only 6 percent of the world's population—that we cannot impose our will upon the other 94 percent—that we cannot right every wrong or reverse each adversity—and that therefore there cannot be an American solution to every world problem.

Kennedy's profound insight was

forgotten when his successor reinstated Dullesism and plunged ahead with the policy of overkill. But today, in the melancholy aftermath of Vietnam, we must at last understand more urgently than ever that "there cannot be an American solution to every world problem," and that we must therefore demand a sense of proportion and priority in the conduct of our foreign affairs.

In light of the Vietnam tragedy and of the current world mood, what would be the basic principles for a new American policy? What are the lessons of Vietnam?

First, that everything in the world is not of equal importance to us. Asia and Africa are of vital importance for Asians and Africans, and they are of some importance to us. But they are not so important for us as they are to Asians and Africans, nor are they as important for us as are Europe, Latin America, and Soviet Russia. In the last three years we have given most of our attention and resources to a marginal problem on the mainland of Asia while our position has steadily deteriorated in parts of the world far more indispensable to our national security.

Second, that we cannot do everything in the world. The universalism of the other generation was spacious in design and noble in intent. Its flaw was that it overcommitted our country—it overcommitted our policy, our resources, and our rhetoric. It estranged our friends without intimidating our enemies. Vietnam should teach us that in the last half of the twentieth century armed white men cannot determine the destiny of a nation on the mainland of Asia. It should teach us, more generally, that any American policies which involve the denial of local nationalism are doomed to failure.

Third, that we cannot be the permanent guarantor of stability in a world of turbulence. Violence is epidemic in the developing world; and we cannot regard every outbreak as a summons for the American fire brigade. "Every country," a wise Englishman said, "has a right to its own War of the Roses." Not every revolution, not every change in political and economic systems, not every assertion of belligerent nationalism is necessarily a mortal threat to the security of the United States.

Fourth, that all problems in the world are not military problems, and that military force is not necessarily the most effective form of national power. So long as we continue to define our world problems in military terms, so long will we strengthen our own warrior class and plunge the nation into further military intervention. This is a self-defeating course. We have never had more military power in the world than we have today—and we have seldom in recent times had less influence. As General de Gaulle observed to President Kennedy in Paris in 1961, the French had learned that exerting influence in Southeast Asia and taking military action there were almost incompatible. We should ponder this statement. And, as we free ourselves from the military hang-ups of our foreign policy, we can begin to combat the militarization of our domestic thought and institutions.

Fifth, that the basis for our international influence in the coming period will lie less in the power of our arms than in the power of our example. As the Superpowers themselves begin to realize that their time is over, then they will recognize that future world leadership will demand persuasion as well as power. Political ties, economic assistance, cultural relations: these we must strengthen as we can. But military intervention is another matter.

We should undertake military intervention only when the national security of the United States is directly and vitally involved, when the people whom we think we are supporting display a capacity for resistance themselves, and when there are reasonable prospects for success—all conditions rejected and trampled on by those who made American policy for Vietnam. We must take advantage of the fact that modern military technology—intercontinental missiles, nuclear submarines, rapid means of airlift—reduces the need for the physical presence of American troops and bases in foreign lands. The time has come for a policy of "selective disengagement."

Of course, it seems easier in the short run to throw military weight around like an international bully than it is to appeal to the reason and conscience of mankind and to validate that appeal by the values we display in our national community. Yet we have exerted our greatest influence in the world precisely when—as in the days of Woodrow Wilson, of Franklin Roosevelt, of John Kennedy—American leadership, in great part because of its identification with progressive policies at home, has been able to command the confidence of ordinary people everywhere. Mr. Nixon's goal of "clear-cut military superiority" will never be a substitute for American idealism as exemplified in action.

The Price of Progress

We can restore our influence only as we contract our military presence around the world and begin to display reason, restraint, and magnanimity in our dealings with other nations. Above all, we can restore our influence only as we live up to our highest ideals of our national community. "Those are not wrong," Carl Schurz wrote seventy years ago, "who maintain that the nation which would assume the office of a general dispenser of justice and righteousness in the world . . . should be held to prove itself as a model of justice and righteousness in its own home concerns." The industrial order is undergoing vast and fundamental changes as the mechanical society created by the first industrial revolution is evolving into the new electronic society. "Because your country is further on the path of industrial development than ours," Jean-Jacques Servan-

Schreiber told a meeting of American intellectuals, "many of the crises you are living through today are the ones we shall increasingly have to face in the future." If America is in turmoil, he continued, this was not the proof of decay but the price of progress. America seems in crisis because Americans have reached the point in social transformation where they are raising and debating fundamental questions long buried in tradition and dogma: the relationships between rich and poor, between black and white, between parent and child, between structure and spontaneity. "From the answers that you will find to this new set of questions will come a new 'social contract,' a new definition of the relationship between man and society with this second industrial revolution."

The experience of Vietnam has shown that we cannot run two crusades at once—that we cannot wage even a small war against an underdeveloped country and at the same time move creatively to meet the problems of our own land. The policy of total involvement in the world is incompatible with the policy of social reconstruction at home. It would appear that in the years ahead America will exercise international influence less by trying to run the planet than by trying to solve the new problems of the high-technology state—the accelerating pace of technical change, the humanization of the city, the dilemmas of racial justice, the reform of education, the light of the individual in a world of great organizations. In the years immediately to come, the world will follow us less because of our armed might than because of our capacity to heal the disruptions and fulfill the potentialities of the electronic society. If this is so, then we return to an earlier conception of the way America should seek to lead the world. "She will recommend the general cause by the countenance of her voice, and by the benignant sympathy of her example," said John Quincy Adams. ". . . But she goes not abroad in search of monsters to destroy."

FOREIGN POLICY FOR THE '70's *

STANLEY HOFFMANN

If we agree that the U.S. foreign policy of the 1950's and 60's is obsolete, there is far less agreement on new policies to replace the old. What have we learned about the limits of military power? Why has economic assistance failed to

* Reprinted from Stanley Hoffmann, "Foreign Policy For the '70's," Life, March 21, 1971. Reprinted by permission of the author.

secure the total allegiance of client states? Why might it be to our disadvantage if Russia were drastically weakened? How do our critics view our role in world affairs? Why must we abandon the ideas of containment and the American role as world policeman? What domestic reaction is provoked by overinvolvement abroad? For what kind of world order should we strive? What limited objectives should it have? To achieve such a world order what guidelines should we use?

American foreign policy needs a new stance and some new conceptions. As the [Nixon] administration seems to have understood, the policies of the past have all brought us to dead ends. Vietnam has provoked a trauma here at home. Bridge-building in Europe ended with the Soviet invasion of Czechoslovakia. Tensions rise in the Middle East. And the nuclear arms race continues at increasing cost.

The United States is still the most powerful nation in the world, but it is a world in which the great powers no longer can control events directly, in which familiar instruments of power are often ineffective, in which there are too many problems for any one state to master. Reacting to our setbacks, we feel uneasy, even guilty. Yet our chief fault is that we have not understood what caused them, and have not yet drawn the necessary lessons from our failures.

The American stance should be characterized by the words "active self-restraint." Our desire to control world affairs should be abandoned and we should think of our moves in terms of their likely impact instead. No great power can abdicate its responsibility in shaping world politics. But neither can even a great power today hope to be effective unless it displays moderation, discrimination and self-control in the use of its power. The world order our statecraft seeks must be one that can accommodate not only differences and diversity, but also conflicts and violence, which are inevitable no matter how well conceived the system might be.

The task, really, is to keep disorder manageable. It is possible *if* the burdens of power are more widely shared than they are today, *if* a group of middle powers emerge between the superpowers and the small states, *if* regional balances of power develop to limit the ambitions of the strong, *if* the great and middle powers can combine to discourage the use of force between states and allow other hierarchies of power to emerge instead, and finally, *if* the superpowers continue to manage their own confrontations with prudence.

After 20 years, there are still only two great powers that are capable of engulfing the world in a general war and at the same time are indispensable to the settlement of all major issues. Only the U.S. and the U.S.S.R. possess modern military might—in fact, the means of annihilation—and the resources to be present, in some form, all over the world. But in two decades there has been a fundamental change in the nature of power. To possess the ingredients of power no longer guarantees the achievements of power. And so the mightiest nations are often the most frustrated. The very elements of power that distinguish the strong from the weak have become either less usable or less potent.

Power no longer means control. Military might was once the most direct means of control. Indeed, it was the criterion of power. But its most important use today is to prevent an adversary from making gains at one's expense. If one wants to extend one's own control by force—to make gains rather then avoid losses—then one encounters sharp limits. For the superpowers, there is the danger of becoming enmeshed in a conflict so unstable that the nuclear holocaust could come out of it. Even on a less dangerous level, the cost of using force can be prohibitive. The Soviets' avoidance of a showdown with Yugoslavia, their decision to withdraw their missiles from Cuba rather than chance war, our consistent refusal to challenge the Soviets in Eastern Europe, and our own experience in Vietnam are evidence of the limits of military power to do more than prevent loss.

The enormous potential might of the great powers has been diminished further by the multiplication of states, many of which are weak, vulnerable and open to subversion.

But the unassailable legitimacy of these nation-states—of any nation-state—obliges the great powers to attempt subtle, indirect methods of influence—and at this game they are not necessarily any better endowed than lesser states. Even when the great powers employ means of persuasion which they alone possess—economic aid, for instance, and military assistance—the fact that the recipients are formally independent states, not colonies, sharply reduces the donors' control. Attempts at control through subversion or domestic manipulation have often backfired, or made the great powers embarrassingly dependent on dubious clients.

Finally, the great powers are unable to exert their control in many disputes where the issues are bitter and local and transcend cold war allegiances—in fact, have little or nothing to do with them. The conflicts in the Middle East, in Cyprus, in Kashmir, and between South Africa and its neighbors, are not reducible to the cold war—although, as in the Middle East, they have often been aggravated by it. In any of the these conflicts, a meeting of the minds between us and the Soviets could contribute to a solution—but the solution would still have to be accepted by the parties concerned.

The present international system is thus full of paradoxes both unfamiliar and unsettling to Americans who have been prepared by history and instinct for a world in black and white, in which there is either harmony or all-out contest.

We have been at loggerheads with Russia everywhere for 20 years— and the confrontation still exists, with no clear winner. In fact, each side has a clear interest in seeing that the other is *not* knocked out, in defending at least some part of the status quo. It is just what Americans dislike: stalemate, uncertainty, protracted conflict. And so we find it difficult to accept our limited adversary relationship with the Soviet Union. We have not yet fully understood that our traditional weapons—military might and economic resources, especially the former—are still important but no longer dominant in international relations. Particularly have these tools disappointed us when we have tried to use them to influence the domestic affairs of other countries —Vietnam, for example. We have not yet grasped a basic truth about the world: that all states are more capable of frustrating each others' dreams than of realizing their own, better at preserving the status quo than at altering it substantially in their favor.

Nor are we used to looking at ourselves in perspective. We tend to see the United States as the gallant champion of democracy, self-determination and stability, waging a worldwide defensive battle against forces of oppression and chaos. Our self-image is based on our good intentions. But others see us quite differently: as a stumbling giant who maintains military bases, advisers and armed forces in most parts of the world, whose clients rule dozens of countries, who supports—in South Vietnam, Guatemala, Greece or South Africa —regimes as oppressive as those he fights, who, in short, acts just the way imperial powers have always acted.

To be truly effective as a nation, we must first of all learn to cope with the world as it is and to rid ourselves of irrelevant concepts and habits. For two decades, we have based our foreign policy on two notions. One was the idea that world Communism must be contained, and the other was that America's mission was to preserve —single-handedly, if necessary— world order everywhere. These notions have now become useless: worse, they are dangerous.

Containment—the building up of "situations of strength" by military means, by economic aid and by frequent although not always visible interventions—gave a sense of direction and mission to our actions. It also provided our foreign policy with its greatest achievement: NATO and the rebirth of Western Europe. But its very success worked fundamental transformations in the international order: the emergence within our alliance of restless, powerful nations; the Sino-Soviet split; the appearance of other more emancipated strains of Communism in Cuba, North Vietnam or North Korea. For these and other reasons, the old guideline has become irrelevant—and Vietnam was its Waterloo. We treated the war for South Vietnam as if it were a repetition of Korea, only to discover through much painful trial and error that it was not. The anti-Communist imperative is of little use when the forces on our side are unable to establish a legitimate and effective government, or when the other side has a strong national appeal and superior organization. It does not work when the fear of escalation limits our use of military power at the point where pursuit of victory would mean both an enlarged war and the destruction of the people we are supposed to be protecting. Moreover, the irrelevance of the old guideline leaves us exposed in various parts of the world as the active supporters of an unsavory status quo against Communist threats that are often remote or even fictitious.

It is true that the United States is the only major non-Communist state possessing both great power and a sense of world mission. But it does not follow that the United States could or should man the front lines at all times everywhere. To proceed as if no one else could be trusted with even a part of the responsibility for creating a satisfactory international order, as if the only thinkable arrangement is one in which we are omnipresent, in which others behave strictly according to *our* notions of "responsibility" and "pragmatism"—the kind of world Walt W. Rostow dreamed of—is dangerous in the extreme. Too often it amounts to choosing flatterers and tyrants in need, rather than listening to the more representative or progressive critics or rebels. And if such be-

havior perpetuates the vicious circle of impotence and dependence abroad, it also results in excessive self-confidence here. It overstretches our resources—especially our psychological resources—and creates the most severe strains in our domestic life. Pretentious overinvolvement abroad leads to breast-beating at home, to demands by the New Left and others for a total reversal of priorities—the proposition that our presence in the world is the only cause of the world's ills, and that our removal from it would insure both the world's salvation and the solution of all our own domestic problems. One kind of "nihilistic perfectionism," to use Henry Kissinger's words, feeds the other. Both reflect impatience and immodesty.

We must somehow escape the familiar cycle in which excessive activism is followed by withdrawal. The persistence of anti-Americanism, even among friends, or the resilience of our adversaries should not become pretexts for a new isolationism. Simply because we cannot shape it to our precise specifications, we cannot escape our part in establishing a new order.

Finally, we must give up the split-level way in which we have heretofore approached world affairs. We *think* about World Order in terms of broad, abstract, mostly unwieldy principles such as "self-determination," "resistance to aggression," or "economic growth." We *handle* issues "pragmatically," case by case, which all too often means that we wait until a crisis breaks out and then deal with it on a short-term basis. Between our airy principles and our emergency rescue efforts, we have failed to develop any long-term *political* objectives, with identifiable goals and ways of reaching them.

This does not mean that we need a so-called master plan. The present world is not receptive to such grand designs. But we do need to think about the kind of international system that would be both possible and desirable.

A world dominated by the United States might appear desirable for us, but it is not acceptable to either our adversaries or our friends. A world jointly ruled by the Soviet Union and by us has great appeal in some quarters. The Soviets themselves would obviously approve of a system in which there would be distinct spheres of influence for each superpower, and in which they would participate in the joint policing of the rest of the world. However, it would be most difficult to establish a Soviet-American condominium on terms acceptable to us, since it would presuppose a settlement of the major questions in which we are on opposite sides, such as the division of Germany. Russia's interest, however, may be to try to seduce us into such an embrace because of her concern for keeping China, Japan and West Germany down, and Eastern Europe crushed. Most of the rest of the world would, however, refuse to accept Soviet-American dictates, and find the means to resist. In the end, such a system

would rely on the superpowers' capacity to use force jointly, and the world is such that the costs of force are prohibitive and most international tasks can be performed only by the consent of all interested parties.

The U.S. interest is, on the contrary, to achieve a more complex and balanced system of world order. Accepting the fact that many present conflicts—including those which oppose us to the Soviet Union and to Red China—are likely to persist, the realistic objective of world order should not be harmony, which is unattainable, but the moderation of conflicts and violence, which could be achieved by a better, more diversified distribution of power and by a multiplicity of institutions and methods for managing conflict.

Such a system will not come into being unless the U.S. finds the right mean between overinvolvement—which fosters irresponsibility by forcing lesser powers either into debilitating reliance on us, or into negative rebellion against us—and retreat into fortress America—which would foster instability by forcing states dependent on the U.S. either into heavy rearmament or into appeasement of our adversaries. In an orderly system, the superpowers would remain the ultimate guarantors of world peace, and the U.S. would not be relieved of the task of deterring major wars. Our power would be used as a supplement to and as a reservoir behind the power of others, not as a substitute. As George Kennan suggested years ago, we should approach world order as gardeners, not as mechanics.

In order to reach such a role, the U.S. should adopt the following guidelines.

First, our task is not to try to force other nations to do our will through coercion, bribes or the black arts of subversion, but to shape the environment in which they operate. This does not mean that we should do nothing. It means taking initiatives that will make it appealing for others to behave in harmony with our common interests, but without obliging them either to sacrifice their own interest to ours, or to harm ours in order to protect their own. This obviously requires us to define our interests in such a way as to get the maximum of freely given cooperation from others, and to ask ourselves not so much whether our moves will have immediate and tangible results but whether they will contribute to an international system which has moderation as an objective. We have often failed to do so. When we display the "arrogance of power," we encourage others to act in the same way. It may be no coincidence that the 1967 war in the Middle East and the Soviet invasion of Czechoslovakia followed our military interventions in Santo Domingo and Vietnam.

Our initiatives must be such as to encourage the lesser powers to play roles both larger and more constructive than the ones we have traditionally assigned them. We will have to rely less on military presence or cloak-and-dagger operations, more on diplomacy and multilateral institutions. We will have to continue our economic assistance, but with fewer expectations of immediate results. We will have to increase efforts toward international cooperation against monetary disruptions and trade distortions.

Secondly, to have a favorable impact on others we must be able to identify and then align ourselves with genuine movements abroad, rather than continuing to deal with precarious clientele. The Soviets, outside of Eastern Europe, have understood this well. In the Middle East they have gained a foothold by exploiting the grievances of a potent, autonomous force—Arab nationalism. It is in our long-term interest to ally ourselves with nationalist forces abroad, even if in the short run they challenge established interests. Only if we take a sympathetic stand will the convergence of interests between the U.S. and nations (developed or not) eager for self-respect manifest itself. This requires of us both greater understanding of what's happening internally in every country and greater detachment from temporary reverses. We must also stop depending on massive interventions to try to put things right. They weaken our fragile partners further, undermine their domestic legitimacy—or remain futile because our partners were fatally weak to begin with.

We must then reassess our national interests. A great power cannot consider itself threatened by every tremor anywhere. It must establish a hierarchy of concerns and have a sense of proportion and perspective. Not every part of the world is of the same importance to us. Some countries are important because of their resources, population, political influence or intimate ties with us. Others are not. Even in an important area, there is a range of interests, and a distinction to be made among threats. A threat of forcible military expansion by one of our major adversaries. Russia or Red China, is far more serious than a threat of similar action by a lesser power. Outright invasion is more serious than a gain of diplomatic influence made by an adversary. Our interest in preserving a key country from attack is greater than our interest in forcing that country to follow a specific line of action.

No foreign policy can be successful if it is so unrelaxed as to view everything on the same level. In Vietnam, we failed to convince our foes that for us the stake—the control of South Vietnam—was worth sacrificing such other American interests as moderate relations with Russia, peace with China, the preservation of NATO, harmony at home. We failed because indeed we did not convince ourselves that this was so.

Nor will we ever achieve a moderate and manageable system of world order unless we accept the fact that occasionally violent internal and social upheavals abroad are inevitable and cannot be stopped or thwarted by us. This does not rule out humanitarian and collective efforts to settle civil wars, as in Nigeria. But we should not eternally try to interfere. We cannot be the perpetual champions of the status quo. The risks both for world order and for domestic peace in this country are too great, and in most cases the damage that a domestic revolution might do to American interests, public and private, is smaller than the damage that would result from our intervention. If an important country is involved, we could not intervene successfully in any case. Thus, in Vietnam, whatever interest many thought we had in keeping an insurgency from taking the country by force—because it was not only Communist but armed and supported by Hanoi—we should have no interest in determining what sort of political regime is set up in Saigon once North Vietnamese and American forces are withdrawn.

These guidelines should help us to achieve the three major objectives of our new foreign policy: the establishment of regional balances of power so as to redistribute responsibilities between the U.S. and other nations; the moderation of third-party disputes dangerous to world peace; and the dampening of conflicts between the U.S. and its two chief opponents. . . .

WEBSTER'S NEW AMERICAN DICTIONARY *

ANTHONY LEWIS

Every nation has a tendency to use or misuse language in a manner that will justify its policies. The United States is no exception. Public relations men in the Pentagon have developed a subvocabulary to explain and defend U.S. military strategy (beginning with the renaming of the War Department as the Defense Department). Nor have American Presidents (with the aid of their speech writers) been immune to this tendency. The tongue-in-cheek dictionary that follows was provoked by the efforts of President Nixon to justify our May, 1970 invasion of Cambodia.

Provocation (n): Dispatch of Russian pilots, at Egyptian Government's request, to help defend Egypt against Israel air attacks. Flying of actual combat mission by Soviet pilots over Egyptian territory is a dangerous provocation.

Action for peace: Dispatch of American troops, bombers and

---

* *Reprinted from* The New York Times, *May 4, 1970. Copyright © 1970 by The New York Times Company. Reprinted by permission.*

helicopters into Cambodia, without informing the Cambodian Government, to prevent attacks that Vietnamese Communist forces there are said to be planning against South Vietnam.

Violation of neutrality: Presence of North Vietnamese and Vietcong in Laos and Cambodia. Usually used with adjective blatant.

Aggression: Similar to above: Communist military activity, as in "massive military aggression in Laos and Cambodia."

Respect for sovereignty and neutrality: Entry of massive American forces into neutral country.

Privileged sanctuary: Area where the enemy can rest and regroup in safety. See Laos, Cambodia. Do not see Thailand, Hawaii or other base and recreation areas for American forces.

Humiliation: What the United States avoids by widening the war in Indochina, alienating her oldest friends abroad and shattering the social peace at home.

Character: What the United States demonstrates by invading Cambodia.

Demilitarized zone: Border strip between North and South Vietnam that may be crossed by air but not by land.

Reckless game: Shooting at American reconnaissance planes that fly over North Vietnam. Americans do not shoot at North Vietnamese planes over South Vietnam since there are none.

Warning: Statement by Pentagon official that American planes will bomb North Vietnam if its troops cross the demilitarized zone. Note: Some philologists think this word refers to events that have already happened.

Threat: Statement by Communist officials in Hanoi, Peking or Moscow criticizing U.S. escalation of the war.

Negotiation: Process leading to confirmation of the Thieu-Ky Government in Saigon.

Intransigence: Communist refusal to join in above process.

Pretext: Excuse put forward by perfidious foreign government for criticism of America; e.g., "any government that chooses to use these actions (the invasion of Cambodia) as a pretext for harming relations with the United States . . ."

Intolerable attitude: Intransigence, aggression or provocation by foreign power justifying American military action.

Constitution: Document empowering the President of the United States to invade any country when he finds an intolerable attitude.

Pitiful helpless giant: What the United States would be if its President did not order an invasion in these circumstances.

Credibility: Maintenance of the belief that the United States is a superpower that angers easily and will use its military force suddenly, without notice or consultation.

Counsels of doubt and defeat: Argument that the United States has no vital interests in Vietnam, is destroying its own fabric and reputation by staying there and should get out.

Patriots: Those who believe that in time of war the U.S. Government is always right. See accompanying historical volume, section on Germany, 1939–45.

Bums: College students who think there is something to protest about in the United States.

Soft-headed liberals: Americans who voted for Richard M. Nixon because they thought he had developed confidence and self-control and would be more likely than Hubert Humphrey to stand up to military pressure and get us out of the Vietnam war.

Allies: Archaic. See previous editions of dictionary.